Twenty Years of World Trade Organization (WTO)

1995-2015

Twenty Years of
WORLD TRADE ORGANIZATION (WTO)

1995-2015

An Exhaustive Description and Documentation of the Demise of GATT and the Birth of WTO, its Present Structure and Functioning, Various Agreements and Declarations, Pending Issues and Ongoing Negotiations

- **Part I:** Advocacy for Open Trade □ General Agreement on Tariffs and Trade (GATT) □ Uruguay Round of Trade Negotiations and the Birth of WTO □ WTO Agreements on Establishment, GATT, Agriculture, Sanitary and Phytosanitary Measures and Textiles □ WTO Agreements on Technical Barriers to Trade, Trade-related Investment, Anti-dumping, Customs Valuation, and Pre-shipment Inspection □ WTO Agreements on Rules of Origin, Import Licensing, Subsidies, and Safeguards □ WTO General Agreement on Trade in Services (GATS) □ WTO Agreement on Trade-related Aspects of Intellectual Property Rights (TRIPS) □ WTO Understanding on Rules and Procedures Governing the Settlement of Disputes
- **Part II:** Discussions, Declarations, Decisions and Agreements of 10 Ministerial Conferences of the WTO held so far: Singapore (December 1996) □ Geneva (May 1998) □ Seattle (November-December 1999) □ Doha (November 2001) □ Cancun (September 2003) □ Hong Kong (December 2005) □ Geneva (November-December 2009) □ Geneva (December 2011) □ Bali (December 2013) □ Nairobi (December 2015).
- **Part III:** Future of WTO □ Appendix □ Bibliography □ Index.

By

O.S. Deol

Associate Professor of Commerce,
Shaheed Bhagat Singh College (Evening),
University of Delhi, Delhi

New Century Publications
New Delhi, India

NEW CENTURY PUBLICATIONS
4800/24, Bharat Ram Road,
Ansari Road, Daryaganj,
New Delhi - 110 002 (India)

Tel.: 011-2324 7798, 4358 7398, 4101 7798
E-mail: indiatax@vsnl.com • info@newcenturypublications.com
www.newcenturypublications.com

Editorial Office:
LG–7, Aakarshan Bhawan
4754-57/23, Ansari Road, Daryaganj,
New Delhi - 110 002

Tel.: 011-4356 0919

Disclaimer: While efforts have been made to explain the contents accurately, they are not legal interpretation of the WTO Agreements. The author shall not be responsible for any loss or damage occurring to anyone on this account. It is advised to consult the documents of the WTO for accuracy and legal interpretation.

First Published: **July 2016**

ISBN: **978-81-7708-431-3**

Published by New Century Publications and printed at Salasar Imaging Systems, New Delhi

Designs: Patch Creative Unit, New Delhi

PRINTED IN INDIA

About the Book

Created by Uruguay Round of Negotiations (1986-1994), WTO was established on January 1, 1995 with headquarters in Geneva, Switzerland. As on January 1, 2016, 162 countries of the world were members of the WTO. The creation of WTO in 1995 marked the biggest reform of international trade since 1948. During those 47 years, international commerce was regulated under the General Agreement on Tariffs and Trade (GATT) which helped to establish a prosperous multilateral trading system. However, by the end of 1980s an overhaul was due.

WTO replaced GATT which remained in existence from 1948 to 1994. GATT was a multilateral treaty, governing trade in goods only. WTO is much wider in scope and coverage. WTO Agreements cover services and intellectual property as well.

WTO is the only international body dealing with the rules of trade between nations. At its heart are the WTO Agreements, the legal ground rules for international commerce and for trade policy. The agreements have three main objectives: (a) to help trade flow as freely as possible, (b) to achieve further liberalisation gradually through negotiations and (c) to set up an impartial means of settling disputes. A number of simple, fundamental principles run throughout all the WTO Agreements. They are the foundation of the multilateral trading system. They include: non-discrimination, freer trade, predictable policies, encouragement to competition and extra provisions for less developed countries.

The present work provides an exhaustive description and documentation of the demise of GATT and the birth of WTO. More importantly, the work focuses on the present structure and functioning of WTO, its various agreements and declarations, dispute settlement mechanism, trade review mechanism, pending issues and ongoing negotiations.

The work consists of three parts.

Part I contains 9 chapters. Chapter 1 advocates the case for open trade. Chapter 2 is devoted to General Agreement on Tariffs and Trade (GATT). Chapter 3 discusses the Uruguay Round of trade negotiations and the birth of WTO. Chapter 4 covers WTO agreements on establishment, GATT, agriculture, sanitary and phytosanitary measures, and textiles. Chapter 5 explains WTO agreements on technical barriers to trade, trade-related investment, anti-dumping, customs valuation, and pre-shipment inspection. Chapter 6 describes WTO agreements on rules of origin, import licensing, subsidies, and safeguards. Chapter 7 is exclusively devoted to General Agreement on Trade in Services (GATS). Likewise, Chapter 8 exclusively deals with Agreement on Trade-related Aspects of Intellectual Property Rights (TRIPS). Chapter 9 spells out WTO understanding on rules and procedures governing the settlement of disputes.

Part II consists of 10 chapters, one each devoted to the discussions, declarations, decisions and agreements of 10 Ministerial Conferences of the WTO held so far.

Part III contains 1 chapter which looks at the future of WTO. It explains and examines the current issues pending before WTO, hurdles in solving them and strategies of member countries/trade blocks in this regard. Besides, Part III also includes an appendix—which provides a list of 162 members of WTO (as on January 1, 2016)—bibliography and index.

Author's Profile

Dr. O.S. Deol is presently Associate Professor of Commerce at Shaheed Bhagat Singh College (Evening), University of Delhi, Delhi. He obtained his M.Phil. and Ph.D. degrees from the Department of Commerce, Delhi School of Economics (DSE), University of Delhi. He has more than 24 years of teaching and research experience.

Specializing in international business and finance, Dr. Deol has authored a book titled *IMF Adjustment Programmes and Developing Countries*. He has published research papers on various aspects of international trade and investment including Purchasing Power Parity (PPP) theory and Foreign Direct Investment (FDI). He has attended and presented papers at numerous seminars/conferences at national and international levels.

Contents

Preface

"No nation was ever ruined by trade"—*Benjamin Franklin*

Created by Uruguay Round of Negotiations (1986-94), WTO was established on January 1, 1995 with its headquarters in Geneva, Switzerland. As on January 1, 2016, 162 countries of the world were members of the WTO. WTO's creation in 1995 marked the biggest reform of international trade since 1948. During those 47 years, international commerce was regulated under the General Agreement on Tariffs and Trade (GATT) which helped establish a prosperous multilateral trading system. However, by the end of 1980s an overhaul was due.

The Eighth Round of multilateral trade negotiations held under GATT and named Uruguay Round, resulted in new legal agreements for trade and strengthening of the settlement system. Following this, there was a Ministerial Conference in Marrakesh, Morocco in April 1994 attended by 125 government representatives from across the world to sign for the establishment of a new successor institution to GATT, namely the World Trade Organization (WTO). WTO entered into force on January 1, 1995, with all assets and liabilities of GATT being transferred to the former. WTO replaced GATT which remained in existence from 1948 to 1994. GATT was a multilateral treaty, governing trade in goods only. WTO is much wider in scope and coverage.

The Uruguay Round provided platform for the largest trade negotiations ever. At a point, the talks seemed doomed to fail, but in the end the Uruguay Round was successful. The task was so immense that some people wondered whether there would ever be another round of negotiations like these. Was it the round to end all the rounds?

WTO is GATT plus a lot more. GATT (the institution) was small and provisional, and not even recognised in law as an international organisation. It was replaced by the WTO. GATT (the agreement) was amended and incorporated into the new WTO Agreements. GATT dealt only with trade in goods. WTO Agreements cover services and intellectual property as well.

WTO is the only international body dealing with the rules of trade between nations. At its heart are the WTO Agreements, the legal ground rules for international commerce and for trade policy. The Agreements have three main objectives: (a) to help trade flow as freely as possible, (b) to achieve further liberalisation gradually through negotiations and (c) to set up an impartial means of settling disputes.

A number of simple, fundamental principles run throughout all the WTO Agreements. They are the foundation of the multilateral trading system. They include: non-discrimination, freer trade, predictable policies, encouragement to competition and extra provisions for less developed countries.

The economic case for an open trading system based on multilaterally agreed rules is simple enough and rests largely on commercial common sense. Protectionism leads to bloated inefficient companies and can in the end lead to factory closures and job losses. One of the WTO's objectives is to reduce protectionism.

Broadly speaking, WTO has set the trend for continued negotiations for agreements in the following areas.

1. Basic telecommunications.
2. Maritime transport.
3. Movement of natural persons.
4. Financial services.
5. General Agreement on Trade in Services (GATS).
6. A reaffirmation of the rule of law in trade and economic relations.
7. A reversal of long standing protectionist practices in agriculture, textiles and clothing.
8. An extension of multilateral rules to services and intellectual property rights.

WTO is run by its member governments. All major decisions are made by the membership as a whole, either by ministers (who meet every two years) or by officials (who meet regularly in Geneva). Decisions are normally taken by consensus. More routine work is supervised by the General Council. Numerous other councils, committees, working parties and negotiating groups cover the wide range of WTO issues.

WTO is directed by a Ministerial Conference which is the highest authority and meets at least once every two years. So far, Ministerial Conferences have been held in Singapore (December 1996), Geneva (May 1998), Seattle (November-December 1999), Doha (November 2001), Cancun (September 2003), Hong Kong (December 2005), Geneva (November-December 2009), Geneva (December 2011), Bali (December 2013) and Nairobi (December 2015).

WTO is based on the principles of non-discrimination, free trade and promotion of fair competition among the member countries. About 98 percent of the global trade is governed by the rules and regulations of WTO.

WTO agreements are permanent and ratified by the Parliaments of member countries.

WTO performs the following functions:

1. Administering WTO trade agreements.
2. Forum for trade negotiations.
3. Handling trade disputes.
4. Monitoring national trade policies.
5. Technical assistance and training for developing countries.
6. Cooperation with other international organisations.

WTO deals with the global rules of trade between nations. Its main function is to ensure that trade flows as smoothly, predictably and freely as possible.

There are various ways of looking at the WTO. It is an organization for trade opening. It is a forum for governments to negotiate trade agreements. It is a place for them to settle trade disputes. It operates a system of trade rules. Essentially, WTO is a place where member governments try to sort out trade problems they face with each other.

WTO was born out of negotiations, and everything the WTO does is the result of negotiations. The bulk of WTO's current work comes from the 1986-94 negotiations called the Uruguay Round and earlier negotiations under the General Agreement on Tariffs and Trade (GATT). WTO is currently host to new negotiations under the Doha Development Agenda launched in 2001.

Where countries have faced trade barriers and wanted them lowered, the negotiations have helped to open markets for trade. However, WTO is not just about opening markets, and in some circumstances its rules support maintaining trade barriers—for example, to protect consumers or prevent the spread of disease.

At its heart are the WTO Agreements, negotiated and signed by the bulk of the world's trading nations. These documents provide the legal ground rules for international commerce. They are essentially contracts, binding governments to keep their trade policies within the agreed limits. Although negotiated and signed by governments, the goal is to help producers of goods and services, exporters, and importers to conduct their business, while allowing governments to meet social and environmental objectives.

The system's overriding purpose is to help trade flow as freely as possible—so long as there are no undesirable side effects—because it is important for economic development and well-being. It partly means removing obstacles. It also means ensuring that individuals, companies and governments know what the trade rules are around the world, and giving them the confidence that there will be no sudden change of policy. In other words, the rules have to be transparent and predictable.

Trade relations often involve conflicting interests. Agreements, including those painstakingly negotiated in the WTO system, often need interpretation. The most harmonious way to settle these differences is through some neutral procedure, based on an agreed legal foundation. That is the purpose behind the dispute settlement process written in the WTO Agreements.

While the WTO is driven by its member states, it could not function without its Secretariat to coordinate the activities. The Secretariat employs over 600 staff, and its experts—lawyers, economists, statisticians and communications experts—assist WTO members to ensure, among other things, that negotiations progress smoothly, and that the rules of international trade are correctly applied and enforced.

WTO agreements cover goods, services and intellectual property. They spell out the principles of liberalization, and the permitted exceptions. They include commitments of individual countries to lower customs tariffs and other trade barriers, and to keep open the services markets. They set procedures for settling disputes. These agreements are not static; they are renegotiated from time to time and new agreements can be added to the package. Many are now being negotiated under the Doha Development Agenda, launched by WTO trade ministers in Doha, Qatar, in November 2001.

WTO agreements require governments to make their trade policies transparent by notifying the WTO about laws in force and measures adopted. Various WTO councils and committees seek to ensure that these requirements are being followed and that WTO agreements are being properly implemented. All WTO members must undergo periodic scrutiny of their trade policies and practices, each review containing reports by the country concerned and the WTO Secretariat.

WTO's procedure for resolving trade quarrels under the Dispute Settlement Understanding is vital for enforcing the rules, thereby ensuring that trade flows smoothly. Countries bring disputes to the WTO if they think their rights under the agreements are being infringed. Judgements by specially appointed independent experts are based on interpretations of the agreements and commitments of individual countries.

WTO Agreements contain special provisions for developing countries, including longer time periods to implement agreements and commitments, measures to increase their trading opportunities, support to help them build their trade capacity, to handle disputes and to implement technical standards. WTO organizes hundreds of technical cooperation missions for developing countries annually. It also holds numerous courses each year in Geneva for government officials. Aid-for-Trade aims to help developing countries develop the skills and infrastructure needed to expand their trade.

WTO maintains regular dialogue with non-governmental organizations, parliamentarians, other international organizations, media and the general public on various aspects of WTO and the ongoing Doha negotiations, with the aim of enhancing cooperation and increasing awareness of the WTO activities.

An attempt has been made in the present work to provide an exhaustive description and documentation of the demise of General Agreement on Tariffs and Trade (GATT) and the birth of the World Trade Organization (WTO). More importantly, the work focuses on the present structure and functioning of WTO, its various agreements and declarations, dispute settlement mechanism, trade review mechanism, pending issues and ongoing negotiations.

The work consists of three parts.

Part I contains 9 chapters. Chapter 1 advocates the case for open trade. Chapter 2 is devoted to General Agreement on Tariffs and Trade (GATT). Chapter 3 discusses the Uruguay Round of trade negotiations and the birth of WTO. Chapter 4 covers WTO agreements on establishment, GATT, agriculture, sanitary and phytosanitary measures, and textiles. Chapter 5 explains WTO agreements on technical barriers to trade, trade-related investment, anti-dumping, customs valuation, and pre-shipment inspection. Chapter 6 describes WTO agreements on rules of origin, import licensing, subsidies, and safeguards. Chapter 7 is exclusively devoted to WTO General Agreement on Trade in Services (GATS). Likewise, Chapter 8 exclusively deals with WTO Agreement on Trade-related Aspects of Intellectual Property Rights (TRIPS). Chapter 9 spells out WTO understanding on rules and procedures governing the settlement of disputes.

Part II consists of 10 chapters, one each devoted to the discussions, declarations, decisions and agreements of 10 Ministerial Conferences of the WTO held so far and mentioned above.

Part III contains 1 chapter which looks at the future of WTO. It explains and examines the current issues pending before the WTO, hurdles in solving them and strategies of member countries/trade blocks in this regard. Besides, Part III also includes an appendix which provides a list of 162 members of WTO (as on January 1, 2016), bibliography and index.

Acknowledgements

I am thankful to Dr. P.K. Khurana, Principal, Shaheed Bhagat Singh College (University of Delhi) for supporting and encouraging me at various stages of the completion of this work. Thanks are also due to my following colleagues for their help and suggestions: Dr. Ramjas,

Dr. N.K. Puri, Dr. V.K. Anand, Mr. Comrade Iqbal, Dr. Vaneeta Chandana, Dr. Prem Kumar and Ms. Pallavi Sethi.

I would like to place on record my deep appreciation and regards for my wife Asha Deol and son Shubhankar Deol for providing moral support and congenial atmosphere at home during the course of completing this work.

Finally, I express my thanks to Mr. Sandeep Sury, Chief Executive, New Century Publications, New Delhi and his team of editors for designing, editing and improving the format and presentation of the book.

New Delhi **O.S. Deol**

WTO-related Abbreviations/Acronyms

ACP	African, Caribbean and Pacific Group
AMS	Aggregate Measure of Support
ASEAN	Association of Southeast Asian Nations
ATC	Agreement on Textiles and Clothing
CCC	Customs Cooperation Council
CRO	Committee on Rules of Origin
CRTA	Committee on Regional Trade Agreements
CTD	Committee on Trade and Development
CTESS	Committee on Trade and Environment in Special Session
CVD	Countervailing Duty
DDA	Doha Development Agenda
DFQF	Duty-free and Quota-free
DG	Director-General
DSB	Dispute Settlement Body
DSU	Dispute Settlement Understanding
EEC	European Economic Community
EIF	Enhanced Integrated Framework
EU	European Union
FAO	Food and Agriculture Organization
FDI	Foreign Direct Investment
FTAs	Free Trade Agreements
GATS	General Agreement on Trade in Services
GATT	General Agreement on Tariffs and Trade
GDP	Gross Domestic Product
GSP	Generalised System of Preferences
GSTP	Global System of Trade Preferences
IBRD	International Bank for Reconstruction and Development
ICC	International Chamber of Commerce
ILO	International Labour Organization
IMF	International Monetary Fund
IPIC	Intellectual Property in Respect of Integrated Circuits
ITC	International Trade Centre
ITO	International Trade Organization
LDCs	Least Developed Countries
MFN	Most-Favoured Nation
NAMA	Non-agricultural Market Access
NTBs	Non-tariff Barriers
OECD	Organisation for Economic Cooperation and Development
OPEC	Organization of the Petroleum Exporting Countries

OTDS	Overall Trade-distorting Domestic Support
PTA	Preferential Trade Agreement
RAM	Recently Acceded Members
RCEP	Regional Comprehensive Economic Partnership
RTAs	Regional Trade Agreements
SAARC	South Asian Association for Regional Cooperation
SADC	South African Development Community
SDT	Special and Differential Treatment
SPS	Sanitary and Phytosanitary Measures
SSM	Special Safeguard Mechanism
TBT	Technical Barriers to Trade
TFA	Trade Facilitation Agreement
TISA	Trade in Services Agreement
TNC	Trade Negotiation Committee
TPP	Trans-Pacific Partnership
TPRB	Trade Policy Review Body
TPRM	Trade Policy Review Mechanism
TRIMs	Trade-related Investment Measures
TRIPS	Trade-related Aspects of Intellectual Property Rights
TTIP	Trans-Atlantic Trade and Investment Partnership
UN	United Nations
UNCTAD	United Nations Conference on Trade and Development
UNDP	United Nations Development Programme
UNEP	United Nations Environment Programme
UPOV	International Union for Protection of New Varieties of Plants
WCO	World Customs Organization
WHOGMP	World Health Organisation Good Manufacturing Practices
WIPO	World Intellectual Property Organization
WTO	World Trade Organization

Part I:
Demise of GATT and the Birth of WTO

1

Advocacy for Open Trade

1.1 Economic Case for Open Trading

The economic case for an open trading system based on multilaterally agreed rules is straightforward. It rests on the commercial common sense of comparative advantage. The principle of "comparative advantage" says that countries prosper first by taking advantage of their resources in order to concentrate on what they can produce best, and then by trading these products for products that other countries produce best.

Comparative advantage is arguably the single most powerful insight into economics. Suppose, country X is better than country Y at making automobiles and country Y is better than country X at making clothing. It is apparent that both would benefit if X specialized in automobiles, Y specialized in clothing and they traded their products. This is a case of absolute advantage. But what if a country is bad at making everything? Will trade drive all producers out of business? The answer, according to Ricardo, is no. The reason is the principle of comparative advantage.

It says that countries X and Y still stand to benefit from trading with each other even if X is better than Y at making everything. If X is much more superior at making automobiles and only slightly superior at making clothing, then X should still invest resources in what it does best—producing automobiles—and export the product to Y. Y should still invest in what it does best—making clothing—and export that product to X, even if it is not as efficient as X. Both would still benefit from the trade. A country does not have to be best at anything to gain from trade. This is comparative advantage. The theory dates back to classical economist David Ricardo. It is one of the most widely accepted among economists. It is also one of the most misunderstood among non-economists because it is confused with absolute advantage. It is often claimed, for example, that some countries have no comparative advantage in anything. That is virtually impossible.

It implies that liberal trade policies allowing the unrestricted flow of goods and services sharpen competition, ground efficient use of resources, motivate innovation and breed success. They multiply the rewards that result from producing the best products, with the best design, at the best price. But the phenomenon of comparative advantage is not static. The ability to compete well in particular products can shift from company to company when the market changes or new technologies make cheaper and better products possible. Producers are encouraged to adapt—gradually and in a relatively painless way—the new techniques and methods. They can focus on new products, find a new "advantage" in their current area or expand into new areas envisaging the advantage. The competitiveness also shifts between whole countries. A country that may have enjoyed an advantage because of lower labour costs or because it had good supplies of some natural resources, could also become uncompetitive in some goods or services as its economy develops. However, with the stimulus of an open economy, the country can move on to become competitive in some other goods or services. This is normally a gradual process.

The experience of world trade and economic growth since the Second World War also supports the economic case of open trade. Tariffs on industrial products have fallen steeply and now average less than 4 percent in industrial countries. During the first 25 years after the War, world economic growth averaged about 5 percent per year, a high rate that was partly the result of lower trade barriers. World trade grew even faster, averaging about 8 percent during the period. Economic theory also points to a definite link between freer trade and economic growth. All countries, including the poorest, have resources—human, industrial, natural, financial—which they can employ to produce goods and services for their domestic markets or to compete overseas. Economics advocates that countries can benefit when these goods and services are traded.

The World Trade Report, 2014, prepared by WTO, has also underpinned the economic progress of developing countries by taking advantage of trade expansion. The Report identified four trends and how the developing countries benefited from these trends.

First, the strong economic performance of many developing countries has been strongly correlated with the reduction in their levels of protection—a significant part undertaken in the context of implementing the WTO commitments. G-20 developing countries reduced their MFN applied rate from 15.6 percent in 1996 to 10.1 percent in 2009-11. They had bound over 80 percent of their tariff lines and reduced their bound rates by a quarter, from 39 percent in 1996 to 29.2 percent in 2009-11. China's accession to the WTO played a major role in its openness to trade and a large body of research shows that the accession has had a positive impact on China's economic growth, trade and investment.

Second, the predictable business environment and the reduction of trade barriers and of trade costs ensued by the implementation of WTO rules made possible the integration of developing countries with global value chains. WTO commitments provided a level playing field that is key not only with respect to trade in intermediate goods, which are largely most-favoured nation and duty free for developing countries, but also for trade in services—a critical sector for the development of global value chains.

Third, high and rising commodity prices from 2002 onwards have created opportunities for developing countries to leverage agricultural and natural resource exports for development.

Finally, the WTO has helped safeguard the economic gains achieved by many developing countries in the past decade despite the world suffering from the biggest economic crisis since the past 70 years. The WTO helped contain protectionism through its system of trade rules and the effectiveness of its monitoring efforts. For this reason, the economic crisis of 2008-09 did not trigger a protectionist surge, bearing resemblance to the experience during the great depression of the 1930s.

The above discussion implies that the rule-based open trade is beneficial in many ways, such as:

1. It creates stability and predictability in the global business environment.
2. It leads to the most efficient utilisation of the resources available worldwide.
3. It mitigates the triggering of protectionism in the world economy.
4. It provides stimulus to the economic growth.
5. It ensures the overall development of the economies and others.

On the other hand, protectionism leads to overfed, inefficient producers supplying consumers with outdated and unattractive products. Protectionism leads to inefficient use of resources also. A country that employs trade barriers remains far behind from its potential development. The overall well-being of the society suffers due to blocked trade. Economists generally believe that the levels of protectionism should move in a countercyclical fashion as regards the economic activity. The Great Depression of the 1930s was a glaring example of the countercyclical behaviour of protectionism. Some empirical studies show the countercyclical behaviour of protectionism, particularly in the case of trade remedies.

In a nutshell, the benefits of rule-based open trade over protectionism makes a clear case for global open trade, ensuring the welfare of the world.

1.2 Open Trade in Practice

Since 1948, the average growth of world trade has outpaced that of the world production. For the first 25 years, world trade grew on an average of 8 percent per year. This higher world trade growth was accompanied by a higher average growth of world production as compared to that before Second World War. Table 1.1 shows that even in the last decade, world merchandise exports grew at an average of 3.5 percent per annum. This is happening since more and more countries are joining the WTO and the attendant reduction in trade barriers.

Table 1.1: Growth in Volume of World Merchandise Exports and Production

(percent)

Exports/GDP	2005-2013	2011	2012	2013
World Merchandise Exports	3.5	5.5	2.5	2.5
World GDP	2.0	2.5	2.0	2.0

Source: International Trade Statistics, WTO, 2014.

Table 1.2 shows the region-wise contribution in the world merchandise exports. There has been an increase in the share of Asian region in world merchandise exports during 1948-2013, especially a massive increase after 1983. The share of all other regions, except the Middle East, in world merchandise exports declined during the same period. Major fall was noticed in the case of North America and South and Central America. The biggest gainer was the Asian region. The share of GATT/WTO Members in world merchandise exports increased from 63.4 percent in 1948 to 97.1 percent in 2013.

Table 1.2: World Merchandise Exports by Region

(US$ billion/percent)

Region	1948	1953	1963	1973	1983	1993	2003	2013
World (US$ billion)	59	84	157	579	1,838	3,684	7,380	18,301
North America	28.1	24.8	19.9	17.3	16.8	18.0	15.8	13.2
South and Central America	11.3	9.7	6.4	4.3	4.5	3.0	3.0	4.0
Europe	35.1	39.4	47.8	50.9	43.5	45.3	45.9	36.3
Africa	7.3	6.5	5.7	4.8	4.5	2.5	2.4	3.3
Middle East	2.0	2.7	3.2	4.1	6.7	3.5	4.1	7.4
Asia	14.0	13.4	12.5	14.9	19.1	26.0	26.1	31.5
World	100.0	100.0	100.0	100.0	100.0	100.0	100.0	100.0
GATT/WTO Members	63.4	69.6	75.0	84.1	77.0	89.0	94.3	97.1

Source: International Trade Statistics, WTO, 2014.

Table 1.3 shows the trend of shares of different regions in world merchandise imports during 1948-2013. The trend followed the expected lines as indicated by world merchandise exports, with one exception. The share of merchandised imports of North America in world merchandise imports remained near constant in contrast to what happened to their share in world merchandise exports. This difference in shares of exports and imports in the case of North America should have been through some adjustment in another sector, otherwise leading to current account deficit. The share of Africa and South and Central America in world merchandise imports declined during the corresponding period. The share of the Middle East in world merchandise imports was almost intact during 1948-2013. The share of merchandise imports increased substantially from 1984 onwards. The data contained in Tables 1.2 and 1.3 prove that the Asian economies integrated with the world economy to a remarkable extent.

The leading exporters and importers in world merchandise trade in 2013 are given Table 1.4. China stood at the top of the list of exporters of merchandise, having an 11.7 percent share of world merchandise exports, followed by the US, Germany and Japan respectively. India was ranked 19th with a share of 1.7 percent in world merchandise exports.

US was a major importer of merchandise, carving out 12.3 percent of world merchandise imports in 2013. China, Germany and Japan followed respectively after the US. India was ranked 12th in the list of merchandise importers and it imported merchandise worth US$ 466 billion in 2013.

Table 1.5 contains information on leading exporters and importers of commercial services in 2013. US was the top exporter, having a share of 14.3 percent of world trade in commercial services followed by UK, Germany and France respectively. India exported commercial services worth US$ 151 billion and secured 6th place in the list of exporters of commercial services in 2013.

Table 1.3: World Merchandise Imports by Region

(US$ billion/percent)

Region	1948	1953	1963	1973	1983	1993	2003	2013
World (US$ billion)	62	85	164	594	1,883	3,800	7,696	18,409
North America	18.5	20.5	16.1	17.2	18.5	21.3	22.4	17.4
South and Central America	10.4	8.3	6.0	4.4	3.9	-3.3	2.5	4.2
Europe	45.3	43.7	52.0	53.3	44.1	44.4	45.0	35.8
Africa	8.1	7.0	5.2	3.9	4.6	2.6	2.2	3.4
Middle East	1.8	2.1	2.3	2.7	6.2	3.3	2.8	4.2
Asia	13.9	15.1	14.1	14.9	18.5	23.6	23.3	31.8
World	100.0	100.0	100.0	100.0	100.0	100.0	100.0	100.0
GATT/WTO Members	58.6	66.9	75.3	85.5	79.7	89.3	96.0	97.5

Source: International Trade Statistics, WTO, 2014.

Table 1.4: Leading Exporters and Importers in World Merchandise Trade in 2013

(US$ billion/percent)

Exporters				Importers			
Rank	Country	Value	Share	Rank	Country	Value	Share
1.	China	2,209	11.7	1.	U.S.	2,329	12.3
2.	U.S.	1,580	8.4	2.	China	1,950	10.3
3.	Germany	1,453	7.7	3.	Germany	1,189	6.3
4.	Japan	715	3.8	4.	Japan	833	4.4
5.	Netherlands	672	3.6	5.	France	681	3.6
6.	France	580	3.1	6.	U.K.	655	3.5
7.	Korea	560	3.0	7.	Hong Kong	622	3.3
8.	U.K.	542	2.9	8.	Netherlands	590	3.1
9.	Hong Kong	536	2.8	9.	Korea	516	2.7
19.	**India**	**313**	**1.7**	**12.**	**India**	**466**	**2.5**
	World	18,816	100.0		World	18,890	100.0

Source: International Trade Statistics, WTO, 2014.

The US imported commercial services valued at US$ 432 billion in 2013. It accounted for 9.8 percent of the total world trade in commercial services and was marked on top place in the list of major importers of commercial services. The US was followed by China, Germany and France respectively in the imports of commercial services. India was on 9th place in the list of imported commercial services, valued at

US$ 125 billion. It attained a 2.8 percent share of the world trade in commercial services in 2013.

Table 1.5: Leading Exporters and Importers in World Trade in Commercial Services in 2013

(US$ billion/percent)

Exporters				Importers			
Rank	Country	Value	Share	Rank	Country	Value	Share
1.	U.S.	622	14.3	1.	U.S.	432	9.8
2.	U.K.	293	6.3	2.	China	329	7.5
3.	Germany	286	6.2	3.	Germany	317	7.2
4.	France	236	5.1	4.	France	189	4.3
5.	China	205	4.4	5.	U.K.	174	4.0
6.	**India**	**151**	**3.2**	6.	Japan	162	3.7
7.	Netherlands	147	3.2	7.	Singapore	128	2.9
8.	Japan	145	3.1	8.	Netherlands	129	2.9
9.	Spain	145	3.1	**9.**	**India**	**125**	**2.8**
10.	Hong Kong	133	2.9	10.	Russia	123	2.8
	World	4,645	100.0		World	4,380	100.0

Source: International Trade Statistics, WTO, 2014.

Nearly two-thirds of the world merchandise exports comprised of industrial products in 2013. Agricultural products accounted for 9.5 percent of the world merchandise exports. The remaining 21.8 percent share in world merchandise exports was carved out by fuel and mining products' exports. In manufactured goods, chemicals, office and telecommunication equipments, and automobile products formed about a half of world exports of manufactured goods in 2013 (Table 1.6).

Table 1.6: World Merchandise Exports by Major Product Groups in 2013

(US$ billion/percent)

Group/Product	Value	Share
Agricultural Products	1,745	9.5
Fuel and Mining Products, of which	3,997	21.8
Fuel	3,258	17.8
Manufactures, of which	11,848	64.7
Iron and Steel	454	2.5
Chemicals	2,001	10.9
Office and telecom equipments	1,750	9.6
Automobiles Products	1,348	7.4
Textiles	306	1.7
Clothing	460	2.5

Source: International Trade Statistics, WTO, 2014.

1.3 Emergence of GATT and WTO

The Great Depression of 1930s led to the adoption of trade protection measures by nations worldwide. The economies started contracting and the issue compelled the countries to devise the ways for the revival of their economies and to mitigate reoccurrence of the events like the Great Depression. Debate on merits and demerits of protectionism generally took place in the economic discussions. The countries sincerely thought about the opening up of the trade to ensure growth and development of the economies. Few industrial countries from Europe started to move in this direction after the Second World War.

Lowering trade barriers is one of the most obvious means of encouraging trade. The barriers concerned include customs duties and measures such as import bans or quotas that restrict quantities selectively. Other measures such as trade distorting subsidies, red tape and exchange rate policies also discourage multilateral trade. There has been a sincere need of such a mechanism to deal with these issues and promoting the global trade, taking the nations together. The efforts to accomplish this started immediately after the Second World War.

A group of 15 countries started talks in 1945 to reduce and bind customs tariffs. They were intended to give a boost to the international trade and to make a beginning of correcting the legacy of protection measures being implemented by the nations. They intended to make this as an interim arrangement to fill the gap until the ITO Charter was approved. The efforts were succeeded in 1947 by making an interim and non-institutional arrangement in the form of the "General Agreement on Tariffs and Trade (GATT)". Thus, the new legal arrangement, namely the 'General Agreement on Tariffs and Trade' was born, with 23 founding members (contracting parties). The first round of negotiations resulted in a set of trade rules and 4,500 tariff concessions affecting US$ 10 billion of trade.

The contracting parties agreed that relations amongst them in the field of trade and economic endeavour should develop in such a way thereby raising standards of living, ensuring full employment and large and steady growth of real income and effective demand, developing the full use of world resources, and expanding the production and trade of goods.

The contracting parties decided to attain these objectives by facilitating negotiations on reciprocal and mutually advantageous arrangements resulting in reduction of tariffs and other trade barriers to trade, and in eliminating discriminating treatment in international commerce.

Since GATT's creation, there have been eight rounds of trade negotiations. A ninth round, under the Doha Development Agenda, is now underway. At first, these focused on lowering tariffs (customs duties) on imported goods. As a result of the negotiations, by the mid-1990s, industrial countries' tariff rates on industrial goods had fallen steadily to less than 4 percent.

But by the 1980s, the negotiations had expanded to cover non-tariff barriers on goods, and to the new areas such as services and intellectual property. GATT, 1947 was a provisional arrangement with a limited field of action and it was successful in promoting and securing the liberalisation of world trade to a limited extent.

As the time passed, the signs of new difficulties were visible. GATT's success in reducing tariffs to a low level in 1970s and severe recession of 1970s and early 1980s, forced the countries to find new ways of protection to tackle increased foreign competition. High unemployment rates and the factory closures drove the governments in Western Europe and North America to seek bilateral market sharing arrangements with the competitors. These governments also increased subsidies in the agricultural sector to maintain their hold on agricultural trade. These developments prompted doubts about the effectiveness and credibility of the GATT.

The world trade had become more complex and important over the time. Trade in services, not covered under the GATT, was expanding and became more lucrative for the countries intending international trade in services. Loopholes in the multilateral system were being exploited in the agricultural sector. International investments were expanding. Even GATT's institutional structure and its dispute settlement system was a matter of concern. The multilateral trading system under GATT 1947 seemed unable to cope up with these issues.

Under GATT 1947, the procedure for settling disputes did not have fixed timetable. It was easier to block rulings, and many cases were dragged on for long time inclusively. Under the GATT 1947 procedure, the rulings could only be adopted by consensus, meaning that a single objection could block the ruling. The new Agreement introduced a more structured process with clearly defined stages in the procedure. It introduced greater discipline for the timely settlement of disputes. The Agreement made it impossible for the country losing a case to block the adoption of the ruling. Now, the rulings are automatically adopted unless there is a consensus to reject the ruling. Now, any country willing to block a ruling has to persuade all other Members (including its opposite party in the case) to share its view.

Another important issue was the integration of developing countries, especially least developed countries, into multilateral trading system. These countries were facing difficulties and their needs were different in some aspects. It was imperative to provide technical assistance to developing countries. For the development of these countries and for their integration into the multilateral trading system, the provision of technology transfer was also vital in trade dealing. There was a dire requirement of special treatment for developing countries.

These issues coupled with other factors, persuaded the GATT members that efforts are needed for the reinforcement and extension of multilateral system. The Uruguay Round was the result of these efforts. The Uruguay Round started in September 1986 at Punta Del Este, Uruguay.

The negotiations were originally scheduled to be completed in four years, but because of the crises and deadlocks that developed from time to time, they dragged on for over seven years. Finally, an agreement to establish the World Trade Organization (WTO) was signed by 123 countries at Marrakesh, Mexico on April 15, 1994.

2

General Agreement on Tariffs and Trade (GATT), 1947

2.1 Introduction

The need was felt to create a third institution to govern the trade side of international economic cooperation, in addition to the two Bretton Woods institutions, namely International Bank for Reconstruction and Development and the International Monetary Fund. The efforts were made to establish an International Trade Organisation at the U.N. Conference on Trade and Employment held in Havana, Cuba in 1947. More than fifty nations took part in the negotiations to establish the third institution, namely, the International Trade Organisation (ITO) as an agency of the United Nations to govern international trade. The Charter of the ITO included rules on employment, commodity agreements, restrictive business practices, international investment and services in addition to trade rules.

The Havana Conference began on November 21, 1947. The 23 founding members of GATT were also part of a larger group which was making negotiations on the ITO Charter. The ITO Charter was finally agreed in Havana in March 1948. But, ratification of the Charter in some national legislatures became difficult. Though the US Government was one of the driving forces for the Charter, the US Congress opposed the Charter. In 1950, the United States government announced that it would not seek the ratification of the Havana Charter by the US congress. Consequently, the International Trade Organisation could not be established.

A group of 15 countries started talks in 1945 to reduce and bind customs tariffs. They intended to give a boost to international trade and to make a beginning of correcting the legacy of protection measures being implemented by the nations. They intended to make this as an interim arrangement to fill the gap until the ITO Charter was approved.

The negotiations that led to the interim arrangement were held in 1946-47 during and after the sessions of the Preparatory Committee of the United Nations Conference on Trade and Employment. The Final Act was signed in Geneva on October 30, 1947 by the group that swelled in numbers to 23. Thus, the new legal arrangement, namely General Agreement on Tariffs and Trade was born, with 23 founding members (contracting parties). The first round of negotiations resulted in a set of trade rules and 4,500 tariff concessions affecting US$ 10 billion of trade. The customs tariff concessions became effective by 1948 through a 'protocol of provisional application'.

There was a provision in GATT, that some of the trade rules of the draft of Havana Charter should be accepted in it. The group agreed that to protect the value of the tariff concessions negotiated, it should be done with pace. They also expressed the possible relationship between GATT and the Havana Charter by incorporating it through Article

XXIX, though the group doubted the creation of ITO.

Since the Havana Charter proved a failed attempt to create the International Trade Organisation, the General Agreement on Tariffs and Trade became the only multilateral instrument governing the international trade. The GATT, 1947 was provisionally applied from January 1, 1948 until December 31, 1994.

The contracting parties agreed that relations amongst them in the field of trade and economic endeavour should develop in a way thereby raising standards of living, ensuring full employment and large and steady growth of real income and effective demand, developing the full use of world resources, and expanding the production and trade of goods.

The contracting parties decided to attain these objectives by facilitating negotiations on reciprocal and mutually advantageous arrangements resulting in reduction of tariffs and other trade barriers, and in eliminating discriminating treatment in international commerce.

2.2 The Agreement

The contents of General Agreement on Tariffs and Trade were divided into four parts. The subject matter of GATT was confined to tariff and non-tariff barriers relating to manufactured goods. The main provisions of GATT are described below. Where reference is made to contracting parties acting jointly they are designated as the *Contracting Parties*.

2.2.1 Part I: It contained the following Articles.

A. Article I: General Most Favoured Nation Treatment: The most-favoured-nation principle says that a contracting party should give equal treatment to all other contacting parties. The principle of most favoured nation treatment also requires that a contracting party should provide no less favourable treatment to all other contracting parties than the treatment provided to any other country.

Article I says that any contracting party granting any advantage, favour, privilege or immunity related to customs duties and charges of any kind imposed on or in connection with imports or exports or imposed on the international transfer of payments for imports and exports, and related to the methods of levying such duties and charges, and related to all rules and formalities in connection with imports and exports to any product originating in or destined for any other country shall accord the same immediately and unconditionally to the like product originating in or destined for the territories of all other contracting parties.

The aim of this provision is to discourage bilateralism and encourage multilateralism to expand global trade in an orderly manner. However, formation of customs unions or free trade areas is permitted by GATT under Article XXIV as long as it does not raise any barrier to the trade of other contracting parties. The generalised system of preferences accepted in Tokyo Round with provision of preferential market access with least developed countries is also an exception to the principle of most favoured nation (MFN).

B. Article II: Schedules of Concessions: The schedules are list of trade concessions committed by the contracting parties contained in Annex. All trade concessions (commitments) must be stated and be a part of the legal agreement. The Article says that no other contracting party may be treated less favourably than the committed concessions in the appropriate Part of the appropriate Schedule annexed to the ‘‘General Agreement on Tariffs and Trade”.

2.2.2 Part II: It contained the following Articles.

A. Article III: National Treatment on Internal Taxation and Regulation: The Article says that the contracting parties shall not use internal measures to discriminate between domestic goods and those imported from the other contracting parties. The product of any contracting party imported by the other contracting party shall be accorded treatment no less favourable than that accorded to domestic products in respect of all laws, regulations and requirements affecting their internal sale, offering for sale, purchase, transportation, distribution or use. In brief, imports by the contracting parties shall be accorded ‘national treatment’.

B. Article IV: Special Provisions Relating to Cinematograph: If any contracting party establishes or maintains internal quantitative regulations pertaining to exposed cinematograph films, such regulations shall take the form of screen quotas which shall conform to specific requirements.

C. Article V: Freedom of Transit: Article V says that traffic in transit shall include passage of goods including baggage, vessels and other means of transport coming from or destined to territories of other contracting parties across the territory of a contracting party. Further, there shall be freedom of transit through the territory of each contracting party, via the routes most convenient for international transit for the traffic in transit to or from the territories of other contracting parties. The traffic in transit shall not be subject to any unnecessary delays or restrictions, except customs laws and regulations, and shall be exempted from customs duties and from all transit duties or other charges in respect of transit. Both the clauses, the most favoured nation as well as the national treatment shall apply to the traffic in transit.

D. Article VI: Anti-dumping and Countervailing Duties: As per Article VI, the contracting parties may apply duties and other measures to the goods originating in other contracting party’s territory which are dumped and/or enjoy export subsidies subject to specifications. There are provisions related to anti-dumping and countervailing measures:

1. The dumping involves the product of one country being introduced into the commerce of another country at less than the normal value of the product.
2. The dumping is condemned if it causes or threatens material injury to an established industry in the territory of the importing contracting party or materially retards the establishment on an industry in the territory of the importing contracting party. There is provision of action on part of the affected party.
3. The affected contracting party may levy on any dumped product, an anti-dumping duty not greater in amount than the margin of dumping in respect of such product in order to offset or prevent dumping.
4. The term ‘countervailing duty’ shall be understood to mean a special duty levied by

an importing contracting party for the purpose of offsetting any bounty or subsidy bestowed directly or indirectly upon the manufacture, production or export of any merchandise originating from the territory of other contracting parties.

5. A countervailing duty may be levied by an importing contracting party on any product originating in another country by an amount not greater than the estimated bounty or the subsidy determined to have been granted, directly or indirectly, on manufacture, production or export of such product in the country of origin or exportation, including any special subsidy to the transportation of a particular product.
6. Anti-dumping or countervailing duty shall not be levied on a product of territory of a contracting party imported into the territory of another contracting party by the reason of the exemption of such product from duties or taxes borne by like product when destined for consumption in the country of origin or exportation or by reason of the refund of such duties or taxes.
7. Anti-dumping or countervailing duty on the importation of any product of the territory of a contracting party into the territory of another contracting party shall not be levied unless it determines that the effect of dumping or subsidisation, as the case may be, is such as to cause or threaten material injury to an established industry, or is such as to retard materially the establishment of an industry in the territory of importing contracting party.
8. The requirement mentioned in point 7 above may be waived by the Contracting Parties so as to permit a contracting party to levy an anti-dumping or countervailing duty on the importation of any product for the purpose of offsetting dumping or subsidisation which causes or threatens material injury to an industry in the territory of another contracting party exporting the product concerned to the territory of the importing contracting party.
9. The sale of a commodity for export at a lower price than the comparable price charged for the like commodity to the domestic buyers resultant to the implementation of a system for the stabilisation of domestic prices or of the return to domestic producers of a primary commodity, independently of the movements of export prices shall be presumed not to result in material injury subject to specifications.

E. Article VII: Valuation for Customs Purposes: The contracting parties accepted the principles of valuation and decided to implement such principles, in respect of all products subject to duties or other charges or restrictions on importation and exportations based upon or regulated in any manner by the value.

1. The value of merchandise for customs purposes or other charges should be based on the actual value of the imported merchandise on which duty is assessed, or of like merchandise and should not be based on the value of merchandise of national origin or on arbitrary or fictitious values.
2. The value of any imported product for customs purposes should not include the amount of any internal tax, applicable within the country of origin or export, from

which the imported product has been exempted or has been or will be relieved by means of refund.

3. Where it is necessary for a contracting party to convert a price expressed in foreign currency into its own currency, the conversion exchange rate to be applied shall be based, for each currency involved, on the par value as established by the Articles of Agreement of the IMF or on the exchange rate recognised by the IMF or on the par value established in accordance with a special exchange agreement entered into pursuant to Article XV of this Agreement.
4. If no such established par value or no such recognised exchange rate exists, the conversion ratc shall reflect effectively the current value of such currency in commercial transaction.
5. The bases and methods used in determining the value of products subject to duties or charges or restrictions based upon or regulated in any manner by value should be stable and should be given sufficient publicity to enable traders to estimate, with reasonable degree of certainty, the value for customs purposes.

F. Article VIII: Fees and Formalities Connected with Importation and Exportation: There should be fair reflection of cost of services provided for importation and exportation by the contracting parties. Further, such cost should not be indirectly used as a mean to give the protection to the domestic industry. The Article has following provisions.

1. The contracting parties shall limit all fees and charges of whatever character (other than import and export duties) imposed on or in connection with importation or exportation to the appropriate cost of services rendered. The imposition of such charges shall not represent an indirect protection to domestic production or a taxation of imports or exports for fiscal purposes.
2. There is a need for minimising the incidence and complexity of import and export formalities and for simplifying and reducing import and export documentation requirements.
3. The contracting parties shall not impose substantial penalties for minor breaches of customs regulations or other procedural requirements. Specifically, no penalty can be imposed for omission or mistake committed in customs documentation with no intention to commit fraud.
4. The provisions of this Article shall extend to fees, charges, formalities and requirements imposed by the government authorities relating to importation and exportation, including those related to:

- Licensing.
- Consular services.
- Exchange control.
- Quantitative restrictions.
- Statistical services.
- Quarantine, sanitation and fumigation.
- Documentation and certification.
- Analysis and inspection.

G. Article IX: Marks of Origin: The most favoured nation treatment should be given to a product regarding marking requirements and it should not increase the cost of the product. The Article has the following provisions:

1. In regarding to marking requirement, each contracting party shall accord treatment to the products of other contracting parties no less favourable than the treatment accorded to like products of third countries.
2. The difficulties and inconveniences to the commerce and industry of exporting countries resultant to the adoption and enforcement of laws and regulations relating to marks of origin should be reduced to the minimum.
3. The contracting parties should permit required marks of origin to be preferably affixed at the time of importation. The consumers should be protected against fraudulent or misleading indications.
4. The compliance of laws and regulations of a contracting party relating to the marking of imported products should not be such as seriously damaging the products, or materially reducing their value, or unnecessarily increasing their cost.
5. A contracting party should not impose any special duty or penalty for failure to comply with marking requirements prior to importation unless the corrective marking is unreasonably delayed or the deceptive marking has been done or the required marking has been intentionally omitted.
6. The contracting parties shall cooperate with each other to prevent the use of trademarks or other marks of origin in such a manner as to misrepresent the true origin of a product.

H. Article X: Publication and Administration of Trade Regulations: The Article says that all trade measures of members should be published and therefore transparent.

1. The contracting parties, to acquaint traders and governments with, shall publish their laws, regulations, judicial decisions and administrative rulings of general applications relating to the classification or the valuation of products for customs purposes, to tariffs, taxes and other charges, or to requirement, restriction on imports or exports or transfer of payments. The rules affecting sale, distribution, transportation, insurance, warehousing, inspection, exhibition, processing, mixing and other uses of imports and exports shall also be published.
2. The measures resulting in an increase in tariffs, or charges on imports, or in imposing new or more burdensome requirement, restriction or prohibition on imports or on the transfer of payments shall be published in advance to their implementation.
3. All laws, regulations, decisions and rulings pertaining to imports and exports shall be administered in uniform, impartial and reasonable manner.
4. A contracting party shall maintain, or institute judicial, arbitral or administrative tribunals or procedures for matters relating to customs.

I. Article XI: General Elimination of Quantitative Restrictions: A contracting party shall not institute or maintain any prohibition or restriction, whether effective through quotas, import or export licenses or other measures, other than duties, taxes or other charges on importation and exportation of any product.

J. Article XII: Restrictions to Safeguard the Balance of Payments: The Article contains conditions relating to use and subsequent removal of emergency trade measures enabling the safeguard of the balance of payments position of the contracting parties. In order to safeguard external financial position and its balance of payments, any contracting party may restrict the quantity or value of merchandise to be imported subject to following provisions:

1. (a) The import restrictions by a contracting party shall not exceed those necessary to stop a serious decline in its monetary reserves or to increase reasonably the reserves from a very low level. (b) A contracting party applying restrictions shall progressively relax them as its balance of payments position improves.
2. (a) A contracting party shall apply trade restrictions in such a way as to give priority to the imports of those products which are more essential. (b) A contracting party applying trade restrictions shall undertake to implement the domestic policies in such a way so as to restore and maintain equilibrium in balance of payments on sound and long lasting basis, and to avoid an uneconomic employment of resources. (c) The application of trade restrictions shall avoid unnecessary damage to the commercial or economic interest of other contracting parties. (d) A contracting party shall undertake not to apply trade restrictions preventing the import of commercial samples or preventing compliance with patent, trademark, copyright, or similar procedures.
3. (a) A contracting party applying new trade restrictions or intensifying restrictions already in effect shall immediately after such application or intensification of the restrictions, consult with the Contracting Parties regarding the severity of balance of payments difficulties, alternative corrective measures, and attendant effect on the economies of other contracting parties. (b) If the Contracting Parties in the course of consultations with the concerned contracting party find that the restrictions applied are inconsistent with the provisions of Articles XII and XIII of this Agreement, they may advise the suitable modification of trade restrictions. (c) If the inconsistency is of serious nature and damaging the trade of any contracting party, the Contracting Parties shall recommend the contracting party applying restrictions to secure conformity with relevant provisions within the specified period. Thereafter, if the concerned contracting party fails to comply with the recommendations within the specified period, the Contracting Parties may release any affected party from such obligations under this Agreement towards the concerned contracting party to apply the restrictions as they determine it to be appropriate in the circumstances.
4. If there is persistent and extensive application of trade restrictions under provisions of this Article, indicating the existence of a general disequilibrium hampering international trade, the Contracting Parties shall initiate discussions with the concerned contracting party and international organisations to remove the underlying causes of the disequilibrium.

K. Article XIII: Non-discriminatory Administration of Quantitative Restrictions: There should be no discrimination between the contracting parties in the application of quantitative restrictions and allocation of such restrictions should reflect their underlying trade shares. Details of any restriction should be transparent and negotiated with affected contracting parties.

L. Article XIV: Exceptions to the Rule of Non-discriminatory Administration of Quantitative Restrictions: A contracting party which is using import restrictions under Article XII or Article XVIII may, with the consent of other contracting parties, temporarily deviate from the provisions of Article XIII (Non-discriminatory administration of quantitative restrictions) in respect of a small part of its external trade where the benefits of the contracting party or contracting parties concerned largely outweigh any injury which may result to the trade of other contracting parties.

M. Article XV: Exchange Arrangements: The Contracting Parties shall consult with the International Monetary Fund to deal with matters relating to monetary reserves, balance of payments, and foreign exchange arrangements. The Contracting Parties shall accept all the findings of the IMF relating to foreign exchange, monetary reserves, and balance of payments. The Contracting Parties shall accept the decision of the IMF regarding consistency of an action taken by a contracting party in foreign exchange matter with the provisions of the Articles of Agreements of the IMF or with the terms of a special exchange arrangement between that contracting party and other contracting parties.

N. Article XVI: Subsidies: The Article has provisions encouraging the avoidance of general and specific use of subsidies.

1. If any contracting party grants or maintains any subsidy, including any form of income or price support, which operates directly or indirectly to increase exports of any product, or reduce imports of any product into its territory, shall notify the Contracting Parties in writing to the extent, nature and its effects. In cases, where it causes serious prejudice to the interest of any other contracting party, the contracting party shall, upon request, discuss with other contracting parties or with Contracting Parties the possibilities of limiting the subsidisation.
2. The contracting parties have a view that providing a subsidy on the export of any product by a contracting party may have harmful effects on exports or imports of other contracting parties, may cause undue disturbance to their commercial interest, and may defeat the objectives of this Agreement.
3. The Contracting Parties should avoid granting subsidies to the export of primary products. If a contracting party grants a subsidy in any way resulting in increasing the exports of any primary product from its territory, such subsidy shall not be applied in a manner resulting in having that contracting party more than an equitable share of world export trade.
4. From January 1, 1958 or the earliest practicable date thereafter, the contracting parties shall not grant directly or indirectly any subsidy on the export of any product other than the primary product resulting in export of such product at a lower price than the comparable price of the like product in the domestic market.
5. The Contracting Parties shall review the provisions of this Article on regular basis to examine the effectiveness in fulfilling the objectives of this Agreement and escaping

the subsidisation harmful to the international trade.

O. Article XVII: State Trading Enterprises: A contracting party should notify the operations of the State Trading Enterprises, including market boards. Government should not provide favourable and discriminating assistance to the state trading enterprises. The state trading enterprises should act in a manner consistent with the commercial considerations.

1. A state enterprise being provided special or exclusive privileges in any form from the government shall make its purchases and sales involving exports or imports consistent with general principles of non-discrimination and without affecting imports or exports of private traders.
2. Further, the state enterprises shall make the purchases and sales involving exports or imports in accordance with the commercial considerations including price, quality, availability, marketability, transportation and other conditions, and shall provide equitable opportunity to the enterprises belonging to other contracting parties in accordance with customary business practices to compete in such purchases and sales.
3. The Contracting Parties shall notify to the contracting parties the products which are imported into or exported from their territories by the state trading enterprises if they have been accorded any favourable government assistance.

P. Article XVIII: Governmental Assistance to Economic Development: The Article has the provisions of granting some concessions from trade measures with respect to the GATT Articles to developing countries desirous to raise general standard of living of people. The developing countries have been divided in two categories as describe below:

1. A contracting party whose economy is in the early stages of development and can only support low standard of living may deviate temporarily from the provisions of other Articles of this Agreement subject to the following provisions:

- If the contracting party with a view to uplift the living standard of its people promotes the establishment of a particular industry needs to modify or withdraw a concession included in the appropriate Schedule annexed to this Agreement, it shall notify this to the contracting parties and enter into negotiations with the contracting party/parties affected by such modification or withdrawal. If the agreement is between the contracting party and the other concerned contracting parties, the contracting party may modify or withdraw a concession, subject to specifications.
- If the contracting party implementing an economic development programme faces balance of payments problems caused by the expansion of its domestic market and unstable terms of trade, and needs to safeguard the level of foreign exchange, may control its imports by restrictive quantity or value of merchandise to be imported, subject to specifications.
- If the contracting party needs governmental assistance to establish a specific industry aiming to uplift the standard of living of people, but finds that measures consistent with the other provisions of this Agreement are not practicable to achieve the aim, it shall notify the Contracting Parties of the difficulties to be faced in achieving the desired aim and shall indicate the specific measure affecting the imports which it

proposes to introduce to remove the difficulties. The contracting party may apply the proposed measure deviating from provisions of the other Articles of this Agreement, subject to other conditions.

2. A contracting party whose economy is not in the early stages of development and desiring the development of its economy, needs governmental assistance to establish a particular industry to raise the general standard of living of people, but finds that measures consistent with the other provisions of this Agreement are not practicable to achieve the objective, it may apply to the Contracting Parties for the approval of proposed measure. The Contracting Parties may release that contracting party from its obligations under Articles of this Agreement to the extent necessary to permit it to apply measure, subject to other conditions.

Q. Article XIX: Emergency Action on Imports of Particular Products: This Article has scope for remedial actions, including suspension of trade measures, if imports of particular products increase in such a manner thereby causing injuries to like products, domestic producers, and competition.

1. If any product being imported by a contracting party is increasing in quantity and is causing or threatening serious injury to the domestic producers in like product, the importing contracting party shall be free, in respect to such product, and to the extent and for such time as may be necessary to prevent or remedy such injury, to suspend the obligations applicable under this Agreement in whole or in part or to withdraw or modify the concession, subject to the prescribed procedure.
2. If any product, subject to a preferential treatment, being imported by a contracting is increasing in quantity and is causing or threatening a serious injury to the domestic producers of like product in the territory of a contracting party receiving preferential treatment, the importing contracting party shall be free, on request by the contacting party receiving preferential treatment, to suspend the obligations applicable under this agreement in whole or in part or to withdraw or modify the concession to the extant and for such time as may be necessary to prevent or remedy such injury, subject to the prescribed procedure.

R. Article XX: General Exceptions: This Article permits non-arbitrary and justifiable measures against certain imports for reasons including public moral grounds, health, prison labour, and cultural treasures. A contracting party may apply measures, which are non-arbitrary, justifiable, and not putting any disguised restriction on international trade, as mentioned below:

1. Necessary to protect public morals.
2. Necessary to protect human, animal or plant life or health.
3. Relating to the products of prison labour.
4. Relating to exports or imports of gold and silver.
5. Relating to secure the compliance of laws and regulations.
6. Relating to protection of national treasures of artistic and historic value.
7. Relating to conservation of exhaustive natural resources.
8. Relating to restriction on exports of domestic material necessary to ensure essential

quantities of such material to a domestic processing industry.

S. Article XXI: Security Exceptions: The contracting parties are not committed to actions contrary to their national security. Nothing in the Agreement shall be construed:

1. To require any contracting party to furnish any information the disclosure of which is contrary to national security,
2. To prevent any contracting party from taking any action considered essential to protect its national security.
3. To prevent any contracting party from taking any action in pursuance of its obligations to the United Nation's Charter for the maintenance of international peace and security.

T. Article XXII: Consultation: A contracting party shall accord and give an opportunity for consultation, if a representation relating to a matter affecting the operation of this agreement is made by another contracting party. If any satisfactory solution does not arrive, the matter may be referred to the Contracting Parties.

U. Article XXIII: Nullification or Impairment: The Article says that if the benefits of any contracting party accruing under this Agreement are being nullified or impaired as the result of:

1. Failure of another party to carry out its obligations under this Agreement.
2. The application by another party of any measure, whether or not consistent with the provisions of this Agreement.
3. The existence of any other situation.

The concerned party may make the representation to the other party seeking a satisfactory adjustment of the matter. If any satisfactory solution does not arrive within a specified period of time, the matter may be referred to the Contracting Parties.

2.2.3 Part III: It contained the following Articles.

A. Article XXIV: Territorial Application-Frontier Traffic-Customs Unions and Free Trade Areas: The Article mentions conditions and measures relating to the formation of customs unions and free trade areas by the contracting parties.

1. A customs territory shall mean any territory with respect to which separate tariffs or other regulations of commerce are maintained for a substantial part of the trade of such territory with other territories.
2. Exclusively for the purpose of the territorial application of this Agreement, each customs territory shall be treated as though it were a contracting party.
3. The contracting parties recognise the desirability to increase free trade by means of the voluntary agreements of closer integration between the economies of the contracting parties.
4. The formation of customs unions or free trade area or the adoption of an interim agreement leading to the formation of a customs union or of a free trade area, subject to:

- Relating to a customs union, or an interim agreement leading to a formation of a customs union, the duties and other commerce regulations imposed at the institutions of any such union or interim agreement relating to trade with contracting parties not party to such union or agreement shall not on the whole be higher or more restrictive than the duties and commerce regulations applicable in the constituent territories prior to the formation of such union or the adoption of such interim agreement.

- Relating to a free trade area, or interim agreement leading to the formation of a free trade area, the duties and other commerce regulations maintained in each of the constituent territories and applicable at the formation of such free trade area or adoption of such interim agreement relating to the trade with contracting parties not included in such area or in such interim agreement shall not be higher or more restrictive than the corresponding duties and regulations existing in the same constituent territories prior to the formation of such free trade area or interim agreement.

5. Any contracting party intending to enter into a customs union or free trade area or an interim agreement leading to the formation of such union or such area shall immediately notify the Contracting Parties.

B. Article XXV: Joint Action by the Contracting Parties: Article XXV has the following provisions:

1. Representatives of the contracting parties shall meet from time to time giving joint action for implementing the provisions, facilitating the operation, and furthering the objectives of this agreement. In joint action, the contracting parties are designated as the Contracting Parties.
2. Each contracting party shall be entitled to have one vote at all meetings of the Contracting Parties.
3. Unless otherwise provided, the decisions of the Contracting Parties shall be taken by a majority of votes cast.
4. The Contracting Parties may, in exceptional circumstances, waive an obligation imposed upon a contracting party under this Agreement, if such decision is taken by a two-thirds majority of the votes cast and such majority shall make of more than half of the contracting parties.

C. Article XXVI: Acceptance, Entry into Force and Registration: The Article contains the provisions:

1. Each government which accepts this Agreement shall deposit an instrument of acceptance with the Executive Secretary to the Contracting Parties, who will inform all interested governments regarding the date of deposit of the instrument of acceptance.
2. This Agreement shall come into force, as among the governments accepting it, on the thirtieth day following the day on which instruments of acceptance have been deposed with the Executive Secretary to the Contacting Parties.
3. The United Nations is authorised to effect registration of this Agreement as soon as it comes into force.

D. Article XXVII: Withholding or Withdrawal of Concessions: A contracting party shall at any time be free to withhold or withdraw in whole or in part any concession, granted in the appropriate Schedule annexed to this Agreement, relating to which such contracting party determines that it was initially negotiated with a government which has ceased to be a contracting party.

E. Article XXVIII: Modification of Schedules: The Article contains regulations concerning the modification of the Schedules of trade concessions on a reciprocal and mutually advantageous basis.

1. The contracting parties shall modify the concessions included in the appropriate Schedule annexed to this Agreement within periods of time specified by the Contracting Parties, subject to prescribed procedure.
2. A contracting party may, by negotiation or agreement with any contracting party with which such concessions were initially negotiated and subject to consultation with other contracting party determined by the Contracting Parties to have substantial interest in such concession, modify or withdraw a concession included in the appropriate Schedule annexed to this Agreement.
3. In such negotiations and agreements, the contracting parties shall make efforts to maintain a general level of reciprocal and mutual concessions not less favourable to trade than that granted in this Agreement prior to such negotiations.

F. Article XXVIII b: Tariff Negotiations: The Article contains the use of negotiations to further reduce tariffs and other trade restrictions on a reciprocal and mutually advantageous basis.

1. The Contracting Parties may sponsor from time to time, negotiations relating to substantial reduction of the general level of tariffs and other charges on exports and imports on reciprocal and mutually advantageous basis.
2. Negotiations may be carried out on a selective product-by-product basis or by the application of such multilateral procedures as may be accepted by the Contracting Parties concerned.

G. Article XXIX: The Relation of This Agreement to the Havana Charter: This Agreement was an interim arrangement subject to the establishment of the International Trade Organisation. The Article says:

1. The contracting parties undertake to observe to the fullest extent of their executive authority, the general principles of Chapter I to VI inclusively and Chapter IX of the pending Havana Charter leading to establishment of the International Trade Organisation.
2. Part II of this Agreement shall be suspended on the day on which the Havana Charter enters into effect.
3. If the Havana Charter does not come into effect, the Contracting Parties shall meet to agree whether this Agreement be amended, supplemented or maintained.

H. Article XXX: Amendments:

1. Amendments to the provisions of Part I of this Agreement or provisions of Article XXIX of this Article shall become effective upon acceptance by all the contracting parties.
2. Other amendments to this Agreement shall come into force upon acceptance by two-thirds of the contracting parties and thereafter, for each other contracting party upon

acceptance by it.

3. Any contracting party accepting an amendment to this Agreement shall deposit an instrument of acceptance with Secretary General of the United Nations within the specified time.

I. Article XXXI: Withdrawals: Subject to the provisions, any contracting party may withdraw from this Agreement, or may separately withdraw on behalf of any of the customs territories for which it has international responsibilities and which at the time possesses full autonomy in the conduct of its external commercial relations and of the other matters provided for in this Agreement.

J. Article XXXII: Contracting Parties: The contracting parties to this Agreement shall mean the governments applying the provisions of this Agreement under Articles XXVI or XXXIII or pursuant to the Protocol of Provisional application.

K. Article XXXIII: Accession: A government not party to this Agreement may accede to this Agreement on terms to be agreed between itself and the Contracting Parties. The decisions shall be taken by a two-thirds majority.

L. Article XXXIV: Annexes: The Article says that the Annexes to this Agreement shall be an integral part of this Agreement.

M. Article XXXV: Non-application of the Agreement between Particular Contracting Parties: This Agreement shall not apply as between a contracting party and another contracting party, if both the contracting parties have not entered into tariff negotiations with each other.

2.2.4 Part IV: It contained the following Articles.

A. Article XXXVI: Principles and Objectives: The Article sets the following objectives.

1. To raise the standards of living and the progressive development of the economies of all the contracting parties, and considering that the attainment of these objectives is particularly urgent for less developed contracting parties.
2. To take individual and joint actions to further the development of the economies of less developed contracting parties and to bring about a rapid advance in the standard of living in these countries.
3. To promote international trade as a means of achieving economic and social advancement and govern it by such rules and procedures, and measures conforming to the objectives set forth in this Article.

The contracting parties to attain these objectives shall observe the following principles:

1. A rapid and substantial expansion of the export earnings of less developed contracting parties.
2. The less developed contracting parties secure a share in the growth in international trade commensurate with the needs of their economic development.
3. Need to provide more favourable and acceptable conditions of access to world markets for primary products of less developed contracting parties.
4. The developed contracting parties do not expect reciprocity for commitments made by them in trade negotiations to reduce or remove tariffs and other barriers to the

trade of less developed contracting parties.

B. Article XXXVII: Commitments: The Article has provisions for endeavours to be made in the interest of less developed contracting parties.

1. The developed contracting parties give, except in compelling circumstances, effect to following provisions:

- To accord higher priority and have special regard to the elimination of trade barriers on the products of interest to less developed parties.
- To refrain from imposing new fiscal measures which would retard significantly the growth of consumption of primary products produced in less developed contracting parties.

2. Less developed contracting parties shall also undertake to accord higher priority and have special regard for the elimination of trade barriers on the products of interest to other less developed contracting parties.

C. Article XXXVIII: Joint Action: The Article says that contracting parties shall collaborate jointly to attain the objective set forth in Article XXXVI of this Agreement.

2.3 The Trade Rounds

The basic aim of GATT was to liberalise world trade and it provided for the contracting parties a forum to discuss their trade problems and to negotiate to enlarge their trading opportunities. The contracting parties made progress in reducing, even in eliminating the trade barriers and tariff and non-tariff barriers, during the trade negotiation rounds. The GATT Trade Rounds are listed in Table 2.1 below.

Table 2.1: The GATT Trade Rounds

Year	Place	Subject	Participants
1947	Geneva	Tariffs	23
1949	Annecy	Tariffs	13
1951	Torquay	Tariffs	38
1956	Geneva	Tariffs	26
1960-61	Geneva (Dillon Round)	Tariffs	26
1964-67	Geneva (Kennedy Round)	Tariffs and anti-dumping measures	62
1973-79	Geneva (Tokyo Round)	Tariffs, non-tariff measures, and framework agreements	102
1986-94	Geneva (Uruguay Round)	Tariffs, non-tariff measures, rules, services, intellectual property, dispute settlements, textiles, agriculture, creation of WTO, and others.	123

2.3.1 Geneva Round, 1947: The first round of trade negotiations was held in

Geneva from April 10 to October 30, 1947 as a part of the establishment of the GATT. The concessions exchanged in the negotiations took the form of:

1. Complete elimination of certain duties and preferences.
2. Reduction of duty preference.
3. Binding of duties of existing levels.
4. Binding of duty free treatment.

The participating countries completed 133 sets of bilateral negotiations, covering two-third of the import trade of the participant countries. The first round of negotiations resulted in a set of trade rules and 4,500 tariff concessions affecting US$ 10 billion of trade. The customs tariff concessions became effective by 1948 through a 'protocol of provisional application'.

2.3.2 Annecy Round, 1949: The second conference for the negotiations was held at Annecy in 1949 to pursue the following agenda:

1. To facilitate the extension of GATT to countries who could not participate in the Geneva conference.
2. To add nine more countries to GATT.

In the conference, 5,000 concessions were negotiated. Participating countries completed 147 bilateral negotiations covering 500 items. World trade of the contracting parties affected by concessions increased from 66 percent to 80 percent.

2.3.3 Torquay Round, 1951: The third conference was held at Torquay in 1951. A number of European countries with comparatively low level of tariff rates agreed to a reduction in tariffs and maintained that they had entered the Torquay negotiations at a disadvantage. The conference was not successful since only 147 out of the 400 accepted negotiations could be completed.

2.3.4 Geneva Round, 1956: The conference was not successful because:

1. Except the U.S., no other country felt satisfied.
2. Several countries including China withdrew from the negotiations owing to inadequate scope.
3. The representatives of European countries returned home with disappointment.

2.3.5 Dillon Round, 1960-61: The tariff reduction negotiations were held during the conference at Geneva. These negotiations were influenced by the events that occurred in the area of economic integration and cooperation.

1. The progress being made by the European Economic Community (EEC) towards the establishment of full customs union comprising the six member states.
2. The U.S. government had obtained authority in the Trade Agreements Extension Act, 1958 to participate in multilateral tariff negotiations during the four years ending in June 30, 1962.

It was decided to hold tariff negotiations especially as these had given an opportunity to negotiate with EEC on its new common tariff. A bilateral trade agreement between the U.K. and the EEC was announced on May 17, 1962. The agreement included the decision to reduce tariffs on a variety of industrial goods by one tariff.

2.3.6 Kennedy Round, 1964-67: After the long discussions, the conference took some important decisions.

1. The participants in the negotiations which made tariff reductions together accounted for 75 percent of the total world trade and the concessions granted by them represented trade valued more than US$ 40,000 million.
2. A Committee on Anti-Dumping Practice was established on July 1, 1968, whereby the signatory countries could consult on matters relating to the administration of anti-dumping systems.
3. The negotiations on grains resulted in agreement on basic minimum and maximum prices for varieties of wheat of major importance in international trade and on the provision of 4.5 million metric tonnes of grains annually, initially for a three year period to the developing countries.
4. The tariff concessions negotiated in the round were to be implemented in stages.

The U.S. President was authorised, by the Congress, to reduce, on a reciprocal basis, almost the entire range of U.S. tariff by 50 percent, spread over five years. The access to world markets for agricultural products was increased.

2.3.7 Tokyo Round, 1973-1979: The Tokyo Round lasted from 1973 to 1979, with 102 countries participating in it. It continued GATT's efforts to progressively reduce tariffs. The results included on an average, one-third cut in customs duties in world's nine major industrial markets, bringing the average tariff on industrial products down to 4.7 percent. The tariff reduction, phased over 8 years, involved an element of 'harmonisation'—higher the tariffs, larger the cut, proportionally.

The Round failed to tackle with the fundamental problems affecting farm trade and also stopped short of providing a modified agreement on 'safeguard'. Nevertheless, a series of agreements on non-tariff barriers did emerge from the negotiations, in some cases interpreting existing GATT rules and in others, breaking entirely new ground. In most cases, only a small number of (mainly industrialised countries) GATT members subscribed to these agreements and arrangements. Since they were not accepted by all members, they were informally called 'codes'. Several codes were eventually amended in the Uruguay Round and turned into multilateral commitments accepted by all WTO Members.

GSP was accepted as an exception to the principle of Most Favoured Nation (MFN). A clause on Generalised System of Preferences was included to give preferential market access to least developed countries and to other developing countries by certain developed countries. In order to have deeper trade integration amongst developing countries, a Global System of Trade Preferences (GSTP) was accepted amongst the G-77 group of developing countries as a boost to South-South cooperation.

2.3.8 Uruguay Round: See chapter 3 of this book.

2.4 Evaluation of the GATT, 1947

The basic principles of GATT remained much as they were in the original agreement for about half a century. A section on development was added in the 1960s. Plurilateral agreements with voluntary membership were added in the 1970s. The Tokyo Round was the first major attempt to deal with trade barriers that do not take the form of tariffs and to reform the system.

GATT was a provisional arrangement with a limited field of action and it was successful in promoting and securing the liberalisation of world trade to some extent. Reductions in tariffs and non-tariff barriers led to the expansion of world trade. During 1950s and 1960s, world trade grew by around 8 percent, even surpassing world production growth. There were only 23 contracting parties at the beginning of the provisional multilateral trade arrangement—the figure substantially rose to 123 in the Uruguay Round (Table 2.2).

Table 2.2: List of Original 23 Contracting Parties to GATT, 1947

Australia	Chile	Lebanon	Southern Rhodesia
Belgium	China	Luxembourg	Syria
Brazil	Cuba	Netherlands	South Africa
Burma	Czechoslovakia	New Zealand	Great Britain
Canada	France	Norway	United States of America
Ceylon	India	Pakistan	

As the time passed, the signs of new difficulties were visible. The GATT's success in reducing tariffs to a low level in 1970s and severe recession of 1970s and early 1980s, forced the countries to find new ways of protection to tackle increased foreign competition. High unemployment rate and the factory closures drove the governments in Western Europe and North America to seek bilateral market sharing arrangements with the competitors. These governments also increased subsidies in the agricultural sector to maintain their hold on agricultural trade. These developments put doubt on the effectiveness and credibility of the GATT.

The world trade had become more complex and important over the time. Trade in services, not covered under the GATT, was expanding and became more lucrative for the countries intending international trade in services. Loopholes in the multilateral system were being exploited in the agricultural sector. International investments were expanding. Even GATT's institutional structure and its dispute settlement system were a matter of concern. The present multilateral trading system seemed unable to cope up with these issues.

These issues coupled with other factors persuaded the GATT members that efforts were needed for the reinforcement and extension of multilateral system. The Uruguay Round was the result of these efforts.

3

Uruguay Round and the Birth of WTO

3.1 The Uruguay Round

The seeds of the Uruguay Round were sown in November 1982 at a Ministerial meeting of the GATT signatories held in Geneva. Ministers intended to launch a major new round of trade negotiations, but the conference stalled on agriculture and was widely regarded as a failure. Nevertheless, it took four more years of exploring, clarifying issues and consensus building, before the Ministers agreed to launch the new round. They launched the eighth round of trade negotiations in September 1986 in Punta del Este, Uruguay. They eventually agreed on an agenda covering virtually every outstanding trade policy issue.

The 15 original subjects for the Uruguay Round were as under:

1. Tariffs.
2. Non-tariff barriers.
3. Natural resource products.
4. Textile and clothing.
5. Agriculture.
6. Tropical products.
7. GATT Articles.
8. Tokyo Round Codes.
9. Anti-dumping.
10. Subsidies.
11. Intellectual property rights.
12. Investment measures.
13. Dispute settlements.
14. The GATT System.
15. Services.

The negotiations were originally supposed to be completed in four years, but because of the crises and deadlocks that developed from time to time, they dragged on for over seven years (Table 3.1). The Ministers met in December 1988, at Montreal, Canada, to assess the progress made. The aim was to clarify the agenda for the remaining two years, but the talks ended in a deadlock that was not resolved until officials met more quietly in Geneva in April 1989.

Regardless of the poor political viewpoint, a considerable amount of technical work continued, leading to the first draft of a final legal agreement in December 1991. The draft was compiled by the then GATT director-general, Arthur Dunkel, who chaired the negotiations at official level. This draft was offered as a single treaty, i.e. in a form of a package—no element of the treaty could be considered agreed unless the total package was agreed. Known as the Dunkel Draft, it came up for intense discussion and debate in developing countries where public opinion was formed against the signing of the draft. The draft was supposed heavily biased in favouring of the developed countries and against the developing countries. It was so designed as to lead to surrender the sovereign authority of the governments of developing countries. The draft fulfilled every part of the Punta Del Este mandate; with one exception—it did not contain the participating members' list of commitments for tariff reduction and opening of their services markets.

Table 3.1: Months and Years of Important Negotiations

Date	Place	Event
September 1986	Punta del	Launch of Uruguay Round
December 1988	Montreal	Ministerial mid-term review
April 1989	Geneva	Mid-term review concluded
December 1990	Brussels	Ministerial meeting ends in deadlock
December 1991	Geneva	First draft of the Final Act completed
November 1992	Washington	US and EU achieve Blair House Agreement
July 1993	Tokyo	Quad achieves market access breakthrough at G-7 Summit
December 1993	Geneva	Except market access, most negotiations concluded
April 1994	Marrakesh	Agreement signed
January 1995	Geneva	WTO established, Agreements effective

The US and the EU settled most of their differences on agriculture in a deal known informally as the Blair House Accord in November 1992. The 'Quad' (US, EU, Japan and Canada) announced significant progress in negotiations on tariffs and market access by July 1993. All issues were finally resolved by the end of 1993. On April 15, 1994, the deal was signed by the Ministers from most of the 123 participating countries at a meeting in Marrakesh, Morocco.

The Uruguay Round was originally planned to be concluded by the end of 1990. The delay allowed some negotiations to progress further that would not have been possible in 1990—for example, some aspect of services and intellectual property, and the creation of the WTO itself. The Uruguay Round agreements contained a time table for new negotiations on a number of topics. There were over 30 items in the original built-in agenda. Some of items of the built-in agenda are given in Table 3.2.

3.2 Objectives of the WTO

The preamble of the Agreement establishing the WTO mentions the objectives of GATT: raising standards of living and incomes, ensuring full employment, expanding production and trade, and optimal use of the world's resources. The preamble extends these objectives to services and:

1. It introduces the idea of 'sustainable development' in relation to the optimal use of

world resources, and the need to protect and preserve the environment in a manner consistent with various levels of national economic development, and

2. It recognises that there is a need for positive efforts to ensure that developing countries, and especially least developed countries among them, secure a better share of the growth in international trade.

Table 3.2: Uruguay Round: The Built-in Agenda

Year	Area	Agenda
1996	Maritime services	Market access negotiations to end by June 30, 1996
	Services and environment	Deadline for working party report by December 1996
	Government procurement	Negotiations to start in 1996
1997	Basic telecommunications	Negotiations to end by February 15, 1997
	Financial services	Negotiations to end by December 30, 1997
	Intellectual property	Negotiations for creating a multilateral system for wines
1998	SPS	Review of the operation and implementation of the Agreement by 1998
	TBT	First triennial review of the operation and implementation of the Agreement by 1998
	DSU	Full review of the rules and procedures starts by the end of 1998
	Rule of origin	Work programme on harmonisation to be completed by July 1998
	Services	Negotiation on emergency safeguard measures in 1998
1999	Government procurement	Further negotiations starting by 1999
	Trade policy review	Appraisal of the operation by 2000
2000	Agriculture	Negotiations for continuing the process of substantial progressive reductions in support and protection starting by 2000
	Services	New negotiations starting in 2000 to achieve a progressive higher level of liberalisation
	TRIPS	Review of the implementation of the Agreement after January 1, 2000
	TRIMS	Review of the operation of the Agreement and discussion on whether provisions on investment and competition be included in the Agreement
2001	ATC	Mandate review of the implementation by 2001
2004	ATC	Mandate review of the implementation by 2004
2005	ATC	Full integration into GATT and Agreement expires on January 1, 2005

Many of the items of the built-in agenda are now a part of the Doha Development Agenda (DDA).

3.3 Functions of the WTO

The primary functions of the WTO are to link all the multilateral trade agreements together, subject them to a common dispute settlement mechanism and provide a framework for the implementation of the results of negotiations on either a multilateral or a plurilateral basis. The WTO also has:

1. To administer and implement the multilateral and plurilateral trade agreements which together make up the WTO.
2. To act as a forum for multilateral trade negotiations.
3. To provide framework to resolve trade disputes.
4. To oversee national trade policies.
5. To provide technical assistance and training for the developing countries.
6. To cooperate with other international institutions concerned with global policy making.

3.4 Structure of the WTO

The highest level decision-making authority in the WTO is the Ministerial Conference comprising of the representatives of all the members. The Ministerial Conference takes decisions on all matters under any of the multilateral trade agreements. The Ministerial Conference has to meet at least once every two years. The second level comprises of the General Council, the Dispute Settlement Body, and the Trade Policy Review Body, all acting on behalf of and reporting to the Ministerial Conference. The third level includes three more councils, the Goods Council, the Services Council, and the Council for Trade Related Aspect of Intellectual Property Rights, dealing with different areas of trade and reporting to the General Council. In addition, there are some committees and working groups dealing with specific subjects and reporting to the General Council.

The fourth level comprises of sub-bodies, the committees and the working groups, of each of the higher level Council. These committees and working groups deal with specific subjects and report to the higher level Councils (Tables 3.3, 3.4 and 3.5).

Table 3.3: Structure of the WTO

Level	Designation	Function
First	The Ministerial Conference	Decisions on all matters related to the Agreements
Second	The General Council, the Dispute Settlement Body and the Trade Policy Review Body	Act on behalf of the Ministerial Conference and report to it
Third	The Goods Council, the Services Council and the TRIPS Council, and six other Committees and Working Parties, and some Working Groups	Deal with different areas of trade and report to the General Council
Fourth	Committees and Working Groups	Work on specialised subjects and report to the higher level council

Table 3.4: Committees, Working Parties, Working Groups and Subsidiaries to Higher Level

Level	Committee	Working Parties	Working Group	Subsidiary
General Council	Trade and Environment	Accession	Trade, Debt and Finance	
	Trade and Development including a sub-committee on LDCs		Trade and Transfer of Technology	
	Regional Trade Agreements		Trade and Investment	
	Balance of Payments Restrictions		Trade and Competition Policy	
	Budget, Finance and Administration		Government Procurement	
Goods Council	Market Access	State Trading Enterprises		
	Agriculture			
	Sanitary and Phytosanitary Measures			
	Technical Barriers to Trade			
	Subsidies and Countervailing Measures			
	Anti-Dumping Practices			
	Customs Valuation			
	Rules of Origin			
	Import Licensing			
	TRIMS			
	Safeguards			
Services Council	Trade in Financial Services			
	Specific Commitments			
TPRB	Trade Negotiations Committee*			
DSB				Appellate Body
				Dispute Settlement Panels

Note: (*) The Committee reports to the General Council.

3.5 Agreements of the WTO

WTO's agreements are often called the Final Act of the Uruguay Round (1986-1994) of trade negotiations. These agreements were signed at the Marrakesh Ministerial meeting on April 15, 1994. There are about 19 Agreements, 24 decisions, 8 understandings, and 3 declarations, totalling 550 pages.

Table 3.5: Basic Structure of the WTO Agreements

Area	Main	Additional	Market Access
Establishment of the WTO	Marrakesh Agreement		
Goods	GATT	Other Goods Agreements and Annexes	Schedules of Commitments
Services	GATS	Services Annexes	Schedules of Commitments
Intellectual Property	TRIPS		
Dispute Settlement	Understanding		
Trade Review Policy	Understanding		

The Final Act signed in Marrakesh in 1994 is like a cover note. The Agreement establishing WTO serves as an umbrella agreement. Everything else is attached to it. Annexed are agreements on goods, services, intellectual property, dispute settlement trade review and the plurilateral negotiations. The national schedules of commitments are also part of the Final Act. The schedules contain commitments made by individual members on specific foreign products or services providers' access to their markets.

The summary of the contents of the Final Act is given below:

Main Agreement: Agreement establishing the WTO.

Annex 1A:

1. General Agreement on Tariffs and Trade, 1994.
2. Agreement on Agriculture.
3. Agreement on Sanitary and Phytosanitary Measures.
4. Agreement on Textile and Clothing.
5. Agreement on Technical Barriers to Trade.
6. Agreement on Trade Related Aspects of Investment Measures.
7. Agreement on Implementation of Article VI (Anti-dumping Measures).
8. Agreement on Implementation of Article VII (Customs Valuation).
9. Agreement on Pre-shipment Inspection.
10. Agreement on Rules of Origin.
11. Agreement on Import Licensing Procedures.
12. Agreement on Subsidies and Countervailing Duties.
13. Agreement on Safeguards.

Annex 1B: Agreement on Trade in Services.

Annex 1C: Agreement on Trade Related Aspects of Intellectual Property Rights.

Annex 2: Understanding on Rules and Procedures Governing the Settlement of Disputes.

Annex 3: Trade Policy Review Mechanism.

Annex 4:

1. Plurilateral Agreements.
2. Agreement on Trade in Civil Aircrafts.
3. Agreement on Government Procurement.
4. In addition to the above agreements, some decisions and declarations were made.

3.6 Uruguay Round Ministerial Decisions and Declarations

3.6.1 Decisions adopted by the Trade Negotiation Committee on December 15, 1994 and April 14, 1994:

1. Measures in favour of least developing countries.
2. Notification procedures.
3. Agriculture: Measures concerning the possible negative effect of the reform programmes on least developing and net food importing countries.
4. Textile and clothing: Notification on First Integration under Article 2.6.
5. Technical barriers to trade: Proposed understanding of the WTO-ISO Standard Information System.
6. Customs Valuation (GATT Article VII).
7. Services: Institutional arrangement for GATS.
8. Government procurement: Accession to agreement.
9. Dispute settlement: Application and review of the dispute settlement understanding.
10. Agreement establishing the WTO: Acceptance of and accession to the agreement.
11. Trade and environment.
12. Organisational and financial consequences.
13. Establishment of the Preparatory Committee of the WTO.

13.6.2 Declarations Adopted by the Trade Negotiation Committee on December 15, 1993:

1. Contribution of the WTO to achieve greater coherence in global economic policy making.
2. Relationship of the WTO with the IMF.

13.6.3 Decisions and Declarations Adopted by the Trade Negotiation Committee on December 15, 1993:

1. Decision on anti-circumvention.
2. Decision on review of Article 17.6 of the Anti-dumping Agreement.
3. Declaration on dispute settlement pursuant to anti-dumping, and subsidies and countervailing measures agreements.

13.6.4 Understanding on Commitments in Financial Services

3.7 Trade Policy Review Mechanism

The Agreement on Trade Policy Review emphasises the importance of awareness about trade conditions among those who are involved in trade. Further, it is important that regulations and policies of the Members are transparent to ensure a fair and rule-based trade. This can be achieved in two ways: first, Members have to apprise the WTO and other Members, of specific measures, policies and laws through their regular notifications; and second, WTO conducts regular reviews of individual Members' trade policies. In the Ministerial meeting held in December 1988, the participants agreed to set up the reviews of trade policies of WTO Members. The first review took place in 1989. After the creation of WTO in 1995, services and intellectual property were also included in the review process. The Trade Policy Review Body comprises of all WTO Members—in other words, it is the General Council in another appearance.

The objectives of the trade policy review are as under:

1. To increase the transparency and understanding of Members' trade policies and practices through regular monitoring.
2. Improve the quality of public and intergovernmental debate on issues.
3. To enable a multilateral assessment of the effects of the policies on world trading system.

In addition to the Members' trade policies and practices, the reviews take into account Members' economic developmental requirements, their policies and objectives and the external economic environment they face. These reviews enable outsiders to understand a Member's policies and economic environment. They also give feedback to the Member being reviewed on its performance in the system. These reviews motivate governments to adhere to the WTO rules and disciplines. They help the Members in fulfilling the commitments made.

The frequency of the trade policy reviews to be carried out depends on the size of the country in terms of share in world trade.

1. The biggest four traders; the EU, the U.S., Japan and China are reviewed approximately once every two years.
2. The next 16 countries (in terms of their share in world trade) are examined every four years.
3. The remaining countries are reviewed every six years, with the possibility of longer interim periods for least developed countries.

A detailed review report independently is written by the WTO Secretariat. Individual country governments under review, prepare a policy statement. These two documents along with the proceedings of the Trade Policy Review Body's meeting are published shortly afterwards.

3.8 Top Ten Benefits of the WTO Trading System

The WTO trading system offers an array of benefits, while some are well-known and others not so obvious. The world is complex. The matter given below is brief, but it tries to reflect the complex and dynamic nature of trade. It highlights some of the benefits of the WTO's trading system, but it doesn't claim that everything is perfect—otherwise there would be no need for further negotiations and for the system to evolve and reform continually. Nor does it claim that everyone agrees with everything in the WTO. That's one of the most important reasons for having the system. It is a forum for countries to flog out their differences on trade issues.

There are many over-riding reasons why we were better off with the system than without it. Here are 10 of them.

1. Promoting peace.
2. Constructive handling of disputes.
3. Rules make life easier for all.
4. Freer trade lowers the living costs.
5. More choice of products and qualities.
6. Trade raises incomes.
7. Trade stimulates economic growth.
8. Basic principles make life more efficient.
9. Governments are shielded from lobbying.
10. System encourages good government.

3.8.1 Promoting Peace: This sounds like an exaggerated claim, and it would be wrong to make too much of it. Nevertheless, the system does contribute to international peace, and if we understand why, we have a clearer picture of what the system actually does.

Peace is partly an outcome of two of the most fundamental principles of the trading system: helping trade to flow smoothly and providing countries with a constructive and fair outlet for dealing with disputes over trade issues. It is also an outcome of the international confidence and cooperation that the system creates and reinforces.

History is littered with examples of trade disputes turning into a war. One of the most vivid is the trade war of the 1930s when countries competed to raise trade barriers in order to protect domestic producers and retaliate against each others' barriers. This worsened the Great Depression and eventually played a part in the outbreak of World War II. Two developments immediately after the World War II helped to avoid a repeat of the pre-War trade tensions. In Europe, international cooperation developed in coal, and in iron and steel. Globally, the General Agreement on Tariffs and Trade (GATT) was created.

Both have proved successful, so much so that they are now considerably expanded—one has become the European Union, the other, the World Trade Organization (WTO).

How does it work? Crudely put, sales people are usually reluctant to fight their customers.

In other words, if trade flows smoothly and both sides enjoy a healthy commercial relationship, political conflict is less likely. What's more, smoothly-flowing trade also helps people all over the world to become better off. People who are more prosperous and contented are also less likely to fight.

But that is not all. The GATT/WTO system is an important confidence builder. The trade wars in the 1930s are proof of how protectionism can easily plunge countries into a situation where no one wins and everyone loses.

The short-sighted protectionist view is that defending particular sectors against imports is beneficial. But that view ignores how other countries are going to respond. The long-term reality is that one protectionist step by one country can easily lead to retaliation from other countries, a loss of confidence in freer trade, and a slide into serious economic trouble for all—including the sectors that were originally protected. Everyone loses.

Confidence is the key to avoiding that kind of no-win scenario. When governments are confident that others will not raise their trade barriers, they will not be tempted to do the same. They will also be in a much better frame of mind to cooperate with each other.

The WTO trading system plays a vital role in creating and reinforcing that confidence. Particularly important are negotiations that lead to agreement by consensus and a focus on abiding by the rules.

3.8.2 Constructive Handling of Disputes: As trade expands in volume, in the number of products traded, and in the number of countries and companies trading, there is a greater chance that disputes will arise. The WTO system helps resolve these disputes peacefully and constructively.

There could be a downside to trade liberalization and expansion. More trade means more opportunities for disputes to arise. Left to themselves, those disputes could lead to serious conflicts. But in reality, a lot of international trade tension is reduced because countries can turn to organizations, in particular the WTO, to settle their trade disputes.

Before World War II, that option was not available. After the War, the world's community of trading nations negotiated trade rules which are now entrusted to the WTO. These rules include an obligation for members to bring their disputes to the WTO and not to act unilaterally.

When they bring disputes to the WTO, the WTO's procedure focuses their attention on the rules. Once a ruling has been made, countries concentrate on trying to comply with the rules, and perhaps later renegotiating the rules—not on declaring war on each other.

A good number of disputes have been brought to the WTO since it was set up in 1995. Without a means of tackling these constructively and harmoniously, some could have led to more serious political conflicts.

The fact that the disputes are based on WTO agreements means that there is a clear basis for judging who is right or wrong. Once the judgement has been made, the agreements provide the focus for any further actions that need to be taken.

As trade expands in volume, in the number of products traded, and in the number of countries and companies trading, there is a greater chance that disputes will arise. The WTO system helps resolve these disputes peacefully and constructively. Countries in dispute always aim to conform to the agreements.

The increasing number of disputes brought to GATT and its successor, the WTO, does not reflect increasing tension in the world. Rather, it reflects the closer economic ties throughout the world—the GATT/WTO's expanding membership and the fact that countries have faith in the system to solve their differences.

Sometimes, exchanges between the countries in conflict can be acrimonious, but they always aim to conform to the agreements and commitments that they themselves negotiated.

3.8.3 Rules Make Life Easier for All: The WTO cannot claim to make all countries equal. But it does reduce some inequalities, giving smaller countries more voice, and at the same time freeing the major powers from the complexity of having to negotiate trade agreements with each of their numerous trading partners.

Decisions in the WTO are made by consensus. The WTO agreements were negotiated by all members, were approved by consensus and were ratified in all members' parliaments. The agreements apply to everyone. Rich and poor countries alike have an equal right to challenge each other in the WTO's dispute settlement procedures.

This makes life easier for all, in several different ways. Smaller countries can enjoy some increased bargaining power. Without a multilateral regime such as the WTO's system, the more powerful countries would be freer to impose their will unilaterally on their smaller trading partners. Smaller countries would have to deal with each of the major economic powers individually, and would be much less able to resist unwanted pressure.

In addition, smaller countries can perform more effectively if they make use of the opportunities to form alliances and pool resources. Several countries are already doing this.

There are matching benefits for larger countries. The major economic powers can use the single forum of the WTO to negotiate with all or most of their trading partners at the same time. This makes life much simpler for the bigger trading countries. The alternative would be continuous and complicated bilateral negotiations with dozens of countries simultaneously. And each country could end up with different conditions for trading with each of its trading partners, making life extremely complicated for its importers and exporters.

The principle of non-discrimination built into the WTO agreements avoids that complexity. The fact that there is a single set of rules applying to all members greatly simplifies the entire trade regime.

And these agreed rules give governments a clearer view of which trade policies are acceptable.

3.8.4 Freer Trade Lowers the Living Costs: We are all consumers. The prices we pay for our food and clothing, our necessities and luxuries, and everything else in between, are affected by trade policies.

Protectionism is expensive. It raises prices. The WTO's global system lowers trade barriers through negotiation and applies the principle of non-discrimination. The result is reduced costs of production (because imports used in production are cheaper) and reduced prices of finished goods and services, and ultimately a lower cost of living.

3.8.5 More Choice of Products and Qualities: Think of all the things we can now have because we can import them: fruits and vegetables out of season, foods, clothing and other products that were considered exotic, cut flowers from any part of the world, all sorts of household goods, books, music, movies, and so on.

Think also of the things people in other countries can have because they buy exports from us and elsewhere. Look around and consider all the things that would disappear if all our imports were taken away from us. Imports allow us more choices—both variety of goods and services to choose from, and a wider range of qualities. Even the quality of locally-produced goods can improve because of the competition from imports.

The wider choice is not simply a question of consumers buying foreign finished products. Imports are used as materials, components and equipment for local production. This expands the range of final products and services that are made by domestic producers, and it increases the range of technologies they can use. When mobile telephone equipment became available, services sprang up even in the countries that did not make the equipment, for example.

Sometimes, the success of an imported product or service on the domestic market can also encourage new local producers to compete, increasing the choice of brands available to consumers as well as increasing the range of goods and services produced locally.

If trade allows us to import more, it also allows others to buy more of our exports. It increases our incomes, providing us with the means of enjoying the increased choice.

3.8.6 Trade Raises Incomes: Lowering trade barriers allows trade to increase, which adds to incomes—national incomes and personal incomes. But some adjustment is necessary.

The WTO's own estimates for the impact of the 1994 Uruguay Round trade deal were between US$ 109 billion and US$ 510 billion added to world income (depending on the assumptions of the calculations and allowing for margins of error).

More recent research has produced similar figures. Economists estimate that cutting trade barriers in agriculture, manufacturing and services by one-third would boost the world economy by US$ 613 billion—equivalent to adding an economy the size of Canada to the world economy.

In Europe, the EU Commission calculates that over 1989–93, EU incomes increased by 1.1–1.5 percent more than they would have done without the Single Market.

So trade clearly boosts incomes. Trade also poses challenges as domestic producers face competition from imports. But the fact that there is additional income means that resources are available for governments to redistribute the benefits from those who gain the most—for example, to help companies and workers adapt by becoming more productive and competitive in what they were already doing, or by switching to new activities.

3.8.7 Trade Stimulates Economic Growth: Trade clearly has the potential to create jobs. In practice, there is often factual evidence that lower trade barriers have been good for employment. But the picture is complicated by a number of factors. Nevertheless, the alternative—protectionism—is not the way to tackle employment problems.

This is a difficult subject to tackle in simple terms. There is strong evidence that trade boosts economic growth, and that economic growth means more jobs. It is also true that some jobs are lost even when trade is expanding. But a reliable analysis of this poses at least two problems.

First, there are other factors at play. For example, technological advancement has also had a strong impact on employment and productivity, benefiting some jobs and hurting others. Second, while trade clearly boosts national income (and prosperity), this is not always translated into new employment for workers who lost their jobs as a result of competition from imports.

The picture is not the same all over the world. The average length of time a worker takes to find a new job can be much longer in one country than for a similar worker in another country experiencing similar conditions.

In other words, some countries are better at making the adjustments than others. This is partly because some countries have more effective adjustment policies. Those without effective policies are missing an opportunity.

There are many instances where the facts show that the opportunity has been grasped—where freer trade has been healthy for employment. The EU Commission calculates that the creation of its Single Market means that there are somewhere in the range of 3,00,000–9,00,000 more jobs than there would be without the Single Market.

Often, job prospects are better in companies involved in trade. In the United States, 12 million people owe their jobs to exports; 1.3 million of those jobs were created between 1994 and 1998. And those jobs tend to be better-paid with better security. In Mexico, the best jobs are those related to export activities: sectors which export 60 percent or more of their production, pay wages 39 percent higher than the rest of the economy and maquiladora (in-bond assembly) plants pay 3.5 times the Mexican minimum wage.

The facts also show how protectionism hurts employment. The example of the US car industry is mentioned here: trade barriers designed to protect US jobs by restricting imports from Japan ended up making cars more expensive in the US, so fewer cars were sold and jobs were lost. In other words, an attempt to tackle a problem in the short-term by restricting trade turned into a bigger problem in the long-term. Even when a country has difficulty making adjustments, the alternative of protectionism would simply make matters worse.

3.8.8 Basic Principles Make Life More Efficient: Many of the benefits of the trading system are more difficult to summarize in numbers, but they are still important. They are the result of essential principles at the heart of the system, and they make life simpler for the enterprises directly involved in trade and for the producers of goods and services.

Trade allows a division of labour between countries. It allows resources to be used more appropriately and effectively for production. But the WTO's trading system offers more than that. It helps to increase efficiency and to cut costs even more because of important principles enshrined in the system.

Imagine a situation where each country sets different rules and different customs duty rates for imports coming from different trading partners. Imagine that a company in one country wants to import raw materials or components—copper for wiring or printed circuit boards for electrical goods, for example—for its own production.

It would not be enough for this company to look at the prices offered by suppliers around the world. The company would also have to make separate calculations about the different duty rates it would be charged on the imports (which would depend on where the imports came from), and it would have to study each of the regulations that apply to products from each country. Buying some copper or circuit boards would become very complicated. That, in simple terms, is one of the problems of discrimination.

Imagine now that the government announces it will charge the same duty rates on imports from all countries, and it will use the same regulations for all products, no matter where they come from, whether imported or locally produced. Life for the company would be much simpler. Sourcing components would become more efficient and would cost less.

Non-discrimination is just one of the key principles of the WTO's trading system. Others include:

1. Transparency (clear information about policies, rules and regulations).
2. Increased certainty about trading conditions (commitments to lower trade barriers and to increase other countries' access to one's markets are legally binding).
3. Simplification and standardization of customs procedure, removal of red tape, centralized databases of information, and other measures designed to simplify trade that come under the heading "trade facilitation".

Together, they make trading simpler, cutting costs and increasing confidence in the future. That in turn also means more jobs and better goods and services for consumers.

3.8.9 Governments are Shielded from Lobbying: The GATT-WTO system which evolved in the second half of the 20th Century helps governments take a more balanced view of the trade policy. Governments are better placed to defend themselves against lobbying from narrow interest groups by focusing on trade-offs that are made in the interest of everyone in the economy.

One of the lessons of the protectionism that dominated the early decades of the 20th century was the damage that can be caused if narrow sectoral interests gain an unbalanced share of political influence. The result was increasingly restrictive policy which turned into a trade war that no one won and everyone lost.

Superficially, restricting imports looks like an effective way of supporting an economic sector. But it biases the economy against other sectors which shouldn't be penalized—if you protect your clothing industry, everyone else has to pay for more expensive clothes, which puts pressure on wages in all sectors, for example.

Protectionism can also escalate as other countries retaliate by raising their own trade barriers. That's exactly what happened in the 1920s and 1930s with disastrous effects. Even the sectors demanding protection ended up losing.

Governments need to be armed against pressure from narrow interest groups, and the WTO system can help.

The WTO system covers a wide range of sectors. So, if during a WTO trade negotiation one pressure group lobbies its government to be considered as a special case in need of protection, the government can reject the protectionist pressure by arguing that it needs a broad-ranging agreement that will benefit all sectors of the economy. Governments do just that, regularly.

3.8.10 System Encourages Good Government: Under WTO rules, once a commitment has been made to liberalize a sector of trade, it is difficult to reverse. The rules also discourage a range of unwise policies. For businesses, that means greater certainty and clarity about trading conditions. For governments it can often mean good discipline.

The rules include commitments not to backslide into unwise policies. Protectionism in general is unwise because of the damage it causes domestically and internationally, as we have already seen. Particular types of trade barriers cause additional damage because they provide opportunities for corruption and other forms of bad government.

One kind of trade barrier that the WTO's rules try to tackle is the quota, for example, restricting imports or exports to no more than a specific amount each year.

Because quotas limit supply, they artificially raise prices, creating abnormally large profits (economists talk about "quota rent"). That profit can be used to influence policies because more money is available for lobbying. It can also provide opportunities for corruption, for example in the allocation of quotas among traders.

There are plenty of cases where that has happened around the world.

The rules reduce opportunities for corruption. In other words, quotas are a particularly bad way of restricting trade. Governments have agreed through the WTO's rules that their use should be discouraged.

Nevertheless, quotas of various types remain in use in most countries, and governments argue strongly that they are needed. But they are controlled by WTO agreements and there are commitments to reduce or eliminate many of them, particularly in textiles.

Many other areas of the WTO's agreements can also help reduce corruption and bad government.

Transparency (such as making available to the public all information on trade regulations), other aspects of "trade facilitation", clearer criteria for regulations dealing with the safety and standards of products, and non-discrimination also help by reducing the scope for arbitrary decision-making and cheating.

Quite often, governments use the WTO as a welcome external constraint on their policies.

3.9 Performance and Issues

Since the establishment of the WTO, the Membership has risen to 162 as on November 30, 2015. The share of WTO Members in world trade rose from 91 percent in 1995 to 98 percent in 2014. Ten Ministerial Conferences have been held so far having different agendas.

The First Ministerial Conference was held in Singapore in 1996. The Members were interested in negotiating on Information Technology Agreement and in launching the work programme on: (i) relationship between trade and investment, (ii) interaction between trade and competition policy, (iii) transparency in government procurement, and (iv) trade facilitation.

The Second Ministerial Conference was timed to coincide with the golden jubilee celebrations of the GATT multilateral trading system in 1998. The Third Ministerial Conference was held in Seattle, U.S.; and collapsed without being able to reach a consensus on the Declaration to be adopted by the Ministers.

The Fourth Ministerial Conference took place at Doha, Qatar in 2001. The Ministerial Conference adopted a comprehensive work programme, known as the "Doha

Development Agenda" launching negotiations on some issues and setting out additional parameters and timeframes for the negotiations on agriculture and services that had commenced on January 1, 2000 in accordance with the mandates in the respective WTO Agreements. A Declaration on TRIPS and Public Health, and a Decision on Implementation of Related Issues and Concerns were also adopted in the Conference.

The Fifth Ministerial Conference was called in Cancun, Mexico in 2003 to review the progress of negotiations under the Doha Work Programme, but ended in a fiasco as serious differences emerged in the ambition levels of the WTO members on two most contentious issues: agriculture and Singapore Issues. The Sixth Ministerial Conference was held in Hong Kong in 2005, aiming the conclusion of Doha Round in 2006.

The Seventh Ministerial Conference took place after a gap of four years in Geneva in 2009 to make general statements about the working of the multilateral trading system. The Eighth Ministerial Conference was held again in Geneva in 2011. Few decisions were taken in the Ministerial Conference and efforts were made to bring negotiations back on track. A text on elements of political guidance was circulated among the Members.

In 2013, the Ninth Ministerial Conference took place at Bali, Indonesia. Ten texts under the Doha Development Agenda relating to agriculture, food security, development and cotton were adopted by the Ministers. A Trade Facilitation Agreement was also concluded. The outcomes of the Conference were dubbed as a success in the light of the Doha Development Agenda.

There was a complete dead lock on negotiations on Doha Development Agenda until the Ministerial Conference held in Geneva in 2011. Even in that Conference, ground was prepared to restart the negotiations on Doha Development Agenda. A little success was achieved at the Bali Ministerial Conference in 2013.

The Tenth Ministerial Conference was held in Nairobi in 2015. The outcome was not satisfactory and resulted in divisive reaffirmation of the Doha Development Agenda.

What are the issues impeding the progress in the conclusion of Doha Round talks? Is there any way out to conclude the talks? What are the possibilities for the conclusion of the Doha talks in near future? These issues are the subject matter of this book along with the study of the performance of the WTO so far.

The WTO allows for various types of flexibilities for developing countries. Special and differential treatment provisions for developing countries are contained across the WTO Agreements, Ministerial Decisions and General Council Decisions. These flexibilities generally aim to make it feasible for developing countries to undertake binding commitments beneficial to their economic development. These flexibilities have been categorised below.

3.9.1 Provisions of Special Interest to Developing Countries: All WTO Members, regardless of their size or level of participation in global trade and economic flows, can in principle participate equally in WTO decision-making, unlike in other international organisations. Certain other provisions for exceptions from WTO disciplines available to all Members also give developing countries a space to address their development aims.

For example, Article XX (b) and XX (g) of the GATT provide exceptions that allow WTO Members to take measures aimed at promoting sustainable development. This includes the situations where the measures are necessary to protect human, animal or plant life or health, or relate to the conservation of exhaustible natural resources.

3.9.2 Provisions Addressing Resource Constraints of Developing Countries: There are numerous provisions in the WTO Agreements that seek to address the resource limitations of developing countries in undertaking certain commitments.

A. Transition Periods: The WTO agreements contain various provisions establishing grace periods or extended timeframes for developing countries to undertake specific obligations.

B. Provisions for Technical Assistance: The WTO addresses the resource limitations of developing countries through various requirements on technical assistance.

3.9.3 Special Flexibilities to Restrict Imports and Promote Exports:

A. Exemptions for Developing Countries: There are few provisions that give special flexibility to developing countries to restrict imports and promote exports. For example, Article 9.1 of the Agreement on Safeguards provides for an exemption from safeguard actions for developing countries product not exceeding 3 percent of the total imports of the product concerned so long as all such developing country products do not exceed 9 percent of the total imports.

B. Special Flexibilities in Preferential Trade Arrangements: The WTO accords developing countries, certain flexibilities in undertaking commitments under preferential trade arrangements that may depart from WTO non-discrimination rules. Paragraph 2(c) of the Enabling Clause permits a departure from MFN treatment for developing countries in the WTO by allowing them to enter into regional or global arrangements with other developing countries for the mutual reduction or elimination of tariff and non-tariff measures for products imported between the parties to the agreements.

3.9.4 Agricultural Policy Distortions and Special Flexibilities for Developing Countries: The threshold (called 'de minimis') for developing countries is 10 percent of the value of the agricultural production in contrast to 5 percent for developed countries, for both product specific support and non-product specific support individually.

3.9.5 Preferential Treatment with Regard to Market Access:

A. Less than Full Reciprocity in Tariff Negotiations: One of the principal ways in which developing countries have been accorded special and differential treatment in the GATT and in the WTO is less than full reciprocity in reduction commitments in the context of negotiations on market access, in particular in tariff reduction. The developing country WTO Members have, on an average, fewer and higher tariff bindings on non-agricultural products and higher tariff bindings on agricultural products than developed countries.

B. Non-reciprocal Preferential Market Access for Developing and LDCs: Most developing countries also enjoy access to developed country markets under non-binding, non-reciprocal preferential schemes. At the Hong Kong Ministerial Conference in 2005, a decision was taken by the WTO Members that developed countries in the WTO and developing countries declaring themselves in a position to do so would provide duty free and quota free (DFQF) market access on a lasting basis, for all products originating from all LDCs by 2008 or no later than the start of the implementation period in manner that ensures stability, security and predictability.

The progress on negotiations relating to trade and development was not as envisaged at the time of establishment of the WTO. In July 2004, three Singapore Issues: competition, investment and transparency in public procurement were withdrawn from the Doha Development Agenda (DDA). The WTO is facing different issues, caused by divergence in the opinions of the Members, impeding the conclusion of the Doha Round. Developing countries raise the problem of implementation of the Agreements. The WTO has to counter these difficult issues for smooth functioning of the multilateral system and to conclude the Doha talks.

4

WTO Agreements on Establishment, GATT, Agriculture, Sanitary Measures and Textiles

4.1 Agreement Establishing the WTO

The Agreement establishing the World Trade Organization (WTO) calls for a single institutional framework encompassing all agreements and arrangements concluded under its auspices and the complete results of the Uruguay Round.

4.1.1 Article I: Establishment of the Organisation: The Article says that the World Trade Organization is hereby established.

4.1.2 Article II: Scope of WTO: The Article mentions about the scope of the World Trade Organization.

1. WTO shall provide the common institutional framework for the conduct of trade relations among its Members in matters related to the Agreement and associated legal instruments included in the Annexes to this Agreement.
2. General Agreement on Tariffs and Trade, 1994 as specified in Annex 1A is legally distinct from General Agreement on Tariffs and Trade dated October 30, 1947, annexed to the Final Act adopted at the conclusion of the second session of the Preparatory Committee of the United Nations Conference on Trade and Employment, as subsequently rectified, amended or modified.

4.1.3 Article III: Functions of the WTO: The Article mentions the following functions:

1. WTO shall facilitate the implementation, administration and operation, and further the objectives of this Agreement and of the Multilateral Trade Agreements, and shall also provide the framework for the implementation, administration and operation of the Plurilateral Trade Agreements.
2. WTO shall provide the forum for negotiations among its Members concerning their multilateral trade relations in matters dealt with under the agreements.
3. WTO shall administer the Understanding on Rules and Procedures Governing the Settlements of Disputes provided in Annex 2 to this Agreement.
4. WTO shall administer the Trade Policy Review Mechanism.
5. With a view to achieving greater coherence in global economic policy making, the WTO shall cooperate, as appropriate, with the International Monetary Fund and with the International Bank for Reconstruction and Development Bank and its affiliated agencies.

4.1.4 Article IV: Structure of the WTO: According to the Article:

1. There shall be a Ministerial Conference composed of representatives of all the Members which shall meet at least once every two years. The Ministerial Conference

shall carry out the functions of the WTO and take actions necessary to this effect.

2. There shall be a General Council composed of representatives of all the Members which shall meet as appropriate. In the intervals between meetings of the Ministerial Conference, its functions shall be conducted by the General Council.
3. The General Council shall convene as appropriate to discharge the responsibilities of the Dispute Settlement Body provided for in the Dispute Settlement Undertaking. The Dispute Settlement Body may have its own chairman and shall establish such rules of procedure as it deems necessary for the fulfilment of those responsibilities.
4. The General Council shall convene as appropriate to discharge the responsibilities of the Trade Policy Review Body provided for in the Trade Policy Review Mechanism. The Trade Policy Review Body may have its own chairman and shall establish such rules of procedure as it deems necessary for the fulfilment of those responsibilities.
5. There shall be a Council for Trade in Goods, a Council for Trade in Services and a Council for Trade Related Aspects of Intellectual Property Rights, which shall operate under the general guidance of the General Council. These Councils shall carry out the functions assigned to them by their respective agreements and by the General Council.
6. These Councils, goods, services and intellectual property rights, shall establish subsidiary bodies as required. These subsidiary bodies shall establish their respective rules of procedure subject to the approval of their respective Councils.
7. The Ministerial Conference shall establish a Committee on Trade and Development, Committee on Balance of Payments Restrictions and a Committee on Budget, Finance and Administration, which shall carry out the functions assigned to them by this Agreement and by the Multilateral Trade Agreements, and any additional functions assigned to them by the General Council and may establish such additional committees with such functions as it may deem appropriate. The committees shall report to the General Council.
8. The bodies provided for under the Plurilateral Trade Agreements shall carry out the functions assigned to them under those Agreements and shall operate within the institutional framework of the WTO. These bodies shall keep the General Council informed of their activities on a regular basis.

4.1.5 Article V: Relationship with other International Organisations: The Article has the following provisions:

1. The General Council shall make appropriate arrangements for the effective cooperation with other intergovernmental organisations that have responsibilities related to those of the WTO.
2. The General Council may make appropriate arrangements for consultation and cooperation with non-governmental organisations concerned with matters related to those of the WTO.

4.1.6 Article VI: The Secretariat: The Article says that:

1. There shall be a Secretariat of the WTO headed by a Director-General.
2. The Ministerial Conference shall appoint the Director-General and adopt regulations

setting out powers, duties, conditions of service, and terms of office of the Director-General.

3. The Director-General shall appoint the members of the staff of the Secretariat and determine their duties and conditions of service in accordance with the regulation adopted by the Ministerial Conference.
4. The responsibilities of the Director-General and of the staff of the Secretariat shall be exclusively international in character.

4.1.7 Article VII: Budget: The Director-General shall present to the Committee on Budget, Finance and Administration the annual budget estimate and financial statement of the WTO. The Committee on Budget, Finance and Administration shall review the annual budget estimate and the financial statement presented by the Director-General and make recommendations thereon to the General Council. The annual budget estimate shall be subject to approval by the General Council. The financial regulations shall be based, as far as practicable, on the regulations and practices of GATT 1947.

4.1.8 Article VIII: Status of the WTO: The WTO shall have legal personality and shall be accorded by each of its Members such legal capacity as may be necessary for the exercise of its functions. The WTO, the officials of WTO and representatives of the Members shall be accorded by each of its Members such privileges and immunity as are necessary for the exercise of its functions.

4.1.9 Article IX: Decision-Making: The decision-making process has been described below:

1. The WTO shall continue the practice of decision-making by consensus followed under GATT 1947. Except as otherwise provided, where a decision cannot be arrived at by consensus, the matter at issue shall be decided by voting.
2. The Ministerial Conference and the General Council shall have the exclusive authority to adopt interpretation of this Agreement and of the Multilateral Trade Agreements. The decision to adopt an interpretation shall be undertaken by a three-fourths majority of the Members.
3. In exceptional circumstances, the Ministerial Conference may decide to waive an obligation imposed on a Member by this Agreement or any of the Multilateral Trade Agreements provided that any such decision shall be taken by three-fourths of the Members unless otherwise provided.
4. Decisions under a Plurilateral Trade Agreement, including any decision on interpretation and waivers, shall be governed by the provisions of that Agreement.

4.1.10 Article X: Amendments: The following provisions shall be applicable regarding an amendment.

1. Any Member of the WTO may initiate a proposal to amend the provisions of this Agreement or the Multilateral Trade Agreements in Annex 1, 2 and 3 by submitting such proposal to the Ministerial Conference.
2. The Goods Council, the Services Council or the Intellectual Property Rights Council may also submit to the Ministerial Conference, proposals to amend the provisions of the corresponding Multilateral Trade Agreements in Annex 1 the functioning of

which they oversee.

3. Amendment shall take effect upon approval by the Ministerial Conference subject to fulfilment of prescribed procedure and rules.
4. Amendments to a Plurilateral Trade Agreement shall be governed by the provisions of that Agreement.

4.1.11 Article XI: Original Membership: The contracting parties to GATT, 1947 as of the date of entry into force of this Agreement, and the European Communities, which accepts this Agreement and the Multilateral Trade Agreements shall become original member of the WTO.

4.1.12 Article XII: Accession: Any state or separate customs territory possessing full autonomy in the conduct of its external commercial relations and of the other matters provided for in this Agreement and the Multilateral Trade Agreements may accede to this Agreement, on terms to be agreed between it and the WTO. The Ministerial Conference shall approve the accession by a two-thirds majority of the Members of the WTO.

4.1.13 Article XIII: Non-Application of Multilateral Trade Agreements between Particular Members: This Agreement and the Multilateral Trade Agreements in Annex 1 and 2 shall not apply as between any Member and any other Member if either of the Members, at the time either becomes a Member, does not consent to such application.

4.1.14 Article XIV: Acceptance, Entry into Force and Deposit: The Article says that:

1. This Agreement shall be open for acceptance, by signature or otherwise, by contracting parties to GATT, 1947, and the European Communities, which are eligible to become original members of the WTO in accordance with Article XI of this Agreement.
2. A Member which accepts this Agreement after its entry into force shall implement those concessions and obligations in the Multilateral Trade Agreements that are to be implemented over a period of time starting with the entry into force of this Agreement as if it had accepted this Agreement on the date of its entry into force.
3. Unless the entry into force of this Agreement, the text of this Agreement and the Multilateral Trade Agreements shall be deposited with the Director–General to the Contracting Parties to GATT, 1947.

4.1.15 Article XV: Withdrawal: Any Member may withdraw from this Agreement. Such withdrawal shall apply both to this Agreement and the Multilateral Trade Agreements and shall take effect upon the expiration of six months from the date on which written notice of withdrawal is received by the Director-General of the WTO.

4.1.16 Article XVI: Miscellaneous Provisions: The Agreement has the following provisions:

1. Except as otherwise provided under this Agreement or the Multilateral Trade Agreements, the WTO shall be guided by the decisions, procedures and customary practices followed by the Contracting Parties to GATT, 1947 and the bodies established in the framework of GATT, 1947.

2. To the extent practicable, the Secretariat of GATT, 1947 shall become the Secretariat of the WTO.

4.2 General Agreement on Tariffs and Trade (GATT), 1994

The provisions of the General Agreement on Tariffs and Trade, 1947 (GATT, 1947), which were in force at the time were included in the General Agreement on Tariffs and Trade, 1994 (GATT, 1994). The following is the text of language incorporating GATT, 1947 and other instruments into GATT, 1994:

The General Agreement on Tariffs and Trade, 1994, shall consist of:

1. The provisions in the General Agreement on Tariffs and Trade, dated October 30, 1947, annexed to the Final Act adopted at the conclusion of the second session of the Preparatory Committee of the United Nations Conference on Trade and Employment (excluding the Protocol of Provisional Application), as rectified, amended or modified by the terms of legal instruments which have entered into force before the date of entry into force of the WTO Agreement.
2. The provisions of the legal instruments set forth below that have entered into force under the GATT, 1947 before the date of entry into force of the WTO Agreement:

- Protocol and certifications relating to tariff concessions.
- Protocols of accession.
- Decisions on waivers granted under Article XXV of GATT, 1947.
- Other decisions of the Contracting Parties to GATT, 1947.

3. Understandings set forth below:

- Understanding on the interpretation of Article II of GATT, 1994.
- Understanding on the interpretation of Article XVII of GATT, 1994.
- Understanding on the interpretation of Article XVIII of GATT, 1994.
- Understanding on the interpretation of Article XXIV of GATT, 1994.
- Understanding on the interpretation of Article XXV of GATT, 1994.
- Understanding on the interpretation of Article XXVIII of GATT, 1994.

4. The Marrakesh Protocol to GATT, 1994.

Explanatory Notes:

1. The references to 'contracting party' in the provisions of GATT, 1994 shall be deemed to read 'member'. The references to 'less developed contracting party' and 'developed contracting party' shall be deemed to read 'developing country member' and 'developed country member'. The references to 'Executive Secretary' shall be deemed to read 'Director-General of the WTO'.
2. The references to the Contracting Parties acting jointly shall be deemed to refer to the WTO. The other functions that the provisions of GATT, 1994 assign to the Contracting Parties acting jointly shall be allocated at the Ministerial Conference.

The provisions of GATT, 1947, as rectified, amended or modified before the date of entry into force of the WTO Agreement, have already been explained earlier. Texts of the interpretation of the following GATT Articles have been included in the Final Act.

1. **Understanding on the Interpretation of Article II-Schedules of Concessions:** This is an Agreement to record in national schedules "other duties or charges" levied in addition to the recorded tariffs and to bind them at the levels prevailing at the date established in the Uruguay Round Protocol.
2. **Understanding on the Interpretation of Article XVII-State Trading Enterprises:** The Agreement seeks increasing surveillance of their activities through stronger notification and review procedures.
3. **Understanding on the Interpretation of Articles XII and XVIII-BOP Provisions:** Agreement that contracting parties imposing restrictions for balance of payments purposes should do so in the least trade disruptive manner and should favour price based measures, like import surcharges and import deposits, rather than quantitative restrictions. It also seeks the procedure for consultations by the GATT Balance of Payments Committee as well as for notification of BOP measures.
4. **Understanding on the Interpretation of Article XXIV:** Agreement on Customs Unions and Free Trade Areas clarifies and reinforces the criteria and procedures for the review of enlarged or new customs unions or free trade areas and for the evaluation of their effects on third parties. The Agreement also clarifies the procedure to be followed for achieving necessary compensatory adjustment in the event of contracting parties forming a customs union seeking to increase a bound tariff.
5. **Understanding on the Interpretation of Article XXV:** The Agreement on waiver seeks new procedures to grant waivers from GATT disciplines, to specify termination dates for any waivers to be granted in future, and to fix expiry dates for existing waivers.
6. **Understanding on the Interpretation of Article XXVIII:** The Agreement calls for new procedures for the negotiation of compensation when tariff bindings are modified or withdrawn, including the creation of a new negotiating right for the country for which the product in question accounts for the highest proportion of its exports. This is intended to increase the ability of smaller and developing countries to participate in the negotiations.
7. **Understanding on the Interpretation of Article XXXV:** The Agreement permits a contracting party or a newly acceding country to invoke GATT's non-application provisions vis-à-vis the other party after having entered into tariff negotiations with each other.
8. **Marrakesh Protocol to GATT, 1994:** The results of the market access negotiations in which participants have made commitments to eliminate or reduce tariff rates and non-tariff measures applicable to trade in goods are recorded in national schedules of concessions annexed to the Uruguay Round Protocol that forms an integral part of the Final Act.

4.3 Agreement on Agriculture

The General Agreement on Tariffs and Trade, 1947 did apply to agricultural trade, but it allowed countries some non-tariff measures such as import quota and subsidies, unlike the non-agricultural trade. The agricultural trade became highly distorted resultant to domestic support policies. The Uruguay Round produced the first multilateral trade agreement on agriculture.

The main objectives of the Agreement are the removal of trade distortions resulting from subsidies, price and market support, and other trade distorting supports; and eventually facilitate a fair, predictable and market-oriented agricultural trading system. The first step in this direction was 'tariffication'. In 'tariffication', all non-tariff barriers such as quota were replaced with tariffs that represented about the same level of protection as the existing non-tariff barriers. These tariff rates are called bound tariff rates acting as ceiling rates. Members are not allowed to increase a bound tariff rate without renegotiating with other Members. The Agreement requires that this bound tariff rate be reduced over a period of time. The tariffs on all agricultural products are now bound tariff rates.

The new rules and commitments apply to:

1. Market Access.
2. Domestic Support.
3. Export Subsidy.

The agreement allows Members to support their rural economies through the policies that cause minimum distortion to trade. Developing country members have been given some flexibility in fulfilling their obligations. To safeguard the interests of net food importing countries and the least developed countries, special provisions have been made in the Agreement.

4.3.1 Market Access: The Agreement requires that all non-trade barriers on the import of an agricultural product be replaced with a single tariff rate. The tariff equivalent to non-tariff measures was calculated on the basis of average world market prices for the product subject to non-tariff measures and its guaranteed price in the importing countries. Tariff rates resulting from such tariffication as well as tariffs applicable to other products have been bound against further increases.

Member countries applying non-tariff barriers on agricultural goods at the time of the Agreement were permitted to adopt Tariff Rate Quotas as a transitional mechanism. Tariff Rate Quota is a system of applying two tariff rates—lower rates for specified quantities, higher rates for quantities that exceed the quota. These Tariff Rate quotas were intended eventually to be transformed into simple tariffs.

The newly committed tariffs and tariff quotas for all agricultural products became effective in 1995. Members agreed that developed countries would cut the tariffs (the higher out of quota rates in the case of tariff quota) by an average of 36 percent in equal steps over six years (1995-2000). Developing countries would cut it by 24 percent over ten years. Several developing countries also used option of offering ceiling tariff rates in cases where duties were not bound before the Uruguay Round. The least developed countries were not required to cut their tariff rates (Table 4.1).

Table 4.1: Tariff Reduction Targets

Measure	Developed Countries: Six Years (1995-2000) (percent)	Developing Countries: Ten Years (1995-2004) (percent)
Tariffs		
Average cut for all agricultural products	36	24
Minimum cut per product	15	10
Domestic Support		
Total AMS cut (base period, 1986-88)	20	13
Exports		
Value of subsidies	36	24
Subsidised quantities (base period, 1986-90)	21	14

Notes: (i) Only the figures for cutting export subsidies appear in the Agreement; (ii) The least developed countries do not need to reduce tariffs or subsidies; (iii) The base level for tariff cuts was the bound rate before January 1, 1995, or for unbound tariffs, the actual rate charged in September 1986 when the Uruguay Round began.

Members used these in preparing their commitment schedules. The commitment schedules are legally binding. For products, where non-tariff barriers were replaced with tariffs, countries are permitted to take 'special safeguards' in order to prevent swiftly falling prices or surge in imports hurting their farmers.

4.3.2 Domestic Support Measures: The policies, which support domestic prices or subsidise production in some other way. The Agreement differentiates between domestic support programmes that encourage the production directly, and those that are considered not directly affecting the production. The domestic support policies that have a direct effect on production and trade have to be cut back. There are four types of domestic support that are useful in the calculation of 'Total Aggregate Measure of Support' (Total AMS)—which is to be reduced as per the Agreement.

A. Red Box Support: These subsidies are not permitted. Red box subsidies refer to income tax exemptions on export profits, concessional interest rate on export credit, special import licenses etc. However, this provision does not apply to those countries having a per capita income lower than US$ 1,000.

B. Green Box Support: These measures can be used freely. These measures include government services such as research, disease control, infrastructure and food security. These also include payment made directly to farmers that do not stimulate production such as certain forms of direct income support, assistance to help farmers restructure agriculture, and direct payment under environmental and regional assistance programmes.

C. Blue Box Support: These measures are also permitted. These are certain direct payments to farmers where the farmers are required to limit production. Such payments are made on fixed areas and yield or a fixed number of livestock.

D. Amber Box Support: These measures include producers' payments and other domestic subsidies that the government has to reduce under the Agreement.

Thus, Amber Box subsidies are to be reduced. The De minimis is the spending on domestic support that is exempted from Total AMS calculations. The Agreement set the De minimis level for developed countries at 5 percent of the total value of all agricultural production for the product specific and the non-product specific each. Developing countries are allowed up to 10 percent of the total value of agricultural production.

Aggregate Measure of Support (AMS) is of two types: Product specific and non product specific. The product specific support refers to subsidies given to producers of specific crops. Non-product specific support includes subsidies on agricultural inputs such as fertilizers, seeds, irrigation, power, credit etc. AMS is calculated separately for either type of support. The total AMS (base year 1986-88) should be reduced by 20 percent over six years (1995-2000) in case of developed countries and by 13 percent over 10 years (1995-2004) in case of developing countries. The least developing countries do not need to make any cuts.

4.3.3 Export Subsidy: The export subsidies are provided by a country to make its goods globally competitive. The Agreement prohibits export subsidies on agricultural products unless the subsidies are specified in a member's lists of commitments. Where these are listed, the Agreement requires the members to reduce both the amount of money they spend on export subsidies and the quantities of exports that are provided subsidies. The developed countries agreed to reduce the value of export subsidies by 36 percent over six years (1995-2000), while developing countries had to cut it by 24 percent over ten years (1995-2004), taking the average for 1986-90 as the base level. The developed countries also agreed to reduce the quantities of subsidised exports by 21 percent over six years (1995-2000), while developing countries had to reduce it by 14 percent over ten years (1995-2004). The least developed countries do not need to make any cut in export subsidies.

Some net food importing poor countries depend on supply of cheap, subsidised food from major industrial countries. Though their farming sector might receive a boost from higher prices caused by reduced export subsidies, they might need temporary assistance to make the necessary adjustment to deal with higher priced imports, and eventually to export. A special ministerial decision sets out the objectives and certain measures for the provision of food aid and for agriculture development. It also refers to the possibility of assistance from the International Monetary Fund and the World Bank to finance commercial food imports.

The Agreement on Agriculture contains 21 Articles as described below:

1. **Article I: Definitions of Terms:** The Article defines aggregate measurement of support (AMS), basic agriculture product, budget outlays, equivalent measurement of support, export subsidies, implementation period, market access concessions, and

total aggregate measurement of support.

2. **Article II: Product Coverage:** This Agreement applies to the product listed in Annex 1 to this Agreement.
3. **Article III: Incorporation of Concessions and Commitments:** The Article has the following provisions:

- The domestic support and export subsidies commitments in Part IV of each Member's Schedule constitute commitments limiting subsidization and are hereby made an integral part of GATT, 1994.
- A Member shall not provide support or subsidise in excess of the commitment levels specified in its Schedule.

4. **Article IV: Market Access:** The Article says:

- Market access concessions contained in Schedules relate to binding and reduction of tariffs and other market access commitments as specified therein.
- A Member shall not maintain, resort to, or revert to any measures of the kind which have been required to be converted into ordinary customs duties, unless otherwise provided.

5. **Article V: Special Safeguard Measures:** For products where non-tariff barriers have to be converted into ordinary tariffs, a Member is permitted to recourse to the provisions of special safeguard.

- If the volume of import exceeds a trigger level, a Member may impose a limited additional duty subject to some provisions.
- If the price of import on the basis of c.i.f. expressed in terms of domestic currency falls below a trigger price equal to the average of 1986-88 reference prices, a Member may impose a limited additional duty subject to some conditions.

6. **Article VI: Domestic Support Commitment:** The Article has the following provisions on domestic support commitment:

- The domestic support reduction commitments of each Member contained in Part IV of its Schedule shall apply to all of its domestic support measures in favour of agricultural producers with the exception of domestic measures which are not subject to reduction in terms of the criteria set out in this Article and in Annex 2 to this Agreement.
- In case of investment subsidies which are part of government measures of assistance, whether direct or indirect, to encourage agricultural and rural development under the development programmes of developing countries and agricultural input subsidies generally available to low income or resource poor producers in developing countries, Members shall be exempt from domestic support reduction commitment that would otherwise be applicable to such measures. This support shall not be required to be included in Member's calculation of its Current Total AMS.
- (a) A Member shall not be required to include in the calculation of its Current Total AMS and shall not be required to reduce: (i) product specific domestic support which would otherwise be required to be included in a Member's calculation of its Current Total AMS where such support does not exceed 5 percent of that Member's

total value of production of a basic agricultural product during the relevant year, and (ii) non-product specific domestic support which would otherwise be required to be included in a Member's calculation of its Current Total AMS where such support does not exceed 5 percent of the value of that Member's total agricultural production. (b) For developing country Members, the de minimis percentage under this paragraph shall be 10 percent.

- (a) Direct payment under production limiting programmes shall not be subject to commitment to reduce domestic support if: (i) Such payments are based on fixed area and yields, or (ii) Such payments are made on 85 percent or less of the base level of products, or (iii) Livestock payments are made on fixed number of head. (b) The domestic support meeting the above criteria shall not be included in Member's calculation of its current Total AMS.

7. **Article VII: General Disciplines on Domestic Support:** Any domestic support measure in favour of agricultural producers, including any modification to such measure, and any measure that is subsequently introduced that cannot be shown to satisfy the criteria in Annex 2 to this Agreement or to be exempt from reduction by reason of any other provision of this Agreement shall be included in the Member's calculation of its Current Total AMS.

- Where no Total AMS commitment exists in Part IV of a Member's Schedule, the Member shall not provide support to agricultural producers in excess of the relevant de minimis level.

8. **Article VIII: Export Competition Commitments:** The Article says that each Member undertakes not to provide export subsidies otherwise than in conformity with this Agreement and with the commitments specified in that Member's Schedule.
9. **Article IX: Export Subsidy Commitments:**

- The following export subsidies are subject to reduction commitments under this agreement: (a) The provision by governments or their agencies of direct subsidies to an industry, to producers of agricultural products, to a cooperative or other association of such producers, or to a marketing board. (b) The sale or disposal for export by governments or their agencies of non-commercial stocks of agricultural products at the lower price. (c) Payment on export of an agricultural product that are financed by virtue of government action. (d) The provision of subsidies to reduce the cost of marketing exports of agricultural products including handling, upgrading and other processing costs, and the costs of international transport and freight. (e) Internal transport and freight charges on export shipments provided or mandated by governments, on terms more favourable than domestic shipments. (f) Subsidies on agricultural products contingent on their incorporation in exported products.
- During the implementation period, developing country Members shall not be required to undertake commitments in respect of the export subsidies listed above in sub-paragraph (d) and (e).

10. **Article X: Prohibition of Circumvention of Export Subsidy Commitment:** The

Article has the following provisions:

- Export subsidies not listed in paragraph 1 of Article IX shall not be applied in a manner which results in circumvention of export subsidy commitment; nor shall non-commercial transactions be used to circumvent such commitments.
- Members undertake to work toward the development of internationally agreed disciplines to govern the provision of export credits, export credit guarantees or insurance programmes and after agreement on such disciplines to provide export credits, export credit guarantees or insurance programmes only in conformity therewith.
- Any Member which claims that any quantity exported in excess of a reduction commitment level is not subsidised must establish that no export subsidy has been granted in respect of the quantity of exports in question.

11. **Article XI: Incorporated Products:** In no case may the per unit subsidy paid on an incorporated agricultural product exceed the per unit export subsidy that would be payable on exports of the primary product as such.
12. **Article XII: Disciplines on Export Prohibitions and Restrictions:** The following provisions are applicable:

- Where any Member institutes any new export prohibition or restriction on foodstuffs in accordance with paragraph 2(a) of Article XI of GATT, 1994, the Member shall observe the following provisions: (a) The Member instituting the export prohibition or restriction shall give due consideration to the effects of such prohibition or restriction on importing Member's food security. (b) Before any Member institutes an export prohibition or restriction, it shall give notice to the Committee on Agriculture comprising such information as the nature and the duration of such measure and shall consult, upon request, with any other Member having a substantial interest as an importer with respect to any matter related to the measure in question.
- The provisions of this Article shall not apply to any developing country Member, unless the measure is taken by a developing country Member which is a net food exporter of the specific foodstuff concerned.

13. **Article XIII: Due Restraint:** During the implementation period, following provisions shall apply:

- Domestic support measures that conform fully to the provisions of Annex 2 to this Agreement shall be non-actionable subsidies for the purpose of countervailing duties and some other provisions.
- Domestic support measures that conform fully to the provisions of Article 6 of this Agreement shall be exempt from imposition of countervailing duties unless a determination of injury is made or some other provisions applicable.
- Export subsidies that conform fully to the provisions of Articles 8-11 shall be subject to countervailing duties only upon a determination of injury or threat thereof or some other provisions.

14. **Article XIV: Sanitary and Phytosanitary Measures:** Article says that Members agree to give effect to the Agreement on the Application of Sanitary and

Phytosanitary Measures.

15. **Article XV: Special and Differential Treatment:** There is provision of special and differential treatment for developing countries.

- In keeping with the recognition that differential and more favourable treatment for developing country Members is an integral part of the negotiations, special and differential treatment in respect of commitments shall be provided as set out in the relevant provisions of this Agreement and embodied in the Schedules of concessions and commitments.
- Developing country Members shall have the flexibility to implement reduction commitments over a period of up to 10 years. Least developed country Members shall not be required to undertake reduction commitments.

16. **Article XVI: Least Developed and Net Food Importing Developing Countries:** Developed country Members shall take such action as is provided for within the framework of the Decision on Measures Concerning the Possible Negative Effect of the Reform Program on Least Developed and Net Food Importing Developing Countries.
17. **Article XVII: Committee on Agriculture:** The Article says that a Committee on Agriculture is hereby established.
18. **Article XVIII: Review of the Implementation of Commitments:** The Agreement has following provisions regarding review process:

- Progress in the implementation of commitments negotiated under the Uruguay Round reform programme shall be reviewed by the Committee on Agriculture.
- The review process shall be undertaken on the basis of notifications submitted by members as well as on the basis of such documentation as the Secretariat may be requested to prepare in order to facilitate the review process.
- In the review process, Members shall be given due consideration to the influence of excessive rates of inflation on the ability of a Member to abide by its domestic support commitments.
- The review process shall provide an opportunity for Members to raise any matter relevant to the implementation of commitments.

19. **Article XIX: Consultation and Commitments:** The provisions of Article XXII and XXIII of GATT, 1994, as elaborated and applied by the Dispute Settlement Undertaking, shall apply to consultations and the settlement of disputes under this Agreement.
20. **Article XX: Continuation of the Reform Process:** Recognising that the long-term objective of substantial progressive reduction in support and protection resulting in fundamental reform is an ongoing process, Members agreed that the negotiations for continuing the process will be initiated one year before the end of the implementation period.
21. **Article XXI: Final Provisions**

- The provisions of GATT, 1994 and other Multilateral Trade Agreements in Annex 1A to the WTO Agreement shall apply subject to the provisions of this agreement.

- The Annexes to this Agreement are hereby made an integral part of this Agreement.

4.4 Agreement on the Application of Sanitary and Phytosanitary Measures

Every country takes measures to ensure that all food, whether domestic or imported, is safe for consumers and to protect animals and plants from pests or diseases. These measures may take many forms such as inspection of products, requiring products to come from disease free area, specific treatment or processing of products, setting allowable maximum level of pesticide residuals or limiting the permitted use of additives in food. There is provision under Article 20 of the GATT, 1994 to protect human, animal or plant life or health, provided this does not lead to discrimination or disguised protectionism. In addition, there are two specific agreements—the Application of Sanitary and Phytosanitary Measures Agreement, and the Agreement on Technical Barriers to Trade—dealing with food safety and animal and plant health and safety, and with standards of products. Sanitary (human and animal health) and Phytosanitary (plant health) measures apply to domestically produced food or local animal and plant diseases, as well as to products being imported from other countries. The Agreement on the Application of Sanitary and Phytosanitary Measures concerns with food safety, and animal and plant health regulations.

For the purpose of the Agreement on the Application of Sanitary and Phytosanitary Measures, sanitary and Phytosanitary measures are defined as any measure applied:

1. To protect human or animal life from risk arising from additives, contaminants, toxins or disease causing organisms in the food or beverages;
2. To protect human life from animal or plant carried diseases;
3. To protect animal or plant life from pests, diseases or disease causing organisms; and
4. To prevent or limit other damages to a country from the entry, establishment or spread of pests.

4.4.1 Justification of Measures: The Agreement on the Application of Sanitary and Phytosanitary Measures permits Members to set their own standards and regulations. But, these regulations and standards must be based on science. They should be applied only to the extent necessary to protect human, animal or plant life or health.

Consistency: Members have to avoid arbitrary or unjustifiable distinctions in the level of protection applied in different situations, if such distinctions result in discrimination or a disguised restriction on international trade.

4.4.2 International Standard: The Agreement encourages Members to apply national sanitary and Phytosanitary measures that are consistent with international standards, guidelines and recommendations. This process is often called 'Harmonisation'. The WTO itself does not develop these standards. These standards are developed by international organisations. These standards are subject to international scrutiny and reviews.

The international organisations include:

1. Food Safety: FAO/WHO-Codex Alimentarius Commission (Codex).
2. Animal Health: The World Organisation for Animal Health (WOAH).

3. Plant Health: FAO-The International Plant Protection Convention (IPPC).

Members can also set higher standards based on appropriate assessment of risks as long as the approach is consistent and not arbitrary. Members can also apply, to some extent, the precautionary measures to deal with scientific uncertainty.

4.4.3 Equivalence: The agreement allows members to apply different standards and regulations of inspecting the products. An importing Member is expected to accept the exporting Member's standards and regulations; if exporting Member demonstrates that the standards and regulations it applies to its exports achieve the same level of health protection as by the importing Member.

4.4.4 Transparency: The Agreement makes sanitary and phytosanitary measures more transparent. Members are required to notify each other, through the WTO Secretariat, of any new or changed sanitary and phytosanitary requirements. Members must also set up offices called 'enquiry point to respond to request for more information on new or existing sanitary and phytosanitary requirements; including justification and application of their food safety, and animal and plant health regulations.

4.4.5 Adaptation to Conditions: Since there may be difference in climate, existing pests or diseases or food safety conditions, it is not always appropriate to apply the same sanitary and phytosanitary requirements on food, animal or plant products coming from different countries.

4.4.6 Risk assessment: The sanitary and phytosanitary measures must be based on an appropriate assessment of the actual risk involved. Members should make known what factors they took into consideration, the assessment procedure applied and the determination of acceptable level of risk.

The main provisions of Articles of the Agreement have been described below:

1. **Article I: General Provisions:** This Article has the following provisions:

- This Agreement applies to all sanitary and phytosanitary measures which may, directly or indirectly, affect international trade. Such measures shall be developed and applied in accordance with the provisions of this Agreement.
- Nothing in this Agreement shall affect the rights of Members under the Agreement on Technical Barriers to trade with respect to measures not within the scope of this Agreement.

2. **Article II: Basic Rights and Obligations:** The Agreement has provisions regarding the rights and obligations of Members.

- Members have the rights to take sanitary and phytosanitary measures necessary for the protection of human, animal or plant life or health, provided that such measures are not inconsistent with the provisions of this Agreement.
- Members shall ensure that any sanitary or phytosanitary measure is applied only to the extent necessary to protect human, animal or plant life or health and is based on scientific principles and not maintained without sufficient scientific evidence, except the provisional application due to inconclusive scientific evidence.

3. **Article III: Harmonisation:** The Agreement has the following provisions relating to harmonisation of the measures:

- To harmonise sanitary and phytosanitary measures, on as wide a basis as possible, Members shall base their sanitary and phytosanitary measures on international standards, guidelines or recommendations, where they exist, unless otherwise provided.
- Members may introduce or maintain sanitary or phytosanitary measures which result in a higher level of sanitary or phytosanitary protection than would be achieved by measures based on the relevant international standards, guidelines or recommendations, if there is a scientific justification.
- Members shall play a full part, within the limits of their resources, in the relevant international organisations and their subsidiary bodies, in particular Codex, WOAH, IPPC to promote within organisations, the development and periodic review of standards, guidelines or recommendations with respect to all aspects of sanitary and phytosanitary measures.
- The Committee on sanitary and phytosanitary measures shall develop a procedure to monitor the process of international harmonisation and coordinate efforts in this regard with the relevant international organisations.

4. **Article IV: Equivalence:** Members shall accept the sanitary or phytosanitary measures of other Members as equivalent, even if these measures differ from their own or from those used by other members trading in the same product, if the exporting Member objectively demonstrates to the importing Member that its measures achieve the importing Member's appropriate level of sanitary or phytosanitary protection.
5. **Article V: Assessment of Risk and Determination of the Appropriate Level of Sanitary or Phytosanitary Measures:** The Article contains the following provisions:

- Members shall ensure that their sanitary or phytosanitary measures are based on an assessment, as appropriate to circumstances, of risks to human, animal or plant life or health, taking into account risk assessment techniques developed by the relevant international organisations.
- In the assessment of risks, Members shall consider available scientific evidence, relevant process and production methods, relevant inspection, sampling and testing methods, prevalence of specific diseases or pests, existence of pest or disease free area, relevant ecological and environmental conditions, and quarantine treatment.
- In the assessment of risks to animal or plant life or health and determination of the measures to be applied to achieve the appropriate level of sanitary or phytosanitary protection from such risks, Members shall take into consideration the relevant factors like cost, damage, loss of production, spread of disease or pest, control etc.
- Members shall determine the appropriate level of sanitary or phytosanitary protection such as to minimise the negative trade effects.
- Members shall maintain consistency and shall avoid arbitrary or unjustifiable distinctions in the level of protection.
- Members shall ensure that measures are not more trade restrictive than required to

achieve their appropriate level of sanitary or phytosanitary protection, taking into account technical and economic feasibility.

- If the relevant scientific evidence is insufficient, a Member may provisionally apply sanitary or phytosanitary measures on the basis of available concerned information.
- If a Member believes that a sanitary or phytosanitary measure adopted by other Member is constraining its exports and the measure is not based on the relevant international standards, guidelines or recommendations; an explanation of the reasons for such measure may be requested and shall be provided by the Member applying the measure.

6. **Article VI: Adaptation to Regional Conditions:** The following are provisions related to the adaptation of regional conditions:

- The sanitary or phytosanitary measures shall be adapted to the sanitary or phytosanitary characteristics of the area—whether a part of country, a whole country or all or parts of several countries—from which the product originated and to which the product is destined.
- Members shall recognise the concept of pest or disease free area and areas of low pest or disease prevalence.
- Members claiming that areas within their territory is a pest or disease free area or areas of low pest or disease prevalence, shall provide necessary evidence of this by objectively demonstrating to the importing Member that such areas are, and likely to remain, pest or disease free areas or areas of low pest or disease prevalence.

7. **Article VII: Transparency:** A member shall notify the change in their sanitary or phytosanitary measures and shall provide information on their sanitary or phytosanitary measures in accordance with the provisions of this Agreement.
8. **Article VIII: Control, Inspection and Approval Procedures:** Members shall observe the provisions of this Agreement in the operation of control, inspection and approval procedures, including the system of approving the use of additives or for establishing tolerances for contaminants in foods, beverages or feedstuffs, and otherwise ensure that their procedures are not inconsistent with the provisions of this Agreement.
9. **Article IX: Technical Assistance:** The Article says that:

- Members agree to facilitate the provisions of technical assistance to other Members especially developing country Members in areas such as processing techniques, research and infrastructure.
- If an exporting developing country Member requires substantial investment in meeting the sanitary or phytosanitary requirements of an importing country Member, the importing country member shall consider providing such technical assistance as will permit developing country member to maintain and expand its market access opportunities for the product in question.

10. **Article X: Special and Differential Treatment:** The Agreement has provisions of special and differential treatment for developing country Members.

- Members shall take into account the special needs of developing country Members and in particular the least developed countries.

- Developing country Members shall be given flexibility in compliance with respect to the introduction of new sanitary or phytosanitary measures, if the appropriate level of sanitary or phytosanitary protection adopted allows this.
- The Committee may grant developing country members, upon request, special and time limiting exemption in whole or part from obligations under this Agreement, taking into account their financial, trade and development needs.
- Members should arrange and facilitate the active participation of developing country Members in the relevant international organisations.

11. **Article XI: Consultation and Dispute Settlement:** The Article says that the provisions of Articles XXII and XXIII of GATT, 1994 as elaborated and applied by the Dispute Settlement Understanding shall apply to consultations and the settlement of disputes under this Agreement, except as otherwise specifically provided therein.
12. **Article XII: Administration:** The Article says that:

- A Committee on sanitary and phytosanitary measures is hereby established to provide a regular forum for consultations. It shall carry out the functions necessary to implement the provisions of this Agreement and achieve its objectives, in particular, the harmonisation.
- The Committee shall maintain close contacts with the relevant international organisations in the field.

13. **Article XIII: Implementation:** The Article says that Members are fully responsible for the observance of all obligations set forth under this Agreement.
14. **Article XIV: Final Provisions:** The least developing country members may delay application of the provisions of this Agreement for a period of five years with respect to their sanitary and phytosanitary measures affecting importation or imported products. Other developing country Members may delay the application of some of the provisions of this Agreement for two years with respect to their existing sanitary or phytosanitary measures affecting importation or imported products, where such application is prevented by insufficient technical expertise.

4.5 Agreement on Textile and Clothing

This Agreement was terminated on January 1, 2005.

5

WTO Agreements on Technical Barriers to Trade, Trade-related Investment, Anti-dumping, Customs Valuation, and Pre-shipment Inspection

5.1 Agreement on Technical Barriers to Trade

The Agreement on Technical Barriers to Trade aims to ensure that regulations, standards, testing and certification procedures do not unnecessarily impede the international trade. The Agreement on Technical Barriers to Trade strengthened and clarified the provisions of the "Standard Code"—the original plurilateral 1979 Tokyo Round Agreement on Technical Barriers to Trade governing regulations and standards.

The Agreement on Technical Barriers to Trade covers all goods, both agricultural and industrial. The following are not covered:

1. Services.
2. Purchase specifications prepared by governmental bodies for production or consumption requirements of governmental bodies.
3. Measures covered by the Agreement on Application of Sanitary and Phytosanitary Measures.

The TBT and SPS Agreements differ in scope. It is not the product, but the measure that determine whether it is covered under TBT Agreement or SPS Agreement. The purpose of the measure is relevant in determining whether it is subject to the SPS Agreement. The type of measure determines whether it is covered by the TBT Agreement. The SPS Agreement concerns with predefined specific risks to human health and animal or plant health or life or protection form pests. While, the TBT Agreement may concern with the prevention of deceptive practices, national security, protection of environment, and protection of human health or animal or plant life or health. Government may draft and implement a broad regulation containing both SPS and TBT measures relating to a product. The SPS Agreement is complementary to the TBT Agreement. Examples are given in Table 5.1.

Table 5.1: TBT and SPS Agreements

Product	Measure	Agreement
Fruit	Regulation on treatment of fruit to prevent pest spreading	SPS
	Regulation on quality, grading and labelling of fruit	TBT
Mineral water	Regulation on minerals safe for human health	SPS
	Regulation on size, volume, shape	TBT

The TBT Agreement distinguishes between three categories of measures: technical regulations, standards, and conformity assessment procedures (Table 5.2).

Table 5.2: Technical Regulations, Standards and Conformity Assessment Procedures

Technical Regulations	Standards	Conformity Assessment Procedures
*Technical regulations lay down product characteristics or their processes and production methods. *They may also deal with terminology, symbols, packaging, marking and labelling. *Compliance is mandatory.	*Standards are approved by a recognised body which is responsible for establishing rules, guidelines or characteristics for products or their processes and production methods. *They may also deal with terminology, symbols, packaging, marking and labelling. *Compliance is not mandatory.	*Conformity procedures are used to determine the relevant requirements in technical regulations or standards are fulfilled. *They include procedures for sampling, testing, inspection; evaluation, verification and assurance of conformity, and registration, accreditation and approval.

Standards are addressed by the TBT Agreement in a separate "Code for Good Practice for the Preparation, Adoption and Application of Standards" (the Code) contained in Annex 3 of the TBT Agreement. This Code, which is open to acceptance by any standardised body, offers guidance on the process of setting standards. The TBT Agreement instructs members to make sure that their central government standardising bodies recognize and comply with the Code.

The TBT Agreement contains fundamental principles of non-discrimination, promoting predictability of access to markets, technical assistance, transparency and special and differential treatment for developing countries in the implementation of the Agreement. The Agreement contains detailed provisions to clarify the entire process of preparing, adopting and applying TBT measures. The TBT Agreement disciplines the Members to differentiate between legitimate and protectionist motivations for TBT measures.

The Agreement recognises that countries have right to adopt technical regulations, which prescribe mandatory product standards. The Agreement on Technical Barriers to Trade strongly encourages the Members to use relevant international standards, guidelines and recommendations. The technical barriers do not create an unnecessary impediment to trade if these are prepared in accordance with relevant international standards. However, harmonisation on the basis of international standards may not be viable in all contexts due to different national preferences and circumstances.

The Agreement on Technical Barriers to Trade contains the provisions of providing special and differential treatment to developing countries. The TBT Agreement consists of three core elements to ensure transparency of regulations: (a) provisions on the notification of draft technical regulations and conformity assessment procedures, as well as one time notification of each member's organisational set up of the implementation of the Agreement, (b) enquiry points and (c) publication requirements for technical regulations, conformity assessment procedures and standards.

The Agreement on Technical Barriers to Trade has the provision of setting up a Committee on Technical Barriers to Trade aimed at reviewing specific measures and the implementation of provisions of this Agreement.

The main provisions of this Agreement have been described below.

1. **Article I: General Provisions:** For the purpose of this Agreement, meaning of the terms given in Annex 1 to this Agreement shall apply. All references in this Agreement to technical regulations, standards and conformity assessment procedures shall be construed to include any amendments thereto and any addition to rules or the product coverage thereof.
2. **Article II: Preparation, Adoption and Application of Technical Regulations by Central Government Bodies:** With respect to their central government bodies:

- Members shall ensure Most Favoured Nation, and National Treatments to the products imported from the territory of any Member in relation to preparation, adoption and application of technical regulations.
- Members shall ensure that technical regulations are prepared, adopted and applied without creating unnecessary obstacles to international trade.
- Technical regulations shall be amended appropriately, if changed circumstances or objectives can be addressed in a less trade restrictive manner.
- Where technical regulations are required and relevant international standards exist or their completion is eminent, Members shall use them, or relevant part of them, as a basis for their technical regulations except when such international standards or relevant part cannot fulfil the legitimate objectives.
- A Member preparing, adopting or applying a technical regulation which may have effect on trade of other countries shall, on the request of another Member, explain the justification for that technical regulation.
- With a vision to harmonising technical regulations, as far as possible, Members shall play full part in preparation by suitable international standardising bodies of international standards for products.
- Members shall positively consider to accepting as equivalent the technical regulations of other Members, even if these regulations differ from their own, provided they are satisfied that these regulations adequately fulfil the objectives of their own regulations.
- Members shall, if appropriate, specify technical regulations based on product requirements in terms of performance rather than design or descriptive characteristics.

- If a relevant international standard does not exist or a proposed technical regulation is not in accordance with the relevant standards and that technical regulation may have significant effect on trade of other members, Members shall notify other Members and upon request provide other Members with the copies of technical regulations. Members shall discuss the comments made by other Members and take into consideration the results of discussion.
- Members shall ensure that all technical regulations which have been adopted are published promptly to enable other Members to become acquainted with them.

3. **Article III: Preparation, Adoption and Application of Technical Regulations by Local Government Bodies and Non-Governmental Bodies:** Members shall take reasonable measures to ensure that local government and non-governmental bodies within their territories comply with the provisions of Article 2 mentioned above.
4. **Article IV: Preparation, Adoption and Application of Standards:** Members shall make sure that their central government standardising bodies accept and comply with the 'Code of Good Practice for the Preparation, Adoption and Application of Standards' in Annex 3 to this Agreement. Members shall take such reasonable measures as may be accessible to them to ensure that local government and non-government standardising bodies within their territories as well regional standardising bodies admit and comply with the 'Code of Good Practice'. The obligations of the members with respect to compliance of standardising bodies with the provisions of the 'Code of Good Practice' shall apply irrespective of whether or not a standardising body has accepted the 'Code of Good Governance'.
5. **Article V: Procedure for Assessment of Conformity by Central Government Bodies:** The Agreement has the following provisions:

- Members shall ensure that their central government bodies apply the following provisions to the imported product: (a) Conformity assessment procedures are prepared, adopted and applied so as to grant access to suppliers of products originating in the territories of other members no less favourable than those accorded to the suppliers of like products of national origin or originating in any other country. (b) Conformity assessment procedures are not prepared, adopted and applied with a view to creating unnecessary impediments to international trade.
- Members shall ensure that: (a) Conformity assessment procedures are undertaken and completed as expeditiously as possible and in no less favourable order for products originating in the territories of other Members than like domestic products. (b) The standard processing period of each conformity assessment procedure is published or communicated to the applicants upon request. (c) Information requirements are limited to what is necessary to conformity and determining fees. (d) The confidentiality of information about product originating in the territories of other Members supplied in connection with such conformity assessment procedure is respected. (e) A procedure exists to review complaints concerning the operation of a conformity assessment procedure and to take corrective action when a complaint is justified.

- A Member can carry out reasonable spot checks within its territory.
- If it is required that products conform with technical regulations or standards, and relevant guides or recommendations issued by international standardising body exist; Members shall ensure that central government bodies use them, or the relevant parts of them as a basis for their conformity assessment procedures.
- With a view to harmonising conformity assessment procedures, as far as possible, Members shall play full part in the preparation by appropriate international standardising bodies of guides and recommendations for conforming assessment procedures.
- If a relevant guide or recommendation issued by international standardising body does not exist or the technical content of a proposed conformity assessment procedure is not in accordance with the relevant guides or recommendations issued by international standardising bodies and conformity assessment procedure may have significant effect on trade of other Members, Member shall publish a notice in this regard, provide copies of the proposed procedure upon request, and shall discuss the comments thereon and take into account the results of such discussions.
- Members shall ensure that all conformity assessment procedures which have adopted are published promptly to enable other Members to acquaint with.

6. **Article VI: Recognition of Conformity Assessment by Central Government Bodies:** Members shall ensure, if possible, that results of conformity assessment procedure in other Members are accepted by their central government bodies, even when these procedures differ from their own, provided they are satisfied that these procedures offer an assurance of conformity with the applicable technical regulations or standards equivalent to their own procedures.
7. **Article VII: Procedures for Assessment of Conformity by Local Government Bodies:** With respect to their local governmental bodies, Members shall take such reasonable measures as may be available to them to ensure the compliance by such bodies with the provisions relating to Procedures for Assessment of Conformity and Recognition of Conformity Assessment of other Members.
8. **Article VIII: Procedure for Assessment of Conformity by Non-Governmental Bodies:** Members shall take such practical measures as may be available to them to make certain that non-governmental bodies within their territories which operate conformity assessment procedures comply with the procedures relating to Procedures for Assessment of Conformity and Recognition of Conformity Assessment of other members.
9. **Article IX: International and Regional Systems:** The Article says that:

- Members shall, if a positive assurance of conformity with a technical regulation or standard is required, wherever applicable, formulate and adopt international systems of conformity assessment and become members thereof or participate therein.
- Members shall take such practical measure as may be available to them to ensure that international and regional systems for conformity assessment in which relevant bodies within their territories are members or participants comply with the

provisions relating to Procedures for Assessment of Conformity and Recognition of Conformity Assessment of other Members.

10. **Article X: Information about Technical Regulations, Standards and Conformity Assessment Procedures:** Each Member shall make certain that an enquiry point exists which is competent to answer all reasonable enquiries from other Members and interested parties in other Member countries as well as to provide relevant documents regarding:

- Any technical regulations adopted or proposed within its territory by central or local governmental bodies, by non-governmental bodies which have a legal power to implement a technical regulation, or by regional standardising bodies of which such bodies are members or participants.
- Any standard adopted or proposed within its territory by central or local governmental bodies, by non-governmental bodies or regional standardising bodies of which such bodies are members or participants.
- Any conformity assessment procedures which are operated by central government or local government bodies or by non-governmental bodies.
- The membership and participation of the Members or of relevant central or local government bodies in international and regional standardising bodies.
- The location of notices pursuant to this Agreement.
- Local enquiry points.

11. **Article XI: Technical Assistance to other Members:** The Agreement has the following provisions:

- Member shall, if requested, advise other Members, especially developing country members, on the preparation of technical regulations.
- Member shall, if requested, advise other Members, especially developing country members, and shall grant them technical assistance on mutually agreed terms and conditions regarding the establishment of national standardising bodies.
- In providing advice and technical assistance to other Members, Members shall give priority to needs of the least developed countries.

12. **Article XII: Special and Differential Treatment:** The Agreement has provisions of special and differential treatment for developing country Members:

- Members shall provide differential and more favourable treatment to developing country Members to this Agreement.
- Members shall give special attention to the provisions of this Agreement concerning developing country Members' rights and obligations and shall take into account the special development, financial and trade needs of developing country Members in the implementation of this Agreement.
- Members shall, in the preparation and application of technical regulations, standards and conformity assessment procedures, consider the special development, financial and trade needs of developing countries.
- Members recognise that, while international standards or guide may exist, in their

particular technological and socio-economic conditions, developing country Members adopt certain technical regulations, standards and conformity assessment procedures intended at preserving indigenous technology and processing methods with their development needs. Members therefore make out that developing country Members should not be expected to use international standards as a basis for their technical regulations or standards, including test methods, which are not suitable to their development, financial and trade needs.

- The Committee on Technical Barriers to Trade is enabled to grant upon request, special and time-bound exemption to developing countries in whole or in part from obligations under this Agreement.

13. **Article XIII: The Committee on Technical Barriers to Trade:** A Committee on Technical Barriers to Trade is established to further the objectives and fulfil the responsibilities assigned to it under this Agreement.
14. **Article XIV: Consultation and Dispute Settlement:** The Article states that the provisions of Articles XXII and XXIII of GATT, 1994 as elaborated and applied by the Dispute Settlement Understanding shall apply to consultations and the settlement of disputes under this Agreement, except as otherwise specifically provided therein.
15. **Article XV: Final Provisions:** The Agreement has the provisions:

- Reservations may not be entered in respect of any of the provisions of this Agreement without the consent of other Members.
- The Committee shall review annually the implementation and operation of this Agreement taking into account the objectives thereof.

5.2 Agreement on Trade-related Investment Measures (TRIMs)

Governments sometimes impose conditions on foreign direct investment to meet certain national priorities such as export performance or local input requirements and others like. These measures may prohibit and distort the international trade. The Agreement on TRIMs states that no Member shall apply a measure that is prohibited by provisions of Article III (National Treatment) or Article XI (Quantitative Restrictions) of GATT, 1994. This Agreement applies only to measures that affect trade in goods. The Agreement prohibits five TRIMs given in Annex to this Agreement.

TRIMs are prohibited because they infringe the principle of National Treatment by extending favourable treatment to domestic enterprises. The following measures are prohibited on this ground:

1. Requiring the purchase or use by an enterprise of products of domestic origin or from any domestic source (local inputs requirement).
2. Requiring the purchase or use of imported products by an enterprise to be limited to an amount related to the volume or value of the local product it exports (balance of payments requirement).

The following measures are also prohibited for being inconsistent with the provisions of Article XI of GATT, 1994 against the use of quantitative restrictions on imports and exports:

1. Restricting the imports used by an enterprise to an amount related to the quantity or value of the product exported (balance of payments requirement).
2. Importation of the products used by an enterprise restricting access to foreign exchange to an amount of foreign exchange inflows attributable to the enterprise (balance of payment requirement).
3. Specifying exports or sale for exports in terms of the volume or value of local production by the enterprise (export performance requirement).

The Agreement on TRIMs requires mandatory notification of all non-conforming TRIMs and their elimination within two years for developed country Members, within five years for developing country Members and within seven years for least developed country Members. The Agreement established a Committee on TRIMs which will, among other things, observe the implementation of these commitments. The Agreement also provides for consideration, at a later stage, of whether it should be complemented with provisions on investment and competition policy more broadly.

Main provisions of the Agreement have been described below:

1. **Article I: Coverage:** This Agreement applies to investment measures related to trade in goods.
2. **Article II: National Treatment and Quantitative Restrictions:** The Article says that:

- Without prejudice to other rights and obligations under GATT, 1994, no Member shall apply any TRIM that is inconsistent with the provisions of Article III or Article XI of GATT, 1994.
- An illustrative list of TRIMs that are inconsistent with the provisions of Article III or Article XI of GATT, 1994 is contained in the Annex to this Agreement.

3. **Article III: Exceptions:** All exceptions under GATT, 1994 shall apply, as appropriate, to the provisions of this Agreement.
4. **Article IV: Developing Country Members:** A developing country member shall be free to deviate temporarily from the provisions of Article II to the extent and in such a manner as Article XVIII of GATT, 1994, the Understanding on the Balance of Payments Provisions of GATT, 1994, and Declaration on Trade Measures Taken for Balance of Payments Purposes adopted on November 28, 1979.
5. **Article V: Notification and Transitional Arrangements:** The Agreement has the following provisions:

- Members shall notify all TRIMs they are applying that are not in conformity with the provisions of this Agreement.
- Members shall eliminate all TRIMs that have been notified within two years in the case of developed country Members, within five years in the case of developing country Members and within seven years in the case of least developed country Members.
- The Council for Trade in Goods may, upon request, extend the transition period for elimination of TRIMs notified for developing country Members which demonstrate particular difficulties in implementing the provisions of this Agreement.

- In order not to disadvantage established enterprises which are subject to a notified TRIM, a Member may apply during the transition period, the same TRIM to new enterprises.

6. **Article VI: Transparency:** The Article states that:

- Members shall notify the Secretariat of Publications in which TRIMs may be found, including those applied by regional and local governments and authorities within their territories.
- Members shall accord thoughtful consideration to the requests for information and provide sufficient opportunities for consultation on any matter arising from this Agreement raised by another Member.

7. **Article VII: Committee on Trade Related Investment Measures:** The Agreement contains:

- A Committee on TRIMs has been established.
- The Committee shall carry out responsibilities assigned to it by Council for Trade in Goods and shall provide opportunity to Members to consult on any matter relating to the operation and implementation of this Agreement.
- The Committee shall monitor the operation and implementation of this Agreement and shall report thereon annually to the Council for Trade in Goods.

8. **Article VIII: Consultation and Dispute Settlement:** The Provisions of Article XXII and XXIII of GATT, 1994, as elaborated and applied by the Dispute Settlement Understanding, shall apply to consultations and the Settlement of Disputes under this Agreement.
9. **Article IX: Review by the Council for Trade in Goods:** The Council for Trade in Goods shall review the operation of this Agreement within five years and shall consider whether the agreement should be complemented with the provisions on investment and competition policy.

5.3 Agreement on Implementation of Article VI (Anti-dumping Measures)

Article VI of the GATT, 1994 has provisions for the right of contracting parties to apply anti-dumping measures against imports of a product being priced below its normal value; if such dumped imports cause injury to a domestic industry of importing contracting party. An Anti-dumping Agreement consisting rules to administer the application of such measures was concluded in Tokyo Round. Agreement on Implementation of Article VI adopted at Uruguay Round had resulted in a revision of the Tokyo Round Agreement and providing more detailed rules.

The Agreement contains more clarified and detailed rules in relation to the method of determining whether a product is being dumped, the criteria to be applied in determining that dumped product is causing injury to the domestic industry, the procedures to be followed in initiating and conducting anti-dumping investigations, and the implementation and duration of anti-dumping measures. The Agreement also has provisions relating to role of dispute settlement panels in disputes relating to anti-dumping duties.

The importing country Member has to establish a clear causal relationship between dumped import and injury to the domestic industry. The Agreement has provisions that all interested parties are given an opportunity to present evidence. Provisions on the application of provisional measures, use of price undertaking in anti-dumping cases, and on the duration of anti-dumping measures have been strengthened.

There is provision for the immediate termination of an anti-dumping investigation in cases where authorities determine that the margin of dumping is de minimis (which is defined as less than 2 percent, expressed as percentage of the export price of the product) or that the volume of dumped imports is negligible (generally when the volume of dumped imports from an individual country accounts for less than 3 percent of the imports of the product in question into the importing country).

A Member has to immediately notify in detail all anti-dumping measures to the Committee on anti-dumping practice. Members shall be given an opportunity of consultation on any matter relating to the operation of the Agreement.

Main provisions of the Agreement are given below:

1. **Article I: Principles:** An anti-dumping measure shall be applied under the circumstances provided for in Article VI of GATT, 1994 and pursuant to the investigations initiated and conducted in accordance with the provisions of this Agreement.
2. **Article II: Determination of Dumping:** In relation to dumping, the Agreement states that:

- A product is to be considered as being dumped if the export price of the product exported from one country to another country is less than the comparable, in the ordinary course of trade, for the like product when destined for consumption in the exporting country.
- In the case where products are not imported directly from the country of origin but are exported to the importing Member from an intermediate country, the price at which the products are sold from the country of export to the importing Member shall normally be compared with the comparable price in the country of export.

3. **Article III: Determination of Injury:** The Agreement has the following provisions regarding the determination of injury:

- The injury shall be determined on the basis of a positive evidence and objective examination of both: (a) the volume of the dumped imports and the effects of the imports on prices in domestic market for like products, and (b) the subsequent impact of these imports on domestic producers of such products.
- The investigating authorities shall consider whether there has been a significant increase in the volume of dumped imports, either in absolute term or in relation to production or consumption in the importing member country.
- The assessment of the impact of the dumped imports on domestic industry concerned shall include an evaluation of all relevant economic factors and indices having a bearing on the state of the industry.
- It must be demonstrated that the dumped products are, through the effect of

dumping, causing injury within the meaning of this Agreement.

- The effect of the dumped imports shall be determined relative to the domestic production of the like product when available data allows separate identification of that production on the basis of such criteria like the production process, producer's sale and profits.
- The determination of threat of material injury shall be based on evidence and not merely on allegations, supposition or remote possibility.

4. **Article IV: Definition of Domestic Industry:** The term 'industry' shall be interpreted as referring to the domestic producers as a whole of the like products or to those of them whose collective output of the products constitutes a major proportion of the total domestic production of those products unless otherwise provided.
5. **Article V: Initiation and Subsequent Investigation:** Provisions regarding initiation of investigation are given below:

- An investigation to determine the existence, degree and effect of any alleged dumping of imports shall be initiated upon a written application by or on behalf of the domestic industry or may be initiated by authorities itself on the basis of evidence.
- When an application is made on the behalf of domestic industry it shall include evidence of: (a) dumping, (b) injury, and (c) casual relationship between the dumped imports and alleged injury.
- The authorities shall look at the accuracy and adequacy of the evidence provided in the application to determine whether there is sufficient evidence to justify the initiation of an investigation.
- The authorities shall evade, unless a decision has been made to initiate an investigation, any publicizing of the application for the initiation of an investigation.
- An application shall be rejected and an investigation shall be terminated promptly as soon as the authorities concerned are satisfied that there is not sufficient evidence of either dumping or of injury to justify proceeding with the case. There shall be the immediate termination of an anti-dumping investigation in cases where authorities determine that the margin of dumping is de minimis (which is defined as less than 2 percent, expressed as percentage of the export price of the product) or that the volume of dumped imports is negligible (generally when the volume of dumped imports from an individual country accounts for less than 3 percent of the imports of the product in question into importing country).
- An anti-dumping proceeding shall not hamper the procedures of customs clearance.

6. **Article VI: Evidence:** The Article says that:

- All interested parties in an anti-dumping investigation shall be given notice of the information which the authorities require and ample opportunity to present in writing all evidence which they consider relevant in respect of the investigation in question.
- The interested parties shall include: (a) an exporter or foreign producer or the importer of a product subject to investigation or a business association in which a

majority of the members consists of producers, exporters or importers of such product, (b) the government of the exporting Member and (c) a producer of the like product in the importing Member or a trade and business association in which a majority of the Members produce like products in the territory of the importing Member.

7. **Article VII: Provisional Measures:** The Article has the following provisions:

- Provisional measures may be applied only if: (a) a public notice, after the initiation of investigation, has been given to and interested parties have been given adequate opportunities to submit information and make comments, (b) a preliminary affirmative determination has been made of dumping and consequent injury to a domestic industry, and (c) the authorities concerned judge such measures necessary to prevent injury being caused during the investigation.
- Provisional measures may be applied only after 60 days from the date of initiation of the investigation.
- The application of provisional measures shall be limited to as short a period as possible and not exceeding the time limits prescribed in this Agreement.

8. **Article VIII: Price Undertakings:** The Agreement has the following provisions regarding price undertaking:

- When satisfactory voluntary undertakings are received from any exporter to revise its prices or to cease to export to the area in question at dumped prices so that the authorities are satisfied that the injury effect of the dumping is eliminated, the proceedings may be suspended or terminated without the imposition of provisional measures or anti-dumping duties. Price increases under such undertakings shall not be higher than necessary to eliminate the margin of dumping.
- Price undertakings shall not be required or accepted from exporters unless the authorities of the importing Member have made preliminary confirmatory determination of dumping and injury caused by such dumping.
- If an undertaking is accepted, the investigation of dumping and injury shall however be completed if the exporter so desires or authorities so decide. The undertaking shall be consistent with its terms and the provisions of this Agreement, in case a positive determination of dumping and injury is made.

9. **Article IX: Imposition and Collection of Anti-dumping Duties:** The Agreement has the following provisions:

- The authorities of the importing Member shall make decisions on whether or not to impose an anti-dumping duty in cases where all requirements for the imposition have been fulfilled, or on whether the amount of the anti-dumping duty to be imposed shall be full margin of dumping or less.
- If any anti-dumping is imposed in respect of any product, such anti-dumping duty shall be collected in the suitable amounts in each case, on a non-discriminatory basis on imports of such product from all sources found to be dumped and causing injury except as to imports from those sources from which price undertakings under the terms of this agreement have been accepted.

- The amount of the anti-dumping duty shall not exceed the margin of dumping as determined under the provisions of this Agreement. A refund shall be made promptly and normally in not more than 90 days following the assessment of final liability arising owing to excess collection.

10. **Article X: Retroactivity:** Provisional measures and anti-dumping duties shall only be applied to products which enter for consumption after the time when the decision of imposing such measures was taken subject to some exceptions.
11. **Article XI: Duration and Review of Anti-dumping Duties and Price Undertakings:** The Article says:

- An anti-dumping duty shall remain in force only as long as and to the extent necessary to offset dumping which is causing injury.
- The authorities shall review the need for the continued imposition of the duty, where justified, on their own proposal or upon request by an interesting party which submits affirmative information substantiating the need for review, provided that a reasonable period of time has elapsed since the imposition of the definitive anti-dumping duty.

12. **Article XII: Public Notice and Explanation of Determination:** The Agreement has the following provisions:

- When the authorities are content that there is adequate evidence to justify the initiation of an anti-dumping investigation, the Member or Members, the product of which are subject to such investigation and other interested parties acknowledged to the investigating authorities to have an interest there, shall be notified and a public notice shall be given.
- The public notice shall be given of any preliminary or final determination of any decision to accept an undertaking of the termination of an anti-dumping duty, and of the termination of a definitive anti-dumping duty.

13. **Article XIII: Judicial Review:** Each Member whose national legislation contains provisions on anti-dumping measures shall maintain judicial, arbitral or administrative tribunals or procedures for the purpose of the prompt review of administrative action relating to final determination and review of determination.
14. **Article XIV: Anti-dumping Action on Behalf of a Third Country:** An application for anti-dumping action on the behalf of a third country shall be made by the authorities of the third country requesting the action.
15. **Article XV: Developing Country Members:** It is recognised that special regard must be given by developed country Members to the special situation of developing country Members when considering the application of anti-dumping measures under this Agreement.
16. **Article XVI: Committee on Anti-dumping Practices:** The Agreement has the provision for setting up of the committee.

- A Committee on Anti-Dumping Practices comprising representatives from each of the Members is established.
- The Committee may set up subsidiary bodies as it thinks fit.

- Members shall inform without delay to the Committee all preliminary or final anti-dumping actions taken. The semi-annual reports shall be submitted on an agreed standard form.
- Each Member shall notify the Committee: (a) which of its authorities are capable to initiate and conduct investigations and (b) its domestic procedures governing the initiation and conduct of such investigations.

17. **Article XVII: Consultation and Dispute Settlement:** The agreement has the provisions regarding the settlement of disputes:

- The Dispute Settlement Undertaking is applicable to consultations and the settlement of disputes under this Agreement, unless otherwise provided.
- Each Member shall give sympathetic consideration to, and shall give adequate opportunity for consultation concerning representations made by another Member with respect to any matter affecting the operation of this Agreement.
- The Dispute Settlement Body shall, at the appeal of the complaining party, establish a panel to examine the matter concerned.
- Confidential information provided to the panel by a person, body or authority shall not be disclosed without their formal authorisation.

18. **Article XVIII: Final Provisions:** The Agreement also has some other provisions:

- No specific action against dumping of exports from another Member can be taken except in accordance with the provisions of GATT, 1994.
- Each Member shall take all required steps, whether of general or specific nature, to make certain, not later than the date of entry into force of the WTO Agreement for it, the conformity of its laws, regulations and administrative procedures with the provisions of this Agreement as they may apply for Member in question.
- The Committee on Anti-Dumping Practices shall review annually the implementation and operation of this Agreement taking into account the objectives thereof. The Committee shall inform the Council for Trade in Goods of developments during the period covered by such reviews.

5.4 Agreement on Implementation of Article VII (Customs Valuation)

Customs authorities have the right to seek further information of importers where they reasonably doubt on the accuracy of the declared value of imported goods. If authorities still have a reason to doubt that the customs value of imported goods cannot be determined on the basis of the declared value, they would establish the value according to relevant provisions of the Agreement. The Agreement also has provisions relating to developing countries, importations by sole agents, sole distributors and sole concessionaires.

The main provisions of the Agreement have been mentioned below:

1. **Article I: Rules on Customs Valuation:**

- The customs value of imported goods shall be the transaction value, which is the price actually paid or payable for goods sold to the importing Member adjusted according to the provisions of Article 8, subject to: (a) There are no restrictions as to the disposition or use of goods by the buyer other than restrictions prescribed. (b) The sale or price is not subject to some condition or consideration for which a value cannot be determined relating to the goods being valued. (c) No part of the proceeds of a subsequent resale, disposal or use of goods by the buyer will accrue to the seller. (d) The buyer and seller are not related.

- When buyer and seller are related: (a) It shall not in itself be a ground for regarding the transaction value as unacceptable. In such a case, the conditions surrounding the sale shall be examined and the transaction value shall be accepted provided that the relationship did not influence the price. (b) If the administration has grounds for considering that the relationship influenced the price, it shall communicate this to the importer. (c) The transaction value shall be accepted if the importer demonstrates that such value closely approximates to one of the following occurring at or about the same time: (i) the transaction value in sales to unrelated buyers of identical or similar goods for export to the same country of importation and (ii) the customs value of identical goods.

2. **Article II: Customs Valuation Based on Transaction Value of Identical Goods:** When the customs value of the imported goods cannot be determined under the provisions of Article 1, the customs value shall be the transaction value of identical goods sold for export to the same country of importation and exported at or about the same time as the goods being valued.
3. **Article III: Customs Valuation Based on Transaction Value of Similar Goods:** When the customs value of the imported goods cannot be determined under the provisions of Articles 1 and 2, the customs value shall be the transaction value of similar goods sold for export to the same country of importation and exported at or about the same time as the goods being valued.
4. **Article IV: Rules on Customs Valuation:** When the customs value of the imported goods cannot be determined under the provisions of Articles 1, 2 and 3, the customs value shall be determined under the provisions of Article 5 or under the provisions of Article 6, when the customs value cannot be determined under Article 5.
5. **Article V: Customs Valuation Based on Unit Price:** If the imported goods or identical or similar goods are sold in the country of importation in condition as imported, the customs value of the imported goods shall be based on the unit price at which such goods are sold in the greatest aggregate quantity, subject to following deductions: (a) The commission or additions usually made for profit and general expenses, (b) The cost of transportation, insurance and associated costs incurred within the country of importation, (c) When appropriate, the cost of transportation of the imported goods to the port or place of importation, loading, unloading and handling charges, cost of insurance in the exporting country, and (d) The customs duties and other national taxes.
6. **Article VI: Customs Valuation on Computed Value:** The customs value of imported goods shall be based on computed value. Computed value shall consist of the sum of: (a) Cost or value of materials and fabrication in producing the imported

goods, (b) An amount of profit and general expenses made by producers in the country of exportation for exports, and (c) Cost of transportation of the imported goods to the port or place of importation, loading, unloading and handling charges, and cost of insurance in the exporting country.

7. **Article VII: Rules on Customs Valuation:** The customs valuation has the following provisions:

- When customs value of the imported goods cannot be determined under the provisions of Articles 1, 2, 3, 4, 5 and 6, the customs value shall be determined using logical means consistent with the principles and general provisions of this Agreement and of Article VII of GATT, 1994 and on the basis of data on hand in the country of importation.
- No customs value shall be determined under the provisions of this Article on the basis of: (a) The selling price in the country of importation of goods produced in such country, (b) A system which provides for the acceptance for customs purposes of the higher of two alternative values, (c) The price of goods in the domestic market of the exporting country, (d) Cost of production other than computed value determined under the provisions of Article 6, (e) The price of the goods for export to a country other than the country of importation, (f) Minimum customs values, or (g) Arbitrary or fictitious values.

8. **Article VIII: Rules on Customs Valuation:** The Agreement has the following provisions:

- In assessing the customs value on the basis of transactional value, there shall be added to the price actually paid or payable for the imported goods: (a) The following, to the extent that they are incurred by the buyer but are not included in the price actually paid or payable for goods: (i) Commission and brokerage, except buying commission, (ii) The cost of containers which are treated as being one for customs purposes for the goods in question, and (iii) The cost of packing whether for labour or materials. (b) The value, as relevant, provided by the buyer free of charge or at a reduced price in connection with the production of goods in exporting country: (i) Materials, components, parts and similar items used in the imported goods, (ii) Tools, dies, moulds and similar items used in the production of the imported goods, and (iii) Engineering, development, artwork, design work, plans and sketches necessary for the production of imported goods. (c) Royalties and license fees paid by the buyer, and (d) The value of any part of the proceeds to the seller.
- Each Member shall, in framing its legislation, provide for the inclusion in or the exclusion from the customs value, partial or whole, of the following: (a) The cost of transport of the imported goods to the port or place of importation, (b) Loading, unloading and handling charges associated with the transport of the imported goods to the port or place of importation, and (c) The insurance cost.

9. **Article IX: Exchange Rate:** Where the conversion of currency is necessary for the determination of the customs value, the rate of exchange to be used shall be that which is duly published by the competent authorities of the country of importation.

10. **Article X: Confidentiality:** All information which is by nature confidential or which is provided on a confidential basis for the purpose of customs valuation shall be treated strictly confidential by the authorities concerned.
11. **Article XI: Appeal:** The Agreement says that:

- Each Member shall, in its legislation, provide in regard to a determination of customs value for the right of appeal by the importer or any other person liable for the payment of duty.
- An initial right of appeal without penalty may be to an authority within the customs administration or to an independent body, but the legislation of each Member shall provide for the right of appeal without penalty to a judicial authority.

12. **Article XII: Publication:** The laws, regulations, judicial decisions and administrative rulings of general application giving effect to this Agreement shall be published in conformity with Article X of GATT, 1994 by the country of importation.
13. **Article XIII: Guarantee in the Form of Surety, Deposit:** Where it becomes necessary to delay the final determination of the customs value of the imported goods, the importer of goods shall nevertheless be able to withdraw the goods from customs if, as per the requirement, the importer furnishes sufficient guarantee in the form of surety, a deposit or some other suitable instrument, covering the ultimate payment of customs duties for which the goods may be liable.
14. **Article XIV: Annexes:** The Article says that Annexes I, II and III are an integral part of this Agreement.
15. **Article XV: Definitions:** In this Agreement:

- Customs value of imported goods means the value of goods for the purpose of levying ad valorem duties of customs on imported goods.
- 'Country of importation' means country or territory importing the goods.
- Produced includes grown, manufactured and mined.
- 'Identical goods' mean goods which are the same in all respects, including physical, quality and reputation.
- 'Similar goods' mean goods which, although not alike in all respects, have like characteristics and like component materials which enable them to perform the same functions and to be commercially interchangeable.
- Goods shall not be regarded as 'identical goods' or 'similar goods' unless they were produced in the same country as the goods being valued.

16. **Article XVI: Explanation:** The importer shall have the right to an explanation in writing from the customs administration of the country of importation as how the customs value of the imported goods was determined.
17. **Article XVII: Administration:** Nothing in this Agreement shall be construed as restricting or calling into question the rights of customs administration to satisfy itself as to the truth or correctness of any statement, document or declaration presented for customs valuation purposes.
18. **Article XVIII: Institutions:** The Article says:

- A Committee on Customs Valuation (the Committee) comprising representatives of all Members is established.
- There shall be a 'Technical Committee on Customs Valuation' (the Technical Committee) under the auspices of Customs Cooperation Council, which shall carryout responsibilities described in the Agreement.

19. **Article XIX: Consultation and Dispute Settlement:**

- The Dispute Settlement Undertaking is applicable to consultations and the settlement of disputes under this Agreement, unless otherwise provided.
- At the request of a party to the dispute or on its own initiative, a panel is established to examine dispute relating to the provisions of this Agreement.
- The Technical Committee shall provide advice and assistance to the Members engaged in the consultations.

20. **Article XX: Special Differential Treatment:** Developed country Members shall provide, on mutually agreed terms, technical assistance to developing country Members requesting so. On this basis, developed country Members shall chalk out programmes of technical assistance which may include personnel's training, assistance in preparing implementation measures, access to sources of information regarding customs valuation methodology, and advice on the application of the provisions of this Agreement.
21. **Article XXI: Final Provisions:** Reservations may not be entered in respect of any of the provisions of this Agreement without the consent of the other Members.
22. **Article XXII: National Legislation:** Members shall ensure, not later than the date of application of the provisions of this Agreement for them, the conformity of their laws, regulations and administrative procedures with the provisions of this Agreement.
23. **Article XXIII: Review:** The Committee shall review annually the implementation and operation of this Agreement taking into account its objectives. The Committee shall annually inform the Council for Trade in Goods of developments during the period covered by such reviews.
24. **Article XXIV: Secretariat:** This Agreement shall be serviced by the WTO Secretariat except in regard to those responsibilities which are specifically assigned to the Technical Committee.

5.5 Agreement on Pre-shipment Inspection

Pre-shipment inspection (PSI) is the practice of employing specialised private agencies to check shipment details—basically price, quantity, and quality—of goods ordered abroad. Governments of developing countries use this practice aiming to safeguard national financial interests (for example, prevention of capital flight, financial fraud, customs duty avoidance) and to overcome inadequacies in administrative infrastructures.

This Agreement recognises that GATT principles and obligations apply to the activities of pre-shipment inspection agencies mandated by governments. Obligations on the part of governments contacting or mandating pre-shipment inspection agencies include non-discrimination, transparency, avoidance of unreasonable delay, the use of specific guidelines for conducting price verification and avoidance of conflicts of interest by the agencies. The obligations of exporting Members towards pre-shipment inspection users include non-discrimination in the application of domestic laws and regulations, timely publication of such laws and regulations, and the provision of technical assistance where requested.

The Agreement sets up an independent review procedure—administered jointly by an organisation representing pre-shipment inspection agencies and an organisation representing exporters—to resolve disputes between an exporter and an agency.

1. **Article I: Coverage/Definitions:** The Agreement has the following provisions:

- This Agreement shall apply to all pre-shipment inspection activities carried out on the territory of Members, whether such activities are contracted or mandated by the government or any government body of a Member.
- The term 'User Member' means a Member of which the government or any government body contracts for or mandates the use of pre-shipment inspection activities.
- Pre-shipment inspection activities are all activities relating to the verification of the quality, the quantity, the price, including exchange rate and financial terms, and customs classification of goods to be exported to the country of the User Member.
- The term 'pre-shipment inspection entity' is any entity contracted or mandated by a Member to carry out pre-shipment inspection activities.

2. **Article II: Obligations of User Members:** The Agreement has the provision of certain obligations towards User Members as mentioned below:

- **Non-discrimination:** User Members shall ensure that pre-shipment inspection activities are carried out in a non-discriminatory manner and on objective and equality basis by all the inspectors of the pre-shipment inspection entities.
- **Government Requirements:** User Members shall ensure that in the course of pre-shipment inspection, activities relating to their laws, regulations and requirements, national treatment is accorded.
- **Site of Inspection:** User Members shall ensure that all pre-shipment inspection activities are carried either in customs territory from which goods are exported or in the customs territory in which goods are manufactured.
- **Standards:** User Members shall ensure that pre-shipment inspection is carried out in accordance with the standard defined in the purchase agreement or with international standards.
- **Transparency:** User Members shall ensure that all pre-shipment inspection activities are to be conducted in transparent manner.
- **Protection of Confidential Business Information:** User Members shall ensure that the pre-shipment inspection entities treat all information received in the course of the inspection as business confidential to the extent required.

- **Conflict of Interest:** User Members shall ensure that pre-shipment inspection entities maintain procedures to avoid conflict of interest between pre-shipment inspection entities.
- **Delays:** User Members shall ensure that pre-shipment inspection entities avoid unreasonable delays in the inspection of shipments.
- **Price Verification:** User Members shall ensure that in order to prevent over and under invoicing and fraud, pre-shipment inspection entities conduct price verification according to the prescribed guidelines.
- **Appeal Procedures:** User Members shall ensure that pre-shipment inspection entities establish procedures, to receive, consider and render decisions concerning grievances raised by exporters, to be developed and maintained according to the prescribed guidelines.
- **Derogation:** User Members shall provide that shipments whose value is less than a minimum value applicable as defined by the User Members shall not be inspected, except in exceptional circumstances.

3. **Article III: Obligations of Exporter Members:** There are certain obligations on the part of exporter Members as described below:

- **Non-discrimination:** Exporter Members shall ensure that their laws and regulations relating to pre-shipment inspection activities are applied in a non-discriminatory manner.
- **Transparency:** Exporter Members shall publish promptly all applicable laws and regulations relating to pre-shipment inspection activities in such a manner as to enable other governments and traders to become acquainted with them.
- **Technical Assistance:** Exporter Members shall offer to provide to User Members, upon request, technical assistance directed towards the achievement of the objectives of this Agreement on mutually agreed terms.

4. **Article IV: Independent Review Procedures:** Members shall encourage pre-shipment inspection entities and exporters mutually to resolve their disputes. Members shall ensure that independent review procedures are established and maintained to settle the disputes.
5. **Article V: Notification:** Members shall submit to the Secretariat, copies of the laws and regulations by which they put this Agreement into force as well as copies of any other laws and regulations relating to pre-shipment inspection.
6. **Article VI: Review:** The Ministerial Conference shall review the provisions, implementation and operation of this Agreement every three years taking into account its objectives.
7. **Article VII: Consultation:** Members shall consult with other members, if requested, with respect to any matter affecting the operation of this Agreement.
8. **Article VIII: Dispute Settlement:** Disputes arising among Members regarding the operation of this Agreement shall be subject to the provisions of Article XXIII of GATT, 1994, as elaborated and applied by the Dispute Settlement Understanding.
9. **Article IX: Final Provisions:** The Agreement has some other provisions as

mentioned below:

- Members shall take the necessary measures for the implementation of this Agreement.
- Members shall ensure that their laws and regulations shall not be contrary to the provisions of this Agreement.

6

WTO Agreements on Rules of Origin, Import Licensing, Subsidies, and Safeguards

6.1 Agreement on Rules of Origin

The purpose of this Agreement is to harmonise the rules of origin other than rules of origin relating to the granting of tariff preferences and make sure that such rules of origin do not create preventable obstacles to trade. The Agreement has set up a harmonisation work programme, starting as early as possible after the conclusion of the Uruguay Round and to be completed within three years of initiation. The programme would make the rules of origin objective, understandable and predictable. A Committee on Rules of Origin in the WTO and a Technical Committee under the auspices of the Customs Cooperation Council would conduct the work.

Until the completion of the harmonisation programme, Members were be expected to ensure that their rules of origin are transparent; they do not restrict and distort the international trade; they are administered in a consistent, uniform, impartial and reasonable manner, and they are based on positive standard. Annex II to this Agreement sets out a 'common declaration' with respect to the operation of rules of origin on goods which qualify for preferential treatment.

1. **Article I: Definition and Coverage:**

- Rules of origin shall be defined as those laws, regulations and administrative determinations of general application applied by any Member to determine the country of origin of goods, provided such rules of origin are not related to contractual or autonomous trade regimes leading to granting of tariff preferences.
- Rules of origin shall include all rules of origin used in non-preferential commercial policy instruments.

2. **Article II: Disciplines during the Transition Period:** Until the harmonisation work programme for rules of origin is completed, Members shall ensure that:

- When they issue administrative determination of general application, the requirements to be fulfilled are clearly defined.
- Their rules of origin are not used as instruments to pursue trade objectives directly or indirectly.
- Rules of origin shall not themselves create restrictive, distorting, or disruptive effects on international trade.
- The rules of origin that they apply to imports and exports are not more stringent than the rules of origin they apply to determine whether or not a good is domestic and shall not discriminate between other Members.

- Their rules of origin are administered in a consistent, uniform, impartial and reasonable manner.
- Their rules of origin are based on a positive standard.
- Their laws, regulations, judicial decisions and administrative rulings of general application relating to rules of origin are published.
- On the request of an exporter, importer or any other person with a justifiable cause, determination of the origin they would accord to a good are issued as soon as possible.
- Any administrative action which they take in relation to the determination of origin is reviewable promptly by judicial, arbitral or administrative tribunals or procedures, independent of the authority issuing the determination, which can effect modification or reversal of the determination.

3. **Article III: Disciplines after the Transition Period:** Members shall ensure, upon the implementation of the results of the harmonisation work programme, that:

- They apply rules of origin equally for all purposes,
- The country to be determined as origin of a particular good is either the country where the good has been wholly obtained or, where more than one country are related with the production of the good, the country where the last substantial transformation has been carried out,
- The rules of origin that they apply to imports and exports are not more stringent than the rules of origin they apply to determine whether or not a good is domestic and shall not discriminate between other Members,
- Their rules of origin are administered in a consistent, uniform, impartial and reasonable manner,
- Their laws, regulations, judicial decisions and administrative rulings of general application relating to rules of origin are published,
- On the request of an exporter, importer or any other person with a justifiable cause, determination of the origin they would accord to a good are issued as soon as possible,
- Any administrative action which they take in relation to the determination of origin is reviewable promptly by judicial, arbitral or administrative tribunals or procedures, independent of the authority issuing the determination, which can effect modification or reversal of the determination, and
- All the information which is by nature confidential or which is provided on a confidential basis for the purpose of the application of rule of origin is treated strictly confidential by the authorities concerned.

4. **Article IV: Institutions:** The Agreement has provisions regarding the institutions:

- A Committee on Rules of Origin composed of the representatives from each of the Members is established. The Committee shall afford Members the opportunity to consult on the matters relating to the operation and furtherance of the objectives of this Agreement. The Committee shall carry out responsibilities assigned to it by the

Council for Trade in Goods.

- A Technical Committee on Rules of Origin under the auspices of the Customs Cooperation Council shall be established. The Technical Committee shall, if relevant, request information and advice from the Committee on Rules of Origin on matters relating to this Agreement. The CCC Secretariat shall act as the Secretariat to the Technical Committee.

5. **Article V: Information and Procedures for Modification and Introduction of New Rules of Origin:**

- Members shall provide to the Secretariat, within 90 days after the date of entry into force of the WTO Agreement for it, their rules of origin, judicial decisions, and administrative rulings of general application relating to rules of origin in effect on that date.
- Members introducing modifications to their rules of origin or introducing new rules of origin shall publish a notice to that effect at least 60 days before the entry into force of the modified or new rules.

6. **Article VI: Review:** The Article says that:

- The Committee shall review annually the implementation and operation of this Agreement keeping in view its objectives.
- The Committee shall review the provisions of this Agreement and propose amendments as necessary to reflect the results of the harmonisation work programme.
- The Committee, in cooperation with the Technical Committee, shall set up a mechanism to consider and propose amendments to the results of the harmonisation work programme, taking into account the objectives and principles of this Agreement.

7. **Article VII: Consultation:** The provisions of Article XXII of GATT, 1994, as elaborated and applied by the Dispute Settlement Understanding, are applicable to this Agreement.
8. **Article VIII: Dispute Settlement:** The provisions of Article XXIII of GATT, 1994, as elaborated and applied by the Dispute Settlement Understanding, are applicable to this Agreement.
9. **Article IX: Harmonisation of Rules of Origin:**

- Keeping in view the objectives of harmonising rules of origin and providing more predictability in the conduct of world trade, the Ministerial Conference shall undertake the work programme in conjunction with the CCC, applying the following principles: (a) Rule of origin should apply equally for all purposes, (b) Rules of origin should provide for the country to be determined as the origin of a particular good to be either country where the good has been wholly obtained or, if more than one country are involved in the production of the good, the country where the last substantial transformation has been carried out, (c) Rules of origin should be objective, understandable and predictable, (d) Their rules of origin are not used as instruments to pursue trade objectives directly or indirectly, (e) Their rules of origin are administered in a consistent, uniform, impartial and reasonable manner, (f) Rules of origin should be coherent, and (g) Rules of origin should be based on a positive standard.

- There would be a harmonisation work programme on rules of origin: (a) The work programme shall be initiated as soon after the entry into force of the WTO Agreement as possible and will be completed within three years of initiation. (b) The Committee and the Technical Committee shall be the appropriate bodies to conduct this work. (c) To provide for detailed inputs by the CCC, the Committee shall request the Technical Committee to provide its interpretations and opinions resulting from the work as given below: (i) Wholly obtained and minimal operations or processes, (ii) Substantial transformation—change in tariff classification and (iii) Substantial transformation—supplementary criteria.
- There is an important role of the Committee: (a) The Committee shall consider the interpretations and opinions of the Technical Committee periodically with a view to endorsing such interpretations and opinions, (b) After the completion of all the work, the Committee shall consider the results in terms of their overall coherence, and (c) The Ministerial Conference shall establish the results of the harmonisation work programme in an annex as an integral part of this Agreement. The Ministerial Conference shall establish a timeframe for the entry into force of this annex.

6.2 Agreement on Import Licensing Procedures

The Agreement on Import Licensing Procedures refines the Tokyo Round (1979) Agreement on import licensing. The Agreement requires more discipline, transparency and predictability in import licensing systems. The users of import licensing systems should not create unnecessary restrictions on international trade by implementing such systems. The Agreement requires Members to publish sufficient information for traders to know the basis on which licenses are granted. The Agreement has strengthened rules for the notification of the institution of import licensing procedures or changes therein. It also offers guidance on the assessment of applications.

The Agreement lays down the criteria under which automatic licensing procedures are assumed not to have trade restrictive effects. In the case of non-automatic procedures, the administrative obligation on exporters and importers should not be beyond what is necessary to administer the measures to which they apply. The Agreement requires the consideration of applications within 60 days.

The main provisions of the Agreement have been described below:

1. **Article I: General Provisions:** The Agreement has the following general provisions:

- Import licensing is defined as administrative procedures applied in the operation of import licensing regimes requiring the submission of an application and other documents to the relevant administrative body as a prerequisite for the importation of goods.
- Members shall ensure that administrative procedures are applied with a view to

preventing trade distortions that may arise from an inappropriate operation of these procedures.

- The rules of import licensing procedures shall be rational, fair and equitable.
- The rules and all information relating to administrative procedures shall be published.
- Application forms and procedures shall be simple.
- No application shall be refused for minor documentation errors which do not alter basic data contained therein.
- Licensed imports shall not be refused for minor variation in value, quantity or weight from the amount designated on the license due to difference occurring during shipment, differences incidental to bulk loading and other minor differences consistent with normal commercial practice.
- The foreign exchange necessary to pay for licensed imports shall be made available to license holders on the same basis as to importers of goods not requiring import licenses.
- The provisions of this Agreement shall not require any Member to disclose confidential information which would prejudice legitimate commercial interests of particular enterprises.

2. **Article II: Automatic Import Licensing:** The Article says that:

- Automatic import licensing is defined as import licensing where approval of the application is granted in all cases.
- Automatic licensing procedures shall not be administered in such a manner as to have restrictive effect on imports subject to automatic licensing. Automatic licensing procedures shall be deemed to have trade restricting effects unless: (a) Any person, firm or institution which fulfils the legal requirements of the importing Member for engaging in import operations involving product subject to automatic import licensing is equally eligible to apply for and to get import licenses; (b) Application for licensing may be submitted on any working day prior to the customs clearing of the goods; (c) Applications for licenses when submitted in appropriate and complete form are approved without delay on receipt, to the extent administratively possible, but within a maximum 10 working days.
- Members recognise that automatic import licensing may be necessary whenever other appropriate procedures are not available.

3. **Article III: Non-automatic Import Licensing:** The following provisions are applicable in non-automatic import licensing procedures:

- Non automatic import licensing procedures shall correspond in scope and duration to the measure they are used to implement, and shall be no more administratively troublesome than absolutely indispensable to administer the measure.
- Members shall publish sufficient information for other Members and traders to know the basis for granting and allocating licenses.
- In import licensing procedures: (a) Members shall provide, upon the request of any

Member having an interest in the trade in the product concerned, all relevant information about the procedures of import; (b) Any person, firm or institution which fulfils legal and administrative requirements of the importing Member shall be equally eligible to apply and to be considered for a license. If the license application is not approved, the applicant shall, on request, be given the reasons therefore and shall have a right of appeal or review in accordance with the domestic legislation or procedures of the importing Member; (c) The period for processing the applications shall be no longer than 60 days; (d) The period of license validity shall be of rational duration and not be so short as to preclude imports; (e) While issuing the import licenses, Members should consider the import performance of the applicant; and (f) When issuing licenses, Members shall take into account the desirability of issuing licensing for products in economic quantities.

4. **Article IV: Institutions:** A Committee on Import Licensing composed of representatives from each of the Members has been established. The Committee shall meet as necessary for the purpose of affording Members the opportunity of consulting on any matters relating to the operation of this Agreement or continuance of its objectives.
5. **Article V: Notification:** The Article says that:

- Members who institute procedures or change in the procedures shall notify the Committee of such within 60 days of publication.
- Any interested Member which considers that another Member has not notified the institution of a licensing procedure or change therein may bring the matter to the attention of such other Member.

6. **Article VI: Consultation and Dispute Settlement:** Consultations and Settlement of Disputes with respect to any matter affecting the operation of this Agreement shall be subject to the provisions of Article XXII and XXIII of GATT, 1994, as elaborated and applied by the Dispute Settlement Understanding.
7. **Article VII: Review:** The Article has the following provisions:

- The Committee shall review as necessary, but at least once every two years, the implementation and operation of this Agreement, keeping in mind the objectives thereof, and the rights and obligations contained therein.
- The Committee shall inform the Council for Trade in Goods of developments during the period covered by such reviews.

8. **Article VIII: Final Provisions:** The Agreement has the following final provisions:

- Reservations may not be entered in respect of any of the provisions of this Agreement without the consent of other Members.
- Each Member shall ensure, not later than the date of entry into force of the WTO Agreement for it, the conformity of its laws, regulations and administrative procedures with the provisions of this Agreement.
- Each Member shall inform the Committee of any changes in its laws or regulations relevant to this Agreement and in the administration of such laws or regulations.

6.3 Agreement on Subsidies and Countervailing Measures

The Agreement has two basic aims: first, it disciplines the use of subsidies and second, it regulates the actions countries can take to counter the effects of subsidies. A Member can use the WTO's dispute settlement procedure to seek the withdrawal of the subsidy or the removal of its adverse effects. A Member can initiate its own investigations and may impose countervailing duty on subsidised imports provided they are found to be hurting domestic producers.

The Agreement defines subsidy. It also contains the concept of 'specific subsidy', i.e. subsidy available only to an enterprise, industry, group of enterprises, or a group of industries in a country which provides the subsidy. The disciplines contained in the Agreement only apply to specific subsidies. These subsidies can be domestic or export subsidies.

The Agreement defines two categories of subsidies: prohibited and actionable. A third category, non-actionable subsidies, existed for five years, ending on December 31, 1999, and was not extended further.

The prohibited subsidies require the recipients to achieve definite export targets, or to use domestic goods over imported goods. These subsidies are specifically designed to distort international trade. Since such subsidies are likely to hurt other countries' trade, they are challengeable in the Dispute Settlement Procedures. They must be withdrawn immediately if the Dispute Settlement Procedure finds the subsidy prohibited. Otherwise the complaining Member can apply counter measures. If the import of subsidised products is damaging the interest of domestic producers, the concerned Member can apply countervailing duties.

In the case of actionable subsidies, the subsidies are permissible unless a Member shows the adverse effects of subsidies on its interest. The Agreement defines three types of damages these subsidies can cause. These subsidies can hurt a domestic industry in an importing country. These subsidies can hurt rival exporters from another country when the two compete in third markets. Domestic subsidies in one country can hurt exporters trying to compete in the subsidising country's domestic market. Such subsidies must be withdrawn or the adverse effect must be removed, if Dispute Settlement Body finds the subsidies having an adverse effect. The countervailing duty can be imposed, if domestic producers are hurt by imports of subsidised products.

The Agreement sets out disciplines on the initiation of countervailing cases, investigations by national authorities and rules of evidence to make sure that all interested parties can present information and argument. The basis to determine the amount of subsidy and resultant injury to domestic industry are outlined. All relevant factors must be taken into account in establishing the link between the subsidised imports and the alleged injury. Investigations shall be terminated immediately when the amount of the subsidy is de minimis or when the volume of subsidised imports or the injury is negligible. All countervailing duties have to be terminated within five years of their imposition unless the authorities determine on the basis of review that the expiry of the duty may lead to continuation or recurrence of subsidisation and injury.

The Agreement recognises that subsidies play an important role in developing countries and in the transformation of centrally planned economies to market economies. Developing countries also receive preferential treatment if their exports are subject to countervailing duty investigations.

The main provisions of the agreement are given below:

Part I: Coverage

1. **Article I: Definition of a Subsidy:** A subsidy shall be deemed to exist if:

- There is financial contribution by a government or any public body within the territory of a Member, or
- There is any form of income or price support, and
- A benefit is thereby conferred.

2. **Article II: Specificity:**

- In order to determine whether a subsidy is specific to an enterprise or industry or group of enterprises or industries within the jurisdiction of the granting authority, the following principles shall apply: (a) Where the granting authority, or the legislation pursuant to which the granting authority operates, explicitly limits access to a subsidy to certain enterprises, such subsidy shall be specific. (b) Where the granting authority, or the legislation pursuant to which the granting authority operates, establishes objective criteria or conditions governing the eligibility for and the amount of, a subsidy, specificity shall not exist, provided that the eligibility is automatic and that such criteria and conditions are strictly adhered to. (c) If there are reasons to believe that the subsidy may in fact be specific, other factors may be considered.
- A subsidy which is limited to certain enterprises located within a designated geographical region within the jurisdiction of granting authority shall be specific.
- Any subsidy falling under the provisions of Article 3 shall be deemed to be specific.

Part II: Prohibited Subsidies:

3. **Article III: Prohibition:** The following subsidies shall be prohibited, except as provided in the Agreement on Agriculture:

- Subsidies contingent upon export performance.
- Subsidies contingent upon the use of domestic over imported goods.

4. **Article IV: Remedies:** The following remedies are available to the complaining Member:

- Wherever a Member has reason to believe that a prohibited subsidy is being provided by another Member, such Member may request consultations with such other Member.
- If no mutually agreed solution has been reached within 30 days of the request for consultation, the Members may refer the matter to the Dispute Settlement Body for immediate set up of a panel.
- If the measure is found to be a prohibited subsidy, the panel shall recommend that the subsidising Member withdraw the subsidy immediately.

- Where a panel report is appealed, the Appellate Body shall issue its decision within 30 days. The appellate report shall be adopted by the Dispute Settlement Body.
- In the event, the recommendation of the Dispute Settlement Body is not followed, the Dispute Settlement Body shall grant authorisation to the complaining Member to take appropriate counter measures, unless the DSB decides by consensus to reject the request.
- In the case, a party to the dispute requests arbitration, the arbitrator shall determine whether the counter measures are appropriate or not.

Part III: Actionable Subsidies:

5. **Article V: Adverse Effects:** No Member shall cause, through the use of any subsidy, adverse effects to the interest of other Members, i.e.

- Injury to the domestic industry of another Member,
- Nullification or impairment of benefits accruing directly or indirectly to other Members under GATT, 1994, and
- Serious prejudice to the interest of another Member.
- This Article does not apply to the subsidies maintained on agricultural products as provided in Article XIII of the Agreement on Agriculture.

6. **Article VI: Serious Prejudice:** The Agreement has the following provisions:

- Serious prejudice shall be deemed to exist in the case of: (a) The total ad valorem subsidisation of a product exceeding 5 percent, (b) Subsidies to cover operating losses sustained by an industry, (c) Subsidies to cover operating losses sustained by an enterprise, other than one time measures given merely to provide time for the development of long-term solution, and (d) Direct forgiveness of debt.
- Notwithstanding the above provisions, serious prejudice shall not be found if the subsidising Member demonstrates that the subsidy has not resulted in any of the effects mentioned below: (a) The effect of the subsidy is to displace or impede the imports of a like product of another Member into the market of the subsidising Member, (b) The effect of the subsidy is to displace or impede the exports of a like product of another Member from a third country market, (c) The effect of the subsidy is a consistent increase in the world market share of the subsidising Member, and (d) The effect of the subsidy is a significant price undercutting by the subsidised product as compared with the price of a like product of another Member in the same market.
- This Article does not apply to the subsidies maintained on agricultural products as provided in Article XIII of the Agreement on Agriculture.

7. **Article VII: Remedies to Serious Prejudice:** The following provisions shall apply to find the remedies:

- When a Member has reason to believe that any subsidy granted or maintained by another Member results in injury to its domestic industry, nullification or impairment, or serious prejudice, such Member may request consultations with the concerned Member.
- If consultations do not result in a mutually agreed solution within 60 days, Members

may refer the matter to the DSB for the establishment of a panel.

- The report of the panel shall be adopted by the DSB unless one of the parties to the dispute formally notifies the DSB of its decision to appeal or the DSB decides by consensus not to adopt the report.
- When a panel report is appealed, the Appellate Body shall issue its decision within 60 days.
- When a panel report or an appellate body report is adopted in which it is determined any subsidy has resulted in adverse effects to the interest of another Member, the Member providing such subsidy shall take appropriate steps to remove the adverse effects or shall withdraw the subsidy.
- In case the Member has not taken appropriate steps to remove the adverse effects or to withdraw the subsidy within 6 months, the DSB shall grant authorisation to the complaining Member to take counter measures.
- In case a party to the dispute requests arbitration, the arbitrator shall determine whether the counter measures are commensurate with the degree and the nature of the adverse effects.

Part IV: Non-actionable Subsidies:

8. **Article VIII: Identification of Non-actionable Subsidies:** The Agreement has the following provisions regarding the non-actionable subsidies:

- The following subsidies shall be considered as non-actionable: (a) Subsidies which are not specific, (b) Assistance for research activities conducted by firms or by higher education or research establishments on contract basis with the firms if the assistance covers not more than 75 percent of the costs of research or 50 percent of the costs of pre-competitive development activity and provided that such assistance is limited exclusively to: (i) Cost of personnel, (ii) Cost of instrument, equipment, land and buildings for research, (iii) Costs of consultancy and equivalent services, (iv) Additional overhead costs incurred directly, and (v) Other running costs incurred directly as result of the research activity. (c) Assistance to disadvantaged regions within the territory of a Member given pursuant to a general framework of regional development, and (d) Assistance to promote adaptation of existing facilities to new environmental requirements imposed by law subject to some provisions.
- A subsidy programme, which is non-actionable, shall be notified in advance of its implementation to the Committee.

9. **Article IX: Consultations and Authorised Remedies:** The Agreement states that:

- If in the course of implementation of a programme related to non-actionable subsidy, a Member has reason to believe that this programme has resulted in serious adverse effects on its domestic industry such Member may request consultations with the Member providing or maintaining the subsidy.
- If no mutually acceptable solution has been reached in consultations within 60 days, the requesting Member may refer the matter to the Committee.
- If the Committee determines that such effect exists, it may recommend to the subsidising Member to modify this programme in a way to remove these effects.

- In the event the recommendation is not followed within six months, the Committee shall authorise the requesting Member to take appropriate counter measures commensurate with the nature and the degree of the effects determined to exist.

Part V: Countervailing Measures:

10. **Article X: Application of Article VI of GATT, 1994:** Members shall take all necessary steps to ensure that in the imposition of a countervailing duty on any product of any Member imported by another Member is in the accordance with the provisions of Article VI of GATT, 1994 and the terms of this Agreement. Countervailing duty may only be imposed subject to investigations initiated and conducted in accordance with the provisions of this Agreement and the Agreement on Agriculture.
11. **Article XI: Initiation and Subsequent Investigation:** The following provisions are applicable in an investigation:

- An investigation to determine the existence, degree and effect of any alleged subsidy shall be initiated upon a written request by or on the behalf of domestic industry to the authorities or by the authorities themselves.
- The authorities shall review the accuracy and adequacy of the evidence provided in the application to determine whether the evidence is sufficient to justify the initiation of an investigation.
- If in a particular situation, the authorities concerned decide to initiate an investigation without receiving a written application by or on behalf of a domestic industry for the initiation of such investigation, they shall proceed only if they have adequate evidence of existence of subsidy, injury and causal link to justify the initiation of an investigation.
- If products are not imported directly from the country of origin but are exported to the importing country from an intermediary country, the provisions of this Agreement shall be fully applicable and the transaction shall be regarded as having taken place between the country of origin and the importing country.
- An application shall be discarded and an investigation shall be ended immediately as soon as the authorities are satisfied that there is no adequate evidence of either subsidisation or of injury to justify the proceedings. There shall be prompt termination where the amount of a subsidy is de minimis, or where the volume of subsidised imports or the injury is negligible. The amount of the subsidy shall be considered to be de minimis if the subsidy is less than 1 percent ad valorem.
- An investigation shall not impede the procedures of customs clearance.

12. **Article XII: Evidence:** The Agreement has following provisions:

- The authorities shall give notice of the information and ample opportunity to interested Members and parties in countervailing duty investigation to present in writing all evidences relevant to such investigation.
- The authorities shall treat the information, which is by nature confidential or it is provided on the confidential basis by the parties to the countervailing duty investigation, as confidential.

13. **Article XIII: Consultation:** The Agreement has the following provisions related to consultation:

- Before the initiation of any investigation, the authorities shall invite the Members, product of which may be subject to such investigation, for consultations with a view to arriving at mutually agreed solution.
- During the investigation, the authorities shall afford a reasonable opportunity to the Members, product of which may be subject to such investigation, to continue consultations with a view to clarifying the accurate situation and to attempt a mutually agreed solution.

14. **Article XIV: Calculation of Amount of Subsidy:** Any method, to calculate the benefit to the recipient, used by the investigating authority shall be provided in the national legislation or implementing regulations of the Member concerned. The methods used in the calculation of benefits shall be transparent and properly explained.
15. **Article XV: Determination of Injury:** The determination of injury shall be based on positive evidence and involve an objective examination of both: (a) volume of the subsidised imports and the effects of the subsidised imports on prices in the domestic market for like products and (b) the resultant impact of these imports on the domestic producers of such products.
16. **Article XVI: Definition of Domestic Industry:** The term 'domestic industry' be interpreted as referring to the domestic producers as a whole of the like products or to those of them whose collective output of the products constitutes a major proportion of the total domestic production of those products, except that when producers are related to the exporters or importers or are themselves importers of the alleged subsidised product or a like product from other countries, the term 'domestic industry' may be interpreted as referring to the rest of producers.
17. **Article XVII: Provisional Measures:** The Article has the following provisions regarding the provisional measures:

- Provisional measures may be applied only if: (a) An investigation has begun and a public notice has been given to that effect and interested Members and interested parties have been given adequate opportunities to submit information and make comments, (b) A preliminary affirmative determination has been made that a subsidy exists and that there is injury to a domestic industry caused by subsidised imports, and (c) The authorities concerned judge such measures necessary to stop injury being caused during the investigation.
- Provisional measures may take the form of provisional countervailing duties guaranteed by cash deposits or bonds equal to the amount of the temporarily calculated amount of subsidisation.
- Provisional measures can be applied only after 60 days from the date of initiation of the investigation.
- The application of provisional measures shall be limited to as short a period as possible, not exceeding four months.

18. **Article XVIII: Undertakings:** The following provisions are applicable regarding the undertakings:

- Proceedings may be suspended or terminated without imposing provisional measures or countervailing duties after receiving satisfactory voluntary undertakings under which: (a) The exporting Member agrees to eliminate or limit the subsidy or take other measures concerning its effects, or (b) The exporter agrees to revise its prices so that the investigating authorities are satisfied that the injurious effect of the subsidy is eliminated.
- If an undertaking is accepted, the investigation of subsidisation and injury shall however be completed if the exporting Member so requests or the importing Member so decides.

19. **Article XIX: Imposition and Calculation of Countervailing Duties:** The Agreement has the following provisions:

- When a countervailing duty is imposed in respect of any product, such countervailing duty shall be levied on a non-discriminating basis on imports of such product from all sources found to be subsidised and causing injury.
- Countervailing duty shall not be levied on any imported product in excess of the amount of the subsidy found to exist, calculated in terms of subsidisation per unit of the subsidised product.

20. **Article XX: Retroactivity:** Provisional measures and countervailing duties shall only be applied to products which enters for consumption after the time when the decision to impose the provisional measures enters into force, subject to some exceptions.

21. **Article XXI: Duration and Review of Countervailing Duties:** There is provision for the review of countervailing duties as mentioned below:

- A countervailing duty shall stay in force as long as and to the extent necessary to counteract subsidisation which is causing injury.
- The authorities shall review the need for continued imposition of the duty, where justified, on their own proposal or upon request by any interested party after elapse of reasonable period of time.

22. **Article XXII: Public Notice and Explanation of Notice:** The Agreement has the following provisions regarding the notices:

- When the authorities are contented that there is ample evidence to justify the initiation of an investigation, the Member the product of which is subject to such investigation and other interested parties known to the investigating authorities to have interest in the investigation shall be notified and a public notice shall be given.
- Public notice shall be given of any preliminary or final determination, or of any decision to accept an undertaking, of termination of such undertaking, and of the termination of a definitive countervailing duty.
- Public notice shall be given of imposition of provisional measures, of winding up of confirmatory determination, of imposing a definitive duty or suspension of an investigation.

23. **Article XXIII: Judicial Review:** Members whose national legislation contains provisions on countervailing duty measures shall maintain judicial, arbitral or administrative tribunals or procedures aiming at a prompt review of administrative actions relating to final determination and review of determinations. These tribunals or procedures shall be independent of the authorities responsible for the determination or review and shall provide all interested parties those participated in the administrative proceedings and individually affected by the administrative actions with access to review.

Part VI: Committee on Countervailing Measures and Subsidiary Bodies:

24. **Article XXIV: Committee on Subsidies and Countervailing Duties:** There is provision of establishing the Committee as given below:

- A Committee on Subsidies and Countervailing Measures composed of representatives from each of the Members is established. The Committee shall carry out responsibilities as assigned to it under this Agreement and it shall afford Members the opportunity of consulting on any matter relating to the operation of this Agreement or the furtherance of the objectives.
- The Committee may set up subsidiary bodies as appropriate.
- The Committee shall establish a Permanent Group of Experts (PGE) of 5 independent persons, highly qualified in the field of subsidies and trade relations.
- The PGE may be consulted by any Member and may give advisory opinions on any subsidy proposed to be introduced or currently maintained by that Member. Such advisory opinion will be confidential.
- In carrying out their functions, the Committee and any subsidiary body may consult with and seek information from any source they deem appropriate.

Part VII: Notification and Surveillance:

25. **Article XXV: Notifications:** The Agreement has the following provisions:

- Members agree that their notification of subsidies shall be submitted not later than June 30 of each year and shall conform to the provisions of this Agreement.
- Members shall notify any subsidy, which is specific, maintained or granted.
- The contents of notifications should be adequately specific to enable other members to appraise the trade effects and to understand the operation of notified subsidy programmes.
- Members shall report without delay to the Committee all preliminary or final actions taken with respect to countervailing duty. Members shall submit, on a semi-annual basis, reports on any countervailing duty actions taken within the proceeding six months.
- Members shall notify the Committee about: (a) competent authority to initiate and conduct investigations and (b) their domestic procedures governing the initiation and conduct of such investigations.

26. **Article XXVI: Surveillance:** The Committee shall examine notifications and reports submitted at each regular meeting of the Committee.

Part VIII: Developing Country Members:

27. **Article XXVII: Special and Differential Treatment:** The Agreement has provision of special and differential treatment for developing Members:

- Members recognise that subsidies may play an important role in economic development programmes of developing country Members.
- The prohibition of subsidies shall apply to developing country Members subject to some exemptions.
- Any countervailing duty investigation of a product originating in a developing country Member shall be terminated as soon as the authorities concerned determine that: (a) The overall level of subsidies granted upon the product does not exceed 2 percent of its value calculated on per unit basis, or (b) The volume of subsidised imports represents less than 4 percent of the total imports of the like product in the importing Member, unless imports from developing country Members collectively account for more than 9 percent of total imports of the like product in the importing country.

Part IX: Transitional Arrangements:

28. **Article XXVIII: Existing Programmes:** The subsidy programmes which have been established within the territory of any Member before the date on which such a Member signed WTO Agreement and which are inconsistent with the provisions of this Agreement shall be brought into conformity with the provisions of this Agreement within three years of the date of entry into force of the WTO Agreement for such Members.
29. **Article XXIX: Transformation into Market Economy:** A Member in the process of transformation from a centrally planned into a market economy may apply for programmes and measures necessary for such transformation. For such Members, subsidy programmes shall be phased out or will be brought into conformity within a period of 7 years from the date of entry into force of the WTO Agreement for such Members.

Part X: Dispute Settlement:

30. **Article XXX: Dispute Settlement:** Consultations and Settlement of Disputes with respect to any matter affecting the operation of this Agreement shall be subject to the provisions of Article XXII and XXIII of GATT, 1994, as elaborated and applied by the Dispute Settlement Understanding, unless otherwise provided.

Part XI: Final Provisions:

31. **Article XXXI: Provisional Application:** The Committee shall review after five years from the date of entry into force of the WTO Agreement, the provisions of Articles 6, 8 and 9, with a view to determine whether to extend their application for a further period.
32. **Article XXXII: Other Final Provisions:** The Agreement contains the following provisions:

- No specific action against a subsidy of another Member can be taken except in accordance with the provisions of GATT, 1994.
- Reservations may not be entered in respect of any of the provisions of this

Agreement without the consent of the other Members.

- Each Member shall take all necessary steps, of a general or particular nature, to ensure, not later than the date of entry into force of the WTO Agreement for it, the conformity of its laws, regulations and administrative procedures with the provisions of this Agreement.
- The Committee shall review annually the implementation and operation of this Agreement, taking into account its objectives.

6.4 Agreement on Safeguards

If a surge in imports is causing or threatening a serious injury to domestic industry of a WTO Member, the Member may restrict imports of a product temporarily. The safeguard measures were always available in Article 19 under GATT, 1947. These measures were, however, rarely used. Some countries preferred to protect their domestic industries through 'grey area' measures such as using bilateral negotiations outside GATT's auspices—they convinced exporting countries to restrain exports voluntarily or to agree to other means of sharing markets.

The Agreement on Safeguards prohibits 'grey area' measures and puts time limits on all safeguard measures. The Agreement prohibits applying or maintaining any voluntary export restraints, orderly marketing arrangements, or any other similar measures on the export or the import side. The bilateral measures that were not modified to conform to this Agreement were phased out at the end of 1998. Countries were allowed to continue one of these measures an extra year (until the end of 1999).

The heave in imports justifying safeguard as an action can be real increase in imports (an absolute increase), or it can be an increase in the import's share of a shrinking market, even if the import quantity has not increased (relative increase). The safeguard measures can be applied if surge in imports is causing or threatening to cause serious injury to the domestic industry that produces the like or directly competitive products.

A Member may apply a safeguard only following an investigation by its competent authority according to the provisions of established procedures and giving a public notice to all concerned parties. The emphasis is on transparency and on implementing established rules and practices in the course of determination—avoiding arbitrary methods of determination. The authorities shall provide opportunity for interested parties to present evidence. The evidence must include arguments on whether a measure is in public interest or not.

The Agreement defines criteria for assessing whether 'serious injury' is being caused or threatened, and the factors which must be considered in determining the impact of imports on domestic industry. If required, the safeguard measure should be applied to the extent necessary to avert or remedy serious injury and to help the domestic industry to adjust. If quantitative restrictions are applied, the quantity of imports should not be reduced below the annual average for the last three years for which statistics are available, unless a different level necessary to avert or remedy serious injury is justified.

Safeguard measures shall be applied to a product being imported irrespective of its source. However, the Agreement does describe how quota can be allocated among supplying countries, including in the exceptional circumstances where imports from certain countries have increased excessively in speed. A safeguard measure should not last more than four years, although it can be extended up to eight years, provided the authorities determine that the measure is required and the industry is adjusting. Measures imposed for more than a year must be gradually liberalised.

The Agreement has provision that an exporting country can seek compensation from the country imposing measures through consultations. If no agreement is reached, the exporting country can retaliate by taking equivalent action—for example, it can raise tariffs on exports from the country that is imposing safeguard measures. In some conditions, the exporting country has to wait for three years after the safeguard measure was introduced before it can retaliate in such way.

The Agreement shields to some extent the exports of developing countries from safeguard actions. An importing country can only apply a safeguard measure to a product from developing country if the developing country is supplying more than 3 percent of imports of that product, or if developing country Members with less than 3 percent import share collectively account for more than 9 percent of total imports of the product concerned.

The Committee on Safeguards oversees the operation of this Agreement and is responsible for the supervision of Members' commitments. The Committee reviews the reports provided by the Members relating to safeguard investigations and decisions thereon.

The main provisions of the Agreement are given below:

1. **Article I: General Provisions:** This Agreement establishes rules for the application of safeguard measures which shall be understood to those measures provided in Article XIX of GATT, 1994.
2. **Article II: Conditions:** The application of safeguard measures shall meet the following conditions:

- A Member may apply a safeguard measure to a product only if such product is being imported in increased quantities, absolute or relative to domestic production, and under such conditions as to cause or threaten to cause serious injury to the domestic industry that produces like or directly competitive products.
- Safeguard measures shall be applied to a product being imported irrespective of its source.

3. **Article III: Investigation:** The Article says:

- A Member may apply a safeguard measure only following an investigation by its competent authority carried out pursuant to the provisions of established procedures and giving a public notice to all concerned parties. The Member shall provide opportunity to importers, exporters and other interested parties to present facts and their views and to respond to the presentations of other parties. The authorities shall publish a report setting forth their findings and conclusions reached on all relevant issues of facts and law.
- Any information which is by nature confidential or which is provided on confidential

basis shall be treated as such by the authorities.

4. **Article IV: Determination of Serious Injury or Threat:** The Agreement has provisions on the determination of serious injury:

- For the purpose of this Agreement: (a) 'Serious injury' shall be understood to mean a significant overall impairment in the position of a domestic industry. (b) 'Threat of serious injury' shall be understood to mean serious injury that is clearly imminent according to the findings of prescribed investigation carried out for determination of such threat. (c) 'Domestic industry' shall mean all producers of the like products or directly competitive products operating within the territory of a Member, or the producers whose collective output of the like products or directly competitive products constitutes a major proportion of the total domestic production of those products.
- The following provisions are applicable in the investigation: (a) In the investigation to determine whether increased imports have caused or are threatening to cause serious injury to a domestic industry, the authorities shall consider all relevant factors of an objective and quantifiable nature having a bearing on the situation of that industry. (b) The determination shall not be made unless the investigation demonstrates the causal link between increased imports of the product and serious injury or threat of it. (c) The authorities shall publish promptly a detailed analysis of the case under investigation as well as a demonstration of the relevance of the factors examined.

5. **Article V: Application of Safeguard Measures:** Members shall apply safeguard actions only to the extent necessary to prevent or remedy serious injury and to facilitate adjustment of the industry. If a quantitative restriction is used, such a restriction shall not reduce the quantity of imports below the level of a recent period which shall be the average of imports in the last three representative years, unless clear justification is given to a different level that is necessary to prevent or remedy serious injury.
6. **Article VI: Provisional Safeguard Measures:** In critical situations where delay in action would cause damage which would be difficult to repair, Members may take provisional safeguard measures pursuant to a preliminary determination that there is clear evidence that increased imports have caused or are threatening to cause serious injury.
7. **Article VII: Duration and Review of Safeguard Measures:** The Agreement has the following provisions:

- Members shall apply safeguard actions only for such period of time as may be necessary to prevent or remedy serious injury and to facilitate adjustment of the industry. The period of the application shall not exceed four years, unless it is extended by the authorities of the importing Member under the requirements of continuation of such measures.
- The total period of application of a safeguard measure including the period of application of any provisional measures, the period of initial application and any

extension thereof, shall not exceed eight years.

8. **Article VIII: Level of Concessions and Other Measures:** A Member proposing to apply a safeguard measure or seeking an extension of a safeguard measure shall make an effort to maintain to a large extent an equivalent level of concessions and other obligations to the exporting Members which would be affected by the application of such a measure. To accomplish this purpose, the Members affected may agree on any adequate means of trade compensation for the adverse effects of the measure on their trade.
9. **Article IX: Developing Country Members:** The Agreement has provisions for preferential treatment to developing country Members:

- An importing country can only apply a safeguard measure to a product from developing country if the developing country is supplying more than 3 percent of imports of that product, or if developing country Members with less than 3 percent import share collectively account for more than 9 percent of total imports of the product concerned.
- A developing country Member shall have the right to extend the period of application of a safeguard measure for a period up to two years beyond the maximum period of eight years.

10. **Article X: Pre existing Article XIX Measures:** Members shall terminate all safeguard measures taken pursuant to Article XIX of GATT, 1947 that were in existence on the date of entry into force of the WTO agreement not later than eight years after the date on which they were first imposed or five years after the date of entry into force of the WTO Agreement, which ever comes later.
11. **Article XI: Prohibition and Elimination of Certain Measures:** The Agreement has the following provisions:

- This Agreement only applies to measures sought, taken or maintained under provisions of Article XIX of GATT, 1994.
- A Member shall not take any emergency action on imports of particular products unless such action conforms to the provisions of Article XIX of GATT, 1994 in accordance with this Agreement.

12. **Article XII: Notification and Consultation:** The Article states that:

- A Member shall promptly notify the Committee on Safeguards upon: (a) Initiating an investigation relating to serious injury and reasons for it, (b) Making a finding of serious injury or its threat caused by increased imports, and (c) Taking a decision to apply or extend a safeguard measure.
- A Member proposing to apply or extend a safeguard measure shall provide adequate opportunity for prior consultation with those Members having a substantial interest as exporters of the product.
- A Member shall make a notification to the Committee on Safeguards before taking a provisional safeguard measure. Consultations shall be initiated immediately after the measure is imposed.
- A Member shall notify immediately the results of consultations, results of mid-term

reviews, any form of compensation, proposed suspension of concessions and other obligations to the Council for Trade in Goods.

- Members shall notify promptly the Committee on Safeguard of their laws, regulations and administrative procedures relating to safeguard measures as well as any modifications made to them.
- All notifications to the Council for Trade in Goods shall normally be made through the Committee on Safeguards.

13. **Article XIII: Surveillance:** The Agreement has provisions for surveillance of the implementation:

- A Committee on Safeguards is established, under the authority of the Council for Trade in Goods, which shall be open to the participation of any Member indicating its wish to serve on it. The Committee will have the following functions: (a) To monitor and report to the Council for Trade in Goods on the general implementation of this Agreement and make recommendations towards its improvement, (b) To assist Members, if they so request, in their consultations under the provisions of this Agreement, (c) To receive and review all notifications provided for in this Agreement and report as appropriate to the Council for Trade in Goods, and (d) To perform any other functions related to this Agreement that the Council for Trade in Goods may decide.
- To assist the Committee in carrying out its surveillance function, the Secretariat shall prepare annually, a factual report on the operation of this Agreement based on the notifications and other reliable information available to it.

14. **Article XIV: Dispute Settlement:** The provisions of Articles XXII and XXIII of GATT, 1994, as elaborated and applied by the Dispute Settlement Understanding, are applicable to this Agreement.

7

WTO General Agreement on Trade in Services (GATS)

Services represent the fastest growing sector of the global economy accounting for 70 percent of global output, one third of global employment and nearly 20 percent of global trade. The idea of bringing rules on services into the multilateral trading system was coined in early 1980s. The General Agreement on Trade in Services was developed in the Uruguay Round which concluded in 1994.

A number of countries were sceptical and even opposed the move. They believed such an agreement could undermine governments' ability to pursue national policy objectives and constrain their regulatory powers. But, the agreement allows a higher degree of flexibility, both within the framework of rules and also in terms of the market access commitments.

7.1 Three Pillars of the Agreement

The Agreement rests on three pillars. The first is a Framework Agreement containing basic obligations, which applies to all member countries. The second contains national commitments, which will be the subject of a continuing process of liberalisation. The third is a number of annexes addressing the special situations of individual services sector.

The Agreement covers all internationally traded services—for example, banking, telecommunications, tourism, and professional services etc. Government services are explicitly carved out of the Agreement.

Part I of the basic Agreement defines its scope. The Agreement defines four modes of trading services:

Mode I: Services supplied from one country to another, officially known as 'cross border supply', e.g. international telephone calls.

Mode II: Consumers making use of a service in another country, officially known as 'consumption abroad', e.g. tourism.

Mode III: A foreign company setting up subsidiary or branches to provide services in another country, officially known as 'commercial presence', e.g. a foreign bank setting up operations in a country.

Mode IV: Individuals travelling from their own country to supply services in another country, officially known as 'presence of natural persons'.

Part II contains general obligations and disciplines. A basic most-favoured nation obligation states that each Member 'shall accord immediately and unconditionally to services and service providers of any other Member country, treatment no less favourable than that it accords to like services and service providers of any other country'. Secondly, favour one, favour all. MFN treatment means treating ones' trading partners equally on the principle of non-discrimination. Under GATS, if a country allows foreign competition in a sector, equal opportunities in that sector should be given to service providers from all other WTO Members.

MFN treatment applies to all services, but some special temporary exemptions have been allowed. When GATS came into existence, a number of countries already had preferential agreements in services that they had signed with trading partners, either bilateral or in small groups. The need was felt to maintain these preferences temporarily. It was decided to continue giving more favourable treatment to particular countries, in particular, service activities by listing 'MFN exception' along with their first sets of commitments. In order to make the general MFN principle fully functional, the exceptions could only be made once and making the list completely non-expandable, and eventually not lasting more than ten years.

Transparency requirements include publication of all relevant laws and regulations. Since domestic regulations are the most significant means of exercising influence over services trade, the Agreement says that governments should regulate services reasonably, objectively and impartially. Governments shall have to set up enquiry points to obtain information about regulations in any service sector. Governments have to notify the WTO of any change in the regulations that apply to the services that come under specific commitments. Once a government makes an administrative decision that affects a service, it should also afford an impartial means of reviewing the decision.

When a government has made a commitment to open a service sector to foreign competition, it must not normally restrict money being transferred out of the country as payment for services supplied in that sector. The only exception is when there are balance of payments problems, and even then the restrictions must be temporary and subject to other limits and conditions.

Part III contains provisions on market access and national treatment, which would not be general obligations but would be commitments made in national schedules. The commitments made by countries to open markets in specific sectors, and forms of opening the market are the results of negotiations. The national schedules contain the sector being opened, the extent of market access permissible in these sectors and any limitations on national treatment. For example, if a Member allows foreign banks to do business in its territory, this is market access commitment. If the Member limits number of branches to be opened, this is market access limitation. When domestic banks are allowed numerous branches, but foreign banks are permitted limited number of branches, this is an exception to the national treatment principle.

Like bound tariffs for trade in goods, the commitments made are bound. These bound can only be modified after negotiations with affected parties. Since unbinding is not so easy, the commitments are virtually guaranteed conditions for exporters and importers of services and investors in these service sectors.

Government services are not subject to any GATS disciplines, these are not covered by the negotiations, and commitments on market access and national treatment do not apply to them.

The commitments to liberalise services' market do not affect Members' right to set levels of quality, safety or price, or to introduce regulations to pursue any other policy objectives deemed fit. When two or more Members have agreements recognising each others' qualifications, e.g. licenses, GATS says other Members must be provided an opportunity to negotiate comparable pacts.

Part IV establishes the basis for progressive liberalisation in the services area through successive rounds of negotiations and the development of national schedules. After a period of three years, Members may withdraw or modify commitments made in their national schedules. Where commitments are modified or withdrawn, negotiations should be undertaken with interested Members to make agreement on compensation. When Members fail to arrive on any agreement, the compensation would be determined by arbitration.

Part V contains institutional provisions, including consultation and dispute settlement and the establishment of a Council on Services.

The GATS annexes reflect diversity of services. The annex on telecommunication requires that the market access be accorded to another Member, on reasonable and non-discriminatory basis, to allow the supply of a service included in its schedule. Annex on financial services gives governments wide freedom to take prudential measures, e.g. protection of investors, depositors and insurance policy holders and ensure the integrity and stability of the financial system. The annex on movement of natural persons deals with negotiations on individuals' rights to stay temporarily in a country with the aim of providing a service. It specifies that the Agreement does not apply to people seeking permanent employment or to condition for obtaining citizenship/permanent residence.

7.2 Main Provisions of the Agreement

Part I: Scope and Definitions:

1. **Article I: Scope and Definition:** The Agreement incorporates the following:

- This Agreement applies to measures adopted by Members affecting trade in services.
- Trade in services is defined as the supply of a service: (a) From the territory of one Member into the territory of any other Member, (b) In the territory of one Member to service consumer of any other Member, (c) By a service supplier of one Member, through commercial presence in the territory of any other Member, (d) By a service supplier of one Member, through the presence of natural persons in the territory of any other Member.
- For the purpose of this Agreement: (a) 'Services' includes any service except services supplied in the exercise of governmental authority. (b) 'A service supplied in the exercise of governmental authority' means any service which is supplied neither on commercial basis nor in competition with one or more service suppliers.

Part II: Most-Favoured Nation Treatment

2. **Article II: Most-Favoured-Nation Treatment:** With respect to any measure covered by this Agreement, each Member shall accord immediately and unconditionally to services and service providers of any other Member, treatment no

less favourable than that it accords to like services and service providers of any other country.

3. **Article III: Transparency:** The Article has the provisions related to transparency:

- Members shall publish immediately, at the latest by the time of their entry into force, all relevant measures of general application which concern to or affect the operation of this Agreement.
- Members shall immediately and at least annually inform the Council for Trade in Services of the introduction of any new, or any changes to existing laws, regulations or administrative rules which significantly affect trade in services covered by its specific commitments under this Agreement.
- Members shall respond immediately to the requests by any other Member for specific information on any of their measures of general application or international agreements on trade in services to which such members are signatories.

Article IIIa: Confidential Information: This Agreement shall not require any Member to provide confidential information, the disclosure of which would obstruct law enforcement, or otherwise be converse to public interest, or which would be an injustice to the lawful commercial interests of particular enterprises.

4. **Article IV: Increasing Participation of Developing Countries:** The Article says that:

- To increase the participation of developing country Members in world trade, different Members shall facilitate negotiations on specific commitments relating to: (a) The strengthening of their domestic services capacity and its effectiveness and competitiveness through access to technology on commercial basis, (b) The improvement of their access to distribution channels and information networks, and (c) The liberalisation of market access in sectors and modes of supply of exports of their interest.
- Developed country Members shall establish contact points to facilitate the access of developing country Members' suppliers to information, pertinent to their respective markets concerning: (a) Commercial and technical aspects of the supply of services, (b) Registration, recognition and obtaining of professional qualifications, and (c) The availability of service technologies.
- Special preferences should be given to the least developing country Members.

5. **Article V: Economic Integration:** The Agreement has following provisions regarding the economic integration:

- This Agreement shall not stop the Members from being a party to or entering into an agreement liberalising trade in services between or among the parties to such an agreement, provided such agreement: (a) has substantial sectoral coverage, and (b) provides for the absence or elimination of discrimination.
- The above mentioned agreement shall be formulated to make easy trade between parties to such agreement and shall not in respect of any Member outside the agreement elevate the overall level of barriers to trade in services within the respective sectors or sub-sectors compared to the level applicable prior to such agreement.

- Members that are parties to any above mentioned agreement shall immediately notify such agreement or any changes in this agreement to the Council for Trade in Services.
- A Member that is party to any above mentioned agreement may not seek compensation for trade benefits that may accrue to any other Member from such agreement.

6. **Article VI: Domestic Regulation:** The Agreement has following provisions relating to domestic regulations:

- Members shall make sure that all measures of general application affecting trade in services are administered in a rational, objective and unbiased manner in sectors where specific commitments are undertaken.
- Members shall maintain or institute as soon as practicable, judicial, arbitral or administrative tribunals or procedures which provide for the immediate review of and appropriate remedies for, administrative decisions affecting trade in services.
- The Council for Trade in Services shall develop necessary disciplines to ensure that measures relating to qualification requirements and procedures, technical standards and licensing requirements do not amount to unnecessary barriers to trade in services.

7. **Article VII: Recognition:** The Agreement has following provisions pertaining to the recognition:

- For the purpose of accomplishment of its standards or criteria for the authorisation, licensing or certification of service providers, a Member may recognise the education or the experience, requirements for licenses or certificates granted in a particular country.
- A Member making any above mentioned arrangement or an agreement to that effect shall afford adequate opportunity for other interested Members to negotiate their accession to such arrangement or agreement.
- A Member shall not accord recognition in a manner which would constitute as means of discrimination between countries in the application of its standards or criteria for the authorisation, licensing or certification of services suppliers, or a concealed restriction on trade in services.
- Members shall inform the Council for Trade in Services about any above mentioned arrangement or agreements.
- Members shall, as appropriate, work in cooperation with relevant intergovernmental and non-governmental organisations towards the establishment and adoption of common international standards and criteria for recognition and common international standards for the practice of relevant services trades and professions.

8. **Article VIII: Monopolies and Exclusive Service Suppliers:** The Agreement has following provisions:

- Members shall ensure that any monopoly supplier of a service in their territories does not, in the supply of the monopoly service in the relevant market, act in a manner inconsistent with those of Members' obligations under Article II and its specific commitments.

- When a monopoly supplier competes in the supply of a service outside the scope of its monopoly rights and which is subject to that Member's specific commitments, the Member shall make certain that such a supplier does not misuse its monopoly position to operate in its territory in a manner inconsistent with such commitments.

9. **Article IX: Business Practices:** The Article says that:

- Members recognise that certain business practices of service suppliers, other than those falling under Article VIII, may contain competition and thereby restrict trade in services.
- Members shall, at the request of any other Member, enter into consultations with a view to eliminating the practices mentioned above.

10. **Article X: Emergency Safeguard Measures:** There shall be multilateral negotiations on the issue of emergency safeguard course, based on the principle of non-discrimination. The results of such negotiations shall enter into effect on a date not later than three years from the date of entry into force of the WTO Agreement.
11. **Article XI: Payments and Transfers:** A Member shall not apply restrictions on international transfers and payments for current transactions relating to its specific commitments except in the event of serious balance of payments and external financial difficulties.
12. **Article XII: Restrictions to Safeguard the Balance of Payments:** The Agreement has the following provisions:

- In the event of serious balance of payments and external financial difficulties or threat thereof, a Member may adopt or maintain restrictions on trade in services on which it has undertaken specific commitments, including on payments and transfers for transactions related to such commitments. Such restrictions: (a) Shall not discriminate among members, (b) Shall be consistent with the Articles of Agreement of the IMF, (c) Shall avoid unnecessary damage to the commercial, economic and financial interests of any other Member, (d) Shall not exceed those necessary to deal with the circumstances, and (e) Shall be temporary and be phased out progressively as the situation improves.
- In determining the incidence of such restrictions, Members may give priority to the supply of services which are more vital to their economic or development programmes. However, such restrictions shall not be maintained for the purpose of defending a particular service sector.
- Any such restriction adopted or maintained or any change therein shall be immediately notified to the General Council.
- Members applying the provisions of this Article shall immediately consult the Committee on BOP restrictions.

13. **Article XIII: Government Procurement:** Articles II, XVI and XVII shall not apply to laws, regulations or requirements governing the procurement of services by governmental agencies for governmental purposes and not with a view to commercial

resale or with a view to use in the supply of services for commercial sale.

14. **Article XIV: General Exceptions:** The Agreement has following exceptions:

- Nothing in this Agreement shall be construed to prevent the application by any Member of following measures, subject to that such measures are not applied in a manner which would comprise a means of arbitrary or unjustifiable discrimination between countries where like conditions exist: (a) Necessary to protect public morals or to maintain public order, (b) Necessary to protect human, animal, or plant life or health, (c) Laws or regulations relating to prevention of deceptive and fraudulent practices, protection of personal confidentiality or maintaining safety.
- Nothing in this Agreement shall be construed: (a) To require any Member to provide any information, the disclosure of which it considers converse to its essential security interests, or (b) To prevent any Member from taking any action which it considers necessary for the protection of its essential servicing interests.
- The Council for Trade in Services shall be informed of the Measures, both their imposition and termination.

15. **Article XV: Subsidies:** The Article says that:

- In certain circumstances, subsidy may distort trade in services. Members shall make negotiations with a view to developing the necessary multilateral disciplines to avoid such trade distortive effects. The negotiations shall also address the suitability of countervailing procedures. For the purpose of such negotiations, Members shall exchange information relating to all subsidies associated to trade in services that they provide to their domestic services suppliers.
- Any Member, which considers that it is negatively affected by a subsidy of another Member, may ask for consultations with that Member on such issues. Such requests shall be accorded sympathetic consideration.

Part III: Special Commitments:

16. **Article XVI: Market Access:** The Agreement has the following provisions:

- Pertaining to market access, Members shall accord services and service suppliers of any other Member treatment no less favourable than that provided for under the terms, limitations and conditions agreed and specified in their schedules of commitments.
- In sectors where market access commitments are undertaken, the measures which a Member shall not maintain or adopt, unless otherwise specified in its schedules of commitments are defined as: (a) Limitation on the number of service suppliers, (b) Limitation on the total value of service transactions or assets, (c) Limitation on the total number of service operations or on the total quantity of service output, (d) Limitation on the total number of natural persons that may be employed in a particular sector, (e) Measures which restrict or require specific types of legal entity or joint venture through which a service supplier may supply a service, and (f) Limitations on the participation of foreign capital in terms of maximum percentage limit on foreign shareholding or the total value of individual or aggregate foreign investment.

17. **Article XVII: National Treatment:** Each Member shall accord to services and service providers of any other Member, in respect of all measures affecting the supply of services, treatment no less favourable than that it accords to its own like services and service providers, subject to conditional qualifications set out in its schedules of commitments.
18. **Article XVIII: Additional Commitment:** Members may negotiate commitments with respect to measures affecting trade in services not subject to scheduling under Articles XVI or XVII, including those regarding qualifications, standards or licensing matters.

Part IV. Progressive Liberalisation:

19. **Article XIX: Negotiation of Specific Commitments:** The Agreement has the following provisions:
- Members shall enter into successive rounds of negotiations, beginning not later than five years from the date of entry into force of the WTO Agreement and periodically thereafter, with a view to achieving a progressively higher level of liberalisation.
- The liberalisation process shall take place keeping in mind the national policy objectives and the level of development of individual Members, both overall and in individual sectors. There shall be suitable flexibility for individual developing country Members for opening fewer sectors, liberalising fewer types of transactions and progressively extending market access in line with their development position.
- Guidelines and procedures for negotiations for each round shall be established. The Council for Trade in Services shall carry out an assessment of trade in services in overall terms and on a sectoral basis with the aim of framing the guidelines.
- The process of progressive liberalisation shall be advanced in each such round through bilateral, plurilateral or multilateral negotiations directed towards increasing the general level of specific commitments undertaken by Members under this Agreement.

20. **Article XX: Schedules of Specific Commitments:** The Members have to make specific commitments as mentioned below:
- Members shall make in schedules the specific commitments they undertake. Where such commitments are undertaken relating to different sectors, each schedule shall specify: (a) Terms, limitations and conditions on market access, (b) Conditions and qualifications on national treatment, (c) Undertakings relating to additional commitments, (d) The timeframe for the implementation of such commitments, and (e) The date of entry into force of such commitments.
- Measures inconsistent with both Articles XVI and XVII shall be inscribed in the column relating to Article XVI.

21. **Article XXI: Modification of Schedules:** The Article has the following provisions:
- A Member may modify or withdraw any commitment in its schedule, at any time after three years have elapsed from the date on which that commitment entered into force, in accordance with the provisions of this Article.
- A Member shall notify its intention to modify or withdraw a commitment pursuant to

this Article to the Council for Trade in Services.

- At the request of any Member the benefit of which under this Agreement may be affected by a proposed modification or withdrawal, the modifying Member shall enter into negotiations with a view to getting agreement on any necessary compensatory adjustment.
- The principle of Most-Favoured Nation shall be applied in making any compensatory adjustment.
- If no agreement is reached between the modifying Member and the affected Member within the prescribed period for negotiations, such affected Member may refer the matter to arbitration.
- The modifying Member may not modify or withdraw the commitment until it has made compensatory adjustment in conformity with the findings of the arbitration.

Part V: Institutional Provisions:

22. **Article XXII: Consultation:** Each Member shall accord kind consideration to, and shall afford sufficient opportunity for, consultation regarding such representation as may be made by any other Member with respect to any matter affecting the operation of this Agreement. The Dispute Settlement Understanding (DSU) shall apply to such consultations.
23. **Article XXIII: Dispute Settlement:** The Agreement says:

- If a Member considers that any other Member fails to carry out its obligations or specific commitments under this Agreement, it may with a view to reaching a mutually satisfactory resolution of the matter have recourse to the DSU.
- If a Member considers that any benefit it could rationally have expected to accrue to it under a specific commitment of another Member is being nullified or impaired as a result of the application of any measure which does not clash with the provisions of this Agreement, it may have recourse to the DSU.

24. **Article XXIV: Council for Trade in Services:** The Council for Trade in services shall carry out such functions as may be assigned to it to facilitate the operation of this Agreement and further its objectives. The Council may establish subsidiary bodies as it considers appropriate for the effective discharge of its functions.
25. **Article XXV: Technical Cooperation:** The Agreement says:

- Service suppliers of Members shall have access to the services of contact points for needful assistance.
- Technical assistance to developing countries shall be provided at the multilateral level by the Secretariat and shall be decided upon by the Council for Trade in Services.

26. **Article XXVI: Relationship with Other International Organisations:** The General Council shall make suitable arrangements for consultation and cooperation with the United Nations and its specialised agencies as well as with other intergovernmental organisations concerned with services.

Part VI Final Provisions:

27. **Article XXVII: Denial of Benefits:** A Member may deny the benefits of this Agreement:

- To the supply of a service, if it establishes that the service is supplied from or in the territory of a non-Member or of a Member to which the denying Member does not apply the WTO agreement, or
- In the case of the supply of a maritime transport service subject to conditions, or
- To a service supplier that is a juridical person, if it establishes that it is not a service supplier of another Member, or that it is a service supplier of a Member to which the denying Member does not apply the WTO Agreement.

28. **Article XXVIII: Definitions:** For the purpose of this Agreement:

- 'Measure' means any measure by a Member, whether in the form of a law, regulation, rule, procedure, decision, administrative action, or any other form.
- 'Supply of Services' includes the production, distribution, marketing, sales and delivery of service.
- 'Service Supplier' mean any person that supplies a service.

29. **Article XXIX: Annexes:** The annexes to this Agreement are an integral part of this Agreement.

8

WTO Agreement on Trade-related Aspects of Intellectual Property Rights (TRIPS)

8.1 Coverage of the Agreement

The Agreement on Trade-related Aspects of Intellectual Property Rights (TRIPS), negotiated in the Uruguay Round, introduced intellectual property rights into the trading system of the WTO for the first time. The Agreement recognises that varying standards in the protection and enforcement of intellectual property rights and the lack of a multilateral framework of principles, rules and disciplines dealing with international trade in counterfeit goods have been a source of tension in international economic relations.

The TRIPS Agreement is an attempt to fill the gaps in the ways these rights are protected around the world and to bring them under common international rules. The Agreement establishes minimum level of protection that each Member has to give to the intellectual property of other Members.

The Agreement covers five broad issues:

1. The application of basic GATT principles and relevant international intellectual property agreements.
2. The provision of adequate intellectual property rights.
3. The provision of effective enforcement measures for those rights.
4. Multilateral dispute settlement.
5. Transitional arrangements.

Part I of the Agreement sets out general provisions and basic principles. Part II addresses each intellectual property right in succession. Part III sets out the obligations of Member governments to provide procedures and remedies under their domestic law to ensure that intellectual property rights can be effectively enforced by foreign right holders as well as by their own nationals. Part IV contains provisions on acquisition and maintenance of intellectual property rights. Part V relates to dispute settlement procedures. Part VI relates to transitional arrangements. Part VII contains final arrangements.

The prominent feature of the Agreement is non-discrimination: national treatment (treating one's own nationals and foreigners equally), and most-favoured nation treatment (providing no less favourable treatment to all trading partners in the WTO than treatment given to any other party). The Agreement has an additional important principle that intellectual property protection should contribute to technical innovation and the transfer of technology.

The World Intellectual Property Organisation (WIPO) adopted conventions laying down international obligations to protect the rights of owners of IPRs even before the birth of the WTO:

1. The Paris Convention for the protection of industrial property (industrial design and patents), and
2. The Berne Convention for the protection of literary and artistic works (copyrights).

The TRIPS Agreement builds on the main international conventions on intellectual property rights by incorporating most of their provisions. In some cases, the standards of protection prescribed were thought inadequate. Consequently, the Agreement adds a significant number of new or higher standards.

8.2 Main Provisions of the Agreement

Part I: General Provisions and Basic Principles:

Part I of the Agreement sets out general provisions and basic principles.

1. **Article I: Nature and Scope:** The Article says that Members shall give effect to the provisions of this Agreement. Members may, but shall not be obliged to, implement in their law more extensive protection than that is required by this Agreement, provided that such protection does not contravene the provisions of this Agreement. Members shall be free to determine the appropriate method of implementing the provisions of this Agreement within their own legal system and practice.
2. **Article II: Intellectual Property Conventions:** The Article says:

- In respect of Part II, III and IV of this Agreement, Members shall comply with Articles 1-12 and Article 19 of the Paris Convention, 1967.
- Nothing in Part I- IV of this Agreement shall derogate from existing obligations that Members may have to each other under the Paris Convention, the Berne Convention, the Rome Convention and the Treaty on Intellectual Property in Respect of Integrated Circuits.

3. **Article III: National Treatment:** The Agreement says that each Member shall accord to the nationals of other Members treatment no less favourable than that it accords to its own nationals with regard to the protection of intellectual property, subject to the exceptions already provided in, respectively, the Paris Convention, the Berne Convention, the Rome Convention and the Treaty on Intellectual Property in Respect of Integrated Circuits.
4. **Article IV: Most-Favoured Nation Treatment:** The Agreement says that any advantage, favour, privilege or immunity regarding the protection of intellectual property granted by a Member to the nationals of any other country shall be accorded immediately and unconditionally to the nationals of all other Members, subject to some exceptions.
5. **Article V: Multilateral Agreement:** According to the Article, the obligations under Articles III and IV do not apply to procedures provided in multilateral agreements concluded under the auspices of WIPO relating to the acquisition or maintenance of intellectual property rights.
6. **Article VI: Exhaustion:** The Article says that for the purposes of dispute settlement

under this Agreement, subject to the provisions of Articles III and IV, nothing in this Agreement shall be used to address the issue of the exhaustion of intellectual property rights.

7. **Article VII: Objectives:** The Article says that the protection and enforcement of intellectual property rights should contribute to the promotion of technological innovation and to the transfer and dissemination of technology, to the mutual advantage of producers and users of technological knowledge and in a manner conducive to social and economic welfare and to a balance of rights and obligations.
8. **Article VIII: Principles:** The Agreement says that:

- Members may, in formulating or amending their laws and regulations, adopt measures necessary to protect public health and nutrition, and to promote the public interest in sectors of vital importance to their socio-economic and technological development, provided that such measures are consistent with the provisions of this Agreement.
- Appropriate measures, provided that they are consistent with the provisions of this Agreement, may be needed to prevent the abuse of intellectual property rights by right holders or the resort to practices which unreasonably restrain trade or adversely affect the international transfer of technology.

Part II: Relevant Standards:

Part II addresses each intellectual property right in succession.

Copy Right and Related Rights: The TRIPS Agreement ensures that computer programme will be protected as literary work under the Berne Convention and outlines how databases should be protected. Authors of computer programmes and producers of sound recordings must have the right to forbid the commercial rental of their works to the public. A similar restricted right applies to films where commercial rental has led to extensive copying affecting copyright owners' potential earnings from their films.

The Agreement says performers must also have the right to prevent unauthorised recording, reproduction and broadcast of live performances for no less than 50 years. Producers of sound recordings must have the right to prevent the unauthorised reproduction of recordings for a period of 50 years.

9. **Article IX: Relation to the Berne Convention:** According to the Article:

- Members shall comply with Articles I- XXI of the Berne Convention (1971) and the appendix thereto.
- Copyright protection shall extend to expressions and not to ideas, procedures, and methods of operation or mathematical concept as such.

10. **Article X: Computer Programmes and Compilation of Data:** The Article says that:

- Computer programmes, whether in source or object code, shall be protected as literary works under the Berne Convention.
- Compilation of data or other material, whether in machine readable or other form, which by reason of the selection or arrangement of their contents constitute

intellectual creations shall be protected as such. Such protection, which shall not extend to the data or material itself, shall be without prejudice to any copyright subsisting in the data or material itself.

11. **Article XI: Rental Rights:** In respect of at least computer programmes and cinematographic works, a Member shall provide authors and their successors in title the right to authorise or to prohibit the commercial rental to the public of original or copies of their copyright works.
12. **Article XII: Terms of Protection:** Whenever the term of protection of a work, other than a photographic work or a work of applied art, is calculated on a basis other than the life of a natural person, such term shall bc no less than 50 years from the end of the calendar year of authorised publication, or, failing such authorised publication within 50 years from the making of the work, 50 years from the end of the calendar year of making.
13. **Article XIII: Limitations and Exceptions:** Members shall confine limitations or exceptions to exclusive rights to certain special cases which do not conflict with a normal exploitation of the work and do not unreasonably prejudice the legitimate interest of the right holder.
14. **Article XIV: Protection of Performers, Producers of phonograms and Broadcasting Organisations:** The Agreement says that:

- In respect of a fixation of their performance on a phonogram, performers shall have the possibility of preventing the following acts when undertaken without their authorisation: the fixation of their unfixed performance and the reproduction of such fixation. Performers shall also have the possibility of preventing the following acts when undertaken without their authorisation: the broadcasting by wireless means and the communication to the public of their live performance.
- Producers of phonograms shall enjoy the right to authorise or prohibit the direct or indirect reproduction of their phonograms.
- Broadcasting organisations shall have the right to prohibit the following acts when undertaken without their authorisation: the fixation, the reproduction of fixation, and the rebroadcasting by wireless means of broadcasts, as well as the communication to the public of television broadcasts of the same. When Members do not grant such rights to broadcasting organisations, they shall provide owners of copyright in the subject matter of broadcasts with the possibility of preventing the above acts, subject to the provisions of the Berne Convention (1971).
- The provisions of rental rights available in respect of computer programs shall also apply to the producers of phonograms and any other right holders in phonograms as determined in a Member's law.
- The term of the protection available under this Agreement to performers and producers of phonograms shall last at least until the end of a period of 50 years computed from the end of the calendar year in which the fixation was made or the performance took place. The term of protection available to broadcasting organisations or owners of copyright shall last for at least 20 years from the end of

the calendar year in which the broadcast took place.

Trademarks: In respect of trademarks and service marks; the Agreement prescribes what types of signs shall be eligible for protection as a trademark or service mark and the rights conferred on their right holders. The Agreement says that service marks must be protected in the same way as trademarks used for goods. Trademarks that have become well known in a particular country shall enjoy additional protection.

15. **Article XV: Protectable Subject Matter:** The Agreement says that:

- Any sign, or any combination of signs, capable of distinguishing the goods or services of one undertaking from those of other undertakings, shall be capable of constituting a trademark. Such signs, in particular words including personal names, letters, numerical, figurative elements and combinations of colours as well as any combination of such signs, shall be eligible for registration as trademarks.
- Members may make continuity of registration dependent on use. However, actual use of trademark shall not be a condition for filing an application for registration.
- The nature of the goods or services to which a trademark is to be applied shall in no case form a barrier to registration of the trademark.
- Members shall publish each trademark either before it is registered or immediately after it is registered and shall afford a reasonable opportunity for petitions to cancel the registration. Members may also afford an opportunity for the registration of a trademark to be opposed.

16. **Article XVI: Rights Conferred:** The owner of a registered trademark shall have the exclusive right to prevent all third parties not having the owner's permission from using in the course of trade, identical or similar signs for goods or services which are identical or similar to those in respect of which the trademark is registered where such use would result in a possibility of misunderstanding.
17. **Article XVII: Exceptions:** Members may provide limited exceptions to the rights conferred by a trademark, such as fair use of descriptive terms, provided that such exceptions take account of the legitimate interests of the owner of trademark and of third parties.
18. **Article XVIII: Term of Protection:** Initial registration and each renewal of registration of a trademark shall be for a term no less than seven years. The registration of a trademark shall be renewable indefinitely.
19. **Article XIX: Requirement of Use:** According to the Article:

- If use is required to maintain a registration, the registration may be cancelled only after an uninterrupted period of at least three years of non use, unless valid reasons based on the existence of obstacles to such use are shown by the trademark owner.
- When subject to the control of its owner, use of a trademark by another person shall be recognised as use of the trademark for the purpose of maintaining the registration.

20. **Article XX: Other Requirements:** The use of trademark in the course of trade shall not be unduly burdened by special requirements, such as use with another trademark, use in a special form or use in a manner detrimental to its capacity to distinguish the

goods or services of one undertaking from those of other undertakings.

21. **Article XXI: Licensing and Assignments:** Members may determine conditions on the licensing and assignment of trademarks, it being understood that the compulsory licensing of trademarks shall not be permitted and that the owner of a registered trademark shall have the right to assign the trademark with or without the transfer of the business to which the trademark belongs.

    Geographical Indications: Sometimes, a place name is used to identify a product. The Agreement says that the countries have to prevent the misuse of place names. The Agreement says that all parties must provide means to prevent the use of indications which misleads the consumers as to the origin of goods. Exceptions are allowed for names that have already generic terms, but any Member using such exceptions must be willing to negotiate with the country protecting the geographical indications in question.

    For wines and spirits, the Agreement provides higher level of protection, i.e. even where there is no risk of the public being misled. Furthermore, provision is made for further negotiations to institute a multilateral system of notification and registration of geographical indications for wines. This issue is now a part of the Doha Round. Extending the higher level of protection beyond wines and spirits is also being debated in the WTO.

22. **Article XXII: Protection of Geographical Indications:** The Agreement says that:

- Geographical indications are indications which identify a good as originating in the territory of a Member, or a region or locality in that territory, where a given quality, reputation or the characteristics of the good is essentially attributable to its geographical origin.
- In respect of geographical indications, Members shall provide the legal means for interested parties to prevent: (a) The use of any means in the designation or presentation of a good that indicates or suggests that the good in question originates in a geographical area other than the true place of origin in a manner which misleads the public as to the geographical origin of the good. (b) Any use which constitutes an act of unfair competition within the meaning of Article 10 of the Paris Convention (1967).
- A Member shall, on the request, refuse or invalidate the registration of a trademark which contains or consists of a geographical indication with respect to goods not originating in the territory indicated, if the use of the indication in the trademark for such goods in that Member is of such a nature as to mislead the public regarding the true place of origin.

23. **Article XXIII: Additional Protection for Geographical Indications for Wines and Spirits:** The Agreement says that:

- Each Member shall provide the legal means for interested parties to prevent use of a geographical indication identifying wines for wines not originating in the place indicated by the geographical indication in question or identifying spirits for spirits not originating in the place indicated by the geographical indication in question, even where the true origin of the goods is indicated or the geographical indication is used in translation or accompanied by expression such as 'kind', 'type', 'style', 'imitation' or the like.

- The registration of a trademark for wines which contains or consists of a geographical indication identifying wines or for spirits which contains or consists of a geographical indication identifying spirits shall be refused or invalidated, on the request, with respect to such wines or spirits not having this origin.
- In order to facilitate the protection of geographical indications for wines, negotiations shall be undertaken in the Council for TRIPS concerning the establishment of a multilateral system of notification and registration of geographical indication for wines eligible for protection in those Members participating in the system.

24. **Article XXIV: International Negotiations: Exceptions:** The Agreement says that Members shall conduct negotiations to conclude bilateral or multilateral agreements.

- Members agree to enter into negotiations aimed at increasing the protection of individual geographical indications.
- The Council for TRIPS shall keep under review the application of the provisions of the Agreement for geographical indications.
- There shall be no obligation under this Agreement to protect geographical indications which are not or cease to be protected in their country of origin, or which have fallen into disuse in that country.

Industrial Designs: Owners of protected designs must be able to protect the manufacture, sale or importation of articles bearing or embodying a design which is a copy of the protected design. The Agreement says that industrial designs must be protected for at least ten years.

25. **Article XXV: Requirement for Protection:** According to the Article:

- Members shall provide for the protection of independently created industrial designs that are new or original. Members may provide that designs are not new or original if they do not significantly differ from known design or combinations of known design features. Members may provide that such protection shall not extend to designs dictated essentially by technical or functional considerations.
- Each member shall ensure that requirements for security protection for textile designs, in particular in regard to any cost, examination or publication, do not unreasonably impair the opportunities to seek and obtain such protection. Members shall be free to meet this obligation through industrial design law or through copyright law.

26. **Article XXVI: Protection:** The Agreement says that:

- The owner of a protected industrial design shall have the right to prevent third parties not having the owner's consent from manufacturing, selling or importing articles bearing or embodying a design which is a copy of the protected design, when such acts are undertaken for commercial purposes.
- Members may provide exceptions to the protection of industrial designs, provided

that such exceptions do not unreasonably conflict with the normal exploitation of protected industrial designs and do not unnecessarily prejudice the legitimate interests of the owners of the protected designs, taking into account of the legitimate interest of third parties.

- The duration of protection available shall amount to at least ten years.

Patents: In respect of patents, there is a general obligation to comply with the substantive provisions of the Paris Convention (1967). The protection must be available for both products and processes, in almost all fields of technology. The patent protection must be available for inventions for at least twenty years. Members may refuse to provide patent for an invention if its commercial use is prohibited owing to public order or morality. Members can also exclude diagnostic, therapeutic and surgical methods, plants and animals (other than micro organisms), and biological processes for the production of plants or animals (other than microbiological processes).

Plant varieties must be protected by patents or by a special system. If a patent is issued for the production process, then the rights must extend to the product directly obtained from the process. The Agreement describes the minimum rights that a patent owner must enjoy.

To deal with the possibility of abuse of patent rights by owners, for example by failing to supply the product in the market, members can issue 'compulsory licenses', allowing a competitor to produce the product or use the process under license. But this can only be done under special conditions aimed at safeguarding the legitimate interests of the patent owner.

A special declaration by WTO ministers at the Doha Ministerial Conference in November 2001 says the TRIPS Agreement does not and should not prevent Members from taking measures to protect public health. The Ministers agreed to extend exemptions on pharmaceutical patent protection for least developed countries until 2016. They assigned further work to the TRIPS Council to sort out how to provide extra flexibility so that members unable to produce pharmaceuticals domestically can import patented drugs made under compulsory licensing. A waiver providing this flexibility was agreed on August 30, 2003.

The use of information contained in the patent documents for research and development, and imparting education without permission of the patentee does not constitute infringement of the patent. However, commercialisation without permission is definitely an infringement. A patent granted in one country is valid only in the country where it is filed. Therefore, for securing legal rights by patents in different countries, separate applications have to be filed in each of the desired countries, according to the law of the country.

The main provisions of the Agreement regarding patents are described below:

27. **Article XXVII: Patentable Subject Matter:** The Article says that:

- Patents shall be available for any inventions, whether products or processes in all fields of technology, provided they are new, involve an inventive step and are capable of industrial application. Patents shall be available and patent rights enjoyable without discrimination as to the place of invention, the field of technology and whether products are imported or locally produced.

- Members may exclude from patentability inventions, when it is necessary to protect public order or morality, including to protect human, animal or plant life or health or to avoid serious prejudice to the environment, provided that such exclusion is not made merely because the exploitation is prohibited by their law.
- Members may exclude from patentability: (a) Diagnostic, therapeutic and surgical methods for the treatment of humans or animals; (b) Plants and animals other than micro organisms, and essentially biological processes for the production of plants or animals other than non-biological and microbiological processes. However, Members shall provide for the protection of plant varieties.

28. **Article XXVIII: Rights Conferred:** According to the Article:

- A patent shall confer on its owner the following exclusive rights: (a) Where the subject matter of a patent is product, to prevent third parties not having owner's consent from acts of making, using, offering for sale, selling or importing for these purposes that product, (b) Where the subject matter of a patent is a process, to prevent third parties not having owner's consent from the act of using the process and from the acts of using, offering for sale, selling, or importing for these purposes at least the product obtained directly by that process.
- Patent owners shall have the right to assign, or transfer by succession, the patent and to conclude licensing contracts.

29. **Article XXIX: Conditions on Patent Applicants:** The Article says that:

- Members shall require that an applicant for a patent shall disclose the invention in a manner sufficiently clear and complete for the invention to be carried out by a person skilled in the art and may require the applicant to indicate the best mode for carrying out the invention known to the inventor at the filing date.
- Members may require an applicant for a patent to provide information concerning the applicant's corresponding foreign applications and grants.

30. **Article XXX: Exceptions to Rights Conferred:** Members may provide limited exceptions to the exclusive rights conferred by a patent, provided that such exceptions do not unreasonably conflict with a normal exploitation of the patent and do not unreasonably prejudice the legitimate interests of the patent owner, taking account of the legitimate interests of third parties.
31. **Article XXXI: Other Use without Authorisation of the Rights Holder:** Where the law of a Member allows for other use of the subject matter of a patent without the authorisation of the right holder, including use by the government or third parties authorised by the government, the following provisions shall be respected:

- Authorisation of such use shall be considered on its individual merits.
- Such use may only be permitted if, prior to such use, the proposed user has made efforts to obtain authorisation from the right holder on reasonable commercial terms and conditions and that such efforts have not been successful within a reasonable period of time.

- The scope and duration of such use shall be limited to the purpose for which it was authorised.
- Such use shall be non-exclusive.
- Such use shall be non-assignable.
- Any such use shall be authorised predominantly for the supply of the domestic market of the Member authorising such use.
- Authorisation of such use shall be liable to be terminated if and when the circumstances which led to it cease to exist and are unlikely to recur.
- The right holder shall be paid adequate compensation.
- When such use authorised to permit the exploitation of a patent (the second patent) which cannot be exploited without infringing another patent (the first patent), the following additional conditions shall apply: (a) The invention claimed in the second patent shall involve an important technical advance of considerable economic significance in relation to the invention claimed in the first patent, (b) The owner of the first patent shall be entitled to a cross license on reasonable terms to use the invention claimed in the second patent and (c) The use authorised in respect of the first patent shall be non-assignable except with the assignment of the second patent.

32. **Article XXXII: Revocation/Forfeiture:** An opportunity for judicial review of any decision to revoke or forfeit a patent shall be available.
33. **Article XXXIII: Terms of Protection:** The term of protection available shall not end before the expiration of a period of twenty years counted from the filing date.
34. **Article XXXIV: Process Patents: Burden of Proof:** The judicial authorities shall have the authority to order the defendant to prove that the process to obtain an identical product is different from the patented process.

    Layout Design of Integrated Circuits: In the TRIPS Agreement, the Washington Treaty on Intellectual Property in Respect of Integrated Circuits, which comes under the World Intellectual Property Organisation (WIPO), shall be the basis for the protection of integrated circuit designs. The TRIPS Agreement says that the protection must be available for at least ten years. The compulsory licensing and government use is only allowed under a number of strict conditions.
35. **Article XXXV: Relation to the IPIC Treaty:** Members agreed to provide protection to layout designs (topographies) of integrated circuits in accordance with Article 2 through 7 (other than paragraph 3 of Article 6), Article 12 and paragraph 3 of Article 16 of the Treaty on Intellectual Property in Respect of Integrated Circuits and, in addition, to comply with other provisions.
36. **Article XXXVI: Scope of Protection:** Members shall consider unlawful the following acts if performed without the authorisation of the right holder: importing, selling, or otherwise distributing for commercial purposes a protected layout design, an integrated circuit in which a protected layout design is incorporated, or an article incorporating such an integrated circuit only in so far it contains an unlawfully reproduced layout design.

37. **Article XXXVII: Acts not Requiring the Authorisation of the Right Holder:** No Member shall consider unlawful the performance of any of the acts: importing, selling, or otherwise distributing for commercial purposes a protected layout design, an integrated circuit in which a protected layout design is incorporated, or an article incorporating such integrated circuit, where the person performing or ordering such act did not know and had no reasonable ground to know, when acquiring the integrated circuit or article incorporating such an integrated circuit, that it incorporated an unlawfully reproduced layout design.
38. **Article XXXVIII: Terms of Protection:** The Agreement says that:

- In Member countries requiring registration as a condition for protection, the term of protection of layout designs shall not end before the expiration of a period of ten years counted from the date of filing an application for registration or from the first commercial exploitation wherever in the world it occurs.
- In Member countries not requiring registration as a condition for protection, layout designs shall be protected for a term of no less than ten years from the date of the first commercial exploitation wherever in the world it occurs.

Protection of Undisclosed Information: The Agreement says that trade secrets and other type of 'undisclosed information' which have commercial value must be protected against infringement of confidence and other acts against sincere commercial practices. Test data submitted to government in order to get marketing approval for new pharmaceutical or agricultural chemicals must also be protected against unfair commercial use.

39. **Article XXXIX: Protection of Undisclosed Information:** The Agreement says:

- As provided in the Paris Convention (1967), Members shall protect undisclosed information and data submitted to governments or governmental agencies.
- Natural and legal persons shall have the possibility of preventing information lawfully within their control from being disclosed to, acquired by, or used by others without their consent in a manner contrary to honest commercial practices so long as such information: (a) Is secret in the sense that it is not, as a body or in the precise configuration and assembly of its components, generally known among or readily accessible to persons within the circles that normally deal with the kind of information in question, (b) Has commercial value because it is secret; and (c) Has been subject to reasonable steps under the circumstances, by the person lawfully in control of the information, to keep it secret.
- Members, when requiring, as condition for approving the marketing of pharmaceutical or of agricultural chemical products which utilise new chemical entities, the submission of undisclosed test or other data, the organisation of which involves a considerable effort, shall protect such data against unfair commercial use. In addition, Members shall protect such data against disclosure, except where necessary to protect the public or unless steps are taken to ensure that the data are protected against unfair commercial use.

Control of Anti-competitive Practices in Contractual Licenses: The owner of a copyright, patent or other form of intellectual property right can issue a license for someone else to produce or copy the protected trademark, work, inventions, design etc. The Agreement says that under certain conditions government have the right to take action to prevent anti-competitive licensing that abuses intellectual property rights. Governments shall have to consult each other to control anti-competitive licensing.

40. **Article XL: Control of Anti-competitive Practices in Contractual Licenses:** The Agreement says:

- Members agreed that some licensing practices or conditions pertaining to intellectual property rights which restrain competition may have adverse effect on trade and may obstruct the transfer and propagation of technology.
- A Member may adopt, consistent with other provision of this Agreement, appropriate measures to prevent or control such practices.
- Each Member shall enter, upon request, into consultations with any other Member which believes that an intellectual property right owner that is a national or domicile of the Member to which the request has been made is undertaking practices in violation of the requesting Member's laws and regulations on the subject matter and which wishes to secure compliance with such regulations, without prejudice to any action under the law and to the full freedom of an ultimate decision of either Member.

Part III: Enforcement of IPRs:

Part III sets out the obligations of Member governments to provide procedures and remedies under their domestic law to ensure that intellectual property rights can be effectively enforced by foreign right holders as well as by their own nationals. The Agreement says governments have to make sure that intellectual property rights can be enforced under their laws; and that the penalties for infringement are strict as such to deter the abuse. The procedures must be simple, equitable, and transparent and should not impose unreasonable delays.

The Agreement gives details how enforcement should be implemented, and describes rules for obtaining evidence, provisional measures, injunctions, damages and the penalties. It says wilful trademark counterfeiting or copyright piracy on a commercial scale should be treated as a criminal offence. There is provision of compensation for the party who has suffered due to misuse of the enforcement or due to the infringement. Members shall enable the persons concerned to approach a court to review administrative decisions and to appeal a lower court's ruling.

Developing country, in particular, see technology transfer as a means to bargain in which they assure the protection of intellectual property rights. Developed country Members shall provide incentives to enterprises and institutions in their territories for the purpose of promoting and encouraging technology transfer to least developed country Members in order to enable them to create a sound and viable technological base.

Developed country Members were given one year so that their laws and practices conform to the provisions of this Agreement. Developing country Members and transition economy Members were given five years until 2000. Least developed country Members were given 11 years, until 2006, now extended to 2016 for pharmaceutical patents.

The general rule is that obligations in the Agreement apply to intellectual property rights that existed at the end of a country's transition period as well as to new ones. The relevant main provisions have been given below.

41. **Article IXL: General Obligations:** The Article contains general obligations related to the enforcement:

- Members shall ensure that enforcement procedures are available under their law so as to allow effective action against any act of infringement of intellectual property rights covered by this Agreement.
- Procedures concerning the enforcement of intellectual property rights shall be fair and equitable. They shall not be unnecessarily complicated or costly, or entail unreasonable time limits or needless delays.
- Decisions on the merits of a case shall be based only on evidence in respect of which parties were offered the opportunity to be heard.
- Parties to a proceeding shall have an opportunity for review by a judicial authority of final administrative decisions and of at least the legal aspect of initial judicial decisions on the merit of a case.
- It is understood that the enforcement of intellectual property rights does not create any obligation on a Member to put in place a judicial system distinct from that for the enforcement of law in general, nor does it affect the capacity of Member to enforce their law in general.

42. **Article VIIIL: Fair and Equitable Procedures:** Defendants shall have the right to written notice which is timely and contains sufficient detail, including the basis of the claims. Parties shall be allowed to be represented by independent legal counsel, and procedures shall not impose overly troublesome requirements concerning mandatory person appearances. All parties to such procedures shall be duly entitled to authenticate their claims and to present all relevant evidence. The procedures shall provide a means to identify and protect confidential information, unless this would be contrary to existing constitutional requirements.

43. **Article VIIL: Evidence:** The Article says:

- The judicial authorities shall have the authority, where a party has presented reasonably available evidence sufficient to support its claims and has specified evidence relevant to substantiation of its claims which lies in the control of the opposing party, to order that this evidence be produced by the opposing party.
- In cases in which a party to a proceeding voluntarily and without good reason refuses to, or otherwise does not provide necessary information within a reasonable period, or significantly impedes procedure relating to an enforcement action, a Member may accord judicial authorities the authority to make preliminary and final determination on the basis of the information presented to them, subject to providing

the parties an opportunity to be heard on the allegations or evidence.

44. **Article VIL: Injunctions:** The Judicial authorities shall have the authority to order a party to abstain from an infringement, inter alia to prevent the entry into the channels of commerce in their jurisdiction of imported goods that involve infringement of an intellectual property right, immediately after customs clearance of such goods. Members are not obliged to accord such authority in respect of protected subject matter acquired or ordered by a person prior to knowing or having reasonable ground to know that dealing in such subject matter would involve the infringement of an intellectual property right.
45. **Article VL: Damages:** The Agreement has the following provisions relating to damages:

- The judicial authorities shall have the authority to order the infringer to pay the right holder, damages adequate to compensate for the injury the right holder has suffered because of infringement of that person's intellectual property right by the infringer who knowingly, or with reasonable grounds to know, engaged in infringing activity.
- The judicial authorities shall also have the authority to order the infringer to pay the right holder expenses, which may include appropriate attorney fees.

46. **Article IVL: Other Remedies:** In order to create an effective deterrent to infringement, the judicial authorities shall have the authority to order that goods that they have found to be infringed, without compensation of any sort, disposed of outside the channels of commerce in such a manner as to avoid the harm caused to the right holder, or, unless this would be contrary to existing constitutional requirements, destroyed.
47. **Article IIIL: Right of Information:** Members may provide that the judicial authorities shall have the authority, unless this would be out of proportion to the seriousness of the infringement, to order the infringer to inform the right holder of the identity of third persons involved in the production and distribution of the infringing goods or services and of their channels of distribution.
48. **Article IIL: Indemnification of the Defendant:** There are following provisions regarding indemnification of the defendant:

- The judicial authorities shall have the authority to order a party at whose request measures were taken and who has abused enforcement procedures to provide to a party wrongfully enjoined or restraint adequate compensation for the injury suffered because of such abuse.
- In respect of the administration of any law pertaining to the protection or enforcement of intellectual property rights, Members shall only exempt both public authorities and officials from liability to appropriate remedial measures where actions are taken or intended in good faith in the course of the administration of that law.

49. **Article IL: Administrative Procedures:** To the extent that any civil remedy can be ordered as a result of administrative procedures on the merits of a case, such procedures shall conform to principles equivalent in substance to those set forth in this Agreement.

50. **Article L: Provisional Measures:** The following provisions are applicable pertaining to provisional measures:

- The judicial authorities shall have the authority to order prompt and effective provisional measures: (a) To prevent an infringement of any intellectual property right from occurring, and in particular to prevent entry into the channel of commerce in their jurisdiction of goods, including imported goods immediately after customs clearance, (b) To preserve relevant evidence in regard to the alleged infringement.
- The judicial authorities shall have the authority to adopt provisional measures, where appropriate, in particular where any delay is likely to cause irreversible damage to the right holder, or where there is a risk of evidence being destroyed.
- Where provisional measures have been adopted, the parties affected shall be given notice, without delay after the execution of the measures at the latest.
- The applicant may be required to supply other information necessary for the identification of the goods concerned by the authority that will execute the provisional measures.
- Provisional measures shall, upon request by the defendant, be revoked or otherwise cease to have effect, if proceedings leading to a decision on the merits of the case are not initiated within a reasonable period.
- Where the provisional measures are revoked or where they lapse due to any act or omission by the applicant, or where it is subsequently found that there has been no infringement or threat of infringement of an intellectual property right, the judicial authorities shall have the authority to order the applicant, upon request of the defendant, to provide the defendant, appropriate compensation for any injury caused by these measures.

51. **Article LI: Suspension of Release by Customs Authorities:** Members shall adopt procedures to enable a right holder, who has valid grounds for suspecting that the importation of counterfeit trademarks or pirated copyright goods may take place, to lodge an application in writing with competent authorities for the suspension by customs authorities of the release into circulation of such goods. Members may enable such an application to be made in respect of goods which involve other infringements of intellectual property rights. Members may also provide for corresponding procedures concerning the suspension by the customs authorities of the release of infringing goods destined for exportation from their territories.

52. **Article LII: Application:** Any right holder initiating the procedures for the suspension of the release shall be required to provide adequate evidence to satisfy the competent authority that, under the laws of the country of importation, there is prima facie an infringement of the right holder's intellectual property right and to supply a sufficiently detailed description of the goods to make them readily recognised by the customs authorities.

53. **Article LIII: Security or Equivalent Assurance:** The Agreement has following provisions regarding security:

- The competent authorities shall have the authority to require an applicant to provide a security to protect the defendant and the competent authorities and to prevent abuse. Such security or equivalent assurance shall not unreasonably deter recourse to these procedures.

- Where release of goods involving industrial designs, patents, layout-designs or undisclosed information into free circulation has been suspended by customs authorities on the basis of decision other than by a judicial or other independent authority, and a period of 10 working days has expired without any provisional relief by the duly empowered authority, the owner, importer or consignee of such goods shall be entitled to their release on providing a security in an amount sufficient to protect the right holder for any infringement, provided they have complied with all other conditions for importation.

54. **Article LIV: Notice of Suspension:** The importer and the applicant shall be promptly notified of the suspension of the release of goods.
55. **Article LV: Duration of Suspension:** If, within a period not exceeding 10 working days after the applicant has been served notice of the suspension, the customs authorities have not been informed that proceedings leading to a decision have been initiated by a party other than the defendant, or that duly empowered authority has taken provisional measures prolonging the suspension of the release of the goods, the goods shall be released, provided that all other conditions for importation or exportation have been complied with. This time limit may be extended by another 10 working days, if appropriate.
56. **Article LVI: Indemnification of the Importer and of the Owner of Goods:** Relevant authorities shall have the authority to order the applicant to pay the importer, the consignee and the owner of the goods of appropriate compensation for any injury caused to them through the wrongful detention of goods.
57. **Article LVII: Right of Inspection and Information:** Without prejudice to the protection of confidential information, Members shall provide the competent authorities the authority to give the right holder sufficient opportunity to have any goods detained by the customs authorities inspected in order to substantiate the right holder's claims. The competent authorities shall also have authority to give the importer an equivalent opportunity to have any such goods inspected. Members may provide the competent authorities the authority to inform the right holder of the names and addresses of the consignor, the importer and the consignee and of the quality of goods in question.
58. **Article LVIII: Ex-Officio Action:** Where Members require competent authorities to act upon their own initiative and to suspend the release of goods in respect which they have acquired prima facie evidence that an intellectual property right is being infringed: (a) The competent authorities may at any time seek from the right holder any information that may assist them to exercise these powers, (b) The importer and the right holder shall be promptly notified of the suspension, (c) Member shall only exempt both public authorities and officials from the liability to appropriate remedial measures where actions are taken in good faith.

59. **Article LIX: Remedies:** Without prejudice to other rights of action open to the right holder and subject to the right of the defendant to seek review by a judicial authority, competent authorities shall have the authority to order the destruction or disposal of infringed goods in accordance with the prescribed principles. In regard to the counterfeit trademark goods, the authorities shall not allow the re-exportation of the infringing goods in an unaltered state or subject them to a different customs procedure, other than in exceptional circumstances.
60. **Article LX: De Minimis Imports:** Members may exclude from the application of the above provisions small quantities of goods of a non-commercial nature contained in traveller's personal luggage or sent in small consignments.
61. **Article LXI: Criminal Procedures:** Members shall provide for criminal procedures and penalties to be applied at least in cases of wilful trademark counterfeiting or copyright piracy on a commercial scale. Remedies available shall include imprisonment and/or monetary fines sufficient to provide a deterrent, consistently with the level of penalties applied for crimes of a corresponding gravity. In appropriate cases, remedies available shall also include the seizure, forfeiture and destruction of the infringing goods and of any material and implants the predominant use of which has been in the commission of the offence. Members may provide for criminal procedures and penalties to be applied in other cases of infringements of intellectual property rights, in particular, where they are committed wilfully and on a commercial scale.
62. **Article LXII: Acquisition and Maintenance of IPRs:** The provisions pertaining to acquisition and maintenance of IPRs are given below:

- Members may require, as a condition for the acquisition or maintenance of the intellectual property rights, compliance with reasonable procedures and formalities. Such procedures and formalities shall be consistent with the provisions of this Agreement.
- Where the acquisition of an intellectual property right is subject to the right being granted or registered, Members shall make sure that the procedures for grant or registration allow the granting or registration of the right within reasonable period of time so as to avoid unwarranted shortening of the period of protection.
- Article 4 of the Paris Convention (1967) shall apply to service marks.
- Procedures concerning the acquisition or maintenance of intellectual property rights and, where a Member's law provides for such procedures, administrative revocation and inter parte procedures such as opposition, revocation and cancellation, shall be governed by the general principles of this Agreement.
- Final administrative decisions in any of the procedures shall be subject to review by a judicial or quasi-judicial authority.

63. **Article LXIII: Transparency:** The Agreement has provisions related to transparency:

- Laws and regulations, and final judicial decisions and administrative rulings of general application, made effective by a Member pertaining to the subject matter of this Agreement (the availability, scope, acquisition, enforcement and prevention of the abuse of intellectual property right) shall be published, or where such publication is not practicable make publicly available, in a national language, in such manner as to enable governments and right holders to become acquainted with them.

- Members shall notify the laws and regulations to the Council for TRIPS in order to assist the Council in its review of the operation of this Agreement.
- Each Member shall be prepared to supply, subject to a written request from another Member, information on the availability, scope, acquisition, enforcement, and prevention of abuse of intellectual property rights.
- Members shall not disclose confidential information which would hamper law enforcement or otherwise be opposite to the public interest or would prejudice the lawful commercial interests of particular enterprises, public or private.

64. **Article LXIV: Dispute Settlement:** The provisions of Articles XXII and XXIII of GATT, 1994 as elaborated and applied by the Dispute Settlement Undertaking shall apply to consultations and the settlement of disputes under this Agreement except as otherwise specifically provided herein.
65. **Article LXV: Transitional Arrangements:** There are following provisions for transitional arrangements:

- No Member shall be obliged to apply the provisions of this Agreement before the expiry of a general period of one year following the date of entry into force of the WTO Agreement.
- A developing country Member is entitled to delay for a further period of four years from the date of application.
- Any other Member which is in the process of transformation from a centrally planned into market, free enterprises economy may also benefit from delay of 4 years.

66. **Article LXVI: Least Developed Country Members:** The Agreement paid due consideration to the special needs and requirements of least developed country Members.

- In view of the special needs and requirements of least developed country Members, their economic, financial and administrative constraints, and their need for flexibility to create a viable technological base, such Members shall not be required to apply the provisions of this Agreement for a period of 10 years from the date of application.
- Developed country Members shall provide incentives to enterprises and institutions in their territories for the purpose of promoting and encouraging technology transfer to least developed country Members in order to enable them to create a sound and viable technological base.

67. **Article LXVII: Technical Cooperation:** In order to facilitate the implementation of this Agreement, developed country Members shall provide, on request and on mutually agreed terms and conditions, technical and financial cooperation in favour of developing and least developed country Members.
68. **Article LXVIII: Council for TRIPS:** The Council for TRIPS shall monitor the operation of this Agreement and, in particular, Members' compliance with their

obligations, and shall afford Members the opportunity of consulting on matters relating to the trade-related aspects of intellectual property rights.

69. **Article LXIX: International Cooperation:** Members agree to cooperate with each other with a view to eliminating international trade in goods infringing intellectual property rights. For this purpose, they shall establish and notify contract points in their administration and be ready to exchange information on trade in infringing goods.
70. **Article LXX: Protection of Existing Subject Matter:** The Agreement has the provisions for the protection of existing subject matter relating to intellectual property rights:

- This Agreement does not give rise to obligations in respect of acts which occurred before the date of application of the Agreement for the Member in question.
- Except as otherwise provided for in this Agreement, this Agreement gives rise to obligations in respect of all subject matters existing at the date of application of this Agreement for the Member in question, which is protected in that Member on the said date, or which meets or comes subsequently to meet the criteria for protection under the terms of this Agreement.
- There shall be no obligation to restore protection to the subject matter which on the date of application of this Agreement for the Member in question has fallen into public domain.
- In the case of intellectual property rights for which protection is conditional upon registration, applications for protection which are pending on the date of application of this Agreement for the Member in question shall be permitted to be amended to claim any enhanced protection provided under the provisions of this Agreement. Such amendments shall not include new matter.
- Where a Member does not make available as of the date of entry into force of the WTO Agreement, patent protection for pharmaceutical and agricultural chemical products commensurate with its obligations under this Agreement, that Member shall provide a means by which applications for patents for such inventions can be filed.

71. **Article LXXI: Review and Amendment:** The Council for TRIPS shall review the implementation of this Agreement after the expiration of the transitional period. The Council shall, having regard to the experience gained in its implementation, review it two years after that date; and at identical intervals thereafter.
72. **Article LXXII: Reservations:** Reservations may not be entered in respect of any of the provisions of this Agreement without the consent of the other Members.
73. **Article LXXIII: Security Exception:** Nothing in this Agreement shall be construed:

- To require a Member to furnish any information the disclosure of which it considers contrary to its essential security interests, or
- To prevent a Member from taking any action which it considers necessary for the protection of its essential security interests, or
- To prevent a Member from taking any action in pursuant of its obligations under the United Nations Charter for the maintenance of international peace and security.

9

WTO Understanding on Rules and Procedures Governing the Settlement of Disputes

Disputes in the WTO are generally caused by unfulfilled promises. WTO Members have agreed that they will use the multilateral system of settling disputes instead of taking action unilaterally where they believe that other Members are violating trade rules. The Agreement on Understanding on Rules and Procedures Governing the Settlement of Disputes further strengthens the procedures for settling disputes that existed under GATT, 1947.

9.1 Process for Settlement of Disputes

Under GATT, 1947, the procedure for settling disputes did not have fixed timetable. It was easier to block rulings, and many cases were dragged on for long time inclusively. Under the GATT, 1947 procedure, the rulings could only be adopted by consensus, meaning that a single objection could block the ruling.

The new Agreement introduced a more structured process with clearly defined stages in the procedure. It introduced greater discipline for the timely settlement of disputes.

The Agreement makes it impossible for the country losing a case to block the adoption of the ruling. Now, the rulings are automatically adopted unless there is consensus to reject a ruling. Now, any country willing to block a ruling has to persuade all other Members (including its opposite party in the case) to share its view.

Though much of the procedure is like that of a court or tribunal, but the settlement of disputes through discussion by concerned parties is still preferred. The first stage is for consultation between governments concerned, and even when the case has progressed to higher stages, consultation and mediation are still possible.

The dispute settlement is the responsibility of the Dispute Settlement Body (the General Council in another guise) which comprises of all WTO Members. The Dispute Settlement Body (DSB) will exercise the authority of the General Council and the Councils and Committees of the covered agreements. The DSB shall establish panels and also set out specific rules and deadlines for deciding the terms of reference and composition of panels.

The new rules and procedures were to be reviewed within four years after the entry into force of the WTO.

At all stages, the WTO Director-General will be available to offer his good offices, to mediate or to achieve the conciliation. The panel process for settlement of disputes under this understanding has been described in Table 9.1.

Table 9.1: Panel Process for Settlement of Disputes

Stage	Time Taken	Total Time	Article
Consultation	60 days		4
Panel establishment	By the second DSB meeting/45 days		6
Terms of reference and composition	20 days; 30 days if WTO DG asked to pick panel		7, 8
Panel examination	Normally two meeting with the parties and one meeting with third party		10, 12
Interim review stage	Descriptive part of report sent to the parties, and interim report sent to the parties		15
Panel report issued to the parties		6 months from composition of panel, 3 months if urgent	12
Panel report circulated to Members		Up to 9 months from establishment of panel	12
DSB adopts panel/appellate report	60 days for panel report, 90 days for report if appealed	Generally 9 months with no appeal; 12 months with appeal	16, 17
Dispute over implementation	90 days	1 year and 3 months	21
Implementation	Reasonable period of time		21
Compensation	Within 20 days after expiry of reasonable period		22
Retaliation	30 days after expiry of reasonable period		22

9.2 Main Provisions for Settlement of Disputes

1. **Article I: Coverage and Application:** The Agreement is applicable as described below:

- The rules and procedures of this Understanding shall apply to disputes brought pursuant to the consultation and dispute settlement provisions of the agreements listed below (the covered agreements): (a) Agreement establishing the WTO, (b) Multilateral Trade Agreements: (i) Annex 1A: Multilateral Agreements on Trade in Goods, (ii) Annex 1B: General Agreements on Trade in Services, (iii) Annex 1C: Agreement on Trade-related Aspects of Intellectual Property Rights and (iv) Annex 2: Understanding on Rules and Procedures Governing the Settlement of Disputes, (c) Plurilateral Agreements.
- The rules and procedures of this Understanding shall apply subject to such special or

additional rules and procedures on dispute settlement contained in the following covered agreements: (a) Agreement on the Application of Sanitary and Phytosanitary Measures, (b) Agreement on Technical Barriers to Trade, (c) Agreement on Implementation of Article VI of GATT, 1994, (d) Agreement on Implementation of Article VII of GATT, 1994, (e) Agreement on Subsidies and Countervailing Measures, (f) General Agreement on Trade in Services, and (g) Decision on Certain Dispute Settlement Procedures for GATS.

To the extent there is difference between the rules and procedures of this Understanding and the special or additional rules and procedures of the covered agreements mentioned above, the special or additional rules and procedures shall prevail. Where disputes involve rules and procedures under more than one covered agreement and there is difference between special or additional rules and procedures of such agreements, the Chairman of the Dispute Settlement Body (DSB), in consultation with the parties, shall determine the rules and procedures to be followed within 10 days after a request by either Member, provided the parties fail to agree on rules and procedures within 20 days of the establishment of the panel.

2. **Article II: Administration:** The Agreement has the following provisions relating to administration:

- The DSB shall administer these rules and procedures and, except as otherwise provided in a covered agreement, the consultation and dispute settlement provisions of the covered agreements. The DSB shall have the authority to establish panels, adopt panel Appellate Body reports, maintain surveillance of implementation of rulings and recommendations, and to authorise suspension of concessions and other obligations under the covered agreements.
- The DSB shall inform the relevant WTO Councils and Committees of any development in disputes related to provisions of the respective covered agreements.
- The DSB shall meet as often as necessary to carry out its functions within the time frame provided in the Understanding.
- If the rules and procedures of this Understanding require the DSB to take a decision, it shall do so by consensus.

3. **Article III: General Provisions:** The Agreement says:

- Members affirm their adherence to the principles for the management of disputes applied under Articles XXII and XXIII of GATT, 1994, and the rules and procedures as further elaborated and modified.
- The dispute settlement system of the WTO is a central element in providing security and predictability to the multilateral trading system. The Members recognise that it serves to preserve the rights and obligations of Members under the covered agreements.
- The prompt settlement of disputes in which a Member considers that any benefits accruing to it directly or indirectly under the covered agreements are being impaired by measures taken by another Member is essential to the effective functioning of the WTO and the maintenance of a proper balance between the rights and obligations of Members.

- Recommendations and rulings made by the DSB shall be aimed at achieving a satisfactory settlement of the matter in accordance with the rights and obligations under this Understanding and under the covered agreements.
- All solutions to matters formally raised under the consultation and dispute settlement provisions of the covered agreements, including arbitration awards, shall be consistent with those agreements and shall not nullify or impair benefits accruing to any Member under those agreements, nor impede the attainment of any objective of these agreements.
- Mutually agreed solutions to matters formally raised under the consultation and dispute settlement provisions of the covered agreements shall be notified to the DSB and the relevant Councils and Committees.
- Before bringing a case, a Member shall exercise its judgement as to whether action under these procedures would be fruitful. The aim of the Dispute Settlement Mechanism is to secure a positive solution to dispute.
- In cases where there is an infringement of the obligations assumed under a covered agreement, the action is considered prima facie to constitute a case of nullification or impairment.
- The provisions of this Undertaking are without prejudice to the rights of the Members to seek authoritative interpretation of provisions of a covered agreement through decision-making under the WTO Agreement.
- It is understood that requests for conciliation and the use of the dispute settlement procedures should not be intended or considered as contentious acts and that, if a dispute arises, all Members will engage in these procedures in good faith in an effort to resolve the dispute.
- This Understanding shall apply only to new requests for consultations under the consultation provisions of the covered agreements made on or after the date of entry into force of the WTO Agreement.

4. **Article IV: Consultations:** The Agreement has the following provisions regarding consultations:

- Members resolve to strengthen and improve the effectiveness of the consultation procedures employed by Members.
- Each Member undertakes to accord sympathetic consideration to and afford adequate opportunity for consultation regarding any representations made by another Member concerning measures affecting the operation of any covered agreement.
- Where a request for consultations is made pursuant to a covered agreement, the Member to which request is made shall, unless otherwise mutually agreed, reply to the request within 10 days after its receipt and enter into consultations in good faith within a period of 30 days after the receipt of the request, with a view to reaching a mutually satisfactory solution. If the Member does not respond within 10 days after the receipt of the request, or does not enter into consultations within 30 days or a period otherwise mutually agreed after the receipt of the request, then the Member

that requested the consultations may proceed directly to the setting up of a panel.

- All such requests for consultation shall be notified to the DSB and the relevant Councils and Committees by the Member which requested consultations.
- Consultations shall be confidential, and without prejudice to the rights of any Member in any further proceedings.
- If the consultations fail to settle a dispute within 60 days after the date of the receipt of the request for consultations, the complaining party may request the set up of a panel.
- In case of urgency, including those which concern perishable goods, Members shall enter into consultations within a period of 10 days after the receipt of the request. Where the consultations fail to settle the dispute within a period of 20 days after the receipt of the request, the complaining party may request the setting up of a panel.
- During the consultations, Members should give special attention to the particular problems and interests of developing country Members.
- A third party having substantial trade interest in the consultations may notify the consulting Members and the DSB, within 10 days after the date of the circulation of the request for consultations, of its desire to join the consultations.

5. **Article V: Good Offices, Conciliation and Mediation:** There are provisions regarding good offices, conciliation and mediation in the Agreement:

- Good offices, conciliation and mediation are procedures that are undertaken voluntarily if the parties to the dispute agree.
- Proceedings involving good offices, conciliation and mediation, and in particular positions taken by the parties to the dispute, shall be confidential, and without prejudice to the rights of either party in any further proceedings under these procedures.
- Good offices, conciliation and mediation may be requested or terminated at any time by any party to the dispute. Once procedures for good offices, conciliation or mediation are terminated, the complaining party may then proceed with a request for the setting up of a panel.
- When good offices, conciliation or mediation are entered into within 60 days after the receipt of a request for consultations, the complaining party must allow a period of 60 days after the date of receipt of the request for consultations before requesting the establishment of a panel.
- If the parties to a dispute agree, procedures for good offices, conciliation or mediation may continue while the panel process proceeds.
- The Director-General may, acting in an ex-officio capacity, offer good offices, conciliation or mediation with the view to assisting Members to settle a dispute.

6. **Article VI: Establishment of Panels:** Where the complaining party requests, a panel shall be established at the latest at the DSB meeting following that at which the request first appears as an item on the DSB's agenda, unless at that meeting the DSB decides by consensus not to establish a panel.

7. **Article VII: Terms of Reference of Panels:** The Article says:

- The panels shall have the following terms of reference unless the parties to the dispute agree otherwise within 20 days from the set up of the panel:
- "to examine, in the light of the relevant provisions in (name of the covered agreements), the matter referred to the DSB by (name of party) in document ....and to make such findings as will assist the DSB in making the recommendations or in giving the rulings provided for in that/those agreements".
- The DSB may authorise its chairman to draw up the terms of reference of the panel in consultation with the parties to the dispute, if other than standard terms of reference are agreed upon.

8. **Article VIII: Composition of Panels:** The Agreement says:

- Panels shall be composed of well qualified governmental and/or non-governmental individuals, including persons who have served on or presented a case to a panel, served as a representative of a Member or of a contracting party to GATT, 1947 or as representative to the Council or Committee of any covered agreement or its predecessor agreement, or in the secretariat, taught or published on international trade law or policy or served as a senior trade policy official of a Member.
- Panel members should be selected with a view to ensuring the independence of the members, a sufficiently diverse background and a wide spectrum of experience.
- Citizens of Member whose governments are parties to the dispute or third parties shall not serve on a panel concerned with the dispute, unless the parties to the dispute agree otherwise.
- To assist in the selection of panellists, the Secretariat shall maintain an indicative list of governmental and non-governmental individuals possessing the qualifications prescribed.
- Panels shall be composed of three panellists unless the parties to the dispute agree, within 10 days from the establishment of the panel, to a panel composed of five panellists.
- The Secretariat shall propose nominations for the panel to the parties to dispute. The parties to the dispute shall not oppose nominations except for compelling reasons.
- If there is no agreement on the panellists within 20 days after the setting up of a panel, at the request of either party, the Director-General, in consultation with the Chairman of the DSB and the Chairman of the relevant Council or Committee, shall determine the composition of the panel by appointing the panellists whom Director-General considers most appropriate after consulting the parties to the dispute.
- Members shall undertake, as general rule, to permit their officials to serve panellists.
- Panellists shall serve in their individual capacities and not as government representatives, nor as representatives of any organisation.
- When a dispute is between a developing country Member and a developed country Member the panel shall, if the developing country Member so requests, include at least one panellist from a developing country Member.

- Panellists' expenses, including travel and subsistence allowance, shall be met from the WTO's budget.

9. **Article IX: Procedures for Multiple Complainants:** The following provisions are applicable to multiple complaints relating to same matter:

- Where more than one Member requests the setting up of a panel related to the same matter, a single panel may be established to examine these complaints taking into account the rights of all Members concerned.
- The single panel shall organise its examination and present its findings to the DSB in such a manner that the rights which the parties to the dispute would have enjoyed had separate panels examined the complaints, are in no way impaired.
- If more than one panel is established to examine the complaints related to the same matter, to the greatest extent possible the same persons shall serve as panellists on each of the separate panels and the timetable for the panel process in such disputes shall be harmonised.

10. **Article X: Third Parties:** The provisions relating to the recourse available to third parties are given below:

- The interests of the parties to a dispute and those of other Members under a covered agreement at issue in the dispute shall be fully taken into account during the panel process.
- Any Member having a substantial interest in a matter before a panel and having notified its interest to the DSB (referred as third party) shall have an opportunity to be heard by the panel and to make written submission to the panel.
- If a third party considers that a measure already is the subject of a panel proceeding nullifies or impairs benefits accruing to it under any covered agreement, that Member may have recourse to the normal dispute settlement procedures under this Undertaking. Such a dispute shall be referred to the original panel wherever possible.

11. **Article XI: Functions of Panels:** The panel shall make an objective assessment of the matter before it, including an objective assessment of the facts of the case and the applicability of and conformity with the relevant covered agreements, and make other findings which will assist the DSB in making the recommendations or in giving the rulings provided for in the covered agreements.

12. **Article XII: Panel Procedures:** Panels have to follow the working procedures as described below:

- Panels shall follow the working procedures prescribed in this Understanding unless the panel decides otherwise after consulting the parties to the dispute.
- Panel procedures should provide sufficient flexibility so as to make sure high quality panel reports, while not unduly delaying the panel process.
- After consulting the parties to the dispute, the panellists shall, as early as practicable and if possible within one week after the composition and terms of reference of the panel have been agreed upon, fix the timetable for the panel process.
- In fixing the timetable for the panel process, the panel shall provide sufficient time

for the parties to the dispute to prepare their submissions.

- Each party to the dispute shall submit its written submissions with the Secretariat for prompt transmission to the panel and other parties to the dispute.
- Where the parties to the dispute have failed to develop a mutually satisfactory solution, the panel shall submit its findings in the form of a written report to the DSB.
- The panel should submit, as a general rule, final report within six months from the date of the composition and terms of reference of the panel have been agreed.
- In no case should the period from the establishment of the panel to the circulation of the report to the Members exceed nine months.
- Where one or more of the parties is a developing country Member, the panel report shall explicitly indicate the form in which account has been taken of relevant provisions on differential and more favourable treatment, which form part of the covered agreements, for developing country Member.

13. **Article XIII: Right to Seek Information:** The Agreement provides certain rights to a panel to seek the relevant information:

- Each panel shall have the right to seek information and technical advice from any individual or body which it deems appropriate. Confidential information which is provided shall not be revealed without formal authorisation from the individual, body, or authorities of the Member providing the information.
- Panel may seek information from any relevant source and may consult experts to obtain their opinion on certain aspect of the matter.

14. **Article XIV: Confidentiality:** The Agreement says:

- Panel deliberations shall be confidential.
- Opinions expressed in the panel report by individual panellists shall be anonymous.

15. **Article XV: Interim Review Stage:** The Agreement has provisions for the interim review:

- Taking the consideration of rebuttal submissions and oral arguments, the panel shall issue the descriptive (factual and argument) sections of its draft report to the parties to the dispute. Within a period of time set by the panel, the parties shall submit their comments in writing.
- The panel shall issue an interim report to the parties, including both the descriptive sections and the panel's findings and conclusions. A party may submit a written request, within a period of time set by the panel, to the panel to review specific aspects of the interim report prior to circulation of the final report to the Members.
- The findings of the final report shall include a discussion of the arguments made at the interim review stage.

16. **Article XVI: Adoption of Panel Reports:** There are provisions concerning the adoption of the panel report by the DSB:

- In order to provide sufficient time for the Members to consider the panel reports, the reports shall not be considered for adoption by the DSB until 20 days after the date they have been circulated to the Members.

- Members having objections to a panel report shall give written reasons to explain their objections for circulation at least 10 days prior to the DSB meeting at which the panel report will be considered.
- The parties to the dispute shall have the right to participate fully in the consideration of the panel report by the DSB, and their views shall be fully recorded.
- Within 60 days after the circulation of the panel report to the Members, the report shall be adopted at a DSB meeting unless a party to the dispute formally notifies the DSB of its decision to appeal or the DSB decides by consensus not to adopt the report. If a party has notified its decision to appeal, the panel report shall not be considered for adoption by the DSB until after completion of appeal.

17. **Article XVII: Appellate Review:** The Appellate Body shall hear appeals from panel cases:

- A standing Appellate Body shall be established by the DSB. The Appellate Body shall hear appeals from panel cases. It shall be composed of seven persons, three of whom shall serve on any one case. Persons serving on the Appellate Body shall serve in rotation. Such rotation shall be determined in the working procedures of the Appellate Body.
- The DSB shall appoint persons to serve on the Appellate Body for a four year term and each person may be reappointed once.
- The Appellate Body shall comprise persons of recognised authority, with demonstrated expertise in law, international trade and the subject matter of the covered agreements generally. They shall be unaffiliated with any government.
- Only parties to the dispute, not third parties, may appeal a panel report.
- As a general rule, the proceedings shall not exceed 60 days from the date a party to the dispute formally notifies its decision to appeal to the date the Appellate Body circulates its report.
- An appeal shall be limited to issues of law covered in the panel report and legal interpretations developed by the panel.
- Working procedures shall be drawn up by the Appellate Body in consultation with the Chairman of the DSB and the Director-General, and communicated to the Members for their information.
- The proceedings of the Appellate body shall be confidential.
- Opinions expressed in the Appellate Body Report by individuals serving on the Appellate Body shall be anonymous.
- The Appellate Body may uphold, modify or reverse the legal findings and conclusions of the panel.
- An Appellate Body Report shall be adopted by the DSB and unconditionally accepted by the parties to the dispute unless the DSB decides by consensus not to adopt the Appellate Body Report within 30 days following its circulation to the Members.

18. **Article XVIII: Communication with the Panel:** The Agreement says:
- There shall be no ex-parte communication with the panel or Appellate Body concerning matter under consideration by the panel or Appellate Body.
- Written submissions to the panel or the Appellate Body shall be treated as confidential, but shall be made available to the parties to the dispute.

19. **Article XIX: Panel and Appellate Body Recommendations:** There are provisions pertaining to the recommendations made by a panel or the Appellate Body:
- Where a panel or the Appellate Body concludes that a measure is incorrect with a covered agreement, it shall recommend that the Member concerned bring the measure into conformity with that agreement.
- In their findings and recommendations, the panel and Appellate Body cannot add to or diminish the rights and obligations provided in the covered agreements.

20. **Article XX: Timeframe for DSB Decisions:** The period from the date of establishment of the panel by the DSB until the date the DSB considers the panel or Appellate Report for adoption shall as a general rule not exceed nine months where the panel report is not appealed or twelve months where the report is appealed.

21. **Article XXI: Surveillance of Implementation of Recommendations and Rulings:** The Agreement has provisions for surveillance of implementation of recommendations and rulings until the dispute is resolved:
- Prompt compliance with recommendations or rulings of the DSB is essential in order to ensure effective resolution of disputes to the benefit of all Members.
- Particular attention shall be paid to matters affecting the interests of developing country Members with respect to measures which have been subject to dispute settlement.
- At a DSB meeting held within 30 days after the adoption of the panel or Appellate Body Report, the Member concerned shall inform the DSB of its intentions regarding the implementation of the recommendations and rulings of the DSB. If it is impracticable to comply immediately with the recommendations and rulings, the Member shall have a reasonable period of time in which to do so.
- Except where the panel or the Appellate Body has extended the time of providing its report, the period from the date of establishment of the panel by the DSB until the date of determination of reasonable period of time shall not exceed 15 months unless the parties to the dispute agree otherwise.
- Where there is disagreement as to the existence or consistency with a covered agreement of measures taken to comply with the recommendations and rulings such dispute shall be decided through recourse to these dispute settlement procedures, including wherever possible, resorting to the original panel. The panel shall circulate its report within 90 days.
- The DSB shall keep under surveillance the implementation of the adopted recommendations and rulings. Unless the DSB decides otherwise, the issue of implementation of the recommendations and rulings shall be placed on the agenda of the forthcoming meetings of the DSB until the issue is resolved.

- If the case is one brought by a developing country Member, in considering what appropriate action might be taken, the DSB shall take into account not only the trade coverage of measures complained of, but also their impact on the economy of developing country Member concerned.

22. **Article XXII: Compensation and the Suspension of concession:** The Agreement has the following provisions:

- Compensation and the suspension of concessions or other obligations are temporary measures available in the event that the recommendations and rulings are not implemented within a reasonable time.
- If the Member concerned fails to comply with the recommendations and rulings within a reasonable period of time, such Member shall, if requested so, and no later than the expiry of a reasonable period of time, enter into negotiation with any party having invoked the dispute settlement procedures, with a view to developing mutually acceptable compensation. If no satisfactory compensation has been agreed within 20 days after the expiry of the reasonable period of time, the complaining party may request authorisation from the DSB to suspend the application to the Member concerned of concessions or other obligations under the covered agreement.
- In considering what concessions or other obligations to suspend, the complaining party shall apply the following principles and procedures: (a) The general principle is that the complaining party should first seek to suspend concessions or other obligations with respect to the same sector(s) as that in which the panel or the Appellate Body has found violation or other nullification or impairment; (b) If that party considers that it is not practicable or effective to suspend concessions or other obligations with respect to the same sector(s), it may seek to suspend concessions or other obligations in other sectors under the same covered agreement, and (c) If that party considers that it is not practicable or effective to suspend concessions or other obligations with respect to other sectors under the same agreement, and that the circumstances are serious enough, it may seek to suspend the concessions or other obligations under another covered agreement.
- The level of suspension of concessions or other obligations authorised by the DSB shall be equivalent to the level of the nullification or impairment.
- The DSB shall not authorise suspension of concessions or other obligations if a covered agreement prohibits such suspension.
- The DSB, upon request, shall grant authorisation to suspend concessions or other obligations within 30 days of the expiry of the reasonable period of time unless the DSB decides by consensus to reject the request. However, if the Member concerned objects to the level of suspension proposed, or claims that the principles and procedures to suspend concessions or other obligations have not been followed, the matter shall be referred to arbitration. Concessions or other obligations shall not be suspended during the course of arbitration.
- The arbitrator shall not examine the nature of the concessions or other obligations to be suspended but shall determine whether the level of such suspension is equivalent

to the level of nullification or impairment. The parties shall accept the arbitrator's decision as final and the parties concerned shall not seek a second arbitration.

- The suspension of concessions or other obligations shall be temporary and shall only be applied until such time as the measure found to be inconsistent with a covered agreement has been removed, or the Member that must implement recommendations and rulings provides a solution to the nullification or impairment of benefits, or mutually satisfactory solution is reached. The DSB shall continue to keep under surveillance the implementation of adopted recommendations and rulings, including those cases where compensation has been provided or concessions or other obligations have been suspended but the recommendations to bring a measure into conformity with the covered agreements have not been implemented.
- The dispute settlement provisions of the covered agreements may be invoked in respect of measures affecting their observance taken by regional or local governments or authorities within the territory of a Member.

23. **Article XXIII: Strengthening of the Multilateral System:** When Members seek the redress of a violation of obligations or other nullification or impairment of benefits under the covered agreements or an impediment to the attainment of any objectives of the covered agreements, they shall have recourse to, and abide by, the rules and procedures of this Understanding.
24. **Article XXIV: Special Producers Involving Least Developing Country Members:** At all stages of the determination of the causes of a dispute and of dispute settlement procedures involving a least developed country Member, particular consideration shall be given to the special situation of the least developed country Member. If nullification or impairment is found to result from a measure taken by a least developed country Member, complaining parties shall exercise due restraint in asking for compensation or seeking authorisation to suspend the application of concessions or other obligations.
25. **Article XXV: Arbitration:** The Agreement says:

- Expeditious arbitration within the WTO as an alternative means of dispute settlement can facilitate the solution of certain disputes that concern issues that are clearly defined by both the parties.
- Except as otherwise provided in this Understanding, resort to arbitration shall be subject to mutual agreement of the parties which shall agree on the procedures to be followed. Agreements to resort to arbitration shall be notified to all Members sufficiently in advance of the actual commencement of the arbitration process.
- Other Members may become the party to an arbitration proceeding only upon the agreement of the parties which have agreed to have recourse to arbitration.

26. **Article XXVI:** Where some specific provisions of the Article XXIII of GATT, 1994 are applicable to a covered agreement, a panel or the Appellate Body may only make rulings and recommendations subject to prescribed conditions in the Understanding.
27. **Article XXVII: Responsibilities of the Secretariat:** The Agreement says:

- The Secretariat shall have the responsibility of assisting panels, especially on legal, historical and procedural aspects of the matters dealt with, and of providing secretarial and technical support.

- Secretariat shall make available a qualified legal expert from the WTO technical cooperation services to any developing country Member which so requests. This expert shall assist the developing country Member in a manner ensuring the continued impartiality of the secretariat.
- The Secretariat shall conduct special training courses for interested Members concerning these dispute settlement procedures and practices so as to enable Members' experts to be better informed in this regard.

Part II:
WTO Ministerial Conferences and Negotiations

10

Singapore Ministerial Conference, 1996

Chronology of various Ministerial Conferences of the WTO is given in Table 10.1.

Table 10.1: Ministerial Conferences of the WTO

Ministerial Conference	Place	Date
I	Singapore	December 9-13, 1996
II	Geneva	May 18-20, 1998
III	Seattle	November 30-December 3, 1999
IV	Doha	November 9-13, 2001
V	Cancun	September 10-14, 2003
VI	Hong Kong	December 13-18, 2005
VII	Geneva	November 30-December 2, 2009
VIII	Geneva	December 15-17, 2011
IX	Bali	December 3-6, 2013
X	Nairobi	December 15-19, 2015

10.1 Introduction

The First Ministerial Conference of the WTO was held in Singapore from December 9 to 13, 1996. It took stock of the operations of the rule based multilateral trading system, addressed issues pertaining to implementation and determined future course of actions of the WTO. The conference was attended by 5,000 delegates, including officials from over 150 countries, intergovernmental organisations, non-governmental organisations, and members of the press from around the world. The agenda of the Conference included:

1. Assessment of the implementation of commitments of Members under the WTO Agreements and Decisions;
2. Review of the ongoing negotiations and work programmes;
3. Examination of development in world trade; and
4. Addressing the challenges of an evolving world economy.

In the Conference, reports from 26 different WTO bodies, which were presented to the General Council and approved in November 1996, were formally adopted. The special achievements of the Conference were the completion of the Information Technology Agreement and the adoption of the Comprehensive and Integrated Plan of Action designed to lend further assistance to the least developed countries in assessing and sharing the benefits of the multilateral trading system.

Comprehensive discussions took place on core labour standards, investment and competition policy, and, to a lesser level, government procurement and implementation of agreements on agriculture and textiles. New work groups were established to examine the relationship between trade and the areas of investment, competition policy and government procurement. The Committee on Trade and Environment was established as a permanent body of the WTO. The WTO also signed a cooperative agreement with the IMF which, together with a similar agreement with the World Bank, signalled the beginning of a new relationship between the WTO and its Bretton Woods siblings.

Table 10.2: The Conference Proceedings

Issues Raised/Statements Made	Ministerial Declarations
Core labour standards	Trade and economic growth
Regional trade agreements	Integration of economies
Accessions	Core labour standards
Dispute settlement	Marginalisation
Implementation	Role of the WTO
Developing countries and LDCs	Regional agreements
Textiles and clothing	Accession
Trade and environment	Dispute settlement
ITA and telecommunications	Implementation of the WTO Agreements
Work Programme and built-in agenda	Notifications and legislations
Investment and competition	Developing countries
Government procurement	Least developed countries
Other comments	Textiles and clothing
	Trade and environment
	Services negotiations
	ITA and pharmaceuticals
	Work Programmes and built-in agenda
	Investment and competition
	Transparency in government procurement
	Trade facilitation

10.2 Issues Raised and Statements Made

The main issues raised and statements made by the 129 Ministers from WTO Members and observer States, as well as observer organisations during the Conference are given below.

10.2.1 Core Labour Standards: Almost all Members expressed their opinion on whether the WTO should consider the link between core labour standards and trade. A few countries strongly recommended that the WTO should take up the issue in earnest, many suggested that the task be left to the International Labour Organisation, and some suggested for cooperation between the two bodies.

10.2.2 Regional Trade Agreements: Several Ministers advocated the primacy of the multilateral trading system over regional arrangements, while many emphasised on the benefits of regional trade arrangements. A number of Ministers stated that protectionism, not regional blocs, is the enemy.

The South African Development Community (SADC) described its trade protocol and stated that one of its primary objectives is to boost the economic development, diversification and industrialisation of the region. Papua New Guinea said that free trade arrangement in its region has led to improvement in the standards of living. A number of Ministers noted MERCOSUR's (common market of south) effectiveness as a mechanism to promote trade and growth.

10.2.3 Accession: Several Ministers suggested that the accession process for applicants to the WTO be expedited. Poland supported accession as soon as applicants are willing to accept the terms of WTO membership. Jordan stated that acceding countries are being asked to provide more concessions than what is provided for in the Uruguay Round agreements and this could delay accession.

10.2.4 Dispute Settlement: Many countries admitted the success of the dispute settlement mechanism. Costa Rica stated it provides greater certainty in trade relations. Few countries expressed concern about the mechanism. Jamaica said that it should be kept under review to ensure that procedures are fair and transparent. Togo, along with others, called for special treatment for developing countries using the mechanism.

10.2.5 Implementation: Many countries stressed that implementation of the Uruguay Round agreements should be the top priority of the WTO. Some countries emphasised that the introduction of new issues is premature when implementation of existing agreements is currently inadequate. Many countries outlined national efforts to implement the agreements. Several Members expressed concern regarding the implementation of agricultural agreements.

10.2.6 Developing Countries and Least Developed Countries: A number of countries, both developing and developed, stressed on the importance of integrating developing countries into the multilateral system, and asked for technical assistance to facilitate the process. The Netherlands announced it will contribute US$ 2.5 million for a WTO trust fund to finance technical assistance and economies in transition. Bahrain called for technology transfer and direct investment to enable developing countries to become internationally competitive. Many speakers noted that technical assistance to developing countries, including least developed countries, provided in the Uruguay Round agreement has not been forthcoming.

Many developing countries and a number of European countries supported zero tariffs on goods from least developed countries. Many countries suggested increased market access for least developed countries and endorsed the plan of action.

10.2.7 Textiles and Clothing: Many countries expressed their concern that implementation of the Agreement on Textiles and Clothing has been to the letter of the

Uruguay Round agreement, but not to its spirit. India said it is anxious that the sector no longer be an area for bilateral initiatives. The performance of the Textile Monitoring Body was also a concern for many speakers. They emphasised it should be impartial and transparent.

10.2.8 Trade and Environment: Sweden, the EU and the US said that free trade and environment are mutually reinforcing and necessary to achieve the sustainable development. Norway cautioned that trade does not guarantee environmental protection. Many developing countries expressed concern that environmental measures could lead to protectionism and decreased market access. Nigeria said that poverty is the most significant reason for environmental degradation and trade liberalisation will yield environmental dividends.

Few countries approved the work of the Committee on Trade and Environment (CTE), while others said that the progress on trade and environment so far has been disappointing. Sweden stressed for a guarantee of legal security for multilateral environmental agreements.

10.2.9 ITA and Telecommunications: Many countries expressed support for and stressed the importance of concluding negotiations on the Information Technology Agreement (ITA). Italy said the ITA should be joined by all countries and should concern all non-consumer information technology products. Many Ministers also sought the early completion of an agreement on telecommunications. Singapore emphasised the importance of concluding negotiations on basic telecommunication services and the ITA in safeguarding the credibility of the WTO.

10.2.10 Work Programmes and Built-in Agenda: Numerous countries commented on the built-in agenda which prescribes timeframes for further negotiations and reviews. The UK and Australia supported new multilateral trade negotiations before the end of century. Ghana said many developing countries require more time to adjust to the WTO system before rushing into new negotiations. Turkey supported initiating the negotiations called for in the TRIPS agreement as soon as possible. India expressed concern about adverse effects of the TRIPS agreement, including heavy implementation costs in developing countries.

10.2.11 Investment and Competition: Few countries stressed for the establishment of a multilateral framework on trade and investment within the WTO. Many countries called for further study on trade and investment. Some of them emphasised that the study should be undertaken by UNCTAD in consultation with the WTO. India said that a uniform multilateral establishment would not serve equitable global development. Indonesia said a multilateral framework for investment is outside the competence of the WTO.

Germany said multilateral trade and competition rules should be developed to remove impediments to market access. South African Development Community (SADC) said it is premature to address competition policy at this time. Greece recommended that Members discuss what the rules of competition should achieve in order to consolidate progress already achieved by UNCTAD and the OECD.

10.2.12 Transparency in Government Procurement: Many Ministers commented on the proposal that the WTO consider transparency in government procurement. The US said public confidence in the integrity of government procurement decisions would be enhanced if all WTO countries agreed to basic standards of transparency and due process. India expressed an interest in addressing the subject with the sole aim of achieving a procedural agreement providing for transparency. South African Development Council (SADC) expressed it as premature to take the issue of government procurement. Papua New Guinea said it has its own business culture that it wants to preserve.

10.2.13 Other Comments: A large number of countries recommended that the WTO should avoid overloading its agenda with matters that legitimately belong to other multilateral institutions. South Africa called for cooperation and consultation between WTO, UNCTAD and related organisations and said their failure to cooperate is the primary cause for the failure of multilateral organisations to promote development.

The transparency of the WTO decision-making process was also a concern raised by several countries. China said all issues should be discussed among all Members and opposed the practice of conducting negotiations behind closed doors by small groups and the imposition of their decisions on others.

Many Members noted the need to educate the public about the WTO. Slovenia stated that the WTO needs to develop a deeper public understanding of its role.

10.3 Singapore Ministerial Declaration

The Singapore Ministerial Declaration mentioned that the purpose of the biannual meeting of the WTO is strengthening of the WTO as a forum for negotiations, the continuing liberalisation of trade within a ruled based system, and the multilateral review and assessment of trade policies. The meeting assessed implementation of commitments, reviewed ongoing negotiations and work programme, examined developments in world trade, and addressed the challenges of the evolving world economy.

10.3.1 Trade and Economic Growth: The rise in global trade facilitated by trade liberalisation within the rule based system has created more and better paid jobs in many countries. The Ministers said that the achievements of the WTO during its first two years stood witness to our desire to work together to make the most of the possibilities that the multilateral system provides to promote sustainable growth and development while contributing to a more stable and secure climate in international relations.

10.3.2 Integration of Economies, Opportunities and Challenges: The Members believed that the scope and pace of change in the international economy, including the growth in trade in services and direct investment, and the increasing integration of economies offered unprecedented opportunities for improved growth, job creation, and development. These developments require adjustment by economies and societies. They also pose challenges to the trading system. These challenges need to be addressed.

10.3.3 Core Labour Standards: The Ministers renewed their commitment to the observance of internationally recognised core labour standards. The International Labour

Organisation is the competent body to set and deal with these standards, and needs support for its work in promoting them. The Ministers believed that economic growth and development fostered by increased trade and further trade liberalisation contributed to the promotion of these standards. They rejected the use of labour standards for protectionist purposes, and agreed that the comparative advantage of countries, particularly low wage developing countries, must in no way be put into question. In this regard, they noted that the WTO and ILO Secretariats would continue their existing collaboration.

10.3.4 Marginalisation: The Members committed themselves to address the problem of marginalisation for least developed countries, and the risk of it for certain developing countries. They declared that they would continue to work for greater coherence in international economic policy making and for improved coordination between the WTO and other agencies in providing technical assistance.

10.3.5 Role of WTO: To achieve the goal of sustainable growth and development for common good, the Members envisaged a world where trade flows freely. To this end, they renewed their commitment to:

1. Fair, equitable and more open rule-based system;
2. Progressive liberalisation and elimination of tariff and non-tariff barriers to trade in goods;
3. Progressive liberalisation of trade in services;
4. Rejection of all forms of protectionism;
5. Elimination of discriminatory treatment in international trade relations;
6. Integration of developing and least-developed countries and economies in transition into the multilateral system; and
7. The maximum possible level of transparency.

10.3.6 Regional Agreements: The Ministers noted that trade relations of the WTO members were being increasingly influenced by regional trade agreements, which had expanded vastly in number, scope and coverage. Such initiatives can promote further liberalisation and may assist least developed, developing and transition economies in integrating with the international trading system. In this context, they noted the importance of existing regional arrangements involving developing and least developed countries. The expansion and extent of regional trade agreements make it important to analyse whether the system of WTO's rights and obligations as it relates to regional trade agreements needs to be further clarified. They reaffirmed the primacy of the multilateral trading system, which included a framework for the development of regional trade agreements, and renewed their commitments to ensure that regional trade agreements are complementary to it and consistent with its rules. In this context, they welcomed the establishment and endorsed the work of the new Committee on Regional Trade Agreements. They noted that they should continue to work through progressive liberalisation in the WTO as they were committed in the WTO Agreement and doing so facilitated mutually supportive processes of global and regional trade liberalisation.

10.3.7 Accession: It was important that the 28 applicants negotiating accession contributed to completing the accession process by accepting the WTO rules and by offering meaningful market access commitments. The Ministers decided to work to bring these applicants expeditiously into the WTO system.

10.3.8 Dispute Settlement: The Ministers considered impartial and transparent operation of the Dispute Settlement Body to be of fundamental importance in assuring the resolution of trade disputes, and in fostering the implementation and application of the WTO Agreements. The Dispute Settlement Understanding (DSU), with its predictable procedures, including the possibility of appeal of panel decisions to an Appellate Body and provisions on the implementation of recommendations, had improved member's means of resolving their differences. The Ministers believed that the DSU had worked effectively during its first two years. They also noted the role that several WTO bodies had played in helping to avoid disputes. They renewed their determination to abide by the rules and procedures of the DSU and other WTO agreements in the conduct of trade relations and the settlement of disputes. They were confident that longer experience with the DSU, including the implementation of panel and appellate recommendations, would further enhance the effectiveness and credibility of the dispute settlement system.

10.3.9 Implementation of the WTO Agreements: The Ministers gave high priority to full and effective implementation of the WTO Agreements in a manner consistent with the goal of trade liberalisation. Implementation so far had been generally satisfactory, although some members expressed dissatisfaction with certain aspects. It was clear that further effort in this area was required, as indicated by the relevant WTO bodies in their reports. Implementaticn of the specific commitments scheduled by Members with respect to market access in industrial goods and trade in services appeared to proceed smoothly. With respect to industrial market access, monitoring of implementation was to be enhanced by the timely availability of trade and tariff data. Progress had been made in advancing the WTO reform programme in agriculture, including the implementation of the agreed market access concessions and domestic subsidy and export subsidy commitments.

10.3.10 Notifications and Legislation: Compliance with notification requirements had not been entirely satisfactory. Since the WTO system relies on mutual monitoring as a means to assess implementation, Members who had not submitted notifications in a timely manner, or whose notifications were incomplete, needed to renew their efforts. At the same time, the relevant bodies needed to take appropriate steps to promote full compliance while considering practical proposals for simplifying the notification process.

Where legislation was needed to implement WTO rules, Members were mindful of their obligations to complete their domestic legislative process without delay. Members entitled to transition period were urged to take steps, to ensure timely implementation of obligations as they came into effect. Each Member was required to carefully review all its existing or proposed legislations, programmes and measures to ensure their full compatibility with the WTO obligations, and were required to carefully consider points made during review in the relevant WTO bodies regarding the WTO consistency of legislation, programmes and measures, and make appropriate changes where necessary.

10.3.11 Developing Countries: Ministers expressed the importance of the integration of developing countries in the multilateral trading system for their economic development and for global trade expansion. The Ministers reiterated that the WTO Agreements embodied provisions conferring differential and more favourable treatment for developing countries, including special attention to the particular situation of least developed countries. The Ministers acknowledged the fact that developing country members had undertaken significant new commitments, both substantive and procedural, and recognised the range and complexity of the efforts that they were making to comply with. In order to assist them in these efforts, including those with respect to notification and legislative requirements, the Ministers decided to improve the availability of technical assistance under the agreed guidelines. The Ministers also agreed to recommendations relative to the decision taken at Marrakesh concerning the possible negative effects of the agricultural reform programme on least developed and net food importing developing countries.

10.3.12 Least Developed Countries: The Ministers remained concerned by the problems of the least developed countries and agreed to a Plan of Action, including provision for taking positive measures, for example, duty free access, on an autonomous basis, aimed at improving their overall capacity to respond to the opportunities offered by the trading system as under:

1. Seek out to give operational contents to the Plan of Action, for example, by enhancing conditions for investment and providing predictable and favourable market access conditions for the LDCs' products, to foster the expansion and diversification of their exports to the markets of all developed countries; and in the case of relevant developing countries in the context of the Global System of Trade Preferences; and
2. Organise a meeting with UNCTAD and the International Trade Centre as soon as possible in 1997, with the participation of aid agencies, multilateral financial institutions and least developed countries to foster an integrated approach to assisting these countries in enhancing their trade opportunities.

10.3.13 Textiles and Clothing: The Ministers confirmed their commitment to a full and faithful implementation of the provisions of the Agreement on Textiles and Clothing. They stressed the importance of the integration of textile products, as provided into GATT, 1994 under its strengthened rules and disciplines because of its systematic significance for the rule based, non-discriminatory trading system and its contribution to the increase in export earnings of developing countries. The Ministers attached importance to the implementation of this Agreement to ensure an effective transition to GATT, 1994 by way of integration, which is progressive in nature. The use of safeguard measures in accordance with ATC provisions were required to be as sparing as possible. The Ministers noted concern regarding the use of other trade distortive measures and circumvention. They reiterated the importance of fully implementing the provisions of the ATC relating to small suppliers, new entrants and least developed country members, as well as those relating to cotton producing exporting members. The Ministers recognised the importance of wool products for some developing country members. They reaffirmed that as part of the integration process and with reference to the specific commitments undertaken by the Members, all Members should take such action as may be necessary to abide by GATT, 1994 rules and disciplines to achieve improved market access for textiles and clothing products. The Minister agreed that, keeping in view its quasi-judicial nature, the Textiles Monitoring Body should achieve transparency in providing rationale for its findings and recommendations.

10.3.14 Trade and Environment: The Committee on Trade and Environment has made an important contribution towards fulfilling its Work Programme. The Committee has been examining and would continue to examine, inter alia, the scope of the complementarities among trade liberalisation, economic development and environmental protection. Full implementation of the WTO Agreements would make an important contribution to achieving the objectives of sustainable development. The work of the Committee has underlined the importance of policy coordination at the national level in the area of trade and environment. In this connection, the work of the Committee has been enriched by the participation of environmental as well as trade experts from member governments and the further participation of such experts in the Committee's deliberations would be welcomed. The breadth and complexity of the issues covered by the Committee's Work Programme manifested that further work was needed to be undertaken on all items of its agenda, as contained in its report. The Ministers declared that they intended to build on the work accomplished so far, and therefore, directed the Committee to carry out its work, reporting to the General Council, under its existing terms of reference.

10.3.15 Services Negotiations: The fulfilment of the objectives agreed at Marrakesh for negotiations on the improvement of market access in services—in financial services, movement of natural persons, maritime transport services and basic telecommunications—has proved to be difficult. The results have been below expectations, it has been necessary to prolong negotiations beyond the original deadlines in these areas. The Ministers were determined to obtain a progressively higher level of liberalisation in services on a mutually advantageous basis with appropriate flexibility for individual developing countries, as envisaged in the Agreement, in the continuing negotiations and those scheduled to begin no later than January 1, 2000. In this context, the Ministers looked forward to fulfil MFN agreements based on improved market access commitments and national treatment. The Ministers decided:

1. To achieve a successful conclusion to the negotiations on the basic telecommunications in February 1997; and
2. To resume financial services negotiations in April 1997 with the aim of achieving significantly improved market access commitments with a broader level of participation in the agreed timeframe.

With the same broad objectives in mind, the Ministers also looked forward to a successful conclusion of the negotiations on Maritime Transport Services in the next round of negotiations on services liberalisation.

In professional services, the Ministers targeted completing the work on the accountancy sector by the end of 1997, and to continue to develop multilateral disciplines and guidelines. With respect to GATS rules, the Ministers undertook the necessary work with a view to complete the negotiations on safeguards by the end of 1997. They also noted that more analytical work would be needed on emergency safeguard measures, government procurement in services and subsidies.

10.3.16 ITA and Pharmaceuticals: The Ministers welcomed the initiative taken by a number of WTO Members agreeing on a Declaration on Trade in Information Technology Products. The other states which have separate custom territories and applied to accede to the WTO rules have also agreed to tariff elimination for trade in information technology products on a MFN basis. The Members agreed to add more than 400 tariff-free pharmaceutical products to their lists.

10.3.17 Work Programme and Built-in Agenda: The Ministers endorsed the reports of the various WTO bodies. A major share of the Work Programme stemmed from the WTO Agreements and decisions adopted at Marrakesh. As part of these agreements and decisions, the Ministers agreed to a number of provisions calling for future negotiations on agriculture, services and aspect of TRIPS, or reviews and other work on Anti-dumping, Customs Valuation, Dispute Settlement Understanding, Import Licensing, Pre-shipment Inspection, Rules of Origin, Sanitary and Phytosanitary Measures, Safeguards, Subsidies and Countervailing Measures, Technical Barrier to Trade, Textiles and Clothing, Trade Policy Review Mechanism, Trade-related Aspects of Intellectual Property Rights and Trade related Investment Measures. The Ministers agreed to the process of analysis and exchange of information, where provided for in the conclusions and recommendations of the relevant WTO bodies, on the built-in agenda issues, to allow Members to better understand the issues involved and identify their interests before undertaking the agreed negotiations and reviews. They agreed that:

1. The timeframes established in the Agreements would be respected in each case;
2. The work undertaken should not prejudge the scope of future negotiations where such negotiations are called for; and
3. The work undertaken should not prejudge the nature of the activity agreed upon.

10.3.19 Investment and Competition: With regard to the existing WTO provisions on matters related to investment and competition policy and the built-in agenda in these areas, including under the TRIMs Agreement, and on the understanding that the work undertaken shall not prejudge whether negotiations will be initiated in the future, the Ministers also agreed to:

1. Establish a working group to examine the relationship between trade and investment; and
2. Establish a working group to study issues raised by Members relating to the interaction between trade and competition policy, including anti-competitive practices, in order to identify any areas that may merit further consideration in the WTO framework.

These groups would draw upon each other's work and also draw upon and be without prejudice to the work in UNCTAD and other appropriate intergovernmental forum. As regards UNCTAD, the Ministers welcomed the work underway as provided for in the Midrand Declaration and the contribution it could make to the understanding of the issues. In the conduct of the work of the working groups, the Ministers encouraged cooperation with the above organisations to make the best use of available resources and to ensure that the development dimension is taken fully into account. The General Council was asked to keep the work of each body under review, and to determine after two years how the work of each body should proceed. It was clearly understood that future negotiations, if any, regarding multilateral disciplines in these areas, would take place only after an explicit consensus decision is taken among WTO Members regarding such negotiations.

10.3.20 Transparency in Government Procurement and Trade Facilitation: The Ministers further agreed to:

1. Establish a working group to conduct a study on transparency in government procurement practices, taking into account national policies, and, based on this study, to develop elements for inclusion in an appropriate agreement; and
2. Direct the Council for Trade in Goods to undertake exploratory and analytical work, drawing on the work of other relevant international organisations, on the simplification of trade procedures in order to assess the scope for the WTO rules in this area.

In organising the work groups, careful attention was to be given to minimising the burden on delegations, especially those with more limited resources, and to coordinating meetings with those of relevant UNCTAD bodies. It was decided that the Secretariat's technical cooperation programme would be available to developing and, in particular, least developed country members to facilitate their participation in this work.

10.4 Information Technology Agreement

The Information Technology Agreement was formally approved by 28 Members by the end of the Singapore Ministerial Conference, 1996, representing 85 percent of global trade in information technology products. The basic objective of the Agreement was to improve the standard of living and to expand trade in goods through liberalising trade in information technology products. In addition, the Agreement was supposed to enhance research and development in information technology. To accomplish this, the Members decided to promote autonomous and accelerated elimination of customs duties.

The Members agreed to eliminate all customs duties and other duties of any kind for all products defined in the Agreement at an equal rate beginning in 1997 and concluding in the year 2000. The Agreement has provisions for removal of existing non-tariff barriers and prevention of new ones. The Agreement set a particular time table for the Members to submit, review and make consensus on the products covered, and included specific dates to begin the four stages of actual reduction.

The information technology products covered in the Agreement included capacitors, digital photocopiers, LCD/LED panels, fibre optical cables, computer monitors, and graphic display tubes. Items directly related to consumers included computers, calculators, cash registers, automatic teller machines, pagers, telephones sets, videophones, facsimile machines, microphones, loudspeakers, answering machines, magnetic tapes, and local area network (LAN) and wide area network (WAN) products.

10.5 Comprehensive and Integrated Plan of Action

The General Council approved the draft Plan of Action for the least developed countries in November 1996. The Ministerial Conference adopted this plan in its meeting. The Plan of Action aimed at making national and international efforts to achieve growth in the least developed countries through macroeconomic policies, supply-side measures and improved market access. The Plan of Action included measures pertaining to the WTO Decisions in favour of the least developed countries, as well as in the areas of trade capacity building and market access, and envisaged cooperation between the WTO and other multilateral agencies.

To ensure more effective implementation of the WTO Plan of Action for the least developed country Members, four recommendations were made:

1. Increased efforts to improve the least developed countries' capacity to meet notification obligations;
2. A two year review of the implementation of the measures in the least developed countries;
3. The identification of means, by the WTO bodies, to assist the least developed countries in the implementation of the WTO commitments; and
4. The improved disclosure, by Committee on Trade and Development, of Uruguay Round provisions in favour of the least developed countries.

The Members ensured priority to the least developed countries, in the guidelines for the WTO Technical Cooperation and to build human and institutional capacity. The WTO shall work with other relevant agencies, in particular UNCTAD and the International Trade Centre, to assist in institutional capacity building. On the supply side, attention should be given to export diversification by the least developing countries. The Members should facilitate the implementation of commitments to allow the least developed countries to benefit from new market opportunities deriving from the Uruguay Round.

To allow the market access to the least developing countries, the Members were asked, without any legal binding, to take initiatives on an autonomous basis. The initiatives included: granting duty free access to LDCs exports; using relevant provisions of the ATC to increase market access; extending preferential benefits to LDCs' suppliers and expediting relevant Uruguay Round commitments.

The Plan included that the Secretariat shall provide factual and legal information to assist acceding LDCs in drawing up their memorandum on the Foreign Trade Regime. The WTO shall make efforts to work jointly with other relevant multilateral and regional institutions to induce investment in least developing countries.

10.6 Conclusions

The summary and critical evaluation of the business transactions carried out in the Ministerial Conference has been described below:

10.6.1 Built-in Agenda: The Ministerial Conference mainly focussed on agriculture and textiles. Developing countries brought to notice that the efforts by the US, the EU and others on reducing domestic support and export subsidies did not produce the expected gains for other trading partners. They had effectively avoided liberalisation by using high base year values for export subsidies and by continuing domestic support by various other means. Many Members expressed apprehension about the hollow implementation of the ATC and, in particular, the abuse of safeguard measures and the operation of the Trade Monitoring Body.

10.6.2 Ongoing Work: The Ministerial Conference considered how to proceed on the ongoing works for some time, particularly trade and environment and government procurement. The General Council approved by consensus the Report of Committee on Trade and Environment on November 9, 1996. Thus, there was not much scope for negotiations on this issue at the Ministerial Conference. Many developed country Members expressed their disappointment with the Committee on Trade and Environment's lack of progress in its first two years. In contrast, developing country Members were primarily concerned that environmental measures might be used as guise for protectionism. On the issue, North-South divide was clearly visible. A number of Members expressed dissatisfaction that the CTE had made no significant recommendations for environmental reform in the WTO. The conclusions the CTE had reached seemed to suggest that the environment would remain a peripheral issue in the WTO.

Government procurement was an issue of contention between the US, which has pushed for greater transparency in the process of awarding of government contracts, and the EU and Japan, who resisted such push in the past. The Ministerial Conference established a working group on the government procurement, taking into account national policies.

10.6.3 New Issues: Deliberations were made on new issues, namely labour standards, competition policy and investment. No working group was established on labour standards and the issue was handed over to the ILO as the competent body, to deal with labour standards. The OECD made unsuccessful efforts for the draft of a Multilateral Agreement on Investment. A working group was established to conduct a study on investment. A working group was also established to study on competition policy.

The Information Technology Agreement was hailed by some as the biggest 'tariff busting' success since the conclusion of the Uruguay Round. Some noted that the Agreement was considerable victory for the US. They projected that the US, which represents 50 percent of global information technology market, would garner many of the resulting gains.

Developing countries, who were unhappy with non-implementation of the commitments by others, and other countries, those lacking the capacity to fully implement their commitments, expressed their opinion that the WTO should concentrate on a review of the past two years' progress in the light of the Uruguay Round negotiations. While, other countries, in particular developed countries, pressed for having various new issues to be included in the agenda of the WTO to extend the scope of its competence.

In the Ministerial Conference, the past practice of the GATT was visible, as the process was described by some as an 'expandable bilateral between major players'. The review process was below the expectations, while new issues were added to over burden the agenda of the Organization. Few described the Ministerial Conference as a 'shared disappointment'. While the First Ministerial Conference was dubbed as an 'outstanding success' by politicians, most delegates confided that the meeting had resolved very little and the issues of real contention would be taken up in further negotiations.

Since the inception of the WTO, the developed country Members have been pressurising for the expansion of its agenda. They demanded inclusion of environmental standards, labour standards, investment, competition, trade facilitation and government procurement in the negotiating mandate of the WTO. Developing country Members resisted these demands and insisted for the proper implementation of the commitments made in the Uruguay round before. The labour standards and environmental standards were put off the WTO agenda temporarily. On the other four issues, viz. investment, competition, government procurement and trade facilitation, working Groups were setup on investment, competition and government procurement to conduct study processes without any negotiating mandate, while the Council for Trade in Goods was assigned to conduct analytical work on trade facilitation. These four issues are also known as Singapore Issues.

11

Geneva Ministerial Conference, 1998

11.1 Introduction

The Second Ministerial Conference of the WTO was held from May 18 to 20, 1998 at Geneva. The Members agreed at the Conference to launch comprehensive multilateral trade negotiations in the 2000. Since the Singapore meeting, the multilateral trading system achieved many successes. The negotiations on basic telecommunications and on financial services were concluded. The Information Technology Agreement was implemented. The financial turmoil in Asia also took place during this period. The repercussions of this on current account started taking place. The fear of imposing protection measures was obvious in such a situation. On part of the WTO, it became imperative to resist such pressure and to ensure that the implementation of the Agreements was made.

The Ministerial Conference was convened with two main aims among others. The Conference intended to review the implementation of the commitments made by Members under the WTO Agreements. Since the multilateral trading system was completing 50 years of its operation, the Singapore Ministerial Conference had already planned to commemorate the achievements of the trading system on this occasion. But, the Ministerial Conference ultimately seemed more interested in working on expansion of agenda for the Millennium Round of Trade Negotiations supposed to start in 2000.

11.2 Geneva Ministerial Declaration

The Ministers made some declarations at the Geneva Ministerial Conference as described below:

1. The Second Ministerial Conference of the WTO took place at a special time for the multilateral trading system, when the 50th anniversary of its establishment was being commemorated. The Members commended the system's important contribution over the past half a century to growth, employment and stability by promoting the liberalisation and expansion of trade and providing a framework for the conduct of international trade relations, in accordance with the objectives embodied in the preamble to the General Agreement on Tariffs and Trade and the WTO Agreement.
2. The Ministers underlined the crucial importance of the multilateral rule based trading system. They reaffirmed the commitments and assessments made at Singapore, and they noted that the work under existing agreements and decisions had resulted in significant new steps forward since the last meeting. In particular, they welcomed the successful conclusion of the negotiations on basic telecommunications and financial services and noted the implementation of the Information Technology

Agreement. They renewed commitment to achieve progressive liberalisation of trade in goods and services.

3. The 50th anniversary came at such a time when the economies of a number of WTO Members were facing difficulties caused by disturbances in the financial markets. The Ministers took this opportunity to underline that keeping all markets open must be a key element as a durable solution to these difficulties. With this in mind, they rejected the use of any protectionist measures and agreed to work together in the WTO—as in the IMF and the World Bank—to improve the coherence of international economic policy making with a view to maximising the contribution that an open, rule based trading system can help in fostering stable growth for economies at all levels of development.
4. The Ministers recognised the importance of enhancing public understanding of the benefits of the multilateral trading system in order to build support for it and agreed to work towards this end. In this context, they decided to consider how to improve transparency of the WTO operations. They also decided to continue to improve their efforts towards the objective of sustained economic growth and sustainable development.
5. The Ministers renewed their commitment to ensure that the benefits of the multilateral trading system are expanded as widely as possible. They recognised the need for the system to make its own contribution in response to the particular trade interests and development needs of developing country Members. They welcomed the work already underway in the Committee on Trade and Development for reviewing the application of special provisions in the multilateral trade agreements and related Ministerial Decisions in favour of developing country Members, and in particular the least developed among them. They agreed on the need for effective implementation of these special provisions.
6. The Ministers remained deeply concerned over the marginalisation of least developed countries and certain small economies, and recognised the urgent need to address this issue, which had been compounded by the chronic foreign debt problem faced by many of them. In this context, they welcomed the initiatives taken by the WTO in cooperation with other agencies to implement in an integrated manner the Plan of Action for least developed countries, which was agreed at Singapore, especially through the high level meeting on least developed countries held in Geneva in October 1997. They committed themselves to continue to improve the market access conditions for products exported by the least developed countries on as broad and liberal a basis as possible. They urged the Members to implement the market access commitments that they had undertaken at the high level meeting.
7. They welcomed the WTO Members who had joined since they met at Singapore. They recalled that accession to the WTO requires full respect of the WTO rules and disciplines as well as meaningful market access commitments on the part of acceding candidate.
8. Full and faithful implementation of the WTO Agreements and Ministerial Decisions

is imperative for the credibility of the multilateral trading system and indispensable for maintaining the momentum for expanding global trade, fostering job creation and raising standards of living in all parts of the world. They decided to further pursue their evaluation of the implementation of individual agreements and the realisation of objectives concerned at the Third Ministerial Conference to be held in the US. Such evaluation would cover, inter alia, the problems encountered in implementation and the consequent impact on the trade and development prospects of Members. They reaffirmed their commitment to respect the existing schedules for reviews, negotiations and other work to which they had already agreed.

9. They recalled that the Marrakesh Agreement establishing the WTO stated that the WTO shall provide the forum for negotiations among its members concerning their multilateral trade relations in matters dealt with under the agreements in the Annexes to the Agreements, and that it might also provide a forum for further negotiations among its members concerning their multilateral trade relations, and a framework for the implementation of the results of such negotiations, as might be decided by the Ministerial Conference. In this context, they decided that a process will be established under the direction of the General Council to ensure full and faithful implementation of existing agreements, and to prepare for the Third Session of the Ministerial Conference. This process shall enable the General Council to submit recommendations regarding the WTO's Work Programme, including further liberalisation, sufficiently broad-based to respond to the range of interests and concerns of all Members, within the WTO framework, that would enable the Ministers to take decisions at the Third Session of the Ministerial Conference. In this regard, the General Council was to meet in special session in September 1998 and periodically thereafter to ensure full and timely completion of its work, fully respecting the principle of decision-making by consensus. The General Council's work programme was to encompass the following:

- Recommendations concerning: (a) The issues, including those brought forward by Members, relating to implementation of existing agreements and decisions; (b) The negotiations already mandated at Marrakesh, to ensure that such negotiations begin on schedule; (c) Future work already provided for under other existing agreements and decisions taken at Marrakesh.
- Recommendations concerning other possible future work on the basis of the work programme initiated at Singapore.
- Recommendations on the follow up to the high level meeting on least developed countries.
- Recommendations arising from consideration of other matters proposed and agreed to by Members concerning their multilateral trade relations.

10. The General Council was also asked to submit to the Third Session of the Ministerial Conference, on the basis of consensus, recommendations for decisions concerning the future organisation and management of the work programme arising from the above, including the scope, structure and timeframes, that will ensure that the work

programme is begun and concluded expeditiously.

11. The Ministers said the above work programme shall be aimed at achieving the overall balance of interests of all Members.

11.3 Declaration on Global Electronic Commerce

Recognising that global electronic commerce is growing and creating new opportunities for trade, the Ministerial Conference declared that the General Council shall, by its next meeting in special session, establish a comprehensive work programme to examine all trade related issues relating to global electronic commerce, including those issues identified by Members. The work programme will involve the relevant WTO bodies, take into account the economic, financial, and development needs of developing countries, and recognise that work is also being undertaken in other international forum. The General Council should produce a report on the progress of the work programme and any recommendations for action to be submitted at the Third Ministerial Conference. Without discrimination to the outcome of the work programme or the right and obligations of Members under the WTO Agreements, the Ministerial Conference also declared that Member will continue their practices of not imposing customs duties on electronic transmissions. When reporting to the Third Ministerial Conference, the General Council will review this declaration, the extension of which will be decided by consensus, taking into account the progress of the work programme.

11.4 Multilateral System: 50 Years of Achievements

The 50th anniversary of the multilateral trading system was a time for celebration. It was also a time for manifestation and renewed commitments. Two basic ideas have underpinned the system's success over the last fifty years. First, the belief that an open international trading system, and its role in promoting economic prosperity, is an essential element in international peace and stability—that economic order must be at the foundation of a new political and security framework. Policy makers in 1948 had lived through economic destruction of great depression, when turning inward created a descending spiral of declining output and trade. The architects of the post-War system agreed the only route to economic reconstruction and recovery lay in progress towards open markets and liberalised trade, and the experience of 50 years has proved them right. The second idea is that stability and predictability in international trade relations can only be secured through a mutually agreed system of rules, binding on all member governments and enforceable through dispute settlement. The defence of a rule based system on a day to day basis has been greatly facilitated by the fact that this system gave primacy to markets and not governments in determining economic outcomes. This did not mean that governments abrogated responsibility. On the contrary, they focused on creating the underlying conditions for economic prosperity and on promoting liberalisation, contemplating direct intervention only in specific circumstances where markets were found wanting. The rules were not expected to determine outcomes, but rather to establish the conditions for undistorted completion.

The centrepiece and guided idea of the rules based system is non-discrimination, which arose out of the conviction that exclusionary deals and preferential blocs helped fuel inter-war rivalries, insecurities, and conflicts that drove the international community into another world war. The non-discrimination principle was a key to the system's stability in subsequent years. The non-discrimination principle plays an important economic role as well. Non-discrimination is an efficiency principle, both in the sense of ensuring access to low-cost supplies, and of allowing producers to sell in foreign markets without a policy-imposed disadvantage relative to other suppliers. For both political and economic reasons, the non-discrimination principle has served countries well over the last 50 years, be they large or small, developed or developing.

Solutions to the challenges facing governments today and in future will, as always, call for concerted action on a variety of fronts. In considering how the trading system can contribute to meet these challenges, it is useful to remind of what the system has achieved so far. Four achievements stand out, and provide the foundation upon which to build for future.

First, the GATT/WTO trading system has contributed to an extraordinary period of economic growth and increased prosperity. Trade has expanded faster than output by a significant margin over the last five decades. The significant gains in income growth, job creation and prosperity are in part attributable to the success of the multilateral trading system in lowering trade barriers. Since the creation of the WTO, trade liberalisation efforts have been extended to trade in services, covering both cross-border transactions and the rights of enterprises and to establish a commercial presence through direct investment in foreign markets and the right of natural persons to supply services abroad.

Second, the system has widened the circle of participation in the global market place. While early rounds of multilateral trade negotiations, up to the Dillon Round in 1961, typically involved 20 to 30 countries, the Kennedy Round (1964-67) involved over 60 countries, the Tokyo Round (1973-79) more than 100 countries, and the Uruguay Round (1986-94) had 125 participants. The end of the Cold War reflected and reinforced this geographical extension in participation. The walls between East and West collapsed, in part, because centrally planned systems could not meet the challenges posed by free markets and technological change. Divisions between North and South have blurred, as developing countries have increasingly abandoned inward-looking import substitution in favour of more open trade and freer markets.

Third, the dispute settlement system has demonstrated the willingness of governments to respect the rules. The record in this respect has been impressive. Over the past 50 years, the vast majority of cases brought have been settled, either on a bilateral basis before final multilateral determination, or through acceptance of a panel ruling. Dispute settlement arrangements were significantly strengthened in the Uruguay Round, introducing greater automaticity and clear timeframes into the procedures, eliminating the scope for interested parties to block the adoption of panel findings, and establishing an appeals body. These new arrangements have further strengthened the confidence of the Members in the system. As of mid-March 1998, 119 cases have been presented to the WTO, compared to just over 300 cases throughout the life of the GATT, from 1948 to 1994. Moreover, an increasing number of developing countries are making use of dispute settlement procedures.

Fourth, the multilateral trading system had broadened and deepened its agenda to take account of new realties in international economic relations. From its early focus on tariff reduction, the removal of quantitative import restrictions, and the development of rules on such matters as import licensing, customs valuation, and standards, the rules of the system have increasingly extended to the treatment of foreign persons and companies as well as foreign goods and services. The incorporation of trade in services brought an investment dimension into the system, and rules have been developed for the protection of Trade-related Intellectual Property Rights. New initiatives have been launched to examine the relationship between trade and investment, trade and competition policy and procurement.

This preparedness to enable the system to accommodate changing realities will be continually tested in the years ahead. The processes that combine to produce the phenomenon of globalisation—intensified trade and investment flows, supported by the communications revolution, the rise of the information economy and technological advances in transportation—are changing the world in ways that place a premium upon adaptation and flexibility. The constraints of time and space are diminishing, and new technologies are breaking down old barriers. Unprecedented opportunities are being created, but with these new opportunities go the challenges of ensuring that the benefits from these new developments are widely spread.

11.5 Conclusions

The main aim of the Ministerial Conference was, in addition to the commemoration of the achievements of the multilateral trading system on its golden jubilee, to review the implementation part of the WTO Agreements. But, the Conference concluded emphasising more on the work programme to be prepared by the General Council for the Third Ministerial Conference concerning the subject matter of the Millennium Round.

The Conference mentioned the successful conclusion of telecommunications and financial services negotiations, and the implementation of the Information Technology Agreement as main achievements since the Singapore Ministerial Conference. The Ministers also made a Declaration on Global Electronic Commerce.

The Ministers expressed deep concern over the marginalisation of least developed countries and small economies and felt the urgent need to address this issue. They urged the Members to implement the market access commitments that they had undertaken at the high level meeting on LDCs in Geneva in October 1997 pursuant to the WTO Plan of Action for LDCs.

12

Seattle Ministerial Conference, 1999

12.1 Introduction

The Third Ministerial Conference of the WTO was held from November 30 to December 3, 1999 in Seattle, US, which reviewed the differences between the developed and the developing countries that cropped up in the Singapore Ministerial Conference in 1996. The Ministerial Conference was planned to take up the following agenda:

1. To lay a foundation for major future negotiations on agriculture, services, trade and environment, trade and competition, trade and investment, trade in textiles, and other issues.
2. To review the current trade rules.
3. To set up a work programme to look at other important issues.
4. To provide special deal to help least developed countries.

The WTO Director-General, Mike Moore said before the launch of the meeting: "Much work in Seattle will be dedicated to laying a foundation for future negotiations on agriculture, services, trade and environment, trade and investment, trade and competition and trade in textiles. For many developing countries, a very important issue is the implementation of existing agreements. There are areas where we may reach agreements at this Ministerial Conference, i.e. transparency in government procurement and trade facilitation. I would like to see the Member governments agree to increase the amount of money we spend on technical assistance and training".

The preparation for new negotiations kicked off at Second Ministerial Conference in Geneva in May 1998. Proposals for items to be negotiated were first tabled in March 1999 in the General Council. In September 1999, the General Council started to put various ideas together in draft declaration to be issued in Seattle Ministerial Conference. The proposals covered tariffs, anti-dumping, subsidies, safeguards, investment, trade facilitation, e-commerce, competition, fisheries, transparency in government procurement, technical assistance, capacity building and other developmental issues, intellectual property protection and many other subjects in addition to agriculture and services.

Which of these subjects (apart from agriculture and services) will be included in the negotiations and which in the work programmes, was something that WTO Members had been working out in their discussions in the General Council in Geneva. There were also proposals for the Seattle meeting to produce special deal to help the LDCs gain easier access to richer countries' markets and develop further work on technical assistance to the LDCs. Many country Members suggested a deadline of three years for these new negotiations.

Developing countries wanted to examine how the agreement on anti-dumping, subsidies, and textiles and clothing had been implemented. For developing countries, the

Seattle review was of immense importance, as some of the commitments on the part of the developed countries had not been fulfilled. These countries had accrued the maximum benefits at the cost of developing countries especially in matters pertaining to the Trade-related Intellectual Property Rights Agreement. The large protests took place on the opening day of the Seattle Ministerial Conference against the policies being pursued by the WTO. More than 50,000 people, including farmers, politicians, students, non-governmental organisations, traders and others, participated in these street protests.

12.2 Ongoing Work Report

The WTO issued on November 28, 1999, a Press Back leading to the Seattle Ministerial Conference, to describe the implementation position as by the end of October 1999, in respect of the WTO Agreements. The summary of the main findings is given below.

12.2.1 Built-in Agenda: Many of the records agreed during the Uruguay Round specified future dates for continuing reviews or negotiations for specific sectors or subject areas. The situation in respect of the implementation as by the end of October 1999 is given in Table 12.1.

12.2.2 Developing Countries: On the one hand, developing countries lacked the financial and human resources to fulfil their commitments such as the complex requirements of the Intellectual Property Agreement. On the other hand, they said developed countries have failed to implement the Agreement in a way that would have benefited developing countries' trade. The Special and Differential (S&D) provisions are included in all the WTO Agreements. There are two broad categories:

1. More flexible terms within specified time limits: for example, longer transition periods, smaller commitments (like commitments on agriculture), and
2. Clauses which say in broad terms that developed countries should help developing countries in specific areas (such as technology transfer under intellectual property protection), but without defining exactly what action is needed.

In other words, the provisions had been made both to help developing countries implement the agreements and to accentuate the benefits they might enjoy. However, after five years, developing countries were feeling that these provisions had not served any purpose.

Developing countries were eager to see that the Seattle Ministerial Declaration includes the language to correct oversights in the Uruguay Round texts. In their proposals to the General Council, developing countries had identified several difficulties they faced in implementing the WTO Agreements. Most frequently mentioned were:

1. Many developing countries argued that 5 years is not enough to implement the Agreement on Trade-related Aspects of Intellectual Property Rights. These countries said they should be allowed to apply different degrees of intellectual property protection depending on the level of development. The transition period should be extended.

2. Developing countries said that there is too little time for the Agreement of Trade-related Investment Measures. They would like to retain flexibility to choose investment promotion policies that they consider necessary to fulfil their developmental needs, including some of those listed as inconsistent with GATT. They were unable to notify some of their investment measures in time and they cannot now apply these measures.
3. In respect to Sanitary and Phytosanitary, and Technical Barriers to Trade Agreements, developing countries said they feel they are excluded from the creation of international standards and are often expected to comply with standards that go beyond their technical ability or financial capacity.
4. Developing countries said market access has not met expectations for their exports in two areas, namely agriculture and textiles.

Table 12.1: Built-in Agenda Implementation as by the End of October 1999

Year	Area	Mandate	Outcome
1998	SPS	Review of the operation and implementation of the Agreement by 1998	The report on the review was adopted in March 1999
	TBT	First triennial review of the operation and implementation of the Agreement by 1998	The review was completed in November 1997
	DSU	Full review of the rules and procedures	Legal mandate for review expired on July 31, 1999 without a consensus
1999	Government procurement	Further negotiations starting by 1999	Further negotiations started in December 1998
	Trade policy review	Appraisal of the operation by 2000	
2000	Agriculture	Negotiations for continuing the process of substantial progressive reductions in support and protection starting in 2000	
	Services	New negotiations starting in 2000 to achieve a progressive higher level of liberalisation	
	TRIPS	Review of the implementation of the Agreement after January 1, 2000	
	TRIMs	Review of the operation of the Agreement and discussion on whether provisions on investment and competition be included in the Agreement	
2001	ATC	Mandate review of the implementation by 2001	
2004	ATC	Mandate review of the implementation by 2001	

Several developing countries had submitted specific wish lists to the WTO General Council. These included:

1. Creation of a working group to look at implementation basis.
2. Converting all S&D provisions into concrete commitments.
3. Tighter restrictions on the use of anti-dumping measures.
4. Allowing developing countries more flexibility in applying food, animal and plant health and safety measures to their products.
5. Enabling developing countries to participate more in bodies which set food safety and technical standards.
6. Allowing developing countries more time and greater flexibility to implement the agreements on investment measures and intellectual property.
7. Allowing developing countries greater flexibility to subsidise agriculture.
8. Tighter restrictions on the use of subsidies by developed countries in agriculture.

12.2.3 Least Developed Countries: At Singapore Ministerial Conference in 1996, the Ministers adopted a Comprehensive and Integrated Plan of Action for the LDCs. One result of that initiative was the High Level Meeting for LDCs in Geneva in October 1997. At this meeting, Canada, Egypt, the EU, Mauritius, Switzerland, Turkey and the US provided formal notification of their intention to improve access to their markets for the LDCs' exports. The meeting also led to the creation of an Integrated Framework for Trade Related Technical Assistance for LDCs.

For the first time, the secretariats of the WTO, UNCTAD, the World Bank, the International Monetary Fund, the UNDP and the International Trade Centre, combined forces to begin efforts aimed at bringing the LDCs in from sidelines of the multilateral trading system. The idea of the Integrated Framework was to provide a needs driven, coordinated response to the problems the LDCs have faced in taking full advantage of the global trading system. More than 40 LDCs had submitted needs assessments by the end of October 1999 and six agencies had responded with coordinated responses for action.

While acknowledging that trade and the WTO alone cannot provide all the answers to the deep economic difficulties of the LDCs, the Director-General of the WTO, Mr. Mike Moore said that through closer coherence with other international organisations, including the five partner organisations of the Integrated Framework, the international community can and must make an important contribution to raising living standards of families in the world's poorest countries.

Since his first day in the office on September 1, 1999, Mr. Moore had called on WTO Member governments to do away with tariffs and quotas on the products from the LDCs. "Taken together, LDCs constitute only half of one percent of world trade. Removing barriers to trade from these countries poses no serious threat to anyone, but it does provide some of the poorest people on the earth with the gift of opportunity that is vital to their future growth and development", Mr. Moore said.

12.2.4 Agriculture: In the run up to the Seattle Ministerial Conference and the new negotiations, the following issues were among those that were raised:

A. Reductions: Further reductions in tariffs, domestic support and export subsidy were expected to be the main focus of the negotiations. In addition, some countries said the main objective of the new negotiations should be to bring agriculture trade under the same rules and disciplines as trade in other goods. Some countries, mainly developed countries, rejected the idea for a number of reasons, for example non-trade concerns and multi-functionality.

B. Market Access-Tariff Quotas: Several countries expressed interest in further negotiations to deal with tariff quotas.

C. Market Access-Safeguards: There were proposals for negotiations ranging from continuing with the provision in its current form, to its abolition or its revision to prevent its use on products from developing countries.

D. Domestic Support: A number of countries wanted the 'blue box' subsidies scrapped because the payments are only partly decoupled from production. Others said it is an important tool for supporting and reforming agriculture, and for achieving certain non-trade objectives.

E. Export Subsidies: Some countries proposed the total elimination of export subsidies. Others rejected the idea. In addition, a number of countries insisted to examine the rules to prevent governments getting around their commitments, including use of the state trading enterprises and subsidised export credits.

F. Developing Countries: Most members of the 'Cairn Group', which favoured much greater liberalisation in agriculture trade, were developing countries. But like most WTO Members, the Cairn Group favoured developing countries given the special and differential treatment to take account of their needs. Some countries said that the WTO arrangements should be more flexible so that the developing countries could support and protect their agricultural and rural development and ensure the livelihood of the agrarian population.

G. Decision on Net Food Importing Countries: A number of developing countries which depend on imports for their food supply were concerned about possible rise in world food prices as a result of reduction in richer countries' subsidies.

H. Non-trade Concerns and Multi-functionality: The Agreement on Agriculture contains provisions for important non-trade concerns such as food security, the environment, structural adjustment and so on. Some countries said all the objectives can and should be achieved more effectively through the 'green box' subsidies which are targeted directly at these objectives. Other countries said the non-trade concerns are closely linked to production. They believed subsidies based on, or related to, production are needed for these purposes. Many exporting developing countries said multi-functionality is a form of special and differential treatment for rich countries. Several even agreed that any economic activity, whether industrial, services or like, are multi-functional, and therefore, if the WTO has to address this issue, it has to do so in all areas of the negotiations, not only agriculture.

I. Peace Clause: Article 13 of the Agreement on Agriculture (due restraint) protected countries using subsidies which complied with the Agreement from being challenged under the WTO Agreements. The 'peace clause' was due to expire at the end of 2003. Some countries wanted its extension, while others wanted it to lapse.

J. Fisheries and Forestry: The Agreement on Agriculture does not include fishery and forestry products. Some WTO Members wanted to see specific disciplines negotiated for these products. In particular, these proposals were for dealing with fisheries subsidies and their impact on fish stacks and the environment.

12.2.5 Sanitary and Phytosanitary Measures: Sanitary and Phytosanitary measures deal with food safety and animal and plant health standards. The WTO's Agreement on Sanitary and Phytosanitary Measures does not set the standards. It encourages the Members to use standards set by international organisations. The Members may also set their own standards.

A number of Members—developing countries particularly—expressed their desire to see the working of the Agreement tightened, and some voluntary commitments turned into mandatory. Some countries sought clarification as part of improving the implementation of the SPS Agreement. Many Members said the implementation issues had already been discussed in the SPS Committee during the review of the Agreement's operation and implementation.

A number of developing countries had expressed concern about their lack of resources for implementing the Agreement. These countries called for both technical assistance and more time to comply.

12.2.6 Services: The Ministers at Seattle were expected to launch negotiations to further liberalise international trade in services. At the end of the Uruguay Round, governments agreed to continue negotiations in four areas including telecommunications, maritime transport, movement of natural persons and financial services. GATS talks that resumed after the Uruguay Round were to be started as full round of negotiations latest by 2000. Few details in respect of some services negotiations are given below:

1. Basic Telecommunications: completed by February 1997.
2. Maritime Transport: suspended.
3. Financial Services: completed by late 1997.
4. Movement of Natural Persons: completed by July 1995.

The other issues for future negotiations in services were subsidies, government procurement, safeguards, qualifications, technical standards, and licensing.

12.2.7 Agreement on Trade-related Aspects of Intellectual Property Rights: The Member countries tabled a number of proposals regarding the intellectual property rights:

1. A number of countries proposed extending the higher level of protection, under geographical indications, beyond wines and spirits to other products, including handicrafts, agricultural products and other beverages.
2. Several developing countries were asking for more time in order to deal with the large legislative and administrative burden of complying with the TRIPS Agreement.
3. Some Members proposed strengthening technology transfer provisions in general and tightening obligations for developed countries to produce incentives for their

enterprises and institutions to transfer technology to LDCs.

4. Some Members proposed that the WTO's list of essential drugs be exempted from patentability. Alternatively, they said developing countries should be able to issue compulsory licensing for these drugs (i.e. force the patent holder to license other manufacturers, subject to appropriate conditions such as fees) so that the drugs can be supplied at reasonable prices.
5. Topics for Seattle were ensuring that the TRIPS Agreement responds effectively and neutrally to new technological developments and practices; incorporating new trade related intellectual property treaties adopted outside the WTO; and streamlining administrative aspects such as harmonising some aspects of the way governments process patent applications. Many of these proposals came from developed countries.

12.2.8 Agreement on Textiles and Clothing: A group of exporting developing countries suggested that the Ministers secure liberalisation of the sector by requiring major importers, among other things, to remove half of the existing quotas by the beginning of 2002.

12.2.9 Information Technology Products: In the Committee on Information Technology, participants had agreed to examine non-tariff barriers.

12.2.10 Trade and Environment: The Committee on Trade and Environment submitted a report on the progress on all items of its work programme to the Singapore Ministerial Conference, 1996 and the Geneva Ministerial Conference, 1998. The CTE adopted its report for the work undertaken in 1999 for presentation at the Seattle Ministerial Conference.

12.2.11 Trade and Investment: Since 1997, the WTO Members have been engaged in analysis and debate about the relationship between international trade and investment, and its implications for economic growth and development. In the Working Group on the Relationship between Trade and Investment, Members had examined a range of international investment instruments, existing agreements, and debated the possible pros and cons of negotiating a multilateral framework of investment rules in the WTO. UNCTAD has played an important role in this analytical process, particularly helping WTO delegations better understand the development dimension of this project.

In the preparatory process leading up to the Ministerial Conference, eight separate and very similar proposals were tabled by 29 WTO Members recommending that a decision be taken by the Ministers in Seattle to begin negotiating a WTO agreement on FDI.

These Members made it clear that the agreement they are proposing to negotiate in the WTO bears no relationship to the OECD's Multilateral Agreement on Investment. Their proposals accepted support from a number of other WTO Members, both developed and developing.

At the same time, some other WTO Members, both developed and developing countries, made it clear that they are opposed to a negotiation on this subject in the WTO, at least for the time being. They preferred to continue with the analysis and debate that began in 1997.

12.2.12 Trade Facilitation: The issue of trade facilitation brings the WTO right to the customer's gate. Members from both developing and developed countries had long pointed to the vast amount of red tape that existed in moving goods across borders. Documentation requirements often lack transparency and are vastly duplicated in many places, a problem often compounded by lack of cooperation between traders and official agencies. With the lowering of tariffs across the globe, the cost of complying with the customs formalities has been reported to exceed in many instances from the cost of duty to be paid.

Trade facilitation was added to the WTO agenda at the Singapore Ministerial Conference in 1996 when the Ministers requested the Council for Trade in Goods to undertake a work programme to access the scope for WTO rules concerning the simplification of trade procedures.

While agreeing on the benefits of trade facilitation, a number of other delegations questioned the need for a binding WTO agreement in this area subject to dispute settlement rules. They said that such an agreement will add further to implementation burdens of developing countries, which lack resources to modernise customs facilities. Instead, they have called for a comprehensive technical assistance programme in trade facilitation and encourage ongoing work in this area in various WTO bodies, such as the completion of the harmonisation negotiations in rules of origin, and in other international organisations, such as the World Customs Organisation.

12.2.13 Trade and Competition: The WTO working group on the interaction between trade and completion policy was established at the Singapore Ministerial Conference in December 1996 to consider issues raised by the Members concerning the interaction of these two policy fields. Since its initial meeting in July 1997, the group has examined a wide range of such issues. The work focused on the following main elements:

1. The relationship between the objectives, principles, concepts, scope and instruments of trade and completion policy; and their relationship to development and economic growth.
2. Stock taking and analysis of existing instruments, standards and activities regarding trade and competition policy, including of experience with their application.
3. The interaction between trade and completion policy, including consideration of the following sub-elements:

- The impact of anti-competitive practices of enterprises and associations on international trade;
- The impact of state monopolies, exclusive rights and regulatory policies on competition and international trade;
- The relationship between the trade-related aspects of intellectual property rights and completion policy;
- The relationship between investment and competition policy; and
- The impact of trade policy on competition.

A detailed report on the Group's deliberations on the above matters was issued in December 1998. Pursuant to a decision by the General Council of the WTO, the

Working Group examined in 1999 three further topics:

1. The relevance of the fundamental WTO principles of national treatment, transparency and most-favoured nation treatment to competition policy and vice-versa,
2. Approaches to promoting cooperation and communication among Members, including in the field of technical cooperation, and
3. The contribution of completion policy in achieving the objectives of the WTO, including the promotion of international trade.

While a number of Members expressed support for the development of a multilateral framework on competition policy in the WTO, to support the implementation of effective competition policy by Member countries and reduce the potential conflict in this area, others questioned the desirability of such a framework and favoured bilateral and/or regional approaches to cooperation in this field.

12.2.14 Transparency in Government Procurement: The Ministers at Singapore Ministerial Conference mandated to establish a working group to conduct a study on transparency in government procurement policies, and, based on this study, to develop elements for inclusion in an appropriate agreement. A number of the WTO Members had tabled draft agreements and were engaged in intensive consultations with their WTO partners with a view to preparing an agreement on transparency in government procurement that could be adopted by the Ministers at Seattle.

The Working Group on Transparency in Government Procurement, since its first meeting in May 1997, had met nine times. The Working Group initiated its work by hearing presentations from other intergovernmental organisations which had international instruments and activities relevant to transparency in government procurement, notably the United Nations Commission for International Trade Law (UNCITRAL) and the World Bank. It then considered a WTO comparative study of transparency-related provisions in existing international instruments on government procurement procedures as well as national practices. They covered the procedures under plurilateral WTO Agreements on Government Procurement, the UNCITRAL's model law and the World Bank guidelines, as well as available material on national practices.

The next stage in the work of the Working Group was the systematic study of 12 issues that were identified as important in relation to transparency in government procurement. These were: definition and scope of government procurement, procurement methods, publication of information on national legislation and procedures, information on procurement opportunities, tendering and qualification procedures, time periods, transparency of decisions and qualifications, transparency of decisions on contract awards, domestic review procedures, other matters related to transparency, maintenance of records of proceedings, information technology, language; fight against bribery and corruptions; notifications; WTO dispute settlement procedures and technical cooperation and special and differential treatment for developing countries.

The work had shown a high degree of common thinking on many of the issues referred above.

12.2.15 Trade and Labour Standards: Some of the Members in Europe and North America believed that the issue of labour standards must be taken up by the WTO in some form if public confidence in the WTO and the global trading system is to be strengthened. These Members agreed that rights such as the freedom to bargain collectively, freedom of association, elimination of discrimination in the work place and the elimination of work place abuse are matters for consideration in the WTO. Several Members suggested that the issue be brought into the WTO through the formation of a working group to study the issue of trade and core labour standards. These Members believed that the bringing this matter into the WTO will provide incentives for WTO Members to improve conditions for workers around the world.

Most developing countries and many developed countries believed that the issue of core labour standards did not belong to the WTO. They saw the issue of trade and labour standards as guise for protection in developed markets. Developing countries officials said that the efforts to bring labour standards into the WTO represent a smokescreen for undermining the comparative advantage of lower wage developing countries.

Many officials in developing countries argued that better working conditions and improved labour rights arise through economic growth. They said that if the issue of core labour standards becomes enforceable under WTO rules, any sanctions imposed against countries with lower labour standards would merely perpetuate poverty and delay improvement in workplace standards.

At the first WTO Ministerial Conference in Singapore in December 1996, the issue was taken up. The Ministers stated: "we renew our commitment to the observance of internationally recognised core labour standards. The ILO is the competent body to set and deal with these standards, and we affirm our support for its work in promoting them. We believe that economic growth and development fostered by increased trade and further trade liberalisation contribute to the promotion of these standards. We reject the use of labour standards for protectionist purposes, and agree that the comparative advantage of countries, particularly low wage developing countries, must in no way be put into question. In this regard, we note that the WTO and ILO secretariats will continue their existing collaboration".

12.2.16 Disputes: The Dispute Settlement Body conducted the review of operations of the Dispute Settlement Understanding. The review covered many aspects of the Dispute Settlement Understanding. Among the issues the Members highlighted included the following:

1. The Dispute Settlement Understanding does not spell out clear procedures for handling a possible disagreement on whether the accused government had implemented correctly the Dispute Settlement Body's ruling.
2. Panel and Appellate Body reports are published on the WTO website immediately after distribution to the Member governments. However, panel and appeal deliberations are confidential, and there have been complaints, particularly by the non-governmental organisations that the proceedings of the dispute settlement system lack transparency.

3. Some Members said the WTO system is exclusively intergovernmental in nature. In their view, if a non-governmental organisation wants to make an argument to a panel it should convince one of the governments included in the dispute to present that argument to the panel.
4. The developing countries expressed their concern regarding their shortage of resources for participation in the dispute settlement system. As on October 18, 1999, 183 disputes relating to 142 distinct matters were brought to the WTO.

12.2.17 E-commerce: The growing importance of electronic commerce in global trade led the Members of the WTO to adopt a declaration on global electronic commerce on May 20, 1998 at their second Ministerial Conference in Geneva. The declaration directed the General Council of the WTO to establish a comprehensive work programme to examine all trade related issues arising from e-commerce, and to present a report on the progress of the work programme at the Third Ministerial Conference of the WTO.

The following is a summary of the main points from the report presented to the General Council:

1. WTO Member governments identified three types of transactions on internet:
- Transactions for a service which is completed entirely on the internet, from selection to purchase and delivery.
- Transactions involving 'distribution services' in which a product, whether a service or good, is selected and purchased online but delivered by conventional means.
- Transactions involving the telecommunication transport function, including provision of internet services.
2. The general view of the Members was that the vast majority of transactions on the internet are services which are covered by GATS.
3. The WTO Members held the general view that GATS does not distinguish between technical means of delivery.
4. The general view of Members was that all the provisions of the GATS apply to trade in services through electronic means.
5. There is a disagreement on the classification of a small number of products made available on the internet, as to whether or not they are goods or services.

12.3 Conference Proceedings

The Ministers, on December 1, began negotiating on various sections of the Seattle Ministerial Conference in working groups open to all delegations. They were expected to be engaged in nearly continuous work until the close of the Ministerial Conference on Friday, December 3.

12.3.1 Committee of the Whole: Ambassador Charlene Barshefsky opened the meeting by expressing her regret to the Ministers and officials who were harassed by demonstrating parties yesterday. She said that while she reserved the right to hold Green Room Meetings with smaller number of delegations, she much preferred a more inclusive approach in which all delegations could participate. These working groups, she said, were the best way to do that.

She assured the ministers that even if a working group may agree to a text, no element of the Ministerial Declaration is agreed, until all elements are agreed.

12.3.2 Agricultural Working Group: The Ministers discussed new paragraphs on agriculture for the draft ministerial declaration which was supposed to launch the negotiations in agriculture. The text dealt with:

1. The objectives of the negotiations—whether agricultural products should ultimately be treated the same as industrial products;
2. Provisions for developing countries;
3. Further reduction in subsidies and protection;
4. Multi-functionality (how to deal with non-trade objectives such as environmental protection, food security etc.) and other issues; and
5. A proposed time table for the negotiations.

The discussion broadly took two lines. One group favoured the ultimate goal of complete integration of agricultural trade into the same rules as for other products, total elimination of export subsidies, only providing support for non-trade objectives through policies that do not distort the trade, and substantial increase in market access.

The other group stated that agriculture is different from other sectors and therefore, they rejected the ultimate goal of integrating the agriculture into the same disciplines as other products. They said they could not accept eliminating export subsidies and stressed the need to take specific account of 'multi-functionality'.

The chairman of the working group introduced a new one page draft on agriculture—the result of lengthy consultations through the night. Some 60 countries commented. They largely confirmed their existing positions on key issues, for example:

1. Integrating agriculture into the mainstream of WTO rules.
2. Market access.
3. Domestic support.
4. Non-trade concerns and multi-functionality.
5. Developing countries' issues.

The Chairman said he would try to amend his draft according to the comments, but he warned the Members not to raise their expectations too high.

Ending the meeting, the Chairman said he was walking a tight rope. He was being pulled equally in both directions, he said. The danger was that if he moved one way or another he would fall off the rope. But he observed that the text was only for launching new negotiations. The new round is where the real battle begins. If the round is concluded, it will boost global welfare by tens of billions of Dollars.

12.3.3 Working Group on Implementation and Rules: Many developing countries expressed concern and called for action regarding:

1. Difficulties in the implementation of certain WTO agreements and asked for extension of deadlines in TRIPS, TRIMs and customs valuation; and
2. Imbalance in certain agreements and called for changes in certain provisions of the Anti-Dumping, Subsidies and Textiles Agreements. They supported Seattle action on certain issues and for remaining one to be reviewed after Seattle and completed after one year.

The US said it is working with other 'Quad' members for a meaningful market access for LDCs, and welcomed the EU joining its initiatives on trade capacity building for LDCs. It indicated that it could be flexible regarding TRIMs, Customs Valuation, Agriculture, SPS, Rules of Origin, and on making S&D provisions more operational.

The EU said its initiative for duty free treatment of LDCs export is done, and that it has appealed to the US, Japan and Canada to join in. On rules, it supports negotiations on Anti-Dumping, Subsidies, TBT, State Trading, TRIMs, Regional Trade Agreements, and environmental issues. It has certain degree of flexibility regarding implementation issues.

Japan said abusive use of Anti-Dumping measures should be regarded as disguised form of protectionism that nullifies tariff reduction over night. It said that improvement of the Anti-Dumping Agreement is a lynchpin of the new round, and that many developing countries support this.

Jamaica said that the 71 ACP countries have been marginalised regarding certain WTO issues, it called for turning S&D into hard commitments, the extension of transition periods for TRIMs and Customs Valuation, and increase in funding and human resources for technical cooperation.

A new draft text on implementation was circulated by several delegations, which provided for:

1. Immediate decisions: extension of deadlines for implementation of certain provisions of TRIPS, TRIMs, Customs Valuation Agreement, and providing for greater participation of developing countries in formulating international product standards, and
2. Leaving other implementation issues for consideration by the General Council after Seattle.

The Chairman said he will be consulting with delegations and will draw up a new text. The Chairman presented a new text on implementation issues, which he said was his best effort in bridging the sharp differences in this area. He said that one delegation objected strongly to paragraphs on Anti-Dumping, Subsidies and Textiles, and this delegation has submitted its own proposal. He said that there was a significant gap between this delegation's proposal and the position of most delegations. The new text contains proposed immediate decisions, subjects for negotiations, a new plan of action for the full and effective integration of LDCs in the multilateral trading system and reinforcement of technical cooperation for developing countries, particularly the LDCs as well as small, vulnerable and transition economies.

12.3.4 Working Group on Market Access: The portion of the draft declaration on market access (reduction in import duties, access to services' markets) contained a number of unresolved issues. They included:

1. Coverage and scope of the negotiations whether they should cover all non-agricultural products or whether some could be excluded,
2. Overall objectives of the negotiations,
3. Non-tariff measures affecting access to markets,
4. How the negotiations should be organised, and

5. How to address developing countries' concerns—one proposal is for exports from the LDCs to be given 'bound' zero tariffs in richer countries.

A number of delegations proposed a common approach for tariff reduction, unlike in the Uruguay Round where Members cut tariffs on a 'request-offer' basis. This would be a harmonised approach that would facilitate comparison of tariff reduction proposals. Another position was using the combination of request-offer and harmonisation in the negotiations. The accelerated tariff liberalisation initiative for certain product sectors was also raised.

12.3.5 Working Group on Singapore Agenda and Other Issues: The Ministers discussed two issues: investment and competition policy. A large number of delegations called for negotiations to be launched at this Ministerial Conference. Many other delegations said the issue is not yet ripe, the study and analysis of these issues should continue in the working groups on investment and competition, set up in the Singapore Ministerial Conference in December 1996. In summing up, the Chairman said three points seemed to be clear from the Members intervention:

1. There is wide recognition that the issues of investment and competition are important.
2. Because of the recognised importance of these issues, the Members need to move forward on these issues.
3. This forward movement must be credible and not merely an effort to save face.

On TRIPS, delegations reiterated position on extending protection of geographical indications to other products. On Government Procurement, various positions continued to be maintained. On trade facilitation, many developing countries were still reluctant to negotiate new rules in the areas covered by this topic; the need for enhanced technical cooperation was stressed. On coherence and proposed working groups, some developed countries said working groups should all be put under one umbrella, while many developing countries said there was no problem in establishing many separate groups.

12.3.6 Working Group on Systemic Issues: Issues raised by the Member governments in the discussion concerned:

1. De-restriction of documents,
2. WTO organisational structure to improve transparency and decision-making,
3. Improving information flows, and
4. Enhancing public understanding of and participation in the working of the organisation.

There were four proposals on the table. The US proposal called for establishing more formal channels of communications between the WTO and NGO community and the establishment of an advisory body. A number of delegations questioned the role of NGOs in an intergovernmental organisation.

12.3.7 Working Group on Trade and Labour Standards: This working group was set up to discuss proposals for creating a labour standards working group within the WTO or a body operated jointly by a number of international organisations to look at the issues. Opinions differed, with a number of developing countries opposing the creation of either type of body.

The chairpersons did their utmost to ensure that participants represented a cross section of the Members' positions on the relevant subjects. Progress was reported in a number of areas, but there was too little time left to complete the work of narrowing the gaps, bringing the draft declaration back to the plenary working groups, making any additional changes arising from the working groups and then approving the declaration by consensus. The conference had simply run out of time.

The WTO Director-General, Mike Moore said in a press statement issued on December 8, "I feel particularly disappointed because the postponement of our deliberation means the benefits that would have accrued to developing and least developed countries will now be delayed, while the problems facing these countries will not be allayed. A package of results is within reach".

12.4 Conclusions

The main aim of the Seattle Ministerial conference was to adopt an agenda for the new round of negotiations. But, the differences between developing and developed country Members, as well as differences amongst the developed countries themselves, on certain issues could not be sorted out within the prescribed time frame, and ultimately the Seattle Ministerial Conference failed in making any declaration.

The Seattle Ministerial Conference failed owing to an unbridgeable difference in opinions amongst some important developed countries, especially regarding the removal of trade distortions in agricultural trade, unwillingness by the developed countries to consider the implementation concerns of the developing countries, attempts to force non-trade issues like labour standards and environment into the WTO, non-inclusion of all the Members in the decision-making process and others.

13

Doha Ministerial Conference, 2001

13.1 Introduction

The Fourth Ministerial Conference held in Doha, Qatar in November 2001, provided the mandate for negotiations on a range of subjects and other aspects. The Doha Declaration approved by 142 countries ended on a consensus because all the Members, particularly the US, the EU and Japan, did not want a collapse of the multilateral trading system as it happened in Seattle in 1999. The Doha Declaration listed 21 subjects, most of which were connected with negotiations and other works including implementations, analysis, and monitoring of decisions and agreements.

1. Implementation.
2. Agriculture.
3. Services.
4. Market access (non-agriculture).
5. Intellectual property.
6. Investment.
7. Competition.
8. Transparency in government.
9. Trade facilitation.
10. Anti-dumping.
11. Subsidies.
12. Regional agreements.
13. Dispute settlements.
14. Environment.
15. E-commerce.
16. Small economies.
17. Trade, debt and finance.
18. Trade and technology transfer.
19. Technical cooperation.
20. Least developed countries.
21. Special and differential treatment.

The 10 page declaration adopted at the Ministerial Conference, which formed the basis for the new round of negotiations along with implementation and monitoring work, is known as Doha Development Agenda. The work programme also set up two working groups. One group to examine the relationship between trade, debt and finance for suggesting solutions, within the WTO mandate, to the problem of external indebtedness of developing countries and to strengthen the coherence of international trade and financial policies, with a view to safeguarding the multilateral trading system from the effects of financial and monetary instability. The other working group was set up to examine the relationship between trade and transfer of technology and to facilitate, within the WTO mandate, increased flow of technology to the developing countries. The negotiations under the work programme were to be concluded not later than January 1, 2005. The conduct, conclusion and entry into force of the outcome of negotiations were to be treated as parts of a single undertaking, other than for DSU. The overall conduct of the negotiations was to be supervised by a Trade Negotiation Committee under the authority of the General Council.

The performance of the Indian team, led by Mr. Murasoli Maran, was commended whole heartedly by the trade ministers of the developing countries for sticking to the implementation issues of the Uruguay Round resulting in an extra day of negotiations. India was successful in keeping out four contentious issues including investment, competition, government procurement and trade facilitation till the next conference. A few non-governmental organisations, namely Consumer Unity and Trust Society (CUTS), Federation of Indian Chamber of Commerce and Industry (FICCI), Indian Pharmaceutical Alliance and Indian Sugar Mills Association among others also attended the Conference.

13.2 Ministerial Discussions

The meetings were held to address the issues under six headings: (a) agriculture, (b) implementation, (c) environment, (d) rules issues, (e) Singapore issues and (f) intellectual property and access to medicines/public health.

13.2.1 Agriculture: A number of countries, both developed and developing, complained about the trade practices of rich countries, mostly export subsidies, and called for their elimination. They considered the draft's wording on export subsidies to be too weak.

Some developed countries said the text is too strong in what it says on subsidies, and not strong enough on non-trade concerns such as food security, environmental protection and rural development. They rejected the idea of treating agriculture the same way as industrial products.

13.2.2 Implementation: This subject covers developing countries' concern about difficulties they face in implementing current WTO Agreements. Developing countries widely agreed that the text could be accepted as part of an overall package in Doha, even though the text is not as ambitious as they would have liked. However, two significant concerns were raised. Some major trading countries said they had significant difficulties in accepting textiles provisions included in the text. There was also disagreement among developed countries on the question of extending the transition period during which some developing countries, but not others, were exempt from WTO disciplines on export subsidies.

13.2.3 Environment: Some developed countries calling for negotiations to clarify WTO rules relating to the environment said that the current text was not acceptable because it does not include a firm commitment to start negotiations. There was no consensus on the issue as many developing countries expressed concern about negotiations on trade and environment.

13.2.4 Rules: Anti-dumping and subsidies, including fishing subsidies, were the focus here, with developing countries saying that they wanted to see a reduction in anti-dumping actions against their products and the application of Special and Differential Treatment as regards the rules applied to them.

13.2.5 Singapore Issues: The debate was mainly about whether there should be negotiations on these issues and if so, how they should be handled, including whether they would only involve some Members. Developing countries in South Asia and Africa said they are not ready for negotiations, that negotiations should only take place when there is an explicit consensus, which is not the case right now. They would like to continue the study in the working groups.

13.2.6 Trade-related Intellectual Property Rights: Some Members were asked to redraft the text to bridge the differences that have cropped up among the countries.

Finally, agreement was reached on November 14, 2001 after day and night consultations on remaining differences. The Director-General Mike Moore said: "This Conference has been a remarkable experience for all of us. It has been difficult, because we have been dealing with some of the most sensitive issues in international trade policy, and many governments have had to move towards the position of their partners to make this agreement possible".

The negotiations under the Work Programme were to be concluded not later than January 1, 2005. The only exception was the negotiation on improving and clarifying Dispute Settlement Understanding, which was to be concluded by the end of 2002 or by the next Ministerial Conference.

13.3 Doha Ministerial Declaration

The Doha Declaration—comprising of a main Declaration, a Declaration on TRIPS Agreement and Public Health and a decision on implementation-related issues and concerns—launched the future work programme of the WTO and included elaboration and time tables for the ongoing negotiations in agriculture and services and possible negotiations in a range of other issues. The Ministerial Conference made the Declaration on November 14, 2001. The Ministerial Declaration has been mentioned below:

1. The Ministers recognised that the multilateral trading system embodied in the World Trade Organization has contributed significantly to economic growth, development and employment throughout the past fifty years. They determined, particularly in the light of the global economic slowdown, to maintain the process of reform and liberalization of trade policies, thus ensuring that the system plays its full part in promoting recovery, growth and development. Therefore, they strongly reaffirmed the principles and objectives set out in the Marrakesh Agreement establishing the World Trade Organization, and pledged to reject the use of protectionism.
2. The Ministers acknowledged that international trade can play a major role in the promotion of economic development and the alleviation of poverty. They recognized

the need for all our peoples to benefit from the increased opportunities and welfare gains that the multilateral trading system generates. The majority of WTO Members are developing countries. The Ministers decided to place their needs and interests at the heart of the Work Programme adopted in this Declaration. Recalling the Preamble to the Marrakesh Agreement, they decided to continue to make positive efforts designed to ensure that developing countries, and especially the least developed among them, secure a share in the growth of world trade commensurate with the needs of their economic development. In this context, enhanced market access, balanced rules, and well targeted, sustainably financed technical assistance and capacity-building programmes have important roles to play.

3. The Ministers recognized the particular vulnerability of the least developed countries and the special structural difficulties they faced in the global economy. They expressed the commitment to address the marginalization of least developed countries in international trade and to improve their effective participation in the multilateral trading system. They recalled the commitments made by them at their meetings in Marrakesh, Singapore and Geneva, and by the international community at the Third UN Conference on Least Developed Countries in Brussels, to help least developed countries secure beneficial and meaningful integration into the multilateral trading system and the global economy. The Ministers were determined that the WTO will play its part in building effectively on these commitments under the Work Programme to be established.

4. The Ministers stressed their commitment to the WTO as the unique forum for global trade rule making and liberalization, while also recognizing that regional trade agreements can play an important role in promoting the liberalization and expansion of trade and in fostering development.

5. The Ministers were aware that the challenges Members face in a rapidly changing international environment cannot be addressed through measures taken in the trade field alone. They decided to continue to work with the Bretton Woods institutions for greater coherence in global economic policy making.

6. They strongly reaffirmed their commitment to the objective of sustainable development, as stated in the Preamble to the Marrakesh Agreement. They were convinced that the aims of upholding and safeguarding an open and non-discriminatory multilateral trading system, and acting for the protection of the environment and the promotion of sustainable development can and must be mutually supportive. They took note of the efforts by Members to conduct national environmental assessments of trade policies on a voluntary basis. They recognized that under WTO rules no country should be prevented from taking measures for the protection of human, animal or plant life or health, or of the environment at the levels it considers appropriate, subject to the requirement that they are not applied in a manner which would constitute a means of arbitrary or unjustifiable discrimination between countries where the same conditions prevail, or a disguised restriction on international trade, and are otherwise in accordance with the provisions of the WTO

Agreements. They welcomed the WTO's continued co-operation with UNEP and other intergovernmental environmental organizations. They encouraged efforts to promote co-operation between the WTO and relevant international environmental and developmental organizations, especially in the lead up to the World Summit on Sustainable Development to be held in Johannesburg, South Africa in September 2002.

7. They reaffirmed the right of Members under the General Agreement on Trade in Services to regulate, and to introduce new regulations on, the supply of services.
8. They reaffirmed their declaration made at the Singapore Ministerial Conference regarding internationally recognized core labour standards. They took note of work under way in the International Labour Organization (ILO) on the social dimension of globalization.
9. They noted with particular satisfaction that this Conference had completed the WTO accession procedures for China and Chinese Taipei. They also welcomed the accession as new Members, since their last Session, of Albania, Croatia, Georgia, Jordan, Lithuania, Moldova and Oman, and noted the extensive market access commitments already made by these countries on accession. These accessions will greatly strengthen the multilateral trading system, as will those of the 28 countries now negotiating their accession. They therefore attached great importance to concluding accession proceedings as quickly as possible. In particular, they were committed to accelerating the accession of least developed countries.
10. Recognizing the challenges posed by an expanding WTO membership, the Ministers confirmed their collective responsibility to ensure internal transparency and the effective participation of all Members. While emphasizing the intergovernmental character of the organization, they were committed to making the WTO's operations more transparent, including through more effective and prompt dissemination of information, and to improve dialogue with the public. Therefore, they decided to, at the national and multilateral levels, to continue to promote a better public understanding of the WTO and to communicate the benefits of a liberal, rules-based multilateral trading system.
11. In view of these considerations, the Ministers agreed to undertake the broad and balanced Work Programme set out below. This incorporated both an expanded negotiating agenda and other important decisions and activities necessary to address the challenges facing the multilateral trading system.

Implementation-related Issues and Concerns:

12. The Ministers attached the utmost importance to the implementation-related issues and concerns brought by the Members and were determined to find appropriate solutions to them. In this connection, and having regard to the General Council Decisions of May 3 and December 15, 2000, they further adopted the Decision on Implementation-related Issues and Concerns to address a number of implementation problems faced by Members. The Ministers agreed that negotiations on outstanding implementation issues shall be an integral part of the Work Programme, and that agreements reached at an early stage in these negotiations shall be treated in

accordance with the provisions contained therein. In this regard, the Members shall proceed as follows: (a) where the Members provide a specific negotiating mandate in this Declaration, the relevant implementation issues shall be addressed under that mandate; (b) the other outstanding implementation issues shall be addressed as a matter of priority by the relevant WTO bodies, which shall report to the Trade Negotiations Committee, by the end of 2002 for appropriate action.

Agriculture:

13. The Members recognized the work already undertaken in the negotiations initiated in early 2000 under Article 20 of the Agreement on Agriculture, including the large number of negotiation proposals submitted on behalf of a total of 121 Members. They recalled the long-term objective referred to in the Agreement to establish a fair and market-oriented trading system through a programme of fundamental reforms encompassing strengthened rules and specific commitments on support and protection in order to correct and prevent restrictions and distortions in world agricultural markets. They reconfirmed their commitment to this programme. Building on the work carried out to date and without prejudging the outcome of the negotiations they committed themselves to comprehensive negotiations aimed at: substantial improvements in market access; reductions of, with a view to phasing out, all forms of export subsidies; and substantial reductions in trade-distorting domestic support. The Members agreed that special and differential treatment for developing countries shall be an integral part of all elements of the negotiations and shall be embodied in the Schedules of concessions and commitments and as appropriate in the rules and disciplines to be negotiated, so as to be operationally effective and to enable developing countries to effectively take account of their development needs, including food security and rural development. The Ministers took note of the non-trade concerns reflected in the negotiating proposals submitted by Members and confirmed that non-trade concerns will be taken into account in the negotiations as provided for in the Agreement on Agriculture.
14. Modalities for the further commitments, including provisions for special and differential treatment, shall be established no later than March 31, 2003. Participants shall submit their comprehensive draft Schedules based on these modalities no later than the date of the Fifth Session of the Ministerial Conference. The negotiations, including with respect to rules and disciplines and related legal texts, shall be concluded as part and at the date of conclusion of the negotiating agenda as a whole.

Services:

15. The negotiations on trade in services shall be conducted with a view to promoting the economic growth of all trading partners and the development of developing and least developed countries. The Members recognized the work already undertaken in the negotiations, initiated in January 2000, and the large number of proposals submitted by Members on a wide range of sectors and several horizontal issues, as well as on movement of natural persons. The Members reaffirmed the guidelines and procedures for the Negotiations adopted by the Council for Trade in Services on

March 28, 2001 as the basis for continuing the negotiations, with a view to achieving the objectives of the General Agreement on Trade in Services. Participants were asked to submit initial requests for specific commitments by June 30, 2002 and initial offers by March 31, 2003.

Market Access for Non-Agricultural Products:

16. The Ministers agreed to negotiations which were aimed, by modalities to be agreed, to reduce or as appropriate eliminate tariffs, including the reduction or elimination of tariff peaks, high tariffs, and tariff escalation, as well as non-tariff barriers, in particular on products of export interest to developing countries. Product coverage shall be comprehensive and without *a priori* exclusions. The negotiations shall take fully into account the special needs and interests of developing and least developed country participants, including through less than full reciprocity in reduction commitments, in accordance with the relevant provisions of GATT, 1994. To this end, the modalities to be agreed will include appropriate studies and capacity-building measures to assist least developed countries to participate effectively in the negotiations.

Trade-related Aspects of Intellectual Property Rights:

17. The Ministers stressed on the importance they attached to implementation and interpretation of the Agreement on Trade-Related Aspects of Intellectual Property Rights in a manner supportive of public health, by promoting both access to existing medicines and research and development in new medicines. In this connection, the Ministers adopted a separate Declaration.
18. With a view to completing the work started in the Council for Trade-related Aspects of Intellectual Property Rights (Council for TRIPS) on the implementation of Article 23.4, the Ministers agreed to negotiate the establishment of a multilateral system of notification and registration of geographical indications for wines and spirits by the Fifth Session of the Ministerial Conference. They took note that issues related to the extension of the protection of geographical indications provided for in Article 23 to products other than wines and spirits will be addressed in the Council for TRIPS pursuant to this Declaration.
19. They instructed the Council for TRIPS, in pursuing its work programme including under the review of Article 27.3(b), the review of the implementation of the TRIPS Agreement under Article 71.1 and the work foreseen pursuant to paragraph 12 of this Declaration, to examine, *inter alia*, the relationship between the TRIPS Agreement and the Convention on Biological Diversity, the protection of traditional knowledge and folklore, and other relevant new developments raised by Members pursuant to Article 71.1. In undertaking this work, the TRIPS Council shall be guided by the objectives and principles of the TRIPS Agreement and shall take fully into account the development dimension.

Relationship between Trade and Investment:

20. Recognizing the case for a multilateral framework to secure transparent, stable and predictable conditions for long-term cross-border investment, particularly foreign

direct investment, that will contribute to the expansion of trade, and the need for enhanced technical assistance and capacity-building in this area, the Ministers agreed that negotiations will take place after the Fifth Session of the Ministerial Conference on the basis of a decision to be taken, by explicit consensus, at that Session on modalities of negotiations.

21. The Ministers recognized the needs of developing and least developed countries for enhanced support for technical assistance and capacity building in this area, including policy analysis and development so that they may better evaluate the implications of closer multilateral cooperation for their development policies and objectives, and human and institutional development. To this end, the Members decided to work in cooperation with other relevant intergovernmental organisations, including UNCTAD, and through appropriate regional and bilateral channels, to provide strengthened and adequately resourced assistance to respond to these needs.

22. In the period until the Fifth Session, further work in the Working Group on the Relationship Between Trade and Investment will focus on the clarification of: scope and definition; transparency; non-discrimination; modalities for pre-establishment commitments based on a GATS-type, positive list approach; development provisions; exceptions and balance of payments safeguards; and consultation and the settlement of disputes between Members. Any framework should reflect in a balanced manner the interests of home and host countries, and take due account of the development policies and objectives of host governments as well as their right to regulate in the public interest. The special development, trade and financial needs of developing and least developed countries should be taken into account as an integral part of any framework, which should enable Members to undertake obligations and commitments commensurate with their individual needs and circumstances. Due regard should be paid to other relevant WTO provisions. Account should be taken, as appropriate, of existing bilateral and regional arrangements on investment.

Interaction between Trade and Completion Policy:

23. Recognizing the case for a multilateral framework to enhance the contribution of competition policy to international trade and development, and the need for enhanced technical assistance and capacity building in this area, the Members agreed that negotiations will take place after the Fifth Session of the Ministerial Conference on the basis of a decision to be taken, by explicit consensus, at that Session on modalities of negotiations.

24. Members recognized the needs of developing and least developed countries for enhanced support for technical assistance and capacity building in this area, including policy analysis and development so that they may better evaluate the implications of closer multilateral cooperation for their development policies and objectives, and human and institutional development. To this end, the Members shall work in cooperation with other relevant intergovernmental organisations, including UNCTAD, and through appropriate regional and bilateral channels, to provide strengthened and adequately resourced assistance to respond to these needs.

25. In the period until the Fifth Session, further work in the Working Group on the Interaction between Trade and Competition Policy will focus on the clarification of: core principles, including transparency, non-discrimination and procedural fairness, and provisions on hardcore cartels; modalities for voluntary cooperation; and support for progressive reinforcement of competition institutions in developing countries through capacity building. Full account shall be taken of the needs of developing and least developed country participants and appropriate flexibility provided to address them.

Transparency in Government Procurement:

26. Recognizing the case for a multilateral agreement on transparency in government procurement and the need for enhanced technical assistance and capacity building in this area, the Ministers agreed that negotiations will take place after the Fifth Session of the Ministerial Conference on the basis of a decision to be taken, by explicit consensus, at that Session on modalities of negotiations. These negotiations will build on the progress made in the Working Group on Transparency in Government Procurement by that time and take into account participants' development priorities, especially those of least developed country participants. Negotiations shall be limited to the transparency aspects and therefore will not restrict the scope for countries to give preferences to domestic supplies and suppliers. They committed themselves to ensuring adequate technical assistance and support for capacity building both during the negotiations and after their conclusion.

Trade Facilitation:

27. Recognizing the case for further expediting the movement, release and clearance of goods, including goods in transit, and the need for enhanced technical assistance and capacity building in this area, the Ministers agreed that negotiations will take place after the Fifth Session of the Ministerial Conference on the basis of a decision to be taken, by explicit consensus, at that Session on modalities of negotiations. In the period until the Fifth Session, the Council for Trade in Goods shall review and as appropriate, clarify and improve relevant aspects of Articles V, VIII and X of the GATT, 1994 and identify the trade facilitation needs and priorities of Members, in particular, developing and least developed countries. They committed themselves to ensuring adequate technical assistance and support for capacity building in this area.

WTO Rules:

28. In the light of experience and of the increasing application of these instruments by Members, the Ministers agreed to negotiations aimed at clarifying and improving disciplines under the Agreements on Implementation of Article VI of the GATT, 1994 and on Subsidies and Countervailing Measures, while preserving the basic concepts, principles and effectiveness of these Agreements and their instruments and objectives, and taking into account the needs of developing and least developed participants. In the initial phase of the negotiations, participants will indicate the provisions, including disciplines on trade distorting practices, which they seek to clarify and improve in the subsequent phase. In the context of these negotiations,

participants shall also aim to clarify and improve WTO disciplines on fisheries subsidies, taking into account the importance of this sector for developing countries.

29. The Ministers also agreed to negotiations aimed at clarifying and improving disciplines and procedures under the existing WTO provisions applying to regional trade agreements. The negotiations shall take into account the developmental aspects of regional trade agreements.

Dispute Settlement Understanding:

30. The Ministers agreed to negotiations on improvements and clarifications of the Dispute Settlement Understanding. The negotiations should be based on the work done thus far as well as any additional proposals by Members, and aim to agree on improvements and clarifications not later than May 2003, by which time the Members will take steps to ensure that the results enter into force as soon as possible thereafter.

Trade and Environment:

31. With a view to enhancing the mutual supportiveness of trade and environment, the Ministers agreed to negotiations, without prejudging their outcome, on:

- The relationship between existing WTO rules and specific trade obligations set out in multilateral environmental agreements (MEAs). The negotiations shall be limited in scope to the applicability of such existing WTO rules as among parties to the MEA in question. The negotiations shall not prejudice the WTO rights of any Member that is not a party to the MEA in question.
- Procedures for regular information exchange between MEA Secretariats and the relevant WTO committees, and the criteria for the granting of observer status.
- The reduction or, as appropriate, elimination of tariff and non-tariff barriers to environmental goods and services.

The Ministers noted that fisheries subsidies should form part of the negotiations.

32. The Ministers instructed the Committee on Trade and Environment, in pursuing work on all items on its agenda within its current terms of reference, to give particular attention to:

- The effect of environmental measures on market access, especially in relation to developing countries, in particular the least developed among them, and those situations in which the elimination or reduction of trade restrictions and distortions would benefit trade, the environment and development.
- The relevant provisions of the Agreement on Trade-related Aspects of Intellectual Property Rights.
- Labelling requirements for environmental purposes.

Work on these issues should include the identification of any need to clarify relevant WTO rules. The Committee shall report to the Fifth Session of the Ministerial Conference, and make recommendations, where appropriate, with respect to future action, including the desirability of negotiations. The outcome of this work as well as the negotiations shall be compatible with the open and non-discriminatory nature of the multilateral trading system, shall not add to or diminish the rights and obligations of Members under existing WTO agreements, in particular the Agreement on the Application of Sanitary and Phytosanitary Measures, nor alter the balance of these rights and obligations, and will take into account the needs of developing and least developed countries.

33. The Ministers recognized the importance of technical assistance and capacity building in the field of trade and environment for developing countries, in particular the least developed among them. They also encouraged that expertise and experience be shared with Members wishing to perform environmental reviews at the national level. A report shall be prepared on these activities for the Fifth Session.

Electronic Commerce:

34. The Ministers took note of the work which had been done in the General Council and other relevant bodies since the Ministerial Declaration of May 20, 1998 and agreed to continue the Work Programme on electronic commerce. The work to date demonstrated that electronic commerce created new challenges and opportunities for trade for Members at all stages of development. They recognized the importance of creating and maintaining an environment which is favourable for the future development of electronic commerce. The Ministers instructed the General Council to consider the most appropriate institutional arrangements for handling the Work Programme, and to report on further progress to the Fifth Session of the Ministerial Conference. They declared that Members will maintain their current practice of not imposing customs duties on electronic transmissions until the Fifth Session.

Small Economies:

35. The Ministers agreed to a work programme, under the auspices of the General Council, to examine issues relating to the trade of small economies. The objective of this work was to frame responses to the trade-related issues identified for the fuller integration of small, vulnerable economies into the multilateral trading system, and not to create a sub-category of WTO Members. The General Council had to review the work programme and make recommendations for action to the Fifth Session of the Ministerial Conference.

Trade, Debt and Finance:

36. The Ministers agreed to an examination, in a Working Group under the auspices of the General Council, of the relationship between trade, debt and finance, and of any possible recommendations on steps that might be taken within the mandate and competence of the WTO to enhance the capacity of the multilateral trading system to contribute to a durable solution to the problem of external indebtedness of developing and least developed countries, and to strengthen the coherence of international trade and financial policies, with a view to safeguarding the multilateral trading system from the effects of financial and monetary instability. The General Council shall report to the Fifth Session of the Ministerial Conference on progress in the examination.

Trade and Transfer of Technology:

37. The Ministers agreed to an examination, in a Working Group under the auspices of

the General Council, of the relationship between trade and transfer of technology, and of any possible recommendations on steps that might be taken within the mandate of the WTO to increase flows of technology to developing countries. The General Council shall report to the Fifth Session of the Ministerial Conference on progress in the examination.

Technical Co-operation and Capacity Building:

38. The Ministers confirmed that technical cooperation and capacity building are core elements of the development dimension of the multilateral trading system, and they welcomed and endorsed the New Strategy for WTO Technical Cooperation for Capacity Building, Growth and Integration. They instructed the Secretariat, in coordination with other relevant agencies, to support domestic efforts for mainstreaming trade into national plans for economic development and strategies for poverty reduction. The delivery of WTO technical assistance shall be designed to assist developing and least developed countries and low income countries in transition to adjust to WTO rules and disciplines, implement obligations and exercise the rights of membership, including drawing on the benefits of an open, rules-based multilateral trading system. Priority shall also be accorded to small, vulnerable, and transition economies, as well as to Members and Observers without representation in Geneva. The Ministers reaffirmed their support for the valuable work of the International Trade Centre, which should be enhanced.
39. The Ministers underscored the urgent necessity for the effective coordinated delivery of technical assistance with bilateral donors, in the OECD Development Assistance Committee and relevant international and regional intergovernmental institutions, within a coherent policy framework and time table. In the coordinated delivery of technical assistance, they instructed the Director-General to consult with the relevant agencies, bilateral donors and beneficiaries, to identify ways of enhancing and rationalizing the Integrated Framework for Trade-Related Technical Assistance to Least Developed Countries and the Joint Integrated Technical Assistance Programme (JITAP).
40. The Ministers agreed that there was a need for technical assistance to benefit from secure and predictable funding. They, therefore, instructed the Committee on Budget, Finance and Administration to develop a plan for adoption by the General Council in December 2001 that would ensure long-term funding for WTO technical assistance at an overall level no lower than that of the current year and commensurate with the activities outlined above.
41. The Ministers established firm commitments on technical cooperation and capacity building in various paragraphs in this Ministerial Declaration. They reaffirmed these specific commitments contained in paragraphs 16, 21, 24, 26, 27, 33, 38-40, 42 and 43, and also reaffirmed the understanding in paragraph 2 on the important role of sustainably financed technical assistance and capacity building programmes. They instructed the Director-General to report to the Fifth Session of the Ministerial Conference, with an interim report to the General Council in December 2002 on the

implementation and adequacy of these commitments in the identified paragraphs.

Least Developed Countries:

42. The Ministers acknowledged the seriousness of the concerns expressed by the least developed countries (LDCs) in the Zanzibar Declaration adopted by their Ministers in July 2001. They recognized that the integration of the LDCs into the multilateral trading system requires meaningful market access, support for the diversification of their production and export base, and trade-related technical assistance and capacity building. The Ministers agreed that the meaningful integration of LDCs into the trading system and the global economy will involve efforts by all the WTO Members. They committed themselves to the objective of duty-free, quota-free market access for products originating from LDCs. In this regard, they welcomed the significant market access improvements by WTO Members in advance of the Third UN Conference on LDCs (LDC-III), in Brussels in May 2001. They further committed themselves to consider additional measures for progressive improvements in market access for LDCs. Accession of LDCs remains a priority for the Membership. They agreed to work to facilitate and accelerate negotiations with acceding LDCs. They instructed the Secretariat to reflect the priority they attach to LDCs' accessions in the annual plans for technical assistance. The Ministers reaffirmed the commitments they undertook at LDC-III, and agreed that the WTO should take into account, in designing its work programme for LDCs, the trade-related elements of the Brussels Declaration and Programme of Action, consistent with the WTO's mandate, adopted at LDC-III. They instructed the Sub-Committee for Least Developed Countries to design such a work programme and to report on the agreed work programme to the General Council at its first meeting in 2002.
43. The Ministers endorsed the Integrated Framework for Trade-Related Technical Assistance to Least Developed Countries (IF) as a viable model for LDCs' trade development. They urged development partners to significantly increase contributions to the IF Trust Fund and WTO extra-budgetary trust funds in favour of LDCs. They urged the core agencies, in coordination with development partners, to explore the enhancement of the IF with a view to addressing the supply-side constraints of LDCs and the extension of the model to all LDCs, following the review of the IF and the appraisal of the ongoing Pilot Scheme in selected LDCs. They requested the Director-General, following coordination with heads of the other agencies, to provide an interim report to the General Council in December 2002 and a full report to the Fifth Session of the Ministerial Conference on all issues affecting LDCs.

Special and Differential Treatment:

44. The Ministers reaffirmed that provisions for special and differential treatment are an integral part of the WTO Agreements. They noted the concerns expressed regarding their operation in addressing specific constraints faced by developing countries, particularly least developed countries. In that connection, they also noted that some

Members had proposed a Framework Agreement on Special and Differential Treatment. They, therefore, agreed that all special and differential treatment provisions shall be reviewed with a view to strengthening them and making them more precise, effective and operational. In this connection, they endorsed the work programme on special and differential treatment set out in the Decision on Implementation-Related Issues and Concerns.

Organisation and Management of the Work Programme:

45. The negotiations to be pursued under the terms of this Declaration shall be concluded not later than January 1, 2005. The Fifth Session of the Ministerial Conference will take stock of progress in the negotiations, provide any necessary political guidance, and take decisions as necessary. When the results of the negotiations in all areas are established, a Special Session of the Ministerial Conference will be held to take decisions regarding the adoption and implementation of those results.
46. The overall conduct of the negotiations shall be supervised by a Trade Negotiations Committee under the authority of the General Council. The Trade Negotiations Committee shall hold its first meeting not later than January 31, 2002. It shall establish appropriate negotiating mechanisms as required and supervise the progress of the negotiations.
47. With the exception of the improvements and clarifications of the Dispute Settlement Understanding, the conduct, conclusion and entry into force of the outcome of the negotiations shall be treated as part of a single undertaking. However, agreements reached at an early stage may be implemented on a provisional or a definitive basis. Earlier agreements shall be taken into account in assessing the overall balance of the negotiations.
48. Negotiations shall be open to:

- All Members of the WTO.
- States and separate customs territories currently in the process of accession and those that inform Members, at a regular meeting of the General Council, of their intention to negotiate the terms of their membership and for whom an accession working party is established.

Decisions on the outcomes of the negotiations shall be taken only by WTO Members.

49. The negotiations shall be conducted in a transparent manner among participants, in order to facilitate the effective participation of all. They shall be conducted with a view to ensuring benefits to all participants and in achieving an overall balance in the outcome of the negotiations.
50. The negotiations and the other aspects of the Work Programme shall take fully into account the principle of special and differential treatment for developing and least developed countries embodied in Part IV of the GATT, 1994; the Decision of November 28, 1979 on Differential and More Favourable Treatment, Reciprocity and Fuller Participation of Developing Countries; the Uruguay Round Decision on

Measures in Favour of Least Developed Countries; and all other relevant WTO provisions.

51. The Committee on Trade and Development and the Committee on Trade and Environment shall, within their respective mandates, each act as a forum to identify and debate developmental and environmental aspects of the negotiations, in order to help achieve the objective of having sustainable development appropriately reflected.
52. Those elements of the Work Programme which do not involve negotiations are also accorded a high priority. They shall be pursued under the overall supervision of the General Council, which shall report on progress to the Fifth Session of the Ministerial Conference.

13.4 Declaration on the TRIPS Agreement and Public Health

The Ministers made a Declaration on the TRIPS Agreement and Public Health as mentioned below:

1. The Members documented the gravity of the public health problems afflicting many developing and least developed countries, especially those resulting from HIV/AIDS, tuberculosis, malaria and other epidemics.
2. The Members stressed the need for the WTO Agreement on Trade-related Aspects of Intellectual Property Rights (TRIPS Agreement) to be a part of the wider national and international action to address these problems.
3. The Members acknowledged that intellectual property protection is important for the development of new medicines. They also recognized the concerns about its effects on prices.
4. The Members agreed that the TRIPS Agreement does not and should not prevent Members from taking measures to protect public health. Accordingly, while reiterating their commitment to the TRIPS Agreement, they affirmed that the Agreement can and should be interpreted and implemented in a manner supportive of WTO Members' right to protect public health and, in particular, to promote access to medicines for all. In this connection, they reaffirmed the right of WTO Members to use, to the full, the provisions in the TRIPS Agreement, which provide flexibility for this purpose.
5. Accordingly and in the light of the facts above, while maintaining their commitments in the TRIPS Agreement, the Ministers recognized that these flexibilities include:

- In applying the customary rules of interpretation of public international law, each provision of the TRIPS Agreement shall be read in the light of the object and purpose of the Agreement as expressed, in particular, in its objectives and principles.
- Each Member has the right to grant compulsory licences and the freedom to determine the grounds upon which such licences are granted.
- Each Member has the right to determine what constitutes a national emergency or other circumstances of extreme urgency, it being understood that public health crises, including those relating to HIV/AIDS, tuberculosis, malaria and other epidemics, can represent a national emergency or other circumstances of extreme

urgency.

- The effect of the provisions in the TRIPS Agreement that are relevant to the exhaustion of intellectual property rights is to leave each Member free to establish its own regime for such exhaustion without challenge, subject to the MFN and national treatment provisions of Articles 3 and 4.

6. The Ministers recognized that WTO Members with insufficient or no manufacturing capacities in the pharmaceutical sector could face difficulties in making effective use of compulsory licensing under the TRIPS Agreement. They instructed the Council for TRIPS to find an expeditious solution to this problem and to report to the General Council before the end of 2002.
7. The Ministers reaffirmed the commitment of developed country Members to provide incentives to their enterprises and institutions to promote and encourage technology transfer to least developed country Members pursuant to Article 66. They also agreed that the least developed country Members will not be obliged, with respect to pharmaceutical products, to implement or apply Sections 5 and 7 of Part II of the TRIPS Agreement or to enforce rights provided for under these Sections until January 1, 2016, without prejudice to the right of least developed country Members to seek other extensions of the transition periods as provided for in Article 66 of the TRIPS Agreement. They instructed the Council for TRIPS to take the necessary action to give effect to this pursuant to Article 66 of the TRIPS Agreement.

13.5 Decision on Implementation-Related Issues and Concerns

Giving due consideration to the importance that the Members attach to the increased participation of developing countries in the multilateral trading system, and of the need to ensure that the system responds fully to the needs and interest of all participants, the Ministerial Conference, determined to take concrete action to address issues and concerns that had been raised by many developing country Members regarding the implementation of some WTO Agreements and Decisions, including the difficulties and resource constraints that had been encountered in the implementation of obligations in various areas, took the following decisions:

13.5.1 GATT 1994: Reaffirming the provision of a special and differential treatment for developing countries, the Ministerial Conference directed the Market Access Committee to give further consideration to the issue and make recommendations to the General Council as expeditiously as possible, but in any event not later than the end of 2002.

13.5.2 Agreement on Agriculture:

1. The Ministerial Conference urged Members to exercise restraint in challenging measures notified under the 'green box' by developing countries to promote rural development and adequately address food security concerns.
2. The Ministerial Conference took note of the Report of Committee on Agriculture regarding implementation of the Decision on Measures Concerning the Possible Negative Effects of the Reform Programmes on Least Developing Countries and Net Food Importing Developing Countries, and approved the recommendations

contained in the report regarding: (i) food aid, (ii) technical and financial assistance in the aid programmes to improve agricultural productivity and infrastructure; (iii) financing normal levels of commercial imports of basic food stiffs; and (iv) review of follow up .

13.5.3 Agreement on the Applications of Sanitary and Phytosanitary Measures: The Ministerial Conference decided:

1. Where the appropriate level of sanitary and phytosanitary protection allows for the phased introduction of new sanitary and phytosanitary measures, the phrase "longer time frame for compliance" referred to in Article 10 of the Agreement on the Application of Sanitary and Phytosanitary Measures, shall be understood to mean normally a period of not less than 6 months.
2. The Committee on Sanitary and Phytosanitary Measures was instructed to review the operation and implementation of the Agreement on the Application of Sanitary and Phytosanitary at least once every four years.
3. The Ministers urged the Members to provide, to the extent possible, the financial and technical assistance necessary to enable least developed countries to respond adequately to the introduction of any new sanitary and phytosanitary measures which may have significant negative effects on their trade.
4. The Ministers urged the Members to ensure that technical assistance is provided to LDCs with a view to responding to the special problems faced by them in implementing the Agreement on the Application of Sanitary and Phytosanitary Measures.

13.5.4 Agreement on Textiles and Clothing: The Ministerial Conference reaffirmed the commitment to full and faithful implementation of the Agreement on Textiles and Clothing, and agreed that the provisions of the Agreement relating to the early integration of the products and the elimination of quota restrictions should be effectively utilised.

13.5.5 Agreement on Technical Barriers to Trade: The following decisions were taken:

1. The Ministers confirmed the approach to technical assistance being developed by the Committee on Technical Barriers to Trade, reflecting the triennial review work in this area and also mandated this work to continue.
2. The phrase "reasonable interval" in Article 2 of the Agreement on Technical Barriers to Trade shall be understood to mean normally a period of not less than 6 months, except when this would be ineffective in fulfilling the legitimate objectives pursued.
3. The Ministers urged the Members to provide, to the extent possible, the financial and technical assistance necessary to enable least developed countries to respond adequately to the introduction of any new technical barriers to trade measures which might have significant negative effect on their trade.
4. The Ministers urged the Members to ensure that technical assistance is provided to the LDCs with a view to responding to the special problems faced by them in implementing the Agreement on Technical Barriers to Trade.

13.5.6 Agreement on Trade-Related Investment Measures: The following decisions were taken:

1. The Ministers took note of the actions taken by the Council for Trade in Goods in regard to requests from some developing country Members for the extension of the five year transitional period provided for in Article 5.2 of Agreement on Trade-Related Investment Measures.
2. The Ministers urged the Council for Trade in Goods to consider positively the requests that might be made by the LDCs under Article 5.3 of the Agreement on Trade-Related Investment Measures or Article IX of the WTO agreement, as well as to take into consideration the particular circumstances of the LDCs when setting the terms and conditions including time frames.

13.5.7 Agreement on Implementation of Article VI of the GATT, 1994: The Ministers agreed that investigating authorities shall examine with special care any application for the initiation of an anti-dumping investigation where an investigation of the same product from the same Member resulted in a negative finding within 365 days prior to the filing of the application and that, unless the pre-initiation examination indicates that circumstances have changed, the investigation shall not proceed.

13.5.8 Agreement on Implementation of Article VII of the GATT, 1994: The following decisions were taken:

1. The Ministers took note of the actions taken by the Committee on Customs Valuation in regard to the requests from a number of developing country Members for the extension of the five year transition period provided for in Article 20.1 of Agreement on the Implementation of Article VII of GATT, 1994.
2. The Ministers urged the Council for Trade in Goods to give positive consideration to the requests that might be made by the LDCs under Customs Valuation Agreement or under Article IX of the WTO Agreement, as well as to take into consideration the particular circumstances of LDCs when setting the terms and conditions including time frames.

13.5.9 Agreement on Rules of Origin: The Ministers took note of the report of the Committee on Rules of Origin regarding progress on the harmonisation work programme, and urged the Committee to complete its work by the end of 2001.

13.5.10 Agreement on Subsidy and Countervailing Measures: The Ministers took note of proposal to treat measures implemented by developing countries with a view to achieving legitimate development goals, such as regional growth, technology, research and development funding, production diversification and development and implementation of environmentally sound methods of production as non-actionable subsidies. During the course of negotiations, Members were urged to exercise due restraint with respect to challenging such measures.

13.5.11 Agreement on Trade-related Aspects of Intellectual Property Rights: The Ministers directed the Council for Trade-related Aspects of Intellectual Property Rights to continue its examination of the scope and modalities for complaints of the types provided under Article XXIII of GATT, 1994 and make recommendations to the fifth Session of the Ministerial Conference. It was agreed that, in the mean time, the Members shall not initiate such complaints under Agreement on TRIPS.

13.5.12 Cross-cutting Issues: The Ministers instructed the Committee on Trade and Development:

1. To identify those special and differential treatment provisions that are already mandatory in nature and those that are non-binding in character, to consider the legal and practical implications for developed and developing Members of converting special and differential treatment measures into mandatory provisions, to identify those that Members consider should be made mandatory, and to report to the General Council with clear recommendations for a decision by July 2002.
2. To examine additional ways in which special and differential treatment provisions can be made effective, to consider ways, including improved information flows, in which developing countries, particularly the LDCs, may be assisted to make best use of special and differential treatment provisions and to report to the General Council with clear recommendations for a decision by July 2002.
3. To consider, in the context of the work programme adopted at the Doha Ministerial Conference, how special and differential treatment may be incorporated into the architecture of the WTO rules.

13.6 Procedures for Extensions under Subsidies and Countervailing Measures

The Committee on Subsidies and Countervailing Measures shall follow the procedures given below in respect of the extension of the transition period under Article 27 of Agreement on Subsidies and Countervailing Measures for certain developing countries.

1. Programmes eligible for extension pursuant to procedures mentioned in point 2 below, and for which Members shall therefore grant extension for calendar year 2003 are export subsidy programmes:

- In the form of full or partial exemptions from import duties and internal taxes.
- Which were in existence not later than September 1, 2001.
- Which are provided by developing countries.
- Whose share of world merchandise export trade was not greater than 0.10 percent.
- Whose total gross national income for the year 2000 was below US$ 20 billion.

2. Fulfil the following conditions:

- The Members that maintain such programmes shall initiate consultations with the Committee in respect of an extension for eligible subsidy programmes on the basis of documents submitted to the Committee not later than December 31, 2001.
- The Members seeking the extension shall submit to the Committee on Subsidy and Countervailing Measures an initial notification, not later than February 28, 2002.
- Following the receipt of the notification, the Committee on Subsidy and Countervailing Measures shall consider those notifications.
- The extension granted by the Committee on Subsidy and Countervailing Measures shall be subject to annual review in the form of consultations between the Committee

and the Members receiving the extension.

13.7 Conclusions

Before the Ministerial meeting at Doha, the Indian government adopted the 'implementation before expansion' strategy. A number of other developing countries also supported this move as they felt that the trading system had failed in delivering on its promises to them. However, developed countries managed a consensus on the 'Doha Declaration' leading to the launch of a new round of Negotiations. This new round was termed the 'Doha Round'.

The Doha Declaration recognised the work already undertaken in the negotiations including a large number of proposals submitted by Members on a wide range of sectors and several horizontal issues as well as on the movement of natural persons. The time schedule for initial requests for specific commitments and initial offers were June 30, 2002 and March 31, 2003, respectively.

The mandated negotiations in agriculture started in 2000. India submitted its comprehensive proposals in the areas of Domestic Support, Market Access, Export Competition and Food Security. Indian government paid due consideration to the objectives of protecting India's food and livelihood security concerns by having freedom for taking all policy measures for poverty alleviation, rural development and rural employment as also to create opportunities for expansion of agricultural exports by securing meaningful market access in developed countries.

The mandated negotiations under GATS also commenced in 2000. India submitted a proposal on the movement of natural persons since it was an issue of core interest to India. Under TRIPS, India proposed for greater flexibility and clarity in the interpretation of the Agreement on TRIPS in order to ensure affordable access to essential medicines and life saving drugs, in keeping with the public health concerns of developing countries. Major success was achieved by developing countries in the area of intellectual property and public health. The Ministerial Conference adopted separate declaration on the subject stating that 'the Agreement on TRIPS does not and should not prevent the Members from taking measures to protect public health'. The countries without manufacturing capabilities could grant a compulsory license to a company in some other developing country which possesses the necessary capacity.

The Declaration agreed to negotiations aimed, by modalities to be agreed, to reduce or, as appropriate, to eliminate tariffs, including the reduction or elimination of tariff peaks, high tariffs, and tariff escalation, as well as non-tariff barriers, in particular on exports from developing countries.

The developing countries succeeded in preventing negotiations on labour issues by making arguments that for these issues, the International Labour Organisation is a competent authority. However, the Ministerial Conference could not make consensus on initiating negotiations on trade and environment.

The Special and Differential Treatment provisions were incorporated following the recognition of inherent inequality between developed and developing countries and the special needs and concerns of the developing countries. The Doha Ministerial Conference reaffirmed that Special and Differential Treatment provisions are an integral part of the WTO Agreements and agreed that all Special and Differential Treatment provisions shall be reviewed with a view to strengthening these and making them more precise, effective and operational.

At the Singapore Ministerial Conference, it was decided to merely study the issues: investment, competition, government procurement and trade facilitation, and not to make any negotiations on these. The Matter was raised again at the Doha Ministerial Conference. The developing countries managed successfully, to some extent, to drag the issues further. It was recognised that since there was a need for negotiations in these areas they could begin only after there was 'explicit consensus at the Fifth Ministerial Conference to be held at Cancun on the 'modalities of negotiation'.

The real battle was expected to take place when the negotiation process would start and culminate at the stock taking of the work programme by the Ministerial Conference at Cancun in 2003. The controversy would revolve around implementation, rich countries' subsidy and expansion of agenda, in particular 'Singapore Issues', among others.

14

Cancun Ministerial Conference, 2003

14.1 Introduction

The Fifth Ministerial Conference of the WTO was held at Cancun, Mexico from September 10-14, 2003. The Doha Agenda set a number of tasks to be completed before or at the Fifth Ministerial Conference. A consensus was reached on TRIPS and public health issues on August 30, 2003. However, a number of deadlines were missed, including modalities for agriculture and non-agricultural market access negotiations, reform of the Dispute Settlement Understanding, and recommendations on Special and Differential Treatment. Nor the Members were near to agreement on the multilateral geographical indications register for wine and spirits, due to be completed in Cancun.

The Members failed to make a consensus on a number of important issues—launching negotiations on investment, competition policy, transparency in government procurement, and trade facilitation.

But, the Ministerial Conference ended without consensus. The deadlock was broken in Geneva when the General Council agreed on the 'July package' on August 1, 2004. The deal initiated negotiations in trade facilitation, but not on other 'Singapore Issues'.

14.2 The Press Pack

The briefing notes, issued by the WTO, focused on the situation as it existed by mid of August 2003.

The Members assembled for the first meeting of the Trade Negotiation Committee on January 1, 2002 and agreed on the structure of the negotiations launched at Doha. The TNC established negotiating bodies. The work on Special and Differential Treatment was taken up directly by the General Council in February 2003.

14.2.1 Agriculture: From March 2002 to March 2003, the negotiations went through a "modalities phase". Member governments focused their discussions more on technical work—on detailed possibilities for each of the three main areas of the Agriculture Agreement: export subsidies/competition; market access; and domestic support. Special treatment for developing countries was an integral part of all of these, and non-trade concerns were taken into account.

In February 2003, a first draft of the "modalities" was circulated, followed by a revision in March based on negotiators' comments. The draft focused on bridging differences—the search for the compromises that are necessary for a final agreement.

In the March 31, 2003 negotiations meeting, the day for the "modalities" deadline was missed.

14.2.2 Services: More than 150 proposals had been submitted covering sectors such as professional services, telecommunications, tourism, financial services, distribution services, construction services, energy services, maritime transport, postal/courier services and environmental services. There were also several proposals dealing with the movement of natural persons. There were no proposals on health services. On education services, there were four proposals, all of which dealt with private education services, in particular non-academic education such as language training, vocational courses, corporate training and educational testing services.

Member governments started exchanging initial requests for specific market access commitments from July 2002. In response to these initial requests, the 27 members (counting the EU as one member) had submitted initial offers by June 20, 2003.

The initial offers represented improvements relating to 642 specific commitments, 363 of which were improvements to existing commitments and the remaining 279 were new sector-specific commitments.

The bilateral bargaining was in place as members negotiated to get the best possible market access commitments from each other until the deadline of January 1, 2005.

Negotiation work was going on safeguards, MFN exemptions, automatic liberalization and Special Treatment for LDCs.

14.2.3 Market Access: Non-agricultural Products: By June 2003, the negotiating group had met 10 times. Members had submitted more than 40 papers as a contribution to the debate. These proposals dealt with the "modalities" for the negotiations, covering tariff reductions, how to deal with non-tariff barriers, how to give developing countries special and differential treatment, and the possible effects of the reduction in tariffs on the development policies of some countries and on their fiscal revenues, etc. The "modalities" included the criteria to be used to define environmental goods, since the Doha Declaration included a mandate to negotiate the reduction of tariffs in this particular sector of goods, a subject transferred from the Trade and Environment Committee to this negotiating group.

14.2.4 TRIPS: After almost a year of discussion and negotiation, the TRIPS Council considered a draft on December 16, 2002. The draft received very wide support. But there was no consensus and the issue remained unresolved.

The December 16, 2002 draft took the form of a waiver. It would allow countries that could make drugs to export drugs made under compulsory licensing to countries that could not manufacture them. The waiver would last until the TRIPS Agreement is amended.

Negotiations of geographical indications for wine and spirits were in progress. A number of countries wanted to negotiate extending higher level of protection currently being given to wine and spirits and other products.

14.2.5 Anti-dumping and Subsidies: The Negotiating Group on Rules was established by the Trade Negotiations Committee in February 2003. In the Doha Declaration, "rules" covered three subjects: anti-dumping, subsidies, and regional trade agreements.

A number of Members believed that the Anti-Dumping Agreement should be improved to counter what they considered to be an abuse of the way anti-dumping measures were applied.

The United States emphasized the importance of ensuring that anti-dumping actions, and for that matter, countervailing measures, remain effective in addressing unfair trade. It had proposed a number of improvements and clarifications to the agreement.

While the Regional Trade Agreements Committee had continued its examination of specific agreements, Members decided that the Doha mandate should be fulfilled through a specific negotiating channel. A Rules Negotiating Group was set up in 2002 to clarify and improve disciplines on implementation on dumping, subsidies and countervailing measures, fishery subsidies, and regional trade agreements.

14.2.6 Dispute Settlement: On May 16, 2003, the chairman of the negotiations circulated a draft legal text under his own responsibility. The text contained members' proposals on a number of issues, including: enhancing third-party rights; introducing an interim review and "remand" (referring a case back to a panel) at the appeals stage; clarifying and improving the sequence of procedures at the implementation stage; enhancing compensation; strengthening notification requirements for mutually-agreed solutions; and strengthening special and differential treatment for developing countries at various stages of the proceedings.

At its meeting on July 24, 2003, the General Council agreed to extend the negotiations from May 31, 2003 to May 31, 2004.

14.2.7 Trade and Environment: At Doha, Members agreed to launch negotiations on the linkage between trade and environment. However, these negotiations were circumscribed to four issues:

1. The need to clarify the relationship between existing WTO rules and specific trade obligations set out in multilateral environmental agreements (MEAs),
2. The exchange of information between the WTO and MEA Secretariats,
3. The criteria for granting observer status to other international organizations, and
4. The liberalization of trade in environmental goods and services.

The deadline for these negotiations was January 1, 2005 and they were taking place in "special sessions" of the Trade and Environment Committee.

14.2.8 Electronic Commerce: At the Fourth Ministerial Conference in Doha in 2001, the Ministers agreed to continue the Work Programme as well as to extend the moratorium on customs duties. In the Doha Declaration, they instructed the General Council to report on further progress to the Fifth Ministerial in Cancun in 2003.

After the Doha Ministerial Declaration, the General Council agreed to hold "dedicated" discussions on cross-cutting issues, i.e. issues whose potential relevance may "cut across" different agreements of the multilateral system. So far, there had been five discussions dedicated to electronic commerce, held under the General Council's auspices.

The issues discussed included: classification of the content of certain electronic transmissions; development-related issues; fiscal implications of e-commerce;

relationship (and possible substitution effects) between e-commerce and traditional forms of commerce; imposition of customs duties on electronic transmissions; competition; jurisdiction and applicable law/other legal issues.

14.2.9 Small Economies: Small economies counter specific challenges in their participation in world trade, for example, lack of economies of scale or limited natural resources. Studies demonstrate that a small size is likely to limit an economy's possibilities to diversify local production. This in turn makes it more difficult for small economies to adjust to changes in their trade policy regime.

The Doha Declaration mandated the General Council to examine these problems and to make recommendations to the next Ministerial Conference as to what trade-related measures could improve the integration of small economies.

The discussions focused on a paper presented by a group of small economies (Barbados, Belize, Bolivia, Dominican Republic, Guatemala, Honduras, Mauritius and Sri Lanka). The paper included the following proposals:

1. The liberalization process must preserve the existing margins of preference for products exported by small economies.
2. Small economies must not be required to give reciprocal treatment in return for the preferential treatment that they receive from developed members in the context of regional trading arrangements.
3. Small economies must not be required to make concessions that are inconsistent with their development, financial and trade needs.

There was no definition in the WTO of what a "small economy" is. Some members had argued that a definition was necessary before any commitment was made. Other members did not want to embark on such an exercise.

14.2.10 Trade, Debt and Finance: The Working Group on Trade, Debt and Finance was set up at the Fourth Ministerial Conference in Doha in November 2001. Members had seen financial crisis in Asia and the heavy debt burden borne by many developing countries, and they decided to explore how trade could help.

The primary conviction is that markets should be kept open worldwide in periods of financial crisis. This would ensure that crisis-hit economies can continue to count on exports in order to earn foreign exchange, and to help their incomes to grow. If access to foreign markets is constrained, indebted countries may not be able to earn enough foreign exchange and to service their external debt. They may have to resort to further unsustainable borrowing.

The working group had proposed a more focused list of themes and projects for further work after Cancun:

1. Trade liberalization as source of growth.
2. WTO rules and financial stability.
3. The importance of market access and the reduction of other trade barriers in the Doha Development Agenda's negotiations.
4. Trade and financial markets.
5. Trade financing.

6. Better unity in the design and implementation of trade-related reforms and monitoring.
7. The linkages between external liberalization and internal reforms.
8. External financing, commodity markets and export diversification.

14.2.11 Transfer of Technology: A number of provisions in the WTO agreements submit to the need for technology transfer to take place between developed and developing countries. But it is not clear how it takes place in practice and if specific measures might be taken within the WTO to encourage such flows of technology. WTO Ministers decided in Doha to establish a working group to examine the issue. The working group was asked to report to the General Council which itself had to report to the Cancun Ministerial Conference.

The working group had examined a number of studies by the Secretariat and a number of proposals from the members.

A group of developing countries had suggested focusing on the following points:

1. To examine WTO provisions related to technology transfer with a view to making them operational and meaningful.
2. To look at WTO provisions which have the effect of hindering transfer of technology to developing countries (including intellectual property).
3. To examine restrictive practices adopted by multinational enterprises in the area of technology transfer.
4. To examine the impact of developed countries' tariff peaks (relatively high tariffs) and tariff escalation (higher tariffs on processed products than on raw materials and components) on technology transfer.
5. To examine the difficulties, developing countries face in meeting the standards set by different agreements because they lack the relevant technology.
6. To examine the need for and desirability of internationally agreed disciplines on technology transfer.
7. To examine possible internationally agreed commitments on technology transfer.

Repeatedly, developed countries had emphasized the danger in coercing the private sector into giving away its technology. Developed countries believe that this would reduce the appeal for foreign direct investment.

14.2.12 Technical Co-operation: More than three quarters of the WTO's members are developing countries. Of these, 30 are least developed. Developing countries, and countries in transition from central planning, require technical assistance to adjust to WTO rules and disciplines, implement obligations, and exercise their rights as members —including drawing on the benefits of an open, rules-based multilateral trading system.

When WTO members launched a new round of negotiations in Doha, they acknowledged developing countries' increasing need for technical cooperation in order to allow them to participate fully in the negotiations. At Doha, donors—developed countries and international organizations active in trade issues—pledged to provide the needed support to developing countries.

Since the launch of the Doha Development Agenda in November 2001, activities have increased even more. This reflects developing countries' desire to participate actively in the negotiations.

14.2.13 Least Developed Countries: At the Doha Ministerial Conference in November 2001, Members renewed their commitment to help least developed countries. Concretely, they promised to give duty-free, quota-free market access improvements for products from these countries. They also promised to consider additional measures to improve least developed countries' access to their wealthier markets. And they agreed to make it easier for least developed countries to join the WTO.

On February 12, 2002, the Sub-Committee on Least Developed Countries agreed to a Work Programme in order to implement the commitments of the Doha Declaration.

On market access, members were asked to:

1. Work to identify and examine all market access barriers confronting least developed countries' products.
2. Annually review all market access improvements.
3. Examine possible additional measures to improve market access for least developed countries' products.

On technical assistance, priority was to be given to least developed countries. Members were optimistic to significantly increase their contribution to technical assistance programmes for these countries.

14.2.14 Special and Differential Treatment: In the Doha Declaration, member governments agreed that all special and differential treatment provisions should be reviewed with a view to strengthening them and making them more precise, efficient and operational.

More specifically, the Declaration mandated the Trade and Development Committee to identify which special and differential treatment provisions are mandatory, and to consider the legal and practical implications of turning those that are currently non-binding into mandatory obligations.

A total of 88 proposals on special and differential treatment were made by developing and least developed countries. Most proposals came from the African Group and the group of least developed countries.

14.2.15 Implementation: While significant progress had been made in addressing the implementation issues before the WTO bodies, some difficult issues remained to be resolved. There were 23 issues which were before the Trade Negotiations Committee covering issues including balance of payments, customs valuation, market access, safeguards, technical barriers to trade, trade-related investment measures and trade-related intellectual property. The political sensitivity of many of these matters had made resolving them an often difficult exercise.

14.3 Revised Draft Declaration

The draft of declaration, which could not turn into declaration, was revised twice. However, the lack of consensus led to non adoption of the revised Draft Ministerial Declaration. The main points of the second revised draft have been mentioned below:

The Ministers reaffirmed the Declarations made at Doha and the decisions taken there. They also renewed their determination to conclude the negotiations launched at Doha successfully by the agreed date of January 1, 2005. To accomplish these objectives, the Ministers agreed as follows:

1. **TRIPS and Public Health:** They welcomed the decision on implementation of the Doha Declaration on the TRIPS Agreement and Public Health.
2. **Agriculture Negotiations:** The Ministers reaffirmed the commitment to the mandate on agriculture as of the Doha Ministerial Declaration. They directed the Negotiating Group to conclude its work on establishing modalities and to take the necessary further steps to ensure the conclusion of negotiations by the agreed date.
3. **Non-agricultural Market Access Negotiations:** The Ministers reaffirmed the commitment to the mandate for negotiations on market access for non-agricultural products. They directed the Negotiating Group to conclude its work on establishing modalities and take the necessary further steps to ensure the conclusion of negotiations by the agreed date.
4. **Services Negotiations:** The Ministers committed to intensifying the efforts to bring the negotiations on specific commitments in services to conclusion. They called upon those participants who had not yet submitted their initial offers to do so as soon as possible.
5. **Rules Negotiations:** The Ministers instructed the Negotiating Group on Rules to accelerate its work on anti-dumping and subsidies and countervailing measures, including fisheries subsidies, with a view to shifting its emphasis from identifying issues to seeking solutions. They took note of the progress that had been made in the negotiations on improving transparency in Regional Trade Agreements (RTAs) and encouraged the Group to reach a provisional decision soon on its work on transparency and to accelerate its work on the clarification and improvement of RTA disciplines under the existing WTO provisions, taking into account the developmental aspects of RTAs.
6. **TRIPS Negotiations:** They took note of the progress made in the negotiations on the establishment of a multilateral system of notification and registration of geographical indications for wines and spirits and instructed the Special Session of the Council for TRIPS to continue the work as mandated.
7. **Environmental Negotiations:** The Ministers took note of the progress made by the Special Session of the Committee on Trade and Environment in developing a common understanding of the concepts contained in its mandate of the Doha Ministerial Declaration. They agreed that the Committee on Trade and Environment's Special Session continue to invite to its meetings, in accordance with its current practice, the secretariats of the multilateral environmental agreements (MEAs) invited thus far and of the United Nations Environment Programme (UNEP) and the United Nations Conference on Trade and Development (UNCTAD). This invitation shall be for the duration of the negotiations.
8. **Dispute Settlement Understanding:** They took note of the progress that has been

made in the negotiations on dispute settlement. They renewed the determination to pursue these negotiations with the aim of completing them not later than by May 2004.

9. **Special and Differential Treatment:** The Ministers reaffirmed that provisions for special and differential treatment are an integral part of the WTO Agreements. They recalled the decision in Doha to review special and differential treatment provisions with a view to strengthening and making them more precise, effective and operational.
10. **Implementation:** The Ministers noted that, while some progress had been made under the mandates they gave at Doha concerning implementation-related issues and concerns, a number of the issues and concerns raised in this context remained outstanding.
11. **Investment:** The Ministers noted with appreciation the valuable work that had been carried out in the Working Group on the Relationship between Trade and Investment. They committed to provide strengthened and adequately resourced technical assistance to developing and least-developed countries to respond to their needs for enhanced support in this area. They agreed: (a) to intensify the clarification process, (b) to convene the Working Group in Special Session to elaborate procedural and substantive modalities on the basis of the Doha Declaration, and other elements raised by Members and (c) modalities that will allow negotiations on a multilateral investment framework to start shall be adopted by the General Council.
12. **Competition:** They noted with appreciation the discussions that had taken place in the Working Group on the Interaction between Trade and Competition Policy since the Fourth Ministerial Conference. They decided that further clarification of the issues be undertaken in the Working Group, including consideration of possible modalities.
13. **Transparency in Government Procurement:** Taking note of the work done by the Working Group on Transparency in Government Procurement, they decided to commence negotiations on the basis of the modalities prescribed.
14. **Trade Facilitation:** Taking note of the work done on trade facilitation by the Council for Trade in Goods under the mandate of the Doha Ministerial Declaration, the Ministers decided to commence negotiations on the basis of the modalities prescribed.
15. **Small Economies:** The Ministers reaffirmed the commitment to the Work Programme on Small Economies and urged Members to adopt specific measures that would facilitate the fuller integration of small and vulnerable economies into the multilateral trading system.
16. **Trade, Debt and Finance:** The Ministers took note of the report transmitted by the General Council on progress in the examination of the relationship between trade, debt and finance and agreed that this work shall continue on the basis of the mandate contained in paragraph 36 of the Doha Ministerial Declaration and the progress made in the Working Group to date, including consideration of any possible recommendations on steps that might be taken within the mandate and competence

of the WTO. The General Council shall report further to the next Session of the Ministerial Conference.

17. **Trade and Transfer of Technology:** The Ministers took note of the report transmitted by the General Council on progress in the examination of the relationship between trade and transfer of technology and agreed that this work shall continue on the basis of the mandate contained in the Doha Ministerial Declaration. The General Council shall report further to the next Session of the Ministerial Conference.
18. **Committee on Trade and Environment Report:** The Ministers took note of the report transmitted by the General Council on the work undertaken by the Committee on Trade and Environment pursuant to the Doha Ministerial Declaration. They agreed that this work shall continue on the basis of the progress made thus far and instructed the General Council to report to the next Session of the Ministerial Conference.
19. **TRIPS Non-violation:** The Ministers took note of the work done by the Council for Trade-related Aspects of Intellectual Property Rights pursuant to the Doha Decision on Implementation-Related Issues and Concerns and directed it to continue its examination of the scope and modalities for complaints. It was agreed that, in the meantime, Members will not initiate such complaints under the TRIPS Agreement.
20. **Doha Paragraph 19:** The Ministers took note of the work undertaken by the Council for TRIPS pursuant to paragraph 19 of the Doha Ministerial Declaration and agreed that this work shall continue on the basis of paragraph 19 of the Doha Ministerial Declaration and the progress made in the Council for TRIPS to date. The General Council shall report on its work in this regard to the next Session of the Ministerial Conference.
21. **E-commerce:** The Ministers took note of the reports from the General Council and subsidiary bodies on the Work Programme on Electronic Commerce, and agreed to continue the examination of issues under that ongoing Work Programme, with the current institutional arrangements. They instructed the General Council to report on further progress to the next Session of Ministerial Conference. They declared that Members will maintain their current practice of not imposing customs duties on electronic transmissions until the next Session.
22. **Technical Co-operation:** They welcomed the report by the Director-General on the implementation and adequacy of the commitments on technical cooperation and capacity building made in Doha Ministerial Declaration and requested him to report further to the next Session of Ministerial Conference. They also recognized the successful efforts of the International Trade Centre to involve the business communities of the developing and transition economies in the context of the Doha Development Agenda.
23. **Least Developed Countries:** The Ministers welcomed the report by the Director-General on issues affecting Least Developed Countries (LDCs). They reaffirmed the commitment to effectively integrate LDCs into the multilateral trading system. In this regard, they acknowledged the seriousness of the concerns of the LDCs, as

expressed in the Dhaka and adopted by their Ministers in June 2003. They urged Members to adopt and implement rules of origin so as to facilitate exports from LDCs. In this regard, they appreciated the improved market access measures adopted by several Members.

24. **Sectoral Initiative on Cotton:** The Ministers recognised the importance of cotton for the development of a number of developing countries and understood the need for urgent action to address trade distortions in these markets. Accordingly, they instructed the Chairman of the Trade Negotiations Committee to consult with the Chairpersons of the Negotiating Groups on Agriculture, Non-Agricultural Market Access and Rules to address the impact of the distortions that existed in the trade of cotton, man-made fibres, textiles and clothing to ensure comprehensive consideration of the entirety of the sector.
25. **Commodity Issues:** Taking into account the dependence of many developing countries on a few commodities and the problems created by long-term declines and sharp fluctuations in the prices of these commodities, the Ministers instructed the Committee on Trade and Development, within its mandate, to continue with its work on this issue in cooperation with other relevant international organizations and to report on progress to the General Council before the next Session of the Ministerial Conference.
26. **Coherence:** The Ministers appreciated the efforts that had been made by the Director-General to strengthen the WTO's collaboration with the IMF and the World Bank in the context of the Marrakesh mandate on achieving greater coherence in global economic policy-making.
27. **Accession:** The Ministers took note with particular satisfaction that this Conference completed the accession procedures for Cambodia and Nepal.

14.4 Analysis of the Failure

The Cancun Ministerial Conference was very important because it was scheduled to take stock of the progress made on Doha Development Agenda and to decide on many half finished issues. A draft declaration containing a nine page document and a 20 page annexure on modalities was prepared for the approval of the Trade Ministers. The draft declaration could not be adopted, since there was no consensus on some trade issues. Surprisingly, a consensus could not be reached despite mini conferences of 21 Ministers from developing and developed countries that were held at Tokyo in May, Cairo in June, Montreal in July and Geneva in August 2003 to prepare the ground for Cancun.

The draft declaration contained 25 different issues. Out of these, five were contentious issues, namely agriculture, Trade-related Aspects of Intellectual Property Rights, Singapore issues, services and Special and Differential Treatment.

14.4.1 Agriculture: Agriculture was the most important and complicated issue, and very crucial for the success of the Cancun Ministerial Conference. The negotiations held in Geneva in August led to the production of two interest-conflicting drafts. The first was a proposal from the US and the EU. The second proposal was from a group of developing countries including India, China and Brazil. A Ministerial draft was prepared attempting to bring together the two proposals submitted. But, the Ministerial Draft was more tending in contents towards the proposal submitted by the US and the EU.

The developing countries' proposal contained provisions for market access, reduction in domestic support (blue box), export subsidies and special protection for their agricultural products. The Ministerial Draft recommended a very modest reduction in domestic subsidies in rich countries, little reduction in export subsidies and little bit opening of rich country markets. It also suggested special protection for small number of products of developing countries.

There was no decision on the modalities. The original date for a decision on the modalities was March 31, 2003. The deadline was missed and it was decided to negotiate the modalities or the actual formulae to be used in each area later on. Now, the agreement was likely just on the framework. This laid the foundation for the failure of negotiations at Cancun. Finally, the Cancun Ministerial Conference could not reach any framework agreement, and ended in a debacle.

14.4.2 Trade-related Aspects of Intellectual Property Rights and Public Health: In the Doha Ministerial Conference, a separate Ministerial Declaration was made for TRIPS Agreement and Public Health. The Declaration on Public Health was supposed to go a long way in addressing the concerns of the developing countries in respect of public health. First, it acknowledged the enormity of the public health problems resulting from AIDS/HIV, tuberculosis, malaria, and other epidemics in poor countries. Second, it emphasised for more national and international actions to solve these problems and TRIPS to be included in these programmes. Third, while acknowledging that protection of intellectual property is imperative for the development of new medicine, the Ministers agreed that the Agreement on TRIPS does not and should not prevent members from taking measures to protect public health.

The main demand of the developing countries was concerned with the inclusion of public health aspects in Agreement on TRIPS. The Ministers affirmed, keeping this consideration in mind, that the Agreement can and should be interpreted and applied in a manner supportive of the Members' right to protect public health and in particular the right of each Member 'to grant compulsory licenses and the freedom to determine the grounds on which such licenses are granted like the national emergency'.

The Ministers asked the Council for TRIPS to find an early solution to the problem of the Members with insufficient or no manufacturing capacity in the pharmaceutical sector while making effective use of compulsory licensing. The least developing countries are to implement the TRIPS Agreement by January 2016.

In August 2003, a deal on this issue was worked out by India, Brazil, South Africa and Kenya. Developed countries also ended their opposition and agreed to the deal. Developing countries with acknowledged capability to produce generic drugs would be able to export them to other poor countries with no such capability to deal with health emergencies, while agreeing not to take advantage of the arrangements to increase the export of such drugs to nations that are not poor and do not have medical emergency.

The Council for TRIPS agreed to the deal. On part of developing countries, there was a mixed reaction (Table 14.1).

Table 14.1: Deadlines for Negotiations

Negotiation	Date
Agreement on Agriculture Modalities	March 31, 2003
Agreement on Safeguards (Services)	March 31, 2004
Agreement on Market Access Modalities (Non-agricultural products)	March 31, 2003
Solution on compulsory licensing and lack of pharmaceutical production capacity	End of 2002
Action on outstanding implementation issues (TRIPS)	End of 2002
Negotiations on geographical indications registration system	September 14, 2003
Negotiations on trade and environment	January 1, 2005

14.4.3 Singapore Issues: The developing countries opposed the proposals to launch negotiations on the Singapore issues: trade and investment, domestic competition policy, transparency in government procurement and trade facilitation. The Ministerial draft provided two options to the Members. First, all the four issues should be studied further by the working groups or committees concerned and no negotiations could begin immediately. Second, the negotiations should begin as per the suggested framework for talks. The draft suggested the precise modalities for negotiations under the second option. The second option was similar to the one proposed by the EU. The US was even content to start negotiations on transparency in government procurement and trade facilitation.

Developing countries strongly protested against the starting of negotiations. These countries suggested a set of modalities which provided the basis for future discussion, not negotiations.

14.4.4 Services: The work was going on for expansion, MFN treatment, automatic liberalisation, safeguards, movement of natural persons and Special and Differential Treatment for developing countries. The Doha Development Agenda was a good opportunity to pursue liberalisation vital to the interest of developing countries. Negotiations on movement of natural persons were vital to the interest of India. Developing countries insisted on non-reciprocity and Special and Differential Treatment for developing countries. However, the US, the EU and Japan remained stuck to their known ground resulting in the failure of the Cancun Ministerial Conference.

14.4.5 Special and Differential Treatment: The Doha Development Agenda asked the Members to make mandatory the existing clauses that favoured the developing countries. The Ministerial draft incorporated some areas where an agreement could be reached at the Cancun Ministerial Conference. The US and the EU made special efforts to make provisions for Special Differential Treatment to developing and the least developed countries.

The Cancun Ministerial Conference failed because there was no consensus on some important issues as mentioned below.

A. Agricultural Subsidies: The developing countries demanded that developed countries should cut more than US$ 300 billion annual subsidies they provide to their agriculture sector. They argued that such an act motivated to produce unwanted produce which was then discarded in the world markets. But, the EU refused to go forward at accepting a date for eliminating the export subsidies. It agreed only to limit the most trade distorting domestic payments, a concession that would have allowed the developed countries to continue other payments unchecked. It implied that dumping would continue and developing countries would have to compete with heavily subsidised produce from these countries.

B. Market Access: The developed countries looked for access to the markets of developing countries for their industrial goods. Developing countries sought the implementation of the commitments favouring them. They said the Doha Ministerial Conference made several concessions to the developing countries and inaugurated it as 'Doha Development Agenda', rather than as 'Trade Round'. But, nothing happened on these issues. The deadlines for negotiations in the area of agriculture, patents and public health, and Special and Differential Treatment for the developing countries have been missed. At Doha, the Director-General announced that a consensus has been developed on developing countries' case. The WTO listed 40 areas where immediate delivery was promised. Nothing happened on that matter.

C. Singapore Issues: The developing countries opposed the negotiations on trade and investment, trade and competition policy, transparency in government procurement and trade facilitation. They had genuine fear that these issues could bind them to set rules for foreign multinationals.

D. Industrial Tariffs: The developed countries demanded lower tariffs to the exports of industrial goods. The proposed tariff reduction formulae would have forced developing countries to make deeper cuts than the developed countries. The developing countries were not in favour of this. Thus, the Cancun failure spared the developing countries from the negative effect of this premature trade liberalisation on domestic industries.

E. Cotton: Four West African countries—Burkina Faso, Mali, Chad and Benin—demanded that the US cut its massive subsidy to cotton farmers, which was more than the value of their combined harvest. But, the negotiations produced only vague promise of further consultations, with no mention of any deadline for elimination of export subsidies and on commitment of any compensation for West African Producers, who were still suffering from existence of these subsidies.

Cotton was a glaring example of how the developed countries' subsidies could affect the poor countries. In Africa, poor farmers do make their living by growing cotton on their meagre holdings.

These factors were mainly responsible for the failure of the Cancun Ministerial Conference.

14.5 Conclusions

The main agenda of the Cancun Conference was to review the Doha Development Agenda and to develop consensus among the Members for negotiations on the remaining areas, like competition policy, foreign direct investment, transparency in government procurement and trade facilitation. Several deadlines either for negotiations or agreements on modalities had been missed. Barring TRIPS and public health, no consensus could be made on agriculture, market access, geographical indications, services and Singapore issues. Several mini conferences and informal meetings took place before the Cancun Ministerial Conference, but very little success was achieved.

Failure of the Conference was visible in mini conferences and informal meetings. In August 2003, it was decided to form agriculture modalities later on and go ahead on the framework agreement at the Cancun Conference. There was no breakthrough on the Singapore Issues. The rift started on agricultural subsidies. The EU hesitated on committing on any date for phasing out subsidies in the agriculture sector. When developed countries raised the issue of market access for non-agricultural goods, the developing countries made counter attack by complaining about no fulfilment of Special and Differential Treatment commitments by developed countries. Developed countries demanded negotiations on Singapore Issues. No consensus was made on multilateral registration of geographical indications. Developing countries demanded the extension of higher level of protection of geographical indications to other products.

The 'cotton four' countries strongly demanded the elimination of vast subsidies being provided by the US to its cotton farmers.

The Conference ended in a fiasco when its chairman, Mexican foreign minister Luis Ernesto Debrez abruptly declared the Conference closed citing the reason that ministerial negotiations were impossible due to basic differences among the member countries.

The clear divide surfaced between the developed and developing countries on each and every issue. This clear division of approaches could be in a way helpful to develop better agreements through negotiations in coming meetings and conferences.

Although the Cancun Ministerial Conference ended in a debacle, one important development from the point of view of the developing countries was their coming together to push their agenda at WTO negotiations. India played a key role in uniting the developing countries. A 20 nation alliance on agriculture, also known as G-20, under the leadership of Brazil was formed. Another alliance of 16 nations led by Malaysia on Singapore issues was formed. At Cancun, developing countries not only united, but also became more professional in their approach to negotiations. They also presented alternative draft texts to counter the official draft texts.

15

Hong Kong Ministerial Conference, 2005

15.1 Introduction

The Sixth Ministerial Conference was held at Hong Kong, China, from December 13 to18, 2005. Basically, the Conference aimed to conclude the Doha Round negotiations, as original deadline of January 1, 2005 had already been missed. However, the Hong Kong Ministerial Conference could produce only a modest but useful step forward in the 'Doha Round'. Definitive result was achieved in areas of export subsidies in agriculture and NAMA, cotton, and development. But, a lot of work remained to be accomplished in the conclusion of the Doha Round. Finally, a new deadline of December 31, 2006 for the conclusion of the Doha Round was set.

15.2 Ministerial Discussions

On day one, Mr. John Tsang, Chairman of the Hong Kong Ministerial Conference, nominated six facilitators to conduct negotiations in different areas. Ministers started consultations on market access for non-agricultural products. Some excerpts from discussions held among the Member Delegations in respect of trade and concerned areas are given below.

15.2.1 Agriculture: Kenyan Trade and Industry Minister Mukhisa Kitiyu, who facilitated the agriculture discussion, started consultations reporting that "no great advance has been made so far".

The participants made suggestions including: to concentrate on the less developed issues to do with flexibilities in market access particularly for developing countries; to try to settle the end date for export subsidies and deal with the basic level of ambition for market access and domestic support; to plan for a balance where flexibilities and ambition are linked and for 'parallelism' on eliminating export subsidies and disciplining other export measures; and to focus on developing countries' issues such as cotton and market access for tropical products and crops produced as alternatives to narcotics.

A number of countries demanded agreement on an end date for export subsidies with the understanding that disciplines on export credit, food aid and exporting state trading enterprises would also have to be agreed eventually. Some of these also argued that the level of ambition for market access (the tariff reduction formulas) have to be settled before flexibilities can be sorted out.

Some others more broadly stressed the priority they give to market access, one citing World Bank figures indicating that the largest gains from an agreement, including for developing countries, would come from improved market access.

Another group stressed the need to focus on flexibilities first, so that countries could be confident about making ambition commitments more generally, or because they see flexibilities as important for developing countries.

A group of about a dozen Latin American countries stressed their call for developed countries to give duty-free and quota-free market access to tropical products and alternatives to narcotics from developing countries.

One Member stressed the need for balance and parallelism: the tariff reduction formula and flexibilities are linked and should be discussed together, and the end date for subsidies cannot be agreed before the issues of export credit, food aid and exporting state trading enterprises are settled.

15.2.2 Non-agricultural Market Access: The Facilitator said the Members' main differences were about how ambitious the market opening should be and how this is related to flexibility. He said the delegates indicated a willingness to find middle ground but continued to adhere to maximalist positions. He said it was time to start breaking the ice if we are to move at all.

The Facilitator expressed concern that delegations have remained increasingly entrenched in their positions they had adopted in Geneva. They are not flexible enough to turn this Ministerial Conference into a success story. He cautioned that there may be risk of some back sliding on this issue.

The Facilitator said there was broad support for using Swiss Formula (a mathematical formula for cutting tariffs that results in steep cut on higher tariffs) with two coefficients (the numbers in Swiss Formula that determine how steep the cuts are and set ceiling on the final tariffs).

In addition, he said, a group of developing countries which insists on linking tariff reduction in agriculture and non-agriculture market, so that cuts made by developing countries on non-agricultural products are related to the cuts made by developed countries in agriculture.

The group also wanted flexibilities to be independent from the formula. He said differences also remained on the question of unbound tariffs, the erosion of tariff preferences and a sectoral component to the NAMA negotiations (such as having totally free trade for some sector).

15.2.3 Development Issues: The Facilitator on development issues said that while all development issues are important, he intends to concentrate initially on the LDCs' proposals and specifically the question of duty-free, quota-free market access for LDCs.

Members raised issues including, special and differential treatment for developing countries, food importing countries, trade and transfer of technology, trade and debt, commodities, supply side constraints, aid for trade, cotton, implementation (including intellectual property and the convention Biological Diversity) and the erosion of preferences. A number of countries linked some of these issues to technical assistance and capacity building, and some supported the package of proposals for least developed economies and announced new financial assistance.

Facilitator Minister Rohee began by reassuring Members that he fully recognised that the development package was not limited solely to the question of duty-free, quota-free market access for LDCs or to other LDCs' issues alone. He pointed out that he had prioritised his discussion on this issue and that very soon he would take up other development issues.

Some developing countries said they would not let specific development issues be diluted. They spoke favourably about giving preferential access to exports from LDCs, although they asked for flexibilities on such issues as which products would be covered, and how long the preferences would apply.

Services: Facilitator Mr. Kim said the starting point for his consultations was the part on services in the draft ministerial text. Many delegations considered that this offers a sound basis for the way forward, while others wanted the text strengthened. Another group felt that the text was too prescriptive and not in line with the GATS and the Doha negotiating mandate. This group was concerned with provisions in the text dealing with qualitative objectives, sectoral objectives and references to plurilateral "request-offer" negotiations.

15.2.4 Cotton: The four countries that had originally proposed the cotton initiative called for Members to act quickly and concretely, in order to help countries escape a situation that the Chad Minister described as worse than misery. They blamed subsidies in some rich countries on depressed prices and repeated the proposal they submitted to the cotton subcommittee in Geneva a month earlier.

Some other African countries (Niger, Cameroon, Guinea, Uganda, Ghana and Rwanda) supported the proposal and said they are also affected. India described the cotton situation as a 'bleeding wound' on the conscience of the world. Australia said a breakthrough in agriculture negotiations is needed to deal with the cotton problem. The EU appealed to all Members to work for solution, saying it had opened its market and reduced its subsidies.

The US appreciated other countries' self-control in not mentioning the US by name and accepted that as a major subsidiser it has a responsibility to deal with the problem, which it will not shirk. It said part of this is happening with new proposed legislation aimed at scrapping export subsidies that a WTO Panel ruled was illegal.

But the US added that the 11 studies showed that the impact of the subsidies on prices is considerably less than alleged and therefore the problem also arises because of supply constraints, which the African countries also mentioned. For this reason, the US is also working on development assistance for the four cotton countries to help increase yields and tackle other such issues as marketing.

15.2.5 Other Issues, Implementation and Bananas: The Facilitator said a number of countries wanted to discuss trade and environment, electronic commerce, geographical indications, TRIPS Agreement and the convention on Biological Diversity, and "non-violation complaints in intellectual property".

On December 16, 2005, WTO Members ended the fourth day of the Conference working on texts that were the inputs for a revised draft ministerial text. The revised draft was circulated on December 17 to the Members. The text reflected development in talks over the past few days in three key subjects: agriculture, non-agriculture market access and specific development issues—including duty-free, quota-free access for least developed countries' exports.

A. Agriculture: The revised text contained a number of changes while maintaining the basic objectives: to turn the broad agreements currently achieved in the negotiations into something more specific. This was expected to guide the work in coming months on developing the detailed modalities that were to be negotiated by the Members.

B. Non-agriculture Market Access: In the revised text, wording became clear on tariff reduction formula, particularly on preferences that are given with nothing required in return (non-reciprocal preferences) and on small and vulnerable economies. The text also recognised the need to ensure 'commensurably' high levels of ambition in agriculture and NAMA, wording designed to reassure countries that were reluctant to open their market by a large amount in one area without gaining much market access in the other.

C. Development Issues: The revised text reflected a significantly progress on proposals for LDCs designed to do with special treatment for LDCs.

D. Services: In the revised text, the changes were principally to do with reaffirming that text is a prescription for action in negotiations and at the same time aligning the text even more closely with the GATS and the Doha mandate for services negotiations.

15.3 July Package, 2004

After the debacle of the Cancun Ministerial Conference, the Members renewed their efforts and held, at regular intervals, informal and formal meetings. They developed a negotiation package in July 2004. The General council approved the 'July Package' on August 1, 2004.

The General Council reaffirmed the Ministerial Declarations and Decisions adopted at Doha and the full commitment of all Members to give effect to them. The Council took note of the report by the Chairman of the Trade Negotiations Committee (TNC) and agreed to take action as follows:

15.3.1 Agriculture:

The General Council which adopted the framework on modalities in agriculture had the following main aspects:

1. The starting point for the agriculture negotiations had been the mandate set out in the Doha Ministerial Declaration. This in turn has been built on the long-term objective of the Agreement on Agriculture to establish a fair and market-oriented trading system through a programme of fundamental reform. The elements below offered the additional precision required at this stage of the negotiations and thus the basis for the negotiations of full modalities in the next phase.
2. The final balance was to be found only at the conclusion of these subsequent negotiations and within the Single Undertaking. To achieve this balance, the modalities to be developed were needed to incorporate operationally effective and meaningful provisions for special and differential treatment for developing country Members. Agriculture is of critical importance to the economic development of

developing country Members and they must be able to pursue agricultural policies that are supportive of their development goals, poverty reduction strategies, food security and livelihood concerns. Non-trade concerns were to be taken into account.

3. The reforms in all three pillars formed an interconnected whole and were to be approached in a balanced and equitable manner.
4. The General Council acknowledged the importance of cotton for a certain number of countries and its vital importance for developing countries, especially the LDCs. It was to be addressed ambitiously, expeditiously, and specifically, within the agriculture negotiations. The provisions of this framework provided a basis for this approach, as did the sectoral initiative on cotton. The Special Session of the Committee on Agriculture was asked to ensure appropriate prioritization of the cotton issue independently from other sectoral initiatives.

A. Domestic Support:

5. The Doha Ministerial Declaration called for "substantial reductions in trade-distorting domestic support". With a view to achieving these substantial reductions, the negotiations in this pillar were to ensure the following: (a) Special and differential treatment remains an integral component of domestic support. Modalities to be developed were to include longer implementation periods and lower reduction coefficients for all types of trade-distorting domestic support and continued access. (b) There was a strong element of harmonisation in the reductions made by developed Members. Specifically, higher levels of permitted trade-distorting domestic support were subject to deeper cuts. (c) Each such Member had to make a substantial reduction in the overall level of its trade-distorting support from bound levels. (d) As well as this overall commitment, Final Bound Total AMS and permitted *de minimis* levels were subject to substantial reductions and, in the case of the Blue Box, to be capped in order to ensure results to be coherent with the long-term reform objective.

B. Overall Reduction: A Tiered Formula:

6. The overall base level of all trade-distorting domestic support, as measured by the Final Bound Total AMS plus permitted *de minimis* level and the level agreed in paragraph 7 for Blue Box payments, were to be reduced according to a tiered formula. Under this formula, Members having higher levels of trade-distorting domestic support had to make greater overall reductions in order to achieve a harmonizing result. As the first instalment of the overall cut, in the first year and throughout the implementation period, the sum of all trade-distorting support was not to exceed 80 percent of the sum of Final Bound Total AMS plus permitted *de minimis* plus the Blue Box at the level determined in paragraph 14.
7. The following parameters were to guide further negotiations of this tiered formula: (a) This commitment was to apply as a minimum overall commitment. It was not to be applied as a ceiling on reductions of overall trade-distorting domestic support. The separate and complementary formulae was to be developed for Total AMS, *de minimis* and Blue Box payments to make, when taken together, a deeper

cut in overall trade-distorting domestic support for an individual Member. (b) The base for measuring the Blue Box component had to be the higher of existing Blue Box payments during a recent representative period to be agreed and the cap established.

C. Final Bound Total AMS: A Tiered Formula:

8. To achieve reductions with a harmonizing effect: (a) Final Bound Total AMS was to be reduced substantially, using a tiered approach. (b) Members having higher Total AMS were to make greater reductions. (c) To prevent circumvention of the objective of the Agreement through transfers of unchanged domestic support between different support categories, product-specific AMSs were to be capped at their respective average levels according to a methodology to be agreed. (d) Substantial reductions in Final Bound Total AMS were to result in reductions of some product-specific support.
9. Members might make greater than formula reductions in order to achieve the required level of cut in overall trade-distorting domestic support.

D. De Minimis:

10. Reductions in *de minimis* had to be negotiated taking into account the principle of special and differential treatment. Developing countries that allocated almost all *de minimis* support for subsistence and resource-poor farmers were to be exempt.
11. Members might make greater than formula reductions in order to achieve the required level of cut in overall trade-distorting domestic support.

E. Blue Box:

12. Members recognized the role of the Blue Box in promoting agricultural reforms. In this light, Members had recourse to the following measures: (a) Direct payments under production-limiting programmes if: (i) such payments are based on fixed and unchanging areas and yields; or (ii) such payments are made on 85 percent or less of a fixed and unchanging base level of production; or (iii) livestock payments are made on a fixed and unchanging number of head; or (b) Direct payments that do not require production if: (i) such payments are based on fixed and unchanging bases and yields; or (ii) livestock payments made on a fixed and unchanging number of head; and (iii) such payments are made on 85 percent or less of a fixed and unchanging base level of production.
13. The above criteria, along with additional criteria had to be negotiated. Any such criteria had to ensure that Blue Box payments were less trade-distorting than AMS measures, it being understood that: (a) Any new criteria would need to take account of the balance of the WTO rights and obligations. (b) Any new criteria to be agreed would not have the perverse effect of undoing ongoing reforms.
14. Blue Box support was not to exceed 5 percent of a Member's average total value of agricultural production during an historical period. The historical period was to be established in the negotiations.

F. Green Box:

15. Green Box criteria had to be reviewed and clarified with a view to ensuring that

Green Box measures have no, or at most minimal, trade-distorting effects or effects on production. Such a review and clarification was needed to ensure that the basic concepts, principles and effectiveness of the Green Box remain and take due account of non-trade concerns.

G. Export Competition:

16. The Doha Ministerial Declaration called for "reduction of, with a view to phasing out, all forms of export subsidies". Members agreed to establish detailed modalities ensuring the parallel elimination of all forms of export subsidies and disciplines on all export measures with equivalent effect by a credible end date.

H. End Point:

17. The following had to be eliminated by the end date to be agreed: (a) Export subsidies as scheduled, (b) Export credits, export credit guarantees or insurance programmes with repayment periods beyond 180 days, (c) terms and conditions relating to export credits, export credit guarantees or insurance programmes with repayment periods of 180 days and below which were not in accordance with disciplines to be agreed. These disciplines had to cover, *inter alia*, payment of interest, minimum interest rates, minimum premium requirements, and other elements which could constitute subsidies or otherwise distort trade, (d) Trade distorting practices with respect to exporting STEs including eliminating export subsidies provided to or by them, government financing, and the underwriting of losses. The issue of the future use of monopoly powers were of subject to further negotiation, (e) Provision of food aid that was not in conformity with operationally effective disciplines to be agreed. The objective of such disciplines was to prevent commercial displacement. The role of international organizations as regards the provision of food aid by Members, including related humanitarian and developmental issues, had to be addressed in the negotiations.

I. Implementation:

18. Commitments and disciplines in paragraph 17 had to be implemented according to a schedule and modalities to be agreed. Commitments had to be implemented by annual instalments. Their phasing had to take into account the need for some coherence with internal reform steps of Members.
19. The negotiation of the elements in paragraph 17 and their implementation had to ensure equivalent and parallel commitments by Members.

J. Special and Differential Treatment:

20. Developing country Members had to benefit from longer implementation periods for the phasing out of all forms of export subsidies.
21. Developing countries would continue to benefit from special and differential treatment under the provisions of Article 9.4 of the Agreement on Agriculture for a reasonable period, to be negotiated, after the phasing out of all forms of export subsidies and implementation of all disciplines identified above were completed.
22. Members would ensure that the disciplines on export credits, export credit guarantees or insurance programs to be agreed shall make appropriate provision for

differential treatment in favour of least developed and net food importing developing countries as per the Decision on Measures Concerning the Possible Negative Effects of the Reform Programme on Least Developed and Net Food Importing Developing Countries.

23. STEs in developing country Members which enjoyed special privileges to preserve domestic consumer price stability and to ensure food security had to receive special consideration for maintaining monopoly status.

K. Special Circumstances:

24. In exceptional circumstances, which could not be adequately covered by food aid, commercial export credits or preferential international financing facilities, ad hoc temporary financing arrangements relating to exports to developing countries might be agreed by Members. Such agreements must not have the effect of undermining commitments undertaken by Members mentioned above, and would be based on criteria and consultation procedures to be established.

L. Market Access:

25. The Doha Ministerial Declaration had called for "substantial improvements in market access". Members also agreed that special and differential treatment for developing Members would be an integral part of all elements in the negotiations.

M. The Single Approach: A Tiered Formula:

26. To ensure that a single approach for developed and developing country Members meets all the objectives of the Doha mandate, tariff reductions had to be made through a tiered formula that takes into account their different tariff structures.

27. To ensure that such a formula leads to substantial trade expansion, the following principles would guide its further negotiation: (a) Tariff reductions would be made from bound rates. Substantial overall tariff reductions would be achieved as a final result from negotiations. (b) Each Member (other than LDCs) would make a contribution. Operationally effective special and differential provisions for developing country Members would be an integral part of all elements. (c) Progressivity in tariff reductions would be achieved through deeper cuts in higher tariffs with flexibilities for sensitive products. Substantial improvements in market access had to be achieved for all products.

28. The number of bands, the thresholds for defining the bands and the type of tariff reduction in each band remained under negotiation. The role of a tariff cap in a tiered formula with distinct treatment for sensitive products had to be further evaluated.

N. Sensitive Products:

29. Without undermining the overall objective of the tiered approach, Members might designate an appropriate number, to be negotiated, of tariff lines to be treated as sensitive, taking account of existing commitments for these products.

30. The principle of 'substantial improvement' had to be applied to each product.

31. 'Substantial improvement' had to be achieved through combinations of tariff quota commitments and tariff reductions applying to each product. However, balance in

this negotiation had to be found only if the final negotiated result also reflects the sensitivity of the product concerned.

32. Some MFN-based tariff quota expansion was required for all such products. A base for such an expansion was to be established, taking account of coherent and equitable criteria to be developed in the negotiations.

O. Other Elements:

33. Other elements that would give the flexibility required to reach a final balanced result included reduction or elimination of in-quota tariff rates, and operationally effective improvements in tariff quota administration for existing tariff quotas so as to enable Members, and particularly developing country Members, to fully benefit from the market access opportunities under tariff rate quotas.
34. Tariff escalation had to be addressed through a formula to be agreed.
35. The issue of tariff simplification remained under negotiation.
36. The question of the special agricultural safeguard (SSG) remained under negotiation.

P. Special and Differential Treatment:

37. Having regard to their rural development, food security and/or livelihood security needs, special and differential treatment for developing countries would be an integral part of all elements of the negotiation, including the tariff reduction formula, the number and treatment of sensitive products, expansion of tariff rate quotas, and implementation period.
38. Proportionality was be achieved by requiring lesser tariff reduction commitments or tariff quota expansion commitments from developing country Members.
39. Developing country Members were to be given the flexibility to designate an appropriate number of products as Special Products, based on criteria of food security, livelihood security and rural development needs.
40. A Special Safeguard Mechanism (SSM) was to be established for use by developing country Members.
41. Full implementation of the long-standing commitment to achieve the fullest liberalisation of trade in tropical agricultural products and for products of particular importance to the diversification of production from the growing of illicit narcotic crops was overdue and had to be addressed effectively in the market access negotiations.
42. The importance of long-standing preferences was fully recognised. The issue of preference erosion was to be addressed.

Q. Least Developed Countries:

43. Least Developed Countries, which had full access to all special and differential treatment provisions above, were not required to undertake reduction commitments. Developed Members, and developing country Members in a position to do so, should provide duty-free and quota-free market access for products originating from least developed countries.
44. Work on cotton under all the pillars reflected the vital importance of this sector to certain LDC Members and the Members would work to achieve ambitious results expeditiously.

R. Monitoring and Surveillance:

45. Article 18 of the Agreement on Agriculture was to be amended with a view to enhancing monitoring so as to effectively ensure full transparency, including through timely and complete notifications with respect to the commitments in market access, domestic support and export competition. The particular concerns of developing countries in this regard were to be addressed.

15.3.2 Cotton: The General Council reaffirmed the importance of the Sectoral Initiative on Cotton. The General Council also attached importance to the development aspects of the Cotton Initiative and wished to stress the complementarities between the trade and development aspects. Members should work on related issues of development multilaterally with the international financial institutions, continue their bilateral programmes, and all developed countries were urged to participate. In this regard, the General Council instructed the Director General to consult with the relevant international organizations, including the Bretton Woods Institutions, the Food and Agriculture Organization and the International Trade Centre to direct effectively existing programmes and any additional resources towards development of the economies where cotton had vital importance.

15.3.3 Non-agricultural Market Access: The General Council adopted the framework on modalities for non-agricultural market access. The main aspects of the framework are given below:

1. The Framework contained the initial elements for future work on modalities by the Negotiating Group on Market Access. Additional negotiations were required to reach agreement on the specifics of some of these elements. These related to the formula, the issues concerning the treatment of unbound tariffs in indent two of paragraph 5, the flexibilities for developing-country participants, the issue of participation in the sectorial tariff component and the preferences.
2. The General Council reaffirmed that negotiations on market access for non-agricultural products should aim to reduce or as appropriate eliminate tariffs, including the reduction or elimination of tariff peaks, high tariffs, and tariff escalation, as well as non-tariff barriers, in particular on products of export interest to developing countries. It also reaffirmed the importance of special and differential treatment and less than full reciprocity in reduction commitments as integral parts of the modalities.
3. The General Council acknowledged the substantial work undertaken by the Negotiating Group on Market Access and the progress towards achieving an agreement on negotiating modalities.
4. The General Council recognized that a formula approach is the key to reducing tariffs, and reducing or eliminating tariff peaks, high tariffs, and tariff escalation. It agreed that the Negotiating Group should continue its work on a non-linear formula applied on a line-by-line basis which should take fully into account the special needs and interests of developing and least developed country participants, including through less than full reciprocity in reduction commitments.

5. It further agreed on the following elements regarding the formula: (a) product coverage shall be comprehensive without *a priori* exclusions; (b) tariff reductions or elimination shall commence from the bound rates after full implementation of current concessions; however, for unbound tariff lines, the basis for commencing the tariff reductions shall be [two] times the MFN applied rate in the base year; (c) the base year for MFN applied tariff rates shall be 2001 (applicable rates on November 14); (d) credit shall be given for autonomous liberalization by developing countries provided that the tariff lines were bound on an MFN basis in the WTO since the conclusion of the Uruguay Round; (e) all non-*ad valorem* duties shall be converted to *ad valorem* equivalents on the basis of a methodology to be determined and bound in *ad valorem* terms.
6. It furthermore agreed that, as an exception, participants with a binding coverage of non-agricultural tariff lines of less than [35] percent would be exempt from making tariff reductions through the formula. Instead, the Members expect them to bind 100 percent of non-agricultural tariff lines at an average level that does not exceed the overall average of bound tariffs for all developing countries after full implementation of current concessions.
7. The General Council recognized that a sectoral tariff component, aiming at elimination or harmonization is another key element to achieving the objectives of the Doha Ministerial Declaration with regard to the reduction or elimination of tariffs, in particular on products of export interest to developing countries. It recognized that participation by all participants would be important to that effect.
8. It was agreed that developing country participants shall have longer implementation periods for tariff reductions. In addition, they shall be given the following flexibility: (a) applying less than formula cuts to up to 10 percent of the tariff lines provided that the cuts are no less than half the formula cuts and that these tariff lines do not exceed 10 percent of the total value of a Member's imports; or (b) keeping, as an exception, tariff lines unbound, or not applying formula cuts for up to 5 percent of tariff lines provided they do not exceed 5 percent of the total value of a Member's imports.
9. Members agreed that least developed country participants shall not be required to apply the formula nor participate in the sectoral approach; however, as part of their contribution to this round of negotiations, they are expected to substantially increase their level of binding commitments.
10. Furthermore, in recognition of the need to enhance the integration of least developed countries into the multilateral trading system and support the diversification of their production and export base, the Members called upon developed country participants and other participants who so decided, to grant on an autonomous basis, duty-free and quota-free market access for non-agricultural products originating from least developed countries.
11. The General Council recognized that newly acceded Members shall have recourse to special provisions for tariff reductions in order to take into account their extensive

market access commitments undertaken as part of their accession and that staged tariff reductions are still being implemented in many cases. The General Council instructed the Negotiating Group to further elaborate on such provisions.

12. The General Council agreed that pending agreement on core modalities for tariffs, the possibilities of supplementary modalities such as zero-for-zero sector elimination, sectorial harmonization, and request and offer, should be kept open.
13. In addition, the General Council asked developed country participants and other participants who so decided to consider the elimination of low duties.
14. The General Council recognized that NTBs are an integral and equally important part of these negotiations and instructed participants to intensify their work on NTBs. In particular, the General Council encouraged all participants to make notifications on NTBs by October 31, 2004 and to proceed with identification, examination, categorization, and ultimately negotiations on NTBs.
15. The General Council recognized that appropriate studies and capacity building measures should be an integral part of the modalities to be agreed.
16. The General Council recognized the challenges that may be faced by non-reciprocal preference beneficiary Members and those Members that are at present highly dependent on tariff revenue as a result of these negotiations on non-agricultural products. The General Council instructed the Negotiating Group to take into consideration, in the course of its work, the particular needs that might arise for the Members concerned.
17. The General Council furthermore encouraged the Negotiating Group to work closely with the Committee on Trade and Environment in Special Session with a view to addressing the issue of non-agricultural environmental goods covered in the Doha Ministerial Declaration.

15.3.4 Development:

A. Principles: Development concerns formed an integral part of the Doha Ministerial Declaration. The General Council rededicated and recommitted Members to fulfilling the development dimension of the Doha Development Agenda, which placed the needs and interests of developing and least developed countries at the heart of the Doha Work Programme. The Council instructed the Committee on Trade and Development in Special Session to expeditiously complete the review of all the outstanding Agreement-specific proposals and report to the General Council, with clear recommendations for a decision by July 2005.

B. Technical Assistance: The General Council recognized the progress that had been made since the Doha Ministerial Conference in expanding Trade-Related Technical Assistance (TRTA) to developing countries and low-income countries in transition. In this context, the Council welcomed and further encouraged the improved coordination with other agencies, including under the Integrated Framework for TRTA for the LDCs (IF) and the Joint Integrated Technical Assistance Programme (JITAP).

C. Implementation: The Council instructed the Trade Negotiations Committee, negotiating bodies and other WTO bodies concerned to redouble their efforts to find appropriate solutions as a priority. The Council requested the Director-General to continue with his consultative process on all outstanding implementation issues of the Doha Ministerial Declaration, including on issues related to the extension of the protection of geographical indications provided for to the products other than wines and spirits. The Council had to review progress and take any appropriate action no later than July 2005.

D. Other Development Issues: In the ongoing market access negotiations, recognising the fundamental principles of the WTO and relevant provisions of GATT, 1994, special attention shall be given to the specific trade and development related needs and concerns of developing countries, including capacity constraints. These particular concerns of developing countries, including relating to food security, rural development, livelihood, preferences, commodities and net food imports, as well as prior unilateral liberalisation, should be taken into consideration, as appropriate, in the course of the Agriculture and NAMA negotiations.

E. Least-Developed Countries: The General Council reaffirmed the commitments made at Doha concerning the least developed countries and renewed its determination to fulfil these commitments.

15.3.5 Services: The General Council took note of the report to the TNC by the Special Session of the Council for Trade in Services and reaffirmed Members' commitment to progress in this area of the negotiations in line with the Doha mandate. The Council adopted the recommendations agreed by the Special Session on the basis of which further progress in the services negotiations was to be pursued.

15.3.6 Other Negotiating Bodies:

A. Rules, Trade and Environment and TRIPS: The General Council took note of the reports to the TNC by the Negotiating Group on Rules and by the Special Sessions of the Committee on Trade and Environment and the TRIPS Council. The Council reaffirmed Members' commitment to progress in all of these areas of the negotiations in line with the Doha mandates.

B. Dispute Settlement: The General Council took note of the report to the TNC by the Special Session of the Dispute Settlement Body and reaffirmed Members' commitment to progress in this area of the negotiations in line with the Doha mandate. The Council adopted the TNC's recommendation that work in the Special Session should continue on the basis set out by the Chairman of that body in his report to the TNC.

15.3.7 Trade Facilitation: Taking note of the work done on trade facilitation by the Council for Trade in Goods under the mandate of the Doha Ministerial Declaration and the work carried out under the auspices of the General Council both prior to the Fifth Ministerial Conference and after its conclusion, the General Council decided by explicit consensus, to commence negotiations on the basis of the modalities set by it.

A. Relationship between Trade and Investment, Interaction between Trade and Competition Policy and Transparency in Government Procurement: The Council agreed that these issues, mentioned in the Doha Ministerial Declaration, will not form part of the Work Programme set out in that Declaration and therefore no work towards negotiations on any of these issues will take place within the WTO during the Doha Round.

15.3.8 Other Elements of the Work Programme: The General Council reaffirmed the high priority the Ministers at Doha gave to those elements of the Work Programme which do not involve negotiations. Noting that a number of these issues were of particular interest to developing country Members, the Council emphasized its commitment to fulfil the mandates given by Ministers in all these areas. To this end, the General Council and other relevant bodies were asked to report in line with their Doha mandates to the Sixth Session of the Ministerial Conference.

15.4 Ministerial Declaration

The Trade Ministers made a Declaration on December 18, 2005. The main points of the Declaration have been given below:

1. The Ministers reaffirmed the Declarations and Decisions adopted at Doha, as well as the Decision adopted by the General Council on August 1, 2004, and their full commitment to give effect to them. They renewed their resolve to complete the Doha Work Programme fully and to conclude the negotiations launched at Doha successfully in 2006.
2. The Ministers emphasized the central importance of the development dimension in every aspect of the Doha Work Programme and recommitted themselves to making it a meaningful reality, in terms both of the results of the negotiations on market access and rule-making and of the specific development-related issues set out below.
3. In pursuance of these objectives, the Ministers agreed as follows:

15.4.1 Agriculture Negotiations:

4. The Ministers reaffirmed the commitment to the mandate on agriculture as set out at the Doha Ministerial Declaration and to the Framework adopted by the General Council on August 1, 2004. They took note of the report by the Chairman of the Special Session on his own responsibility. They welcomed the progress made by the Special Session of the Committee on Agriculture since 2004 and recorded therein.
5. On domestic support, the Ministers declared that there will be three bands for reductions in Final Bound Total AMS and in the overall cut in trade-distorting domestic support, with higher linear cuts in higher bands. In both cases, the Member with the highest level of permitted support will be in the top band, the two Members with the second and third highest levels of support will be in the middle band and all other Members, including all developing country Members, will be in the bottom band. In addition, developed country Members in the lower bands with high relative levels of Final Bound Total AMS will make an additional effort in AMS reduction. They also noted that there had been some convergence concerning the reductions in Final Bound Total AMS, the overall cut in trade-distorting domestic support and in both product-specific and non product-specific *de minimis* limits. Disciplines will be developed to achieve effective cuts in trade distorting domestic support consistent with the Framework. The overall reduction in trade distorting domestic support will

still need to be made even if the sum of the reductions in Final Bound Total AMS, *de minimis* and Blue Box payments would otherwise be less than that overall reduction. Developing country Members with no AMS commitments will be exempt from reductions in *de minimis* and the overall cut in trade distorting domestic support. Green Box criteria will be reviewed, *inter alia*, to ensure that programmes of developing country Members that cause not more than minimal trade distortion are effectively covered.

6. The Ministers agreed to ensure the parallel elimination of all forms of export subsidies and disciplines on all export measures with equivalent effect to be completed by the end of 2013. They took note of emerging convergence on some elements of disciplines with respect to export credits, export credit guarantees or insurance programmes with repayment periods of 180 days and below. They agreed that such programmes should be self-financing, reflecting market consistency, and that the period should be of a sufficiently short duration so as not to effectively circumvent real commercially-oriented discipline. As a means of ensuring that trade distorting practices of STEs are eliminated, disciplines relating to exporting STEs will extend to the future use of monopoly powers so that such powers cannot be exercised in any way that would circumvent the direct disciplines on STEs on export subsidies, government financing and the underwriting of losses. On food aid, the Ministers reconfirmed the commitment to maintain an adequate level and to take into account the interests of food aid recipient countries. To this end, a "safe box" for bonafide food aid will be provided to ensure that there is no unintended impediment to dealing with emergency situations. Beyond that, they decided to ensure elimination of commercial displacement. To this end, they agreed effective disciplines on in-kind food aid, monetization and re-exports so that there could be no loophole for continuing export subsidization. The disciplines on export credits, export credit guarantees or insurance programmes, exporting state trading enterprises and food aid were to be completed by April 30, 2006 as part of the modalities, including appropriate provision in favour of least developed and net food-importing developing countries.
7. On market access, the Ministers noted the progress made on *ad valorem* equivalents. They adopted four bands for structuring tariff cuts, recognizing that they agreed on the relevant thresholds—including those applicable for developing country Members. They recognized the need to agree on treatment of sensitive products, taking into account all the elements involved. Developing country Members would have the flexibility to self-designate an appropriate number of tariff lines as Special Products guided by indicators based on the criteria of food security, livelihood security and rural development. Developing country Members would also have the right to have recourse to a Special Safeguard Mechanism based on import quantity and price triggers, with precise arrangements to be further defined. Special Products and the Special Safeguard Mechanism should be an integral part of the modalities and the outcome of negotiations in agriculture.

8. On other elements of special and differential treatment, the Ministers noted in particular, the consensus that exists in the Framework on several issues in all three pillars of domestic support, export competition and market access and that some progress has been made on other special and differential treatment issues.
9. The Ministers reaffirmed that nothing they agreed here compromises the agreement already reflected in the Framework on other issues including tropical products and products of particular importance to the diversification of production from the growing of illicit narcotic crops, long-standing preferences and preference erosion.
10. The Ministers agreed to intensify work on all outstanding issues to fulfil the Doha objectives, in particular, they resolved to establish modalities no later than April 30, 2006 and to submit comprehensive draft Schedules based on these modalities no later than July 31, 2006.

15.4.2 Cotton Negotiations:

11. The Ministers recalled the mandate given by the Members in the Decision adopted by the General Council on August 1, 2004 to address cotton ambitiously, expeditiously and specifically, within the agriculture negotiations in relation to all trade distorting policies affecting the sector in all three pillars of market access, domestic support and export competition, as specified in the Doha text and the July 2004 Framework text. They reaffirmed the commitment to ensure having an explicit decision on cotton within the agriculture negotiations and through the Sub-Committee on Cotton ambitiously, expeditiously and specifically as follows: (a) All forms of export subsidies for cotton would be eliminated by developed countries in 2006. (b) On market access, developed countries would give duty and quota-free access for cotton exports from least developed countries (LDCs) from the commencement of the implementation period. (c) Members agreed that the objective is that, as an outcome of the negotiations, trade distorting domestic subsidies for cotton production be reduced more ambitiously than under whatever general formula is agreed and that it should be implemented over a shorter period of time than generally applicable.
12. With regard to the development assistance aspects of cotton, the Ministers welcomed the Consultative Framework process initiated by the Director-General to implement the decisions on these aspects pursuant to the Decision adopted by the General Council on August 1, 2004. The Ministers took note of his Periodic Reports and the positive evolution of development assistance noted therein.

15.4.3 NAMA Negotiations:

13. The Ministers reaffirmed the commitment to the mandate for negotiations on market access for non-agricultural products as set out in the Doha Ministerial Declaration. They also reaffirmed all the elements of the NAMA Framework adopted by the General Council on August 1, 2004. They took note of the report by the Chairman of the Negotiating Group on Market Access on his own responsibility.
14. The Ministers adopted a Swiss Formula with coefficients at levels which shall *inter alia*: (a) Reduce or as appropriate, eliminate tariffs, including the reduction or

elimination of tariff peaks, high tariffs and tariff escalation, in particular, on products of export interest to developing countries; and (b) Take fully into account, the special needs and interests of developing countries, including through less than full reciprocity in reduction commitments. They instructed the Negotiating Group to finalize its structure and details as soon as possible.

15. The Ministers reaffirmed the importance of special and differential treatment and less than full reciprocity in reduction commitments as integral parts of the modalities. They instructed the Negotiating Group to finalize its details as soon as possible.
16. The Ministers recognized that Members were pursuing sectoral initiatives. To this end, they instructed the Negotiating Group to review proposals with a view to identifying those which could garner sufficient participation to be realized.
17. The Ministers adopted a non-linear mark-up approach to establish base rates for commencing tariff reductions. They instructed the Negotiating Group to finalize its details as soon as possible.
18. The Ministers noted of the progress made to convert non *ad valorem* duties to *ad valorem* equivalents on the basis of an agreed methodology.
19. The Ministers took note of the level of common understanding reached on the issue of product coverage and directed the Negotiating Group to resolve differences on the limited issues that remained as quickly as possible.
20. The Ministers recognized the challenges that might be faced by non-reciprocal preference beneficiary Members as a consequence of the MFN liberalization that would result from these negotiations. They instructed the Negotiating Group to intensify work on the assessment of the scope of the problem with a view to finding possible solutions.
21. The Ministers noted the concerns raised by small, vulnerable economies, and instructed the Negotiating Group to establish ways to provide flexibilities for these Members without creating a sub-category of WTO Members.
22. The Ministers noted that the Negotiating Group had made progress in the identification, categorization and examination of notified NTBs. They also took note that Members were developing bilateral, vertical and horizontal approaches to the NTB negotiations, and that some of the NTBs were being addressed in other forum including other Negotiating Groups. They recognized the need for specific negotiating proposals and encourage participants to make such submissions as quickly as possible.
23. The Ministers agreed to intensify work on all outstanding issues to fulfil the Doha objectives, in particular, they resolved to establish modalities no later than April 30, 2006 and to submit comprehensive draft Schedules based on these modalities no later than July 31, 2006.

15.4.4 Balance between Agriculture and NAMA:

24. The Ministers recognized that it is important to advance the development objectives of this Round through enhanced market access for developing countries in both

Agriculture and NAMA. To that end, they instructed the negotiators to ensure that there is a comparably high level of ambition in market access for Agriculture and NAMA. This ambition is to be achieved in a balanced and proportionate manner consistent with the principle of special and differential treatment.

15.4.5 Services Negotiations:

25. The Ministers recalled and reaffirmed the objectives and principles stipulated in the GATS, the Doha Ministerial Declaration, the Guidelines and Procedures for the Negotiations on Trade in Services adopted by the Special Session of the Council for Trade in Services on March 28, 2001 and the Modalities for the Special Treatment for Least Developed Country Members in the Negotiations on Trade in Services adopted on September 3, 2003, as well as the Decision relating to services adopted by the General Council on August 1, 2004.

26. The Ministers urged all Members to participate actively in these negotiations towards achieving a progressively higher level of liberalization of trade in services, with appropriate flexibility for individual developing countries. The Ministers recognized the particular economic situation of LDCs, including the difficulties they faced, and acknowledged that they are not expected to undertake new commitments.

27. The Ministers decided to intensify the negotiations in accordance with the above principles and the Objectives, Approaches and Timelines as given below with a view to expanding the sectoral and modal coverage of commitments and improving their quality: (a) Any outstanding initial offers shall be submitted as soon as possible, (b) Groups of Members presenting plurilateral requests to other Members should submit such requests by February 28, 2006 or as soon as possible thereafter, (c) A second round of revised offers shall be submitted by July 31, 2006 and (d) Final draft schedules of commitments shall be submitted by October 31, 2006.

15.4.6 Other Negotiations:

A. Rules Negotiations:

28. The Ministers recalled the mandates in paragraphs 28 and 29 of the Doha Ministerial Declaration and reaffirmed their commitment to the negotiations on rules.

B. TRIPS Negotiations:

29. The Ministers took note of the report of the Chairman of the Special Session of the Council for TRIPS setting out the progress in the negotiations on the establishment of a multilateral system of notification and registration of geographical indications for wines and spirits and agreed to intensify these negotiations in order to complete them within the overall time frame for the conclusion of the negotiations that were foreseen in the Doha Ministerial Declaration.

C. Environmental Negotiations:

30. The Ministers reaffirmed the mandate in the Doha Ministerial Declaration aimed at enhancing the mutual supportiveness of trade and environment and welcomed the significant work undertaken in the Committee on Trade and Environment (CTE) in Special Session. They instructed Members to intensify the negotiations.

31. The Ministers recognized the progress in the work under paragraph 31(i) of Doha

Declaration based on Members' submissions on the relationship between existing WTO rules and specific trade obligations set out in multilateral environmental agreements (MEAs).

32. The Ministers recognized that recently more work had been carried out under paragraph 31(iii) through numerous submissions by Members and discussions in the CTE in Special Session, including technical discussions, which were also held in informal information exchange sessions without prejudice to Members' positions. They instructed Members to complete the work expeditiously under paragraph 31(iii).

D. Trade Facilitation Negotiations:

33. The Ministers recalled and reaffirmed the mandate and modalities for negotiations on Trade Facilitation contained in the Decision adopted by the General Council on August 1, 2004. They noted with appreciation the report of the Negotiating Group.

E. DSU Negotiations:

34. The Ministers took note of the progress made in the Dispute Settlement Understanding negotiations as reflected in the report by the Chairman of the Special Session of the Dispute Settlement Body to the Trade Negotiations Committee (TNC) and directed the Special Session to continue to work towards a rapid conclusion of the negotiations.

F. Special and Differential Treatment:

35. The Ministers reaffirmed that provisions for special and differential (S&D) treatment are an integral part of the WTO Agreements. They renewed the determination to fulfil the mandate contained in paragraph 44 of the Doha Ministerial Declaration and in the Decision adopted by the General Council on August 1, 2004 that all S&D treatment provisions should be reviewed with a view to strengthening them and making them more precise, effective and operational.

36. The Ministers took note of the work done on the Agreement specific proposals, especially the five LDC proposals. They agreed to adopt the decisions taken in this regard. They instructed the Committee on Trade and Development in Special Session to expeditiously complete the review of all the outstanding Agreement specific proposals and report to the General Council, with clear recommendations for a decision, by December 2006.

37. The Ministers were concerned at the lack of progress on the Category II proposals that had been referred to other WTO bodies and negotiating groups. They instructed these bodies to expeditiously complete the consideration of these proposals and report periodically to the General Council, with the objective of ensuring that clear recommendations for a decision are made no later than December 2006.

38. They further instructed the Special Session, within the parameters of the Doha mandate, to resume work on all other outstanding issues, including on the cross-cutting issues, the monitoring mechanism, and the incorporation of S&D treatment into the architecture of WTO rules, and report on a regular basis to the General Council.

G. Implementation:

39. The Ministers reiterated the instruction in the Decision adopted by the General Council on August 1, 2004 to the TNC, negotiating bodies and other WTO bodies concerned, to redouble their efforts to find appropriate solutions as a priority to outstanding implementation-related issues. They requested the Director-General, without prejudice to the positions of Members, to intensify his consultative process on all outstanding implementation issues under paragraph 12(b), if need be by appointing Chairpersons of concerned WTO bodies as his friends and/or by holding dedicated consultations. The Council had to review progress and take any appropriate action no later than July 31, 2006.

H. TRIPS and Public Health:

40. The Ministers reaffirmed the importance they attached to the General Council Decision of August 30, 2003 on the Implementation of the Doha Declaration on the TRIPS Agreement and Public Health, and to an amendment to the TRIPS Agreement replacing its provisions. They welcomed the work that had taken place in the Council for TRIPS and the Decision of the General Council of December 6, 2005 on an Amendment of the TRIPS Agreement.

I. Small Economies:

41. The Ministers reaffirmed the commitment to the Work Programme on Small Economies and urged Members to adopt specific measures that would facilitate the fuller integration of small, vulnerable economies into the multilateral trading system, without creating a sub-category of WTO Members. They instructed the General Council to report on progress and action taken, together with any further recommendations as appropriate, to the next Session.

J. Trade, Debt and Finance:

42. The Ministers agreed that, building on the work carried out till date, this work should continue on the basis of the Doha mandate. They instructed the General Council to report further to the next Session.

K. Trade and Transfer of Technology:

43. Recognizing the relevance of the relationship between trade and transfer of technology to the development dimension of the Doha Work Programme and building on the work carried out till date, the Ministers agreed that this work should continue on the basis of the mandate of the Doha Ministerial Declaration. They instructed the General Council to report further to the next Session.

L. Doha Paragraph 19:

44. The Ministers took note of the work undertaken by the Council for TRIPS pursuant to paragraph 19 of the Doha Ministerial Declaration and agreed that this work should continue on the basis of the Doha Ministerial Declaration and the progress made in the Council for TRIPS to date. The General Council had to report on its work in this regard to the next Session.

M. TRIPS Non-violation and Situation Complaints:

45. The Ministers took note of the work done by the Council for Trade-related Aspects

of Intellectual Property Rights pursuant to paragraph 11.1 of the Doha Decision on Implementation-Related Issues and Concerns and the Decision adopted by the General Council on August 1, 2004, and directed it to continue its examination of the scope and modalities for complaints of the types provided for under Article XXIII of GATT, 1994 and make recommendations to the next Session. It was agreed that, in the meantime, Members would not initiate such complaints under the TRIPS Agreement.

N. E-commerce:

46. The Ministers agreed to maintain the current institutional arrangements for the Work Programme and to complete the remaining work. They declared that Members will maintain their current practice of not imposing customs duties on electronic transmissions until the next Session.

O. Least Developed Countries (LDCs):

47. The Ministers reaffirmed the commitment to effectively and meaningfully integrate LDCs into the multilateral trading system and shall continue to implement the WTO Work Programme for LDCs adopted in February 2002. Building upon the commitment in the Doha Ministerial Declaration, developed country Members, and developing country Members declaring themselves in a position to do so, agreed to implement duty-free and quota-free market access for products originating from LDCs. In the services negotiations, Members should implement the LDC modalities and give priority to the sectors and modes of supply of export interest to LDCs, particularly with regard to movement of service providers under Mode 4. They reaffirmed the commitment to enhance effective trade-related technical assistance and capacity building to LDCs on a priority basis in helping to overcome their limited human and institutional trade-related capacity to maximize the benefits resulting from the Doha Development Agenda (DDA).

P. Integrated Framework:

48. The Members continued to attach high priority towards the effective implementation of the Integrated Framework (IF) and reiterated their endorsement of the IF as a viable instrument for LDCs' trade development, building on its principles of country ownership and partnership.
49. The Ministers welcomed the establishment of a Task Force by the Integrated Framework Working Group as endorsed by the IF Steering Committee (IFSC) as well as an agreement on the three elements which together constituted an enhanced IF. The Task Force, composed of donor and LDC members, had to provide recommendations to the IFSC by April 2006. The enhanced IF was expected to enter into force no later than December 31, 2006.
50. The Ministers agreed that the Task Force, in line with its Mandate and based on the three elements agreed to, shall provide recommendations on how the implementation of the IF can be improved.
51. The Ministers urged other development partners to significantly increase their contribution to the IF Trust Fund. They also urged the six IF core agencies to

continue to cooperate closely in the implementation of the IF, to increase their investments in this initiative and to intensify their assistance in trade-related infrastructure, private sector development and institution building to help LDCs expand and diversify their export base.

Q. Technical Assistance:

52. The Ministers noted with appreciation the substantial increase in trade-related technical assistance since the Fourth Session, which reflected the enhanced commitment of Members to address the increased demand for technical assistance, through both bilateral and multilateral programmes.
53. The Ministers reaffirmed the priorities established in the Doha Ministerial Declaration for the delivery of technical assistance and urged the Director-General to ensure that programmes focus accordingly on the needs of beneficiary countries and reflect the priorities and mandates adopted by Members. In particular, they encouraged all Members to cooperate with the International Trade Centre, which complements WTO work by providing a platform for business to interact with trade negotiators, and practical advice for small and medium-sized enterprises (SMEs) to benefit from the multilateral trading system.
54. In order to continue progress in the effective and timely delivery of trade-related capacity building, in line with the priority Members attached to it, the relevant structures of the Secretariat should be strengthened and its resources enhanced.

R. Commodity Issues:

55. The Ministers recognized the dependence of several developing and least-developed countries on the export of commodities and the problems they faced because of the adverse impact of the long-term decline and sharp fluctuation in the prices of these commodities. They agreed that the particular trade-related concerns of developing and least-developed countries related to commodities shall also be addressed in the course of the agriculture and NAMA negotiations. They further acknowledged that these countries might need support and technical assistance to overcome the particular problems they faced, and urged Members and relevant international organizations to consider favourably, requests by these countries for support and assistance.

S. Coherence:

56. The Ministers welcomed the Director-General's actions to strengthen the WTO's cooperation with the IMF and the World Bank in the context of the WTO's Marrakesh Mandate on Coherence, and invited him to continue to work closely with the General Council in this area. They agreed to continue building on that experience and expand the debate on international trade and development policymaking and inter-agency cooperation with the participation of relevant UN agencies.

T. Aid for Trade:

57. The Ministers welcomed the discussions of Finance and Development Ministers in various fora, including the Development Committee of the World Bank and the IMF, on expanding Aid for Trade. Aid for Trade should aim to help developing countries,

particularly LDCs, to build the supply-side capacity and trade-related infrastructure that they need to assist them to implement and benefit from WTO Agreements and more broadly to expand their trade. They invited the Director-General to create a task force that will provide recommendations on how to make Aid for Trade operational. The Task Force had to provide recommendations to the General Council by July 2006 on how Aid for Trade might contribute most effectively to the development dimension of the DDA.

U. New Members:

58. The Ministers recognized the special situation of recently-acceded Members who had undertaken extensive market access commitments at the time of accession. This situation was to be taken into account in the negotiations.

V. Accession:

59. The Ministers welcomed those new Members who have completed their accession processes since the last Session, namely Nepal, Cambodia and Saudi Arabia.

15.5 Conclusions

The outcome of the Hong Kong Ministerial Conference was modest. Though no landmark was achieved, the Conference was a step forward towards the Doha mandate. The major consultations were on three points: agriculture, NAMA and development issues. An end date for the elimination of export subsidies in all forms was agreed for on agriculture, including cotton. The Swiss Formula was adopted by Members to decide the market ambition in both areas viz. agriculture and NAMA. It was a positive and helpful decision in framing the modalities in the concerned areas. The agreement on cotton was also a positive development in solving the problem of cotton producing developing countries. From development point of view, the duty-free and quota-free access for exports of least developed countries was an achievement. But, nothing concrete happened in services consultations. A number of new deadlines were set in this Conference (Table 15.1).

Table 15.1: New Deadlines

Establishment of Modalities for Agriculture	April 30, 2006
Establishment of Modalities for Non-Agriculture Market Access	April 30, 2006
Submission of Draft Schedules for Agriculture	July 31, 2006
Submission of Draft Schedules for Non-Agriculture Market Access	July 31, 2006
Revised Offers for Services	July 31, 2006
Submission of Draft Schedules for Services	October 31, 2006
Conclusion of the Doha Negotiations	End of 2006
Elimination of All Forms of Export Subsidies on Cotton by Developed Countries	End of 2006
Elimination of All Forms of Export Subsidies on Agriculture	End of 2013

Further movement was dependent on the fulfilment of deadlines set and progress in the framing modalities on agriculture, NAMA and services. The differences in approaches of the Members were still persisting. The conclusion of the Doha Round by the end of 2006 was a remote possibility. But, the Hong Kong Ministerial Conference set the motion in this direction.

Mr. John Tsang, Chairman of the Ministerial Conference, while outlining the achievements, said:

- We have secured an end date for all export subsidies in agriculture.
- We have an agreement on cotton.
- We have a very solid duty-free, quota-free market access for 32 LDCs.
- In agriculture and NAMA, we have flushed out significant framework for full modalities.
- In services, we now have an agreed text that points positively to the way forward.

The WTO Director-General Mr. Pascal Lamy told the press conference: "we have managed to put the Round back on track after a period of hibernation".

16

Geneva Ministerial Conference, 2009

16.1 Introduction

The Seventh WTO Ministerial Conference was held from November 30 to December 2, 2009 in Geneva, Switzerland. The general theme for discussion was: "The WTO, the Multilateral Trading System and the Current Global Economic Environment". The Conference was a non-negotiating one. The Ministerial Conference took place after a gap of four years. The agenda of the Conference was as given below:

1. Overview of Activities of the WTO: The Ministers will have opportunity to review the operation and function of the multilateral system and to make general statements related thereto.
2. Action by Ministers: At the end of plenary session on December 2, Ministers are expected to take any action they may deem appropriate, including on TRIPS non-violation and situation complaints and e-commerce.
3. Date and venue of the Eighth Session of the Ministerial Conference.
4. Election of Officers.

In his report to the General Council on November 17, 2008, Mr. Pascal Lamy said, "the upcoming WTO Ministerial Conference would not be a negotiating session, it would be a platform for Ministers to review the functioning of this house, including the Doha Round and an occasion to send a number of strong signals to the world with respect to the entire WTO waterfront of issues—from monitoring and surveillance to disputes, accessions, aid for trade, technical assistance and international governance".

16.2 Draft on Agriculture, December 6, 2008

The trade negotiations took place at Ministerial level in July 2008. The Chairman, Negotiation Committee (Agriculture Committee in Special Session) circulated among the Members, a revised draft of framework for modalities on agriculture dated December 6, 2008. He said that the negotiations came somewhat closer, but the text was still square bracketed. There was still certain divergence. There was no formal agreement on any or all contained in the draft.

Main points of the draft are given below:

16.2.1 Domestic Support:

1. The base level for reductions in Overall Trade-Distorting Domestic Support (OTDS) shall be the sum of: (a) the Final Bound Total AMS specified in Part IV of the Member's Schedule; plus (b) for developed country Members, 10 percent of the average total value of agricultural production during the 1995-2000 base period (this being composed of 5 percent of the average total value of production for product-

specific and non-product-specific AMS respectively); plus (c) the higher of average Blue Box payments as notified to the Committee on Agriculture, or 5 percent of the average total value of agricultural production, in the 1995-2000 base period.

2. For developing country Members, item (b) of paragraph 1 above shall be 20 percent of the average total value of agricultural production in the 1995-2000 or 1995-2004 period as may be selected by the Member concerned. For developing country Members, the base period for the purposes of item (c) of paragraph 1 above shall be 1995-2000 or 1995-2004 as may be selected by the Member concerned.
3. The Base OTDS shall be reduced in accordance with the following tiered formula: (a) where the Base OTDS is greater than US$ 60 billion, or the equivalent in the monetary terms in which the binding is expressed, the reduction shall be 80 percent; (b) where the Base OTDS is greater than US$ 10 billion and less than or equal to US$ 60 billion, or the equivalents in the monetary terms in which the binding is expressed, the reduction shall be 70 percent; (c) where the Base OTDS is less than or equal to US$ 10 billion, or the equivalent in the monetary terms in which the binding is expressed, the rate of reduction shall be 55 percent.
4. Developed country Members with high relative levels of Base OTDS in the second tier (i.e. at least 40 percent of the average total value of agricultural production in the 1995-2000) shall undertake an additional effort. The additional reduction to be undertaken shall be equal to one half of the difference between the reduction rates specified in paragraphs 3(a) and 3(b) above.
5. For developed country Members, the reductions shall be implemented in six steps over five years. (a) For Members in the first two tiers specified in paragraphs 3(a) and 3(b) above, the Base OTDS shall be reduced by one-third on the first day of implementation. The remaining reductions shall be implemented annually in five equal steps. (b) For Members in the third tier specified in paragraph 3(c) above, the Base OTDS shall be reduced by 25 percent on the first day of implementation. The remaining reductions shall be implemented annually in five equal steps.
6. Developing country Members with no Final Bound Total AMS commitments shall not be required to undertake reduction commitments in their Base OTDS.
7. For developing country Members with Final Bound Total AMS commitments, the applicable reduction in the Base OTDS shall be two-thirds of the relevant rate specified in paragraph 3(c) above. However, net food-importing developing countries shall not be required to undertake reduction commitments in their Base OTDS.
8. For those developing country Members, the reductions shall be implemented in nine steps over eight years. The Base OTDS shall be reduced by 20 percent on the first day of implementation. The remaining reductions shall be implemented annually in eight equal steps.
9. Saudi Arabia, the Former Yugoslav Republic of Macedonia, Vietnam and Ukraine, as very recently acceded Members shall not be required to undertake reduction commitments in their Base OTDS.

10. For those Members that, under these modalities are subject to reduction commitments in their Base OTDS, such commitments shall apply as a minimum overall commitment. Throughout the implementation period and thereafter, each Member shall guarantee that the sum of the applied levels of trade-distorting support under each OTDS component does not exceed the Annual and Final Bound OTDS levels specified in Part IV of its Schedule.

16.2.2 Final Bound Total AMS: Tiered Formulae:

11. The Final Bound Total AMS shall be reduced in accordance with the following tiered formula: (a) where the Final Bound Total AMS is greater than US$ 40 billion, or the equivalent in the monetary terms in which the binding is expressed, the reduction shall be 70 percent; (b) where the Final Bound Total AMS is greater than US$ 15 billion and less than or equal to US$ 40 billion, or the equivalents in the monetary terms in which the binding is expressed, the reduction shall be 60 percent; (c) where the Final Bound Total AMS is less than or equal to US$ 15 billion, or the equivalent in the monetary terms in which the binding is expressed, the rate of reduction shall be 45 percent.
12. Developed country Members with high relative levels of Final Bound Total AMS (i.e. at least 40 percent of the average total value of agricultural production during the 1995-2000 period) shall undertake an additional effort in the form of a higher cut than would otherwise be applicable for the relevant tier. Where the Member concerned is in the second tier, the additional reduction to be undertaken shall be equal to the difference between the reduction rates specified in paragraphs 11(a) and 11(b) above. Where the Member concerned is in the bottom tier, the additional reduction to be undertaken shall be one half of the difference between the reduction rates specified in paragraphs 11(b) and 11(c) above.
13. For developed country Members, reductions in Final Bound Total AMS shall be implemented in six steps over five years. For developed country Members in the top two tiers specified in paragraphs 11(a) and 11(b) above, this shall be implemented by means of a 25 percent reduction on the first day of implementation, followed by reductions in equal annual instalments over five years. For other developed country Members, the reductions shall be implemented in six equal annual instalments over five years, commencing on the first day of implementation.
14. The reduction in Final Bound Total AMS applicable to developing country Members shall be two-thirds of the reduction applicable for developed country Members under paragraph 11(c) above. The reductions in Final Bound Total AMS shall be implemented in nine equal annual instalments over eight years, commencing on the first day of implementation. However, developing country Members with Final Bound Total AMS levels at or below US$ 100 million shall not be required to undertake reductions.
15. NFIDCs shall not be obligatory to undertake reduction commitments in their Final Bound Total AMS.
16. Saudi Arabia, the Former Yugoslav Republic of Macedonia, Vietnam and Ukraine,

as very recently acceded Members shall not be required to undertake reduction commitments in their Final Bound Total AMS.

16.2.3 Product-Specific AMS Limits:

17. Product-specific AMS limits shall be set fixed in terms of monetary value commitments in Part IV of the Schedule of the Member concerned in accordance with terms and conditions specified in the paragraphs below.
18. The product-specific AMS limits specified in the Schedules of all developed country Members other than the United States shall be the average of the product-specific AMS during the Uruguay Round implementation period (1995-2000) as notified to the Committee on Agriculture.
19. For the United States only, the product-specific AMS limits specified in their Schedule shall be the resultant of applying proportionately the average product-specific AMS in the 1995-2004 period to the average product-specific total AMS support for the Uruguay Round implementation period (1995-2000) as notified to the Committee on Agriculture.
20. The scheduled product-specific AMS limits shall be implemented in full on the first day of the implementation period. Where the average notified product-specific AMS in the two most recent years for which notifications are available was higher, the limits shall be implemented in three equal annual instalments, with the starting point for implementation being the lower of the average of those two years or 130 percent of the scheduled limits.
21. Developing country Members shall establish their product-specific AMS limits by choosing one of the following methods, and scheduling all their product-specific AMS commitments in accordance with the method chosen: (a) the average product-specific AMS during the base period 1995-2000 or 1995-2004 as may be selected by the Member concerned, as notified to the Committee on Agriculture; or (b) two times the Member's product-specific *de minimis* level provided for under Article 6.4 of the Uruguay Round Agreement on Agriculture during the base periods referred to in sub-paragraph (a) above; or (c) 20 percent of the Annual Bound Total AMS in the relevant year during the Doha Round implementation period.

16.2.4 De Minimis:

22. The *de minimis* levels on Agriculture for developed country Members (i.e. 5 percent of a Member's total value of production of a basic agricultural product in the case of product-specific *de minimis* and 5 percent of the value of a Member's total agricultural production in the case of non-product-specific *de minimis*) shall be reduced by no less than 50 percent, effective on the first day of the implementation period. In addition, where, in any year of the implementation period, a lower level of *de minimis* support than that resulting from application of that minimum percentage reduction would still be required to ensure that the Annual or Final Bound OTDS commitment for that year is not exceeded, a Member shall undertake such an additional reduction in what would otherwise be its *de minimis* entitlement.
23. For developing country Members with Final Bound Total AMS commitments, the *de*

minimis level on Agriculture (i.e. 10 percent of a Member's total value of production of a basic agricultural product in the case of product-specific *de minimis* and 10 percent of the value of a Member's total agricultural production in the case of non-product-specific *de minimis*) to which they have access under their existing WTO obligations shall be reduced by at least two-thirds of the reduction rate specified in paragraph 22 above. The time frame for implementation shall be three years from the first day of implementation. Moreover, where, in any year of the implementation period, a lower level of *de minimis* support than that resulting from application of that minimum percentage reduction would still be required to ensure that the Annual Bound or Final OTDS commitment for that year is not exceeded, a Member shall undertake such an additional reduction in what would otherwise be their *de minimis* entitlement.

24. Developing country Members with no Final Bound Total AMS commitments; or with such AMS commitments, but that either allocate almost all that support for subsistence and resource-poor producers, or that are NFIDCs shall continue to have the same access as under their existing WTO obligations to the limits provided for product-specific and non-product-specific *de minimis.*

16.2.5 Blue Box:

25. The value of the following domestic support, provided that it is consistent also with the limits as provided for in the paragraphs below, shall be excluded from a Member's calculation of its Current Total AMS but shall count for purposes of that Member's Blue Box commitments and OTDS: (a) Direct payments under production-limiting programmes if: (i) such payments are based on fixed and unchanging areas and yields; or (ii) such payments are made on 85 percent or less of a fixed and unchanging base level of production; or (iii) livestock payments are made on a fixed and unchanging number of head, or (b) Direct payments that do not require production if: (i) such payments are based on fixed and unchanging bases and yields; or (ii) livestock payments are made on a fixed and unchanging number of head; and (iii) such payments are made on 85 percent or less of a fixed and unchanging base level of production.

26. Each Member shall specify in its Schedule which of these categories 25(a) or 25(b) it has selected for the purposes of establishing all its Blue Box commitments in this Round. Any exception to this universal application would be with the agreement of all Members prior to finalization of Schedules. Under no circumstances, could both domestic support categories be made available for any particular product or products.

27. The maximum value of support that can, under the above criteria of "Blue Box", be given under Article 6.5 shall not exceed 2.5 percent of the average total value of agricultural production in the 1995-2000 base period on the basis of notifications to the Committee on Agriculture where they exist. This limit shall be articulated in monetary terms in Part IV of Members' Schedules and shall apply from the first day of the implementation period.

28. In cases where a Member has, consistent with the terms of Article 6.5(a) of the

Uruguay Round Agreement on Agriculture, placed in the Blue Box an exceptionally large percentage of its trade-distorting support—defined as 40 percent—during the 1995-2000 base period, the limit for that Member shall, instead, be established by application of a percentage reduction in that average base period amount. That percentage reduction shall equal the percentage reduction that the Member concerned is to make in its Final Bound Total AMS. This Blue Box limit shall be expressed in monetary terms and bound in Part IV of that Member's Schedule. An implementation period of no more than 2 years may be provided for any such Member in the event that immediate implementation is overly burdensome.

29. Product-specific limits: For all Members other than the United States, the limit to the value of support that may be provided to specific products as Blue Box entitlements shall be the average value of support provided to those products at an individual product level, consistent with Article 6.5(a) of the Uruguay Round Agreement on Agriculture, during the 1995-2000 period and with notifications to the Committee on Agriculture. These product-specific limits shall be articulated in monetary terms at an individual product level, bound in Part IV of the Schedule of the Member concerned, and shall apply from the first day of the implementation period.
30. In any case where under Article 6.5(a), consistent Blue Box support was not provided for the entirety of the 1995-2000 period, the Member concerned shall use the average value of support for the years notified within that period, provided that there are at least three consecutive notified years within that period.
31. For the United States, the limits to the value of support that may be provided to specific products under paragraph 25(b) above shall be [(110) (120)] percent of the average product-specific amounts that would result from applying proportionately the legislated maximum permissible expenditure under the 2002 Farm Bill for specific products at an individual product level to the overall Blue Box limit of 2.5 percent of the average total value of agricultural production during the 1995-2000 period. These product-specific limits shall be expressed in monetary terms at an individual product level and shall be bound in Part IV of that Member's Schedule.
32. Blue Box entitlements for specific products may nevertheless exceed the limits determined under paragraphs 29-31 above but only where there is a corresponding and irreversible one-for-one reduction in the product-specific AMS limits for the products concerned (except for cotton, where that rate would be two-for-one).
33. Where this arises in the context of this particular negotiation, full documentation must be provided in support of this "transfer" to ensure that the starting point is verifiably, on the one hand, the product-specific AMS limit that would have been otherwise adorned in the Schedule through application of the methodology provided above and, on the other, the Blue Box entitlement otherwise inscribed pursuant to application of the methodology set out above.
34. Where this arises as a result of continuation of the reform process after scheduling and during the implementation period, there must be an exact reciprocal reduction in

the scheduled product-specific AMS limit for, as the case may be, a new, or an increase in the scheduled, product-specific Blue Box limit.

35. In both such situations, the overall Blue Box limit cannot in any case be exceeded.

36. Notwithstanding the above, where, for a particular product, there is no product-specific entitlement to a Blue Box limit under the provisions above, and no Current AMS support in the base period for that particular product, a product-specific Blue Box limit may still be scheduled but only where the total support for any such products concerned does not exceed 5 percent of the overall Blue Box limit; there is a maximum for any single product of 2.5 percent of the overall Blue Box limit; and the overall Blue Box limit is still respected. This is available to developed country Members with direct payments of the kind that meet the terms of paragraph 25(a) above, and is a once-only provision for commitment in this Round of negotiations. The monetary value and the products concerned shall be inscribed in a Member's Schedule.

37. For developing country Members, the maximum permitted value of support shall be 5 percent of the average total value of agricultural production in the 1995-2000 or the 1995-2004 base period as may be selected by the Member concerned. That limit shall be expressed in monetary terms and bound in Part IV of developing country Members' Schedules. However, in cases where there is a movement from AMS to Blue subsequent to the conclusion of this negotiation, the developing country Member concerned shall have the option of selecting as its base period, the most recent five year period for which data at that time are available. An NFIDC which chooses not to avail itself of its Blue Box entitlement and thereby is not obliged to Schedule its OTDS, shall so indicate by marking "nil" in the appropriate section of Part IV of its Schedule.

38. Where a product accounted both for more than 25 percent of the average total value of agricultural production and 80 percent of the average Annual Bound Total AMS during the base period, a developing country Member that chooses to switch its support from AMS to Blue for that product, on a one-for-one and irreversible basis, shall be entitled to do so even if this would otherwise lead to exceeding the overall Blue Box limit provided.

Where, for a particular product, a developing country Member has no product-specific entitlement to a Blue Box limit for that product under the provisions, and no Current AMS support in the base period for it, a product-specific Blue Box limit may still be scheduled but only where the total support for the totality of any such products concerned does not exceed 30 percent of the overall Blue Box limit; this is a maximum for any single product of 10 percent of the overall Blue Box limit; and the overall Blue Box limit is still respected. For least-developed country Members and for NFIDCs, these limits shall be 75 percent and 25 percent respectively.

39. For RAMs, the maximum value of support shall be 5 percent of the average total value of agricultural production in the 1995-2000 base period or the 1995-2004 base period as may be selected by the Member concerned. However, in cases where there

is a movement from AMS to Blue subsequent to the conclusion of this negotiation, the Member concerned shall have the option of selecting as its base period the most recent five year period for which data is available at that time.

16.2.6 Green Box: There were provisions for changes to be incorporated in Annex II of Agreement on Agriculture.

16.2.7 Cotton: Domestic Support: Reductions in support for cotton:

40. The development aspects of cotton shall be addressed as provided for in paragraph 12 of the Hong Kong Ministerial Declaration. AMS support for cotton shall be reduced according to the following formula:

$$S = G + \frac{(100 - G) * 100}{3 * G}$$

S = Specific reduction applicable to cotton as a percentage.

G = General reduction in AMS as a percentage.

41. This shall be applied to the base value of support calculated as the arithmetic average of the amounts from 1995 to 2000. The Blue Box limit applicable to cotton shall amount to one-third of the product-specific limit that would otherwise have been the resultant from the methodology generally applicable above.
42. The reductions for trade-distorting domestic support on cotton shall be implemented over a period which is one-third of the implementation period.
43. Developing country Members with relevant AMS and Blue Box commitments for cotton otherwise applicable under the relevant provisions of this Agreement shall provide a rate of reduction for cotton, that is two-thirds of that which would be applicable.
44. Developing country Members shall implement their reduction commitments for cotton over a longer time period than for developed country Members.

16.2.8 Market Access:

45. Subject to such other specific provisions as may be made, all final bound tariffs shall be reduced using the tiered formula set out in the paragraphs below.
46. In order to place final bound non-*ad valorem* tariffs in the appropriate band of the tiered formula, Members shall follow the methodology to calculate *ad valorem* equivalents (AVEs).
47. Developed country Members shall reduce their final bound tariffs in six equal annual instalments over five years in accordance with the following tiered formula: (a) where the final bound tariff or *ad valorem* equivalent is greater than 0 and less than or equal to 20 percent, the reduction shall be 50 percent; (b) where the final bound tariff or *ad valorem* equivalent is greater than 20 percent and less than or equal to 50 percent, the reduction shall be 57 percent; (c) where the final bound tariff or *ad valorem* equivalent is greater than 50 percent and less than or equal to 75 percent, the reduction shall be 64 percent; and (d) where the final bound tariff or *ad valorem* equivalent is greater than 75 percent, the reduction shall be 70 percent.
48. The minimum average cut on final bound tariffs that a developed country Member shall be obliged to undertake is 54 percent. The application of the tiered formula

treatment above, inclusive of the treatment for sensitive products and additional cuts made as provided for elsewhere in these modalities relating to tariff escalation and tropical products result in an overall average cut less than 54 percent, an additional effort shall be made proportionately across all bands to reach that target.

49. Developing country Members shall reduce their final bound tariffs in eleven equal annual instalments over ten years in accordance with the following tiered formula: (a) where the final bound tariff or *ad valorem* equivalent is greater than 0 and less than or equal to 30 percent, the reduction shall be two-third of the cut for developed country Members; (b) where the final bound tariff or *ad valorem* equivalent is greater than 30 percent and less than or equal to 80 percent, the reduction shall be two-third of the cut for developed country Members; (c) where the final bound tariff or *ad valorem* equivalent is greater than 80 percent and less than or equal to 130 percent, the reduction shall be two-third of the cut for developed country Members; and (d) where the final bound tariff or *ad valorem* equivalent is greater than 130 percent, the reduction shall be 2/3 of the cut for developed country Members.
50. The maximum overall average cut on final bound tariffs any developing country Member shall be required to undertake as a result of application of this formula inclusive of the treatment for Sensitive Products is 36 percent. If the above formula implies an overall average cut of more than 36 percent, the developing country Member shall have the flexibility to apply for lesser reductions in a proportionate manner across the bands, to keep within such an average level.
51. Small, vulnerable economies, including those among them which are ceiling binding and homogenously low binding countries shall be entitled to moderate cuts by a further 10 *ad valorem* percentage points in each band.
52. RAMs shall be entitled to moderate the cuts they would otherwise have been required to make under the tiered formula for developing country Members by up to 8 *ad valorem* percentage points. All RAMs shall be permitted to exempt their final bound tariffs at or below 10 percent from reductions in bound tariffs. The implementation period for RAMs may be prolonged by up to two years after the end of the developing country Members' implementation period.
53. Each developed country Member shall have the right to designate up to 4 percent of tariff lines as "sensitive products".

16.3 Draft on Non-agricultural Market Access, December 6, 2008

The Chairman, Negotiating Group on Market Access circulated among the Members a draft dated December 6, on market access. It was the fourth revised draft of framework of modalities on market access. The Chairman said that the degree of convergence on many issues allowed him to present this draft. However, some areas remained where work was required to be done, such as sectorals, preference erosion etc. There was no formal agreement on any part of this draft. This draft might be helpful in further negotiations on the subject. The main aspects of the draft have been given below:

16.3.1 Introduction:

1. In paragraph 16 of the Doha Ministerial Declaration, Members agreed to negotiations which shall aim, by modalities to be agreed, to reduce or as appropriate eliminate tariffs, including the reduction or elimination of tariff peaks, high tariffs, and tariff escalation, as well as non-tariff barriers, in particular on products of export interest to developing countries. Product coverage shall be comprehensive and without *a priori* exclusions. The negotiations shall take fully into account the special needs and interests of developing and least developed Members, including through less than full reciprocity in reduction commitments.
2. Members decided to establish the following modalities for the non-agricultural market access (NAMA) negotiations which shall be applicable to all non-agricultural tariff lines.
3. The results of the application of these modalities shall be reflected in schedules of concessions which shall be submitted and finalized in the Harmonized System 2002 nomenclature.
4. These modalities do not create a new category or sub-category of WTO Members, nor do they create a precedent for future negotiations. In applying these modalities, existing bindings shall not be raised except as provided by Article XXVIII of GATT, 1994.
5. The following formula shall apply on a line-by-line basis:

$$t_1 = \frac{\{a \text{ or } (x \text{ or } y \text{ or } z)\} * t_0}{\{a \text{ or } (x \text{ or } y \text{ or } z)\} + t_0}$$

where,

t_1 = final bound rate of duty,

t_0 = base rate of duty,

$a = 8$ = Coefficient for developed Members,

$x = 20$, $y = 22$, $z = 25$ = Coefficients for developing Members.

6. The following provisions shall apply: (a) Product coverage shall be comprehensive without *a priori* exclusions; (b) Tariff reductions or elimination shall commence from the bound rates after full implementation of current concessions; however, for unbound tariff lines, a constant, non-linear mark-up shall be applied to establish base rates for commencing tariff reductions as follows: applied rate plus 25 percentage points; (c) The base year for MFN applied tariff rates shall be 2001; (d) All non-*ad valorem* duties shall be converted to *ad valorem* equivalents on the basis of the methodology and bound in *ad valorem* terms; (e) The reference period for import data shall be 1999-2001; (f) The first reduction shall be implemented on January 1 of the year following the entry into force of the DDA results and each successive reduction shall be made effective on January 1 of each of the following years, except as otherwise provided. The tariff reductions for developed Members shall be implemented in 5 years (i.e. 6 equal rate reductions) and for developing Members in 10 years (i.e. 11 equal rate reductions), except as otherwise provided.

7. Developing Members, subject to the formula, shall be granted the flexibility to choose to apply the coefficient and flexibilities in paragraph 7(a) or 7(b) or 7(c) as follows: (a) Coefficient 'x' in the formula and either: (i) less than formula cuts for up to 14 percent of non-agricultural national tariff lines provided that the cuts are no less than half the formula cuts and that these tariff lines do not exceed 16 percent of the total value of a Member's non-agricultural imports; or (ii) keeping, as an exception, tariff lines unbound, or not applying formula cuts for up to 6.5 percent of non-agricultural national tariff lines provided they do not exceed 7.5 percent of the total value of a Member's non-agricultural imports; (b) Coefficient 'y' in the formula and either: (i) less than formula cuts for up to 10 percent of non-agricultural national tariff lines provided that the cuts are no less than half the formula cuts and that these tariff lines do not exceed 10 percent of the total value of a Member's non-agricultural imports; or (ii) keeping, as an exception, tariff lines unbound, or not applying formula cuts for up to 5 percent of non-agricultural national tariff lines provided they do not exceed 5 percent of the total value of a Member's non-agricultural import; and (c) Coefficient z in the formula without recourse to flexibilities.
8. Flexibilities for developing countries: (a) As an exception, developing Members with a binding coverage of non-agricultural tariff lines of less than 35 percent will be exempt from making tariff reductions through the formula. Instead, developing Members with a binding coverage of non-agricultural tariff lines: (i) below 15 percent shall bind 75 percent of non-agricultural tariff lines; (ii) at or above 15 percent shall bind 80 percent of non-agricultural tariff lines; and each Member shall bind at an average level that does not exceed 30 percent. (b) These tariff lines shall be bound on January 1 of the year following the entry into force of the DDA results at initial bound rates. (c) The initial bound rates shall be established as follows: for bound tariff lines, the existing bindings shall be used, and for unbound tariff lines the Member subject to this modality will determine the level of the initial binding of those tariff lines. (d) The overall binding target average shall be made effective at the end of the implementation period as follows: the tariff reductions shall be implemented in 11 equal rate reductions. The first reduction shall be implemented on January 1 of the second year following the entry into force of the DDA results and each successive reduction shall be made effective on January 1 of each of the following years. (e) All duties shall be bound on an *ad valorem* basis. Existing bindings on a non *ad valorem* basis shall be converted to *ad valorem* equivalents on the basis of the methodology.

16.3.2 Sectoral Negotiations:

9. The sectoral tariff reduction component is another key element to achieving the objectives of Paragraph 16 of the DDA, the results of which will form part of the single undertaking as provided for in paragraph 47 of the Doha Ministerial Declaration. Such initiatives shall aim to reduce, harmonize or as appropriate, eliminate tariffs, including the reduction or elimination of tariff peaks, high tariffs

and tariff escalation, over and above that which would be achieved by the formula modality, in particular on products of export interest to developing Members. Participation in sectoral initiatives is on a non-mandatory basis, without prejudging the outcome. However, for some Members, sectoral initiatives that reach a critical mass of participation will help to balance the overall results of the negotiation on non-agricultural market access, which includes the coefficients in paragraph 5 and the levels of flexibilities and related provisions of paragraph 7.

10. At the Hong Kong Ministerial Conference, Ministers instructed Members to identify sectoral initiatives which could garner sufficient participation. Progress has been made in a variety of sectoral initiatives. New proposals on sectors/sub-sectors may be submitted immediately or after the establishment of modalities.
11. After the adoption of modalities, Members shall define, sector by sector, special and differential treatment for developing country Members, for example "zero for x" tariff reductions, longer implementation period, later start of implementation and partial product coverage.
12. For scheduling purposes, Members participating in sectoral initiatives shall: (a) No later than 45 days from the date of the establishment of these modalities: (i) submit any new proposals for sectoral initiatives and (ii) indicate, if not already done so, to the proponents of the relevant sectoral initiatives as well as to the Secretariat, the sectoral initiatives, including any sensitivities, on which they agree to participate in the negotiation of terms, without prejudice to their final decision to incorporate the results of the negotiations in their final comprehensive schedules. (b) In the intervening period time between (a) and (c), in order to ensure transparency, a Chair-led multilateral process shall be undertaken. (c) No later than four months from the date of the establishment of these modalities, notify the terms of all final sectoral initiatives. (d) No later than five months from the date of the establishment of these modalities, incorporate on a conditional basis their sectoral commitments in their comprehensive draft schedules. In the intervening period of time between (d) and (e), Members will hold a multilateral review to assess the sectoral outcome. One month should be provided after such a review to finalize the work. (e) At the time of the submission of final comprehensive schedules, incorporate their sectoral commitments on an unconditional basis for sectors that reach a critical mass.

16.3.3 Small, Vulnerable Economies:

13. With the exception of developed Members, those Members having a share of less than 0.1 percent of world NAMA trade for the reference period 1999 to 2001 or best available data as prescribed, may apply the following modality of tariff reduction instead of the formula modality: (a) Members with a bound tariff average of non-agricultural tariff lines: (i) at or above 50 percent shall bind all of their non-agricultural tariff lines at an average level that does not exceed an overall average of 30 percent; (ii) at or above 30 percent but below 50 percent shall bind all their non-agricultural tariff lines at an average level that does not exceed an overall average of 27 percent; (iii) at or above 20 percent but below 30 shall bind all their non-

agricultural tariff lines at an average level that does not exceed an overall average of 18 percent; and (iv) below 20 percent, shall apply a minimum line-by-line reduction of 5 percent on 95 percent of all non-agricultural tariff lines or bind at the overall average that would result from that line-by-line reduction. (b) All tariff lines shall be bound on January 1 of the year following the entry into force of the DDA results at initial bound rates. As an exception, Fiji shall have the flexibility to maintain 10 percent of non-agricultural tariff lines unbound. (c) The initial bound rates shall be established as follows: for bound tariff lines, the existing bindings shall be used, and for unbound tariff lines, the Member subject to this modality will determine the level of the initial binding of those tariff lines. (d) The overall binding target average shall be made effective at the end of the implementation period as follows: the tariff reductions shall be implemented in 11 equal rate reductions. The first reduction shall be implemented on January 1 of the year following the entry into force of the DDA results and each successive reduction shall be made effective on January 1 of each of the following years. (e) All duties shall be bound on an *ad valorem* basis. Existing bindings on a non *ad valorem* basis shall be converted to *ad valorem* equivalents on the basis of the methodology.

16.3.4 Least Developed Countries (LDCs):

14. LDCs shall be exempt from tariff reductions. However, as part of their contribution to the DDA, LDCs are expected to substantially increase their level of tariff binding commitments.
15. Members reaffirmed the need to facilitate LDCs to secure beneficial and meaningful integration into the multilateral trading system. Members agreed that developed Members shall, and developing country Member declaring themselves in a position to do so should: (a) as given here: (i) Provide duty-free and quota-free market access on a lasting basis, for all products originating from all LDCs no later than the start of the implementation period in a manner that ensures stability, security and predictability; (ii) Members facing difficulties at this time to provide market access as set out above shall provide duty-free and quota-free market access for at least 97 percent of products originating from LDCs, defined at the tariff line level, no later than the start of the implementation period; (iii) Developing country Members shall be permitted to phase in their commitments and shall enjoy appropriate flexibility in coverage. (b) Provide meaningfully enhanced market access for all LDCs. (c) Ensure that preferential rules of origin applicable to imports from LDCs will be transparent, simple and contribute to facilitating market access in respect of non-agricultural products.
16. Accordingly, developed country Members shall inform WTO Members, by a date to be agreed, of the products that will be covered under the commitment to provide duty-free and quota-free market access for at least 97 percent of the products originating from LDCs defined at the tariff line level. The agreement on the date by which this information shall be provided shall be concluded prior to the date of the Special Session of the Ministerial Conference to be held to take decisions regarding

the adoption and implementation of the results of the negotiations in all areas of the DDA (the "Single Undertaking").

17. As part of the review foreseen in the Decision, the Committee on Trade and Development shall monitor progress made in its implementation, including in respect of preferential rules of origin. The details of the monitoring procedure shall be defined and agreed by the Negotiating Group on Market Access by the time of the submission of final schedules. Under the monitoring procedure, Members shall annually notify the Committee on Trade and Development: (a) the implementation of duty-free and quota-free programmes, including the steps taken and possible time frames established to progressively achieve full compliance with the Decision and (b) the corresponding rules of origin. The first notification under this monitoring procedure shall be made by the start of the implementation of the results of the Doha Development Agenda. The Committee on Trade and Development shall review such notifications and shall report annually to the General Council for an appropriate action.
18. The RAMs shall apply the modality provided for in either paragraphs 5, 6 and 7 or paragraph 13, as applicable.
19. In addition, the RAMs applying the formula shall be granted an extended implementation period of 3 equal rate reductions to that provided in paragraph 6(f) to implement their Doha commitments.
20. Members may use the request and offer approach as a supplementary modality. Members engaging in such negotiations shall incorporate any outcomes in their final comprehensive draft schedules.
21. Members are asked to consider the elimination of low duties.

16.3.5 Non-tariff Barriers (NTBs):

22. The reduction or elimination of NTBs is an integral and equally important part of the objectives of paragraph 16 of the DDA. More specifically, initiatives in this area shall aim to reduce or eliminate, as appropriate, NTBs, in particular on products of export interest to developing Members and to enhance market access opportunities achieved through these modalities.
23. Members took note of the ongoing work on the proposals. Members considered that the following proposals merit particular attention in text based negotiations in order to achieve substantive NTB results: (a) The horizontal proposals on: (i) Ministerial Decision on Procedures for the Facilitation of Solutions to Non-Tariff Barriers; and (ii) Ministerial Decision on Trade in Remanufactured Goods. (b) The vertical proposals on: (i) Negotiating Proposal on Non-Tariff Barriers in the Chemical Products and Substances Sector; (ii) Understanding on the Interpretation of the Agreement on Technical Barriers to Trade as Applied to Trade in Electronics; (iii) Agreement on Non-Tariff Barriers Pertaining to the Electrical Safety and Electromagnetic Compatibility (EMC) of Electronic Goods; (iv) Understanding on the Interpretation of the Agreement on Technical Barriers to Trade with Respect to the Labelling of Textiles, Clothing, Footwear, and Travel Goods; and (v) Agreement

on Non-Tariff Barriers pertaining to Standards, Technical Regulations and Conformity Assessment Procedures for Automotive Products. (c) Text based negotiations on vertical proposals would also pay attention to any systemic or cross-cutting issues, including those relating to the TBT Agreement that may arise from these proposals. Negotiations on bilateral requests should proceed in tandem. This will allow for sufficient time to multilateralise the outcomes through *inter alia* incorporating them where appropriate into Part III of the schedules.

24. The text based negotiations shall take place in the context of dedicated NTB sessions and work will continue in accordance with the following time table: (a) text based negotiations shall begin immediately on the NTB proposals; (b) no later than two months from the date of the establishment of these modalities Members shall table any revised legal text suggestions; and (c) Members shall finalize the negotiating texts for the purpose of legal revision as early as possible before the submission of final comprehensive draft schedules.
25. These negotiations shall take fully into account, the principle of special and differential treatment for developing and least developed Members.

16.3.6 Capacity-Building Measures:

26. Members are committed to enhancing trade capacity-building measures to assist Members in the early stages of development, and in particular Least Developed Country Members, to address their inherent supply side capacity constraints and the challenges that may arise from increased competition as a result of MFN tariff reductions. These measures, including the Enhanced Integrated Framework for Least Developed Countries and other Aid-for-Trade initiatives, shall be designed to enable such Members to take advantage of increased market access opportunities, including through diversification of export products and markets, and to meet technical standards/requirements and address other non-tariff measures.

16.3.7 Non-reciprocal Preferences:

27. MFN liberalization resulting from the DDA will wear away non-reciprocal preferences in respect of a limited number of tariff lines which are of vital export importance for developing Members who are beneficiaries of such preferences. As a result, and in order to provide these Members with additional time for adjustment, the reduction of MFN tariffs on those tariff lines shall be implemented in 9 equal rate reductions by the preference-granting developed Members concerned. The first reduction shall be implemented two years after the first reduction required under paragraph 6(f) and each successive reduction shall be made effective on January 1 of each of the following years.
28. To further support preference receiving countries to meet the challenges that will arise from increased competition as a result of MFN tariff reductions, preference granting Members, and other Members in a position to do so, are urged to increase their assistance to these Members through mechanisms including the Enhanced Integrated Framework for Least Developed Countries and other Aid-for-Trade initiatives. They are also urged to simplify the rules of origin in their preference

programs so that preference receiving Members can make more effective use of such preferences. Progress in the implementation of such assistance, and its effectiveness in achieving the objectives of this paragraph, shall be reviewed periodically in the Committee on Trade and Development.

29. As a result of action taken under paragraph 27, some developing Members who do not benefit from these preferences and who export under some of those same tariff lines to those preference granting markets, may be disproportionately affected. For these Members, the reduction agreed in paragraph 5 on the relevant tariff lines shall be implemented, by waiver of Article I of the GATT of sufficient duration to cover the full implementation period, in 6 equal rate reductions, in the relevant preference granting markets. The first reduction shall be implemented on January 1 of the year following the entry into force of the DDA results and each successive reduction shall be made effective on January 1 of each of the following years.

16.3.8 Non-agricultural Environmental Goods:

30. The Committee on Trade and Environment in Special Session (CTESS) is working with a view to reaching an understanding on environmental goods. Members are instructed to take guidance from this work and initiate negotiations, without prejudging their outcome, on the reduction or, as appropriate, elimination of tariffs and NTBs on non-agricultural environmental goods.

16.4 Ministerial Discussion

While opening the 7th WTO Ministerial Conference, the Director-General urged the Members to follow the proverb: "unity is strength", and expressed the hope that we "come out of the next few days stronger, more united and with clear determination to conclude the Round in 2010".

The Chairman of the Conference, Mr. Andres Velasco underlined the stabilising effect of the WTO rules and commitments during the current economic crisis and said that they have prevented a protectionist spiral similar to that of the Great Depression. He said that the role of the WTO has clearly been reaffirmed in this crisis, despite doubts about the functioning of international institutions.

16.4.1 The Doha Round: The Ministers said that the eight year old Doha Round negotiations should be concluded quickly, several of them calling for a political push early in the year so that the talks can end in 2010.

Members such as Australia and Pakistan argued that the Ministers' involvement in early 2010 should be more than simply to take stock of the situation. These Members said Ministers should get down to bridging gaps on outstanding political questions. Some Members said a roadmap for future work will be needed. Some Members envisaged this as a possible outcome of senior officials' meeting going to be held in Geneva for a week starting from December 14, 2009. These monthly meetings of senior officials were being continuously held as per the directive of a group of the Ministers who met in New Delhi in September. India opined that the negotiations have given some structure, but only technical topics have been discussed and therefore substantive negotiations could not move forward.

India called for discussions on "headline" issues, such as cotton, domestic support in agriculture, and 'mode 4' in services. Singapore called for seven issues already pointed out by Mr. Lamy as politically difficult subjects that needed to be settled. These were: in agriculture the special safeguard mechanism for developing countries, resolving conflicting proposals over tropical products and products currently enjoying preferences in richer markets, and cotton; in non-agricultural market access (NAMA) bilateral testing of the implications of various flexibilities and free trade in individual sectors; services; rules; including fisheries subsidies; and intellectual property.

The Members urged that the pace of the negotiations would have to accelerate if the deadline for the conclusion of the Round is to be met. They acknowledged that a lot has been achieved in Doha Round Negotiations since the last Ministerial conference in Hong Kong, but much more is left. The Minister from Hong Kong urged the Members to exercise the maximum flexibility in the Doha round in the coming months.

Many Members articulated that the drafts on agriculture and non-agriculture market access circulated by the Chairman of the negotiating group on December 6, 2008 should stay put the basis for negotiation and that the development dimension should be retained at the heart of the Doha Round.

The Director-General, Mr. Pascal Lamy said, "The longer it takes to conclude negotiations, the longer the WTO's insurance policy to guarantee stability and predictability of the market access to governments and traders will remain unsubscribed". He added, "The amount of progress that has been made since the last Ministerial Conference in 2005 is quite impressive".

16.4.2 Regional Trade Agreements: Members mostly agreed that the proliferation of bilateral or regional agreements was a worry for the multilateral trading system. They said Members need to ensure that the two approaches to trade liberalisation continue to support each other, although different participants had different views about how to do this.

Some Members supported putting a mechanism in place which would make sure the eventual convergence of the two approaches. But, other Members rejected the idea of converting the benefits offered in regional agreements into multilateral system.

16.4.3 Accession: Many Members insisted that negotiations for the WTO membership be streamlined so that neighbouring countries with which they trade actively could join the WTO. They were enthusiastic to see this happen to least developing countries. The Members generally agreed that accession is important for broadening and strengthening of WTO. But, opinions differed on approaches to accomplish these: through closer collective attention (the multilateral part of the membership talks) or through the usual practice of giving priorities to bilateral discussions.

16.4.4 Aid for Trade: The Members also documented that providing market access for developing countries and least developed countries is not enough. They said Aid for trade is important to address the supply side constraints and bottlenecks. Many Members called for donors to live up to their commitments.

The Trade Minister of Canada said that the share of global trade held by least developed countries has more than doubled from 0.6 percent to 1.1 percent since 2000.

16.5 Conclusions

The Ministerial Conference took place after a gap of four years, while the usual interval prescribed amounts to two years. Even after such a long interval, only general statements were made by the Ministers. This indicated deep rooted divergences in the interests of the Members and no smooth going in the multilateral trading system.

The Ministerial Conference 2009 was not aimed at trade negotiations. The Minister overviewed the functioning of the multilateral trading system. They discussed topics such as accession, Aid for trade, regional agreements, e-commerce, intellectual property and others. The Ministers made general statements regarding the progress on Doha Development agenda. All of them expressed their desire of early conclusions of negotiations. They also devised different way outs to conclude negotiations in various trade areas. It was decided to conclude the Doha Round by the end of 2010.

The WTO Members ended their two and a half day Geneva Ministerial Conference on December 2, 2009 having declared that they want to try to conclude the Doha Round talks quickly and agreeing to extend 'moratoriums' on e-commerce and intellectual property.

Although this Conference was not designed for negotiations, almost all Trade Ministers said they wanted the "Doha Round Talks" to achieve an agreement soon, a large number of them calling for this to be done by the end of 2010.

17

Geneva Ministerial Conference, 2011

17.1 Introduction

The Eighth Ministerial Conference was held in Geneva, Switzerland, from December 15 to 17, 2011. In parallel to the plenary session, where ministers made prepared statements, the working sessions took place with following themes: "Importance of the Multilateral Trading System and the WTO", "trade and development" and "Doha Development Agenda". In the final session, Ministers adopted a number of decisions and the Chair made a concluding statement.

The Director-General, Pascal Lamy at the opening of the Conference called on Members to "stand up for the values of multilateralism, and for major players to exercise leadership and to muster political courage to act together for greater trade opening and reform, and to place the interest and needs of developing countries and, in particular, those of the poorest, at its heart".

He said, "So far you have failed in your endeavour to amend the WTO rule book to make global trade fairer and more open. The Doha Development Round is at impasse. At the same time, the bilateral and plurilateral trade agreements keep rising, demonstrating that the benefits of trade opening are not in question. How do we explain this paradox"?

He said, "The multilateral trading system is at crossroads. In an interlinked world economy, in constant transformation, it cannot stay put. Either it advances in the spirit of shared values and enhanced cooperation, or we will face a retreat from multilateralism, at our own peril. Waiting for times will simply not suffice. A consensus for inaction would simply mean a consensus for more pain for all".

In the final Session on December 17, 2011, Ministers adopted a number of decisions on intellectual property, electronic commerce, small economies, least developed countries' accession, a service waiver for least developed countries and trade policy reviews.

Trade Ministers adopted a waiver to enable developing and developed country Members to provide preferential treatment to services and service suppliers of LDC Members. 31 least developed countries were to be benefited from preferential treatment designed to promote their trade in those sectors and modes of supply that were of particular interest to them. This waiver, which will last for 15 years from the date of adoption, released developing and developed country Members from their legal obligation to provide non-discriminatory treatment to all trading partners, so as to give them legal cover when they give preferential treatment to least developed countries.

17.2 Ministerial Discussions

The Ministers made discussions on a number of topics as mentioned next:

17.2.1 Keeping Markets Open and Resisting Protectionism: Ministers highlighted the importance of keeping markets open and the need to defy protectionism particularly in this challenging global economic environment. Many Ministers sought a stronger message against protectionism, stating that the prevailing economic climate had made it all the more essential. In this regard, they urged Members to commit to a standstill on all forms of protectionism; to roll back any protectionist measures that had been introduced during the crisis; to not introduce new protectionist measures while the Doha negotiations were ongoing; and, to exercise maximum restraint in implementing measures that may be WTO-consistent but have a significant protectionist effect. The need for a regular monitoring mechanism was highlighted, including through reinforcing the Trade Policy Review Body. Many Ministers welcomed the Director-General's monitoring reports on recent trade developments.

Other Ministers said that the rules-based nature of the WTO system with its rights and obligations needed to be taken into account. Development aspects also required to be considered. They stressed that in these challenging times, the right of Members to use existing WTO-consistent policy space to achieve economic and development objectives should not be curtailed. Some Ministers also stressed that all forms of protectionism, not only tariffs, should be considered in any commitment.

A number of Ministers expressed concern over the increase of protectionism in agricultural trade in the form of trade-restrictive measures without scientific or technical justification and not in conformity with the SPS and TBT Agreements. Some Ministers also expressed concern with increasing resort to private standards and food labelling requirements.

It was suggested that a technical workshop on protectionism be convened in 2012 to examine all aspects of the issue, with participation by all relevant stakeholders.

Ministers widely acknowledged that improving Members' compliance with notification obligations would enhance transparency across WTO bodies and help to discourage protectionism.

17.2.2 Current Global Challenges: A number of Ministers stressed that for the WTO to remain credible and relevant it needed to address current global challenges. Some of the issues mentioned in this discussion included climate change, energy, food security, trade and exchange rates, competition and investment. Some Ministers stated that it was time to explore these issues in WTO regular bodies to enable the membership to improve understanding of their implications for trade and development while continuing efforts to seek a conclusion of the Doha Round.

Other Ministers expressed reservations about initiating negotiations on new issues. They were concerned about the possibility of addressing issues selectively or shifting the focus away from unresolved issues in the DDA negotiations. They stressed that any new issue should only be brought to committees in accordance with their normal rules and procedures and within their respective mandates.

Some Ministers said that the WTO needed to pay more attention to global value chains. In this regard, calls were made to build on the Secretariat's recent "Made in the World" initiative.

Some Ministers welcomed the decision of the Working Group on Trade, Debt and Finance to convene a seminar on the relationship between exchange rates and trade in the first quarter of 2012. Some Ministers also highlighted the need for greater coherence between the WTO and other international institutions, including the IMF.

17.2.3 Dispute Settlement: The central role of the dispute settlement system in ensuring predictability and security of the multilateral trading system was stressed by many Ministers. The need to improve DSU procedures and make the system more accessible to least developed countries and small, vulnerable economies was stressed. In that regard, many Ministers urged the completion of the DSU negotiations in 2012.

17.2.4 Accessions: There was wide convergence on the importance of accessions to making the multilateral trading system truly universal. Ministers welcomed the adoption of the decision further streamlining LDCs accessions and urged its rapid operationalisation. Some Ministers drew attention to the substantive and procedural challenges in the accession process for other developing countries and urged streamlining of these processes too, including not subjecting acceding countries to commitments beyond their levels of development.

17.2.5 Regional Trade Agreements (RTAs): A large number of Ministers pointed to the growing number of RTAs and stressed the need to ensure that they remain complementary to, not a substitute for, the multilateral trading system. In that regard, many Ministers stressed the need for the WTO to address the systemic implications of RTAs for the multilateral trading system and to study trends in RTAs and report to the Ninth Ministerial Conference.

17.2.6 Role of the Committee on Trade and Development (CTD): The importance of the development dimension of the WTO's work was highlighted by a large number of Ministers, many of whom stressed the need to strengthen the CTD as a focal point for development issues. In that context, some Ministers suggested the full operationalisation of the CTD's mandate including the review and monitoring of special and differential treatment provisions in the WTO. Others expressed support for the finalization of the S&D Monitoring Mechanism and the adoption of Annex C of the draft Cancun text. Other Ministers also suggested that consideration should be given to outstanding implementation issues in line with Paragraph 12 of the Doha Ministerial Declaration.

17.2.7 Food Security: Many Ministers urged WTO Members to commit to remove and not to impose in the future, food export restrictions or extraordinary taxes for food purchased for non-commercial humanitarian purposes by the World Food Programme. Other Ministers stressed the importance of addressing the root causes of food insecurity and underlined the importance of allowing Members to use their rights under the WTO Agreements.

Some Ministers signalled their support for a proposal to establish a work programme on trade-related responses to mitigate the impact of food market prices and volatility, especially on LDCs and NFIDCs, for action by the Ninth Ministerial Conference. Several Ministers noted that the issue of food security was multi-faceted and needed to be looked at in its entirety, including the impact of export restrictions on international prices.

17.2.8 Aid for Trade and the Enhanced Integrated Framework: There was broad recognition of the importance of Aid for Trade to build trade capacity and facilitate the integration of beneficiary countries into the multilateral trading system. The specific role of the Enhanced Integrated Framework for LDCs was underscored. Some Ministers called for ensuring that Aid for Trade funding addresses the need of developing countries, particularly the specific needs of small, vulnerable economies and urged co-operation with other relevant institutions to that effect. The importance of the regional dimension of Aid for Trade and of trade finance was also highlighted.

17.2.9 Doha Round Negotiations: Many Ministers expressed deep unhappiness at the impasse currently facing the Doha Round. They nevertheless reaffirmed their commitment to delivering on the Doha mandate.

On the work ahead, while a number of Ministers emphasised their openness to different negotiating approaches, some expressed strong reservations about plurilateral approaches.

Many Ministers stressed the need for Members to start identifying areas where provisional or definitive agreements could be reached in the shorter term. Others indicated the need to move step by step, bottom-up, to avoid repeating past failed attempts.

Many Members stressed that all different approaches in the work ahead should conform to the Doha mandate, respect the single undertaking, and be truly multilateral, transparent and inclusive.

In looking at future work, a large number of Ministers stressed the centrality of development. Many underlined the need to give priority to issues of interest to LDCs, including cotton. Many mentioned the importance of all three pillars in the agriculture negotiations. Many also mentioned trade facilitation, special and differential treatment, S&D Monitoring Mechanism and non-tariff measures.

There was a shared sense that a key question to unlock the current impasse is the balance in contributions and responsibilities between emerging and advanced economies, although there were different views as to what the appropriate shares in this balance should be.

Several Ministers emphasized the importance of a transparent, inclusive and bottom-up approach in the work ahead while others stressed the need to take account of all Members views and avoid attributing the views of a few to the whole membership.

17.3 Decisions of the Ministerial Conference

The Ministerial Conference took the following decisions:

17.3.1 TRIPS Non-Violation and Situation Complaints: The Ministerial Conference took note of the work done by the Council for Trade-Related Aspects of Intellectual Property Rights pursuant to their Decision of December 2, 2009 on "TRIPS Non-Violation and Situation Complaints" and directed it to continue its examination of the scope and modalities for complaints of the types provided for under subparagraphs 1(b) and 1(c) of Article XXIII of GATT, 1994 and make recommendations to the next Session of the Ministerial Conference. It was agreed that, in the meantime, Members will not initiate such complaints under the TRIPS Agreement.

17.3.2 Work Programme on Electronic Commerce: The Ministerial Conference decided to continue the reinvigoration of the Work Programme on Electronic Commerce adopted on September 25, 1998, based on its existing mandate and guidelines and on the basis of proposals submitted by Members, including the development-related issues under the Work Programme and the discussions on the trade treatment, *inter alia*, of electronically delivered software, and to adhere to the basic principles of the WTO, including non-discrimination, predictability and transparency, in order to enhance internet connectivity and access to all information and telecommunications technologies and public internet sites, for the growth of electronic commerce, with special consideration in developing countries, and particularly in least developed country Members. The Work Programme shall also examine access to electronic commerce by micro, small and medium sized enterprises, including small producers and suppliers.

The Ministers directed the General Council to emphasize and reinvigorate the development dimension in the Work Programme particularly through the CTD to examine and monitor development related issues such as technical assistance, capacity building, and the facilitation of access to electronic commerce by micro, small and medium sized enterprises, including small producers and suppliers, of developing countries and particularly of least developed country Members. Further, any relevant body of the Work Programme may discover appropriate mechanisms to address the relationship between electronic commerce and development in a focused and comprehensive manner.

It was decided that Members will maintain the current practice of not imposing customs duties on electronic transmissions until the next Session of the Ministerial Conference.

17.3.3 Work Programme on Small Economies: The Ministerial Conference recommitted to the Work Programme on Small Economies and took note of all the work conducted so far. The Ministers directed the CTD to continue its work in Dedicated Sessions under the overall responsibility of the General Council. Furthermore, it shall consider in further detail the proposals contained in the various submissions that have been received to date, examine any additional proposals that Members might wish to submit and, where possible, and within its mandate, make recommendations to the General Council, on any of these proposals. The Ministers directed the General Council to direct relevant subsidiary bodies to frame responses to the trade-related issues identified by the CTD with a view to making recommendations for action and instructed the WTO Secretariat to provide relevant information and factual analysis for discussion among Members in the CTD Dedicated Session, *inter alia*, in the relevant areas of the Work Programme on Small Economies, and on the identification and effects of non-tariff measures on small economies. They instructed the CTD in Dedicated Session to continue monitoring the progress of the Small and Vulnerable Economies' proposals in WTO bodies and negotiating groups with the aim of providing responses, as soon as possible, to the trade-related issues identified for the fuller integration of small, vulnerable economies in an appropriate manner in the multilateral trading system.

17.3.4 Extension of Transition Period under TRIPS for LDCs: The Ministerial Conference decided to invite the TRIPS Council to give full consideration to a duly motivated request from Least Developed Country Members for an extension of their transition period under Article 66.1 of the TRIPS Agreement, and report thereon to the WTO Ninth Ministerial Conference.

17.3.5 Accession of Least Developed Countries: The Ministerial Conference recommitted to the LDC accession guidelines adopted in 2002. The Ministers directed the Sub-Committee on LDCs to develop recommendations to further strengthen, streamline and operationalise the 2002 guidelines by, *inter alia*, including benchmarks, in particular in the area of goods, which take into account the level of commitments undertaken by existing LDC Members. Benchmarks in the area of services should also be explored.

The Ministers acknowledged that transparency in the accession negotiations should be enhanced, including by complementing bilateral market access negotiations with multilateral frameworks.

They reiterated that S&D provisions, as stipulated in the 2002 guidelines, shall be applicable to all acceding LDCs, and that requests for additional transition periods will be considered taking into account individual development needs of acceding LDCs.

They underlined the need for enhanced technical assistance and capacity building to help acceding LDCs to complete their accession process, implement their commitments and to integrate them into the multilateral trading system. Appropriate tools should be developed to assess the needs and to ensure greater coordination in the delivery of technical assistance, making optimal use of all facilities, including the EIF. They instructed the Sub-Committee on LDCs to complete this work and make recommendations to the General Council no later than July 2012.

17.3.6 Services Waiver for Least Developed Countries: Considering the 1979 Decision on Differential and More Favourable Treatment, Reciprocity and Fuller Participation of Developing Countries, the 1994 Decision on Measures in Favour of Least Developed Countries, and the 1999 Decision on Preferential Tariff Treatment for Least Developed Countries, and other provisions of the Agreements; and without injustice to the rights of Members to continue to act pursuant to the provisions contained in those Decisions; and noting that the WTO Agreement recognises the need for "positive efforts designed to ensure that developing countries, especially the least developed among them, secure a share in the growth in international trade commensurate with the needs of their economic development", the Ministerial Conference decided as follows:

1. Despite the provisions of Article II of the GATS, Members may provide preferential treatment to services and service suppliers of least developed countries with respect to the application of measures described in Article XVI and any other measures as

may be annexed to this waiver, than to like services and service suppliers of other Members. Any such treatment shall be granted immediately and unconditionally to like services and service suppliers of all least developed country Members. Preferential treatment with respect to the application of measures other than those described in Article XVI, is subject to approval by the Council for Trade in Services in accordance with its procedures and will be annexed to this waiver.

2. Each Member according preferential treatment pursuant to this waiver shall submit a notification to the Council for Trade in Services. The notification shall specify the preferential treatment made available, the sectors or sub-sectors concerned and the period of time during which the Member is intending to maintain those preferences. A supplemental notification shall be made if the preferential treatment is subsequently modified. The notifications shall be made before the preferential treatment is granted or modified.
3. Each Member granting preferential treatment pursuant to this waiver shall, upon request, promptly enter into consultations with any Member with respect to any difficulty or matter that may arise as a result of such treatment. Where a Member considers that any benefit accruing to it under the GATS may be or is being damaged unduly as a result of such treatment, the consultations shall examine the possibility of action for a satisfactory adjustment of the matter.
4. Any preferential treatment accorded pursuant to this Waiver shall be designed to promote the trade of least developed countries in those sectors and modes of supply that are of particular export interest to the least developed countries and not to raise barriers or create undue difficulties for the trade of any other Member. Such preferential treatment shall not constitute an obstruction to the reduction or elimination of market access barriers on a most-favoured nation basis.
5. For the purpose of preferential treatment, a service supplier of a least developed country is: (a) a natural person of a least developed country; or (b) a juridical person.
6. This Waiver shall terminate upon the expiration of a period of 15 years from the date of its adoption.
7. This Waiver shall apply to preferential treatment granted to services and service suppliers of least developed countries designated as such by the United Nations. This Waiver shall terminate with respect to the preferential treatment granted to services and service suppliers of any particular least developed country when graduation of that country from the United Nations list of least developed countries becomes effective.

17.3.7 Trade Policy Review Mechanism: The Ministerial Conference documented the regular work undertaken by the Trade Policy Review Body on the monitoring exercise of trade and trade-related measures in fulfilling its mandate. The Ministers took note of the work initially done in the context of the global financial and economic crisis, and directed it to be continued and strengthened. They therefore invited the Director-General to continue presenting his trade monitoring reports on a regular basis, and asked the TPRB to consider these monitoring reports in addition to its meeting to undertake the Annual Overview of Developments in the International Trading Environment. They committed to duly comply with the existing transparency obligations and reporting requirements needed for the preparation of these monitoring reports, and to continue to support and cooperate with the WTO Secretariat in a constructive fashion. They called upon the TPRB to continue discussing the strengthening of the monitoring exercise of trade and trade-related measures on the basis of Members' inputs.

17.4 Political Guidance

These elements were the subject of consensus in the General Council. They were circulated among the Members. The General Council Chairman, while concluding the Conference reiterated that nothing in this text re-interprets or changes any WTO rules or agreements or prejudices any Member's rights and obligations. In particular, the Doha mandate remains as formally agreed by Members in its entirety. The elements of this text are not legally binding on the Members. The elements of political guidance are given below.

17.4.1 Importance of the Multilateral Trading System and the WTO: Ministers emphasized the value of the rules-based multilateral trading system and agreed to strengthen it and make it more responsive to the needs of Members, especially in the current challenging global economic environment, in order to stimulate economic growth, employment and development.

Ministers underscored that the WTO's role in keeping markets open is particularly critical in light of the challenging global economic environment. The WTO has a vital role to play in the fight against all forms of protectionism and in promoting economic growth and development. Ministers also acknowledged that experience has shown that protectionism tends to deepen global economic downturns. Ministers fully recognized WTO rights and obligations of Members and affirmed their commitment to firmly resist protectionism in all its forms.

Ministers underlined the importance of the work of regular WTO bodies including their role in the oversight of implementing existing Agreements; dispute avoidance; transparency through monitoring and reporting and as a forum for the consideration of trade-related issues raised by Members. Ministers called for strengthening and improving their functioning.

Ministers acknowledged the important asset that the WTO Dispute Settlement system represents and committed themselves to strengthen it, including through concluding the DSU review negotiations.

Ministers welcomed the accessions of Vanuatu, Samoa, the Russian Federation and Montenegro to the WTO and recognized the contribution of accession to strengthening the multilateral trading system. Ministers remain committed to efforts to facilitate accessions, in particular of least developed countries (LDCs).

17.4.2 Trade and Development: Ministers recommitted that development is a core element of the WTO's work. They also reaffirmed the positive link between trade and development and called for focused work in the Committee on Trade and Development (CTD) which was to conduct this work in accordance with its mandate and report the results achieved to Ministers at the Ninth Session. Ministers called on WTO Members to fully operationalize the mandate of the CTD as a focal point for development work.

Ministers reaffirmed the need for the WTO to assist in further integrating developing countries, particularly LDCs and, without creating a sub-category of WTO Members, small, vulnerable economies, into the multilateral trading system.

Ministers acknowledged the needs of LDCs and committed themselves to ensure that LDCs' interests are given due priority in the future work of the WTO. In this regard, they have taken decisions concerning LDC accession, extension of the LDC transition period under Article 66.1 of the TRIPS Agreement, and LDCs services waiver. Ministers also urged the full implementation of Decision of the Hong Kong Ministerial Declaration of 2005 on measures in favour of LDCs. Ministers also welcomed the Istanbul Programme of Action for LDCs for the decade 2011-2020.

Ministers confirmed their commitment to ongoing dialogue and engagement to progress the mandate of the Hong Kong Ministerial Declaration to address cotton "ambitiously, expeditiously and specifically", within the agriculture negotiations. Ministers highlighted the value of ongoing reporting on cotton, and invited the Director-General to continue furnishing periodic reports on the development assistance aspects of cotton to each Ministerial Conference. Ministers commended the work being undertaken within the Director-General's Consultative Process to advance developmental assistance aspects of cotton.

Ministers reaffirmed the internality of special and differential treatment provisions to the WTO agreements and their determination to fulfil the Doha mandate to review them with a view to strengthening them and making them more precise, effective and operational. Ministers agreed to expedite work towards finalizing the Monitoring Mechanism for special and differential treatment. They also agreed to take stock of the 28 Agreement-specific proposals in Annex C of the draft Cancún text with a view to formal adoption of those agreed.

Ministers took note of the progress achieved on Aid for Trade and of the Third Global Aid for Trade Review. They agreed to maintain, beyond 2011, Aid for Trade levels that at least reflect the average of the period 2006-2008 and to work with development banks to make certain the availability of trade finance to low income countries. Ministers reiterated their commitment to funding the WTO Global Trust Fund in a predictable and timely manner to enable the Secretariat to continue to provide the Technical Assistance and Capacity Building required.

Ministers acknowledged the WTO's co-operation with other development-related organizations, in particular, the International Trade Centre (ITC). Ministers reaffirmed the ITC's role in improving and enhancing trade support institutions and policies for the benefit of exporting efforts; and in strengthening the export capacity of enterprises to respond to market opportunities. Ministers encouraged the ITC to support and assist developing countries to address business environment and market access issues affecting the private sector.

17.4.3 Doha Development Agenda: Ministers deeply expressed the regret that, despite full engagement and intensified efforts to conclude the Doha Development Agenda since the last Ministerial Conference, the negotiations were at an impasse.

Ministers acknowledged that there are significantly different perspectives on the possible results that Members could achieve in certain areas of the single undertaking. In this context, it is unlikely that all elements of the Doha Development Round could be concluded simultaneously in the near future.

Regardless of this situation, Ministers remained committed to work actively, in a transparent and inclusive manner, towards a successful multilateral conclusion of the Doha Development Agenda in accordance with its mandate.

In order to achieve this end and to facilitate early progress, Ministers acknowledged that Members need to more fully explore different negotiating approaches while respecting the principles of transparency and inclusiveness.

In this context, Ministers committed to advance negotiations, where progress could be achieved, including focusing on the elements of the Doha Declaration that allow Members to reach provisional or definitive agreements based on consensus earlier than the full conclusion of the single undertaking.

Ministers also stressed that they will intensify their efforts to look into ways that may allow Members to overcome the most critical and fundamental stalemates in the areas where multilateral convergence has proven to be especially challenging.

Ministers maintained that, in their negotiations, they will continue their work based on the progress already made. Ministers affirmed that any agreements reached, at any time, have to respect fully the development component of the mandate.

17.5 Conclusions

Though there was deadlock on the Doha Round, the Eighth Ministerial Conference succeeded in developing the atmosphere for further talks and in bringing, to some extent, the multilateral trading system back on track. The Ministerial Conference took decisions on TRIPS non-violation and situation complaints, work programme on electronic-commerce, work programme on small economies, extension of transition period under TRIPS for LDCs, a services waiver for LDCs, accession of LDCs, and trade policy review mechanism. A text of elements of political guidelines, though not legally binding, was circulated among the Members. It was intended that this text might remind the Members about their responsibilities towards the welfare of the world economy and the importance of multilateral trading system as a means to attain this. The consensus on these elements of political guidelines was in itself a positive step forward to mitigate the hurdles in resuming the negotiations further. The suggestion of making provisional or definitive agreements wherever possible, even before the conclusion of single understanding, was an indication that Members were committed and willing to move forward on negotiations and to end the impasse on Doha development Agenda. All this was to be judged by the outcomes of the Ninth

Ministerial Conference in Bali, Indonesia in 2013.

While concluding the Ministerial Conference, the Chairman said, "I see this Ministerial Conference as significant in three main ways. Firstly, it has produced some positive decisions—the accessions of Russia, Montenegro and Samoa in particular, but also the Government Procurement Agreement and the seven Decisions we have just adopted. Secondly, we have sent a strong collective message that the WTO is more than ever important to the world. And thirdly, we have seen constructive dialogue among Ministers which has improved the WTO's atmosphere and outlook".

18

Bali Ministerial Conference, 2013

18.1 Introduction

The Ninth Session of the WTO Ministerial Conference was held in Bali, Indonesia from December 3 to 7, 2013. A consensus on a package of texts was almost reached by November 26, 2013. There was some divergence on public stockholding for food security purposes. Members were quite hopeful that the negotiations at Bali might lead to the agreement on the package.

On the opening ceremony on December 3, 2013, the Chairman of the Conference, Mr. Gita Wirjawan said, "Success at MC-9, paving the way for further progress under the Doha Development Agenda, will provide a major boost to world trade and economic growth. Over the past few weeks and months, our negotiators in Geneva have been working hard to put together a package of outcomes that would harvest the first results of the Doha Development Agenda. I salute their efforts".

He further said: "This will not be easy. If it were easy, we would have not taken over 12 years to reach this point. But that is the nature of international negotiations. The need for flexibility, compromise and pragmatism is paramount. I trust we can all bear that in mind as we work over the next few days to capitalize on the programme made in Geneva".

On the opening day, the Director-General said, "The package (Bali) contains 10 draft texts comprising: a draft trade facilitation agreement, four texts on agriculture, and five covering development and LDC issues".

He further said, "This is a single package—you cannot remove a pillar, or even a brick from the pillar, without bringing the whole edifice down. We failed to find a full convergence in Geneva. We came truly close to a successful outcome but we did not quite get there. Ministers have a chance to change this".

At the plenary session, Indian trade Minister Mr. Anand Sharma said, "For over 12 years, we have struggled to bring the complex negotiations of the Doha Round to conclusion. The continuing stalemate has led to frustration and cynicism when this was the only round dedicated to development.

India has remained sincerely and constructively engaged in the challenging negotiations in Geneva. A candid evaluation of the proposed package is required. We firmly believe that a package at Bali must be substantive with demonstrable horizontal balance.

We have a half baked agriculture package, statements of pious intent for LDCs and several unresolved issues in the trade facilitation agenda.

Most of the texts that are before us are ostensibly for the benefit of developing countries. In reality, on issues including cotton subsidies, export competition, monitoring mechanism on DFQF, the draft texts contain mere statements of intents with best behaviour precision. Even in trade facilitation, while financial support for LDCs and some developing countries was considered a core element since the commencement of negotiations, it has now been diluted with only a weak and non-binding reference in the footnotes.

None of these texts require the developed countries to make binding commitments for the benefit of developing countries. In contrast, developing countries would be required to undertake significant steps in trade facilitation. If this imbalance in the Bali package is not addressed, the world at large would accuse us collectively making hollow promises and keeping the tank empty on development count.

Historical imbalances in trade rules must be corrected to ensure a rules-based, fair and equitable order.

Public procurement at administered prices is often the only method of supporting farmers and building stocks for food security in developing countries. Need of public stock holding of food grains to ensure food security must be respected.

I bring with me the mandate of my government to expand the coverage of duty-free quota-free market access for LDCs to 96.2 percent of Indian tariff lines".

18.2 Ministerial Declaration

The Ministers made the Declaration and took decisions on December 7, 2013, the last day of the Ministerial Conference. The Decisions and Declarations taken have been divided into three parts: Part I contains decisions relating to the regular work under the General Council; Part II contains decisions and declarations pertaining to the Doha Development Agenda; and Part III has the Declarations made about post-Bali work. The Decisions and Declarations adopted by the Ministers have been described below:

1. The Ministers expressed their deep appreciation to the Government and people of Indonesia for the excellent organisation and the warm hospitality they received in Bali.
2. The Ministers recommitted to the principles and objectives set out in the Marrakesh Agreement Establishing the World Trade Organisation. They also recalled the Declarations and Decisions they adopted at Doha and at the Ministerial Conferences they held since then and reaffirmed their full commitment to give effect to them.
3. The Ministers took note of the reports from the General Council and its subsidiary bodies. They welcomed the progress that these reports, and the decisions stemming from them, shown in the work of the WTO, thereby strengthening its effectiveness and the multilateral trading system as a whole.
4. The Ministers specially welcomed the advances made in the Doha Development Agenda, as represented by the Decisions and Declarations adopted in this Session. These Decisions and Declarations signified that they had taken a major step forward in the negotiations and attested their strong resolve to complete the Doha Development Agenda.

18.2.1 Part I: Regular Work under the General Council:

5. They welcomed the progress in the regular work under the General Council and they adopted the following decisions: (a) TRIPS Non-violation and Situation Complaints, (b) Work Programme on Electronic Commerce, (c) Work Programme on Small Economies, (d) Aid for Trade and (e) Trade and Transfer of Technology.
6. The Ministers further welcomed the following decisions taken in response to the relevant mandate from the Eighth Session of the Ministerial Conference: (a) Decision adopted by the TRIPS Council concerning the extension of the transition period for least developed country Members; (b) Decision adopted by the General Council on the Accession of LDCs.
7. The Ministers welcomed those new Members who completed their accession processes since the Eighth Session of the Ministerial Conference.

18.2.2 Part II: Doha Development Agenda:

8. The Ministers welcomed the progress in the Doha Development Agenda. They adopted the following Decisions and Declarations at the Ninth Session of the Ministerial Conference: (a) Trade Facilitation (i) Agreement on Trade Facilitation, (b) Agriculture: (i) General Services, (ii) Pubic Stockholding for Food Security Purposes, (iii) Understanding on Tariff Rate Quota Administration Provisions of Agriculture products as defined in Article 2 of the Agreement on Agriculture; and (iv) Export Competition, (b) Cotton, (c) Development and LDC Issues: (i) Preferential Rules of Origin for Least Developed Countries, (ii) Operationalisation of the Waiver Concerning Preferential Treatment to Services and Services Suppliers of Least Developed Countries, (iii) Duty Free and Quota-Free Market Access for Least Developed Countries and (iv) Monitoring Mechanism on Special and Differential Treatment.

18.2.3 Part III: Post-Bali Work:

9. The Ministers reaffirmed their commitment to the WTO as a pre-eminent global forum for trade, including negotiating and implementing trade rules, settling disputes and supporting development through the integration of developing countries into the global trading system. They reaffirmed their commitment to the Doha Development Agenda, as well as to the regular work of the WTO.
10. The Ministers took note of the progress that was made towards carrying out the Doha Work Programme, including the decisions they have taken on the Bali Package during this Ministerial Conference. These decisions would be an important stepping stone towards the completion of the Doha Round. They reaffirmed their commitments to the development objectives set out in the Doha Declaration, as well as to all their subsequent decisions and declarations and the Marrakesh Agreement establishing the WTO.
11. The Ministers directed the Trade Negotiations Committee to prepare within the next 12 months, a clearly defined work programme on the remaining Doha Development Agenda issues. This would build on the decisions taken at this Ministerial Conference, particularly on agriculture, development and LDC issues, as well as all

other issues under the Doha mandate that are central to concluding the Round. Issues in the Bali Package where legally binding outcomes could not be achieved were to be prioritised. Work on issues in the Package that were not fully addressed at this Conference was to be resumed in the relevant Committees or Negotiating Groups of the WTO.

12. The work programme was to be developed in a way that was consistent with the guidance that the Ministers provided at the Eighth Ministerial Conference, including the need to look at ways that might allow Members to overcome the most critical and fundamental stumbling blocks.

18.3 Decisions and Declarations Adopted

The Decisions and Declarations adopted at the Ministerial Conference have been described below.

18.3.1 TRIPS Non-violation and Situation Complaints: The Ministerial Conference took note of the work done by the Council for Trade-Related Aspects of Intellectual Property Rights pursuant to the Decision of December 17, 2011 on "TRIPS Non-Violation and Situation Complaints", and directed it to continue its examination of the scope and modalities for complaints of the types provided for under subparagraphs 1(b) and 1(c) of Article XXIII of GATT, 1994 and make recommendations to the next Session of the Ministerial Conference. It was agreed that, in the meantime, Members will not initiate such complaints under the TRIPS Agreement.

18.3.2 Work Programme on Electronic Commerce: The Ministers decided to continue with the positive work under the Work Programme on Electronic Commerce since the last Session, based on its existing mandate and guidelines and on the basis of proposals submitted by Members in the respective WTO bodies. In that regard, the Ministers directed the General Council and its relevant bodies to continue substantially stimulating this work, especially under the initiatives taken in relation to commercial issues, development and evolving technology addressed in the discussions and the two complementary workshops held under the auspices of the CTD and CTS on electronic commerce. Any relevant body of the Work Programme may explore appropriate mechanisms to address the relationship between electronic commerce and development in a focused and comprehensive manner.

The Work Programme should continue to examine the trade related aspects of, *inter alia,* enhancing internet connectivity and access to information and telecommunications technologies and public internet sites, the growth of mobile telephony, electronically delivered software, cloud computing, the protection of confidential data, privacy and consumer protection.

The Ministers further reiterated that the Work Programme shall take forward the issues emerging in the discussions and the evolving application of e-commerce to enhance economic/development opportunities, with special consideration of the situation in developing countries, particularly in least developed country Members and least connected countries. The Work Programme should continue to examine opportunities and challenges for access to electronic commerce by micro, small and medium sized enterprises, including small producers and suppliers.

They directed the General Council to hold periodic reviews in its sessions of July and December 2014 and July 2015, based on the reports submitted by the WTO bodies entrusted with the implementation of the Work Programme. The Ministers decided to assess its progress and consider any recommendations on possible measures related to electronic commerce in the next session of the Ministerial Conference.

It was decided that Members would maintain the current practice of not imposing customs duties on electronic transmissions until the next Session.

18.3.3 Work Programme on Small Economies: The Ministers reaffirmed their commitment to the Work Programme on Small Economies and took note of all the work conducted to date. They took note of the work carried out since 2011 including that on the effects of non-tariff measures on small economies and instructed the CTD to continue its work in Dedicated Sessions under the overall responsibility of the General Council.

Furthermore, the Ministers instructed the Dedicated Session to consider in further detail, the proposals contained in the various submissions that had been received to date, to examine any additional proposals that Members might wish to submit and, where possible, and within its mandate, to make recommendations to the General Council on any of these proposals.

The Ministers instructed the General Council to direct relevant subsidiary bodies to frame responses to the trade-related issues identified by the CTD with a view to making recommendations for action. They instructed the WTO Secretariat to provide relevant information and factual analysis for discussion among Members in the CTD's Dedicated Session, *inter alia*, in the relevant areas identified in the Work Programme on Small Economies and, in particular, the challenges and opportunities experienced by small economies when linking into global value chains in trade in goods and services.

18.3.4 Aid for Trade: The Ministers welcomed progress on Aid for Trade and took note of the deliberations and outcomes of the 4th Global Review of Aid for Trade held from July 8 to 10, 2013. They recognized the continuing need of Aid for Trade for developing countries, and in particular of LDCs.

They reaffirmed their commitment to Aid for Trade and reiterated the mandate given to the Director-General to pursue actions in support of Aid for Trade. The new Aid for Trade Work Programme should be framed by the post-2015 development agenda.

18.3.5 Trade and Transfer of Technology: Pursuant to the mandate contained in paragraph 37 of the Doha Ministerial Declaration, and subsequent affirmation, in paragraph 43, by Ministers in the Hong Kong Declaration, Members had examined the relationship between trade and transfer of technology and had also considered possible recommendations on steps that might be made within the mandate of the WTO to increase flows of technology to developing countries.

The ongoing work, on the basis of submissions by Members and contributions by various intergovernmental organizations had covered a number of issues and helped to enhance Members' understanding of the complex issues that encompass the nexus between trade and transfer of technology.

Although progress had been made, more work remained to be done. In view of this, the Ministers directed that the Working Group should continue its work in order to fully achieve the mandate of the Doha Ministerial Declaration.

18.3.6 Agreement on Trade Facilitation: In December 2013, WTO Members concluded negotiations on a Trade Facilitation Agreement at the Bali Ministerial Conference, as part of a wider 'Bali Package'. Since then, WTO Members have undertaken a legal review of the text. In line with the decision adopted in Bali, WTO Members adopted on November 27, 2014, a Protocol of Amendment into Annex 1A of the WTO Agreement. The Agreement on Trade Facilitation has to be operational once two-third of the Members complete their domestic ratification process.

The Agreement on Trade Facilitation contains provisions for expediting the movement, release and clearance of goods, including goods in transit. It also set out measures for effective cooperation between customs and other appropriate authorities on trade facilitation and customs compliance issues. It further contains provisions for technical assistance and capacity building in this area.

The Agreement allows developing countries and LDCs to choose which parts to implement immediately, which to delay (until an announced date), and which to delay because the countries need technical assistance.

Desiring to clarify and improve relevant aspects of Articles V, VIII and X of the GATT, 1994 with a view to further expediting the movement, release and clearance of goods, including goods in transit; recognizing the particular needs of developing and especially least developed country Members and desiring to enhance assistance and support for capacity building in this area; and recognizing the need for effective cooperation among Members on trade facilitation and customs compliance issues.

18.3.7 Agriculture: General Services: Members accepted the contribution that General Services programmes could make to rural development, food security and poverty alleviation, particularly in developing countries. This included a range of General Services programmes relating to land reform and rural livelihood security that a number of developing countries had highlighted as particularly important in advancing these objectives. Accordingly, Members noted that, subject to Annex 2 of the Agreement on Agriculture, the types of programmes listed below could be considered as falling within the scope of the non-exhaustive list of general services programmes in Annex 2, paragraph 2 of the Agreement on Agriculture.

General Services programmes related to land reform and rural livelihood security in order to promote rural development and poverty alleviation, for example:

1. Land rehabilitation.
2. Soil conservation and resource management.
3. Drought management and flood control.
4. Rural employment programmes.
5. Issuance of property titles.

6. Farmer settlement programmes.

18.3.8 Agriculture: Pubic Stockholding for Food Security Purposes: The following decisions were taken:

1. Members agreed to put in place an interim mechanism as set out below, and to discuss on an agreement for a permanent solution, for the issue of public stockholding for food security purposes for adoption by the Eleventh Ministerial Conference.
2. In the protem, until a permanent solution is found, and provided that the conditions set out below are met, Members shall refrain from challenging through the WTO Dispute Settlement Mechanism, compliance of a developing Member with its obligations under Articles 6.3 and 7.2(b) of the Agreement on Agriculture in relation to support provided for traditional staple food crops in pursuance of public stockholding programmes for food security purposes existing as on the date of this Decision, that are consistent with the criteria of paragraph 3, footnote 5, and footnote 6 of Annex 2 to the Agreement on Agriculture when the developing Member complies with the terms of this Decision.

A. Notification and Transparency:

3. A developing Member benefiting from this Decision must: (a) have notified the Committee on Agriculture that it is exceeding or is at risk of exceeding either or both of its Aggregate Measurement of Support (AMS) limits (the Member's Bound Total AMS or the *de minimis* level) as result of its programmes mentioned above; (b) have fulfilled and continue to fulfil its domestic support notification requirements under the Agreement on Agriculture; (c) have provided, and continue to provide on an annual basis, additional information for each public stockholding programme that it maintains for food security purposes; and (d) provide any additional relevant statistical information in the prescribed statistical format as soon as possible after it becomes available, as well as any information updating or correcting any information earlier submitted.

B. Anti-Circumvention/Safeguards:

4. Any developing Member seeking coverage of programmes under paragraph 2 shall ensure that stocks procured under such programmes do not distort trade or adversely affect the food security of other Members.
5. This Decision shall not be used in a manner that results in an increase of the support subject to the Member's Bound Total AMS or the *de minimis* limits provided under programmes other than those notified under paragraph 3(a).

C. Consultations:

6. A developing Member benefiting from this Decision shall upon request hold consultations with other Members on the operation of its public stockholding programmes.

D. Monitoring:

7. The Committee on Agriculture shall monitor the information submitted under this Decision.

E. Work Programme:

8. Members agreed to establish a work programme to be undertaken in the Committee on Agriculture to pursue this issue with the aim of making recommendations for a permanent solution. This work programme shall take into account Members' existing and future submissions.
9. In the context of the broader post-Bali agenda, Members committed to the work programme mentioned in the previous paragraph with the aim of concluding it no later than the Eleventh Ministerial Conference.
10. The General Council shall report to the Tenth Ministerial Conference for an evaluation of the operation of this Decision, particularly on the progress made on the work programme.

18.3.9 Understanding on Tariff Rate Quota Administration Provisions of Agriculture Products: Without discrimination to the overall conclusion of the Doha Round negotiations based on the single undertaking and to the continuation of the reform process enshrined in Article 20 of the Agreement on Agriculture and agreed in the Doha Development Agenda for negotiations in agriculture, Members agreed as follows:

1. Tariff quota administration of scheduled tariff quotas shall be deemed to be an instance of "import licensing" within the meaning of the Uruguay Round Agreement on Import Licensing Procedures and, accordingly, that Agreement shall apply in full, subject to the Agreement on Agriculture and to the following more specific and additional obligations.
2. As regards the matters referred to in paragraph 4(a) of Article 1 of that Agreement, as these agricultural tariff quotas are negotiated and scheduled commitments, publication of the relevant information shall be effected no later than 90 days prior to the opening date of the tariff quota concerned. Where applications are involved, this shall also be the minimum advance date for the opening of applications.
3. As regards paragraph 6 of Article 1 of that Agreement, applicants for scheduled tariff quotas shall apply to one administrative body only.
4. As regards the matters referred to in paragraph 5(f) of Article 3 of that Agreement, the period for processing applications shall be, unqualifiedly, no longer than 30 days for "as and when received" cases and no longer than 60 days for "concurrent" consideration cases. The issuance of licences shall, therefore, take place no later than the effective opening date of the tariff quota concerned, except where, for the latter category, there has been an extension for applications allowed for under Article 1.6 of that Agreement.
5. As regards Article 3.5(i), licences for scheduled tariff quotas shall be issued in economic quantities.
6. Tariff quota "fill rates" shall be notified.
7. In order to ensure that their administrative procedures are consistent with Article 3.2 of that Agreement, "no more administratively burdensome than absolutely necessary to administer the measure", importing Members shall ensure that unfilled tariff quota access is not attributable to administrative procedures that are more constraining than

an "absolute necessity" test would demand.

8. Where licences held by private operators exhibit a pattern of being less than fully utilized for reasons other than those that would be expected to be followed by a normal commercial operator in the circumstances, the Member allocating the licences shall give this due weight when examining the reasons for under utilization and considering the allocation of new licences as provided for under Article 3.5(j).
9. Where it is evident that a tariff quota is under filled but there would appear to be no reasonable commercial reason for this to be the case, an importing Member shall request those private operators holding unused entitlements whether they would be prepared to make them available to other potential users. Where the tariff quota is held by a private operator in a third country, e.g. as a result of country-specific allocation arrangements, the importing Member shall transmit the request to the holder of the allocation concerned.
10. As regards Article 3.5(a)(ii) of that Agreement, Members shall make available the contact details of those importers holding licences for access to scheduled agricultural tariff quotas, where, subject to the terms of Article 1.11, this is possible and/or with their consent.
11. The Committee on Agriculture shall review and monitor the implementation of Members' obligations established under this Understanding.
12. Members shall provide for an effective re-allocation mechanism in accordance with the procedures outlined in Annex A.
13. A review of the operation of the Decision shall commence no later than four years following the adoption of the Decision, taking into account experience gained up to that time. The objective of this review will be to promote a continuing process of improvement in the utilization of tariff rate quotas. In the context of this review the General Council shall make recommendations to the Twelfth Ministerial Conference.
14. The General Council recommendations in relation to paragraph 4 shall provide for special and differential treatment. Unless the Twelfth Ministerial Conference decides to extend paragraph 4 of Annex A in its current or a modified form, it shall, subject to paragraph 15, no longer apply.
15. Notwithstanding paragraph 14, Members shall continue to apply the provisions of paragraph 4 of Annex A in the absence of a decision to extend that paragraph, except for those Members who wish to reserve their rights not to continue the application of paragraph 4 of Annex A and who are listed in Annex B.

18.3.10 Agriculture: Export Competition: The Ministerial Conference made the Declaration as mentioned below:

1. The Ministers documented that all forms of export subsidies and all export measures with equivalent effect are a highly trade distorting and protectionist form of support, and that, accordingly, export competition remained a key priority of the agriculture negotiations in the context of the continuation of the ongoing reform process set out in Article 20 of the Agreement on Agriculture, in accordance with the Doha work programme on agriculture and the 2005 Hong Kong Ministerial Declaration.

2. In this context, the Ministers therefore reconfirmed their commitment, as an outcome of the negotiations, to the parallel elimination of all forms of export subsidies and disciplines on all export measures with equivalent effect, as set out in the 2005 Hong Kong Ministerial Declaration. They expressed the unhappiness that it had not been possible to achieve this objective in 2013 as thought in that Declaration.
3. The Ministers considered that the revised draft modalities for agriculture, dated December 6, 2008 should remain an important basis for an ambitious final agreement in the export competition pillar, including with regard to special and differential treatment for LDCs and NFIDCs.
4. The Ministers accepted the decrease in recent years in the use of export subsidies subject to reduction commitments under the Agreement on Agriculture, as indicated by information contained in Members' notifications to the WTO, and the positive developments that had also taken place in other areas of the export competition pillar.
5. The Ministers accepted that the reforms undertaken by some Members had contributed to this positive trend. They emphasized however that this generally positive trend was not a substitute for the realization of the final objective on export competition in the Doha negotiations.
6. The Ministers emphasized the importance of consolidating progress in this area within the Doha negotiations so as to achieve as soon as possible the final objective set out in the 2005 Hong Kong Ministerial Declaration and they underscored the importance of further engagement among Members to this end.
7. The Ministers therefore reiterated the importance of Members maintaining and advancing their domestic reform processes in the field of export competition. They were strongly optimistic about those Members who had agreed for the reforms to continue in that direction and Members yet to undertake reforms to do so, given the positive impact that such reforms could have and the significant negative consequences that failure to reform would generate.
8. With the objective on export competition set out in the 2005 Hong Kong Ministerial Declaration in mind and with a view to maintaining the positive trend noted previously, they shall exercise utmost restraint with regard to any recourse to all forms of export subsidies and all export measures with equivalent effect. To this end, they undertook to ensure to the maximum extent possible that: (a) The progress towards the parallel elimination of all forms of export subsidies and disciplines on all export measures with equivalent effect will be maintained; (b) The level of export subsidies will remain significantly below the Members' export subsidy commitments; and (c) A similar level of discipline will be maintained on the use of all export measures with equivalent effect.
9. The Ministers agreed that fulfilling the objective set out in the 2005 Hong Kong Ministerial Declaration on export competition remains a priority issue for the post-Bali work programme. They agreed to continue to work actively to further concretise progress in this area as early as feasible.

10. Accordingly, the Ministers committed to boost transparency and to improve monitoring in relation to all forms of export subsidies and all export measures with equivalent effect, in order to support the reform process.
11. The Ministers therefore agreed to hold dedicated discussions on an annual basis in the Committee on Agriculture to examine developments in the field of export competition. This examination process should provide an opportunity for Members to raise any matter relevant to the export competition pillar, in furtherance of the final objective set out in the 2005 Hong Kong Ministerial Declaration.
12. This examination process shall be undertaken on the basis of timely notifications under the relevant provisions of the Agreement on Agriculture and related decisions, complemented by information compiled by the WTO Secretariat, consistent with the practice followed in 2013.
13. The Ministers agreed to review the situation regarding export competition at the Tenth Ministerial Conference. They also agreed that the terms of this declaration do not affect the rights and obligations of Members under the covered agreements nor shall they be used to interpret those rights and obligations.

18.3.11 Cotton: The Ministerial Conference decided as follows:

1. The Ministers stressed the vital importance of cotton to a number of developing country economies and particularly the least developed amongst them.
2. The Ministers reaffirmed the Decision adopted by the General Council on August 1, 2004, the 2005 Hong Kong Ministerial Declaration, and the commitment, expressed at the 2011 Geneva WTO Ministerial Conference, to ongoing dialogue and engagement to progress the mandate in paragraph 11 of the 2005 Hong Kong Ministerial Declaration to address cotton "ambitiously, expeditiously and specifically", within the agriculture negotiations.
3. They expressed disappointment that they were yet to deliver on the trade-related components of the 2005 Hong Kong Ministerial Declaration, but agreed on the importance of pursuing progress in this area.
4. In that regard, the Ministers considered that the Decision adopted by the General Council on August 1, 2004 and the 2005 Hong Kong Ministerial Declaration, remained a useful basis for the future work. They acknowledged the work on cotton that had been done in the Committee on Agriculture in Special Session in connection with the revised draft agriculture modalities dated December 6, 2008, which provided a reference point for further work.
5. In this context, the Ministers therefore undertook to enhance transparency and monitoring in relation to the trade-related aspects of cotton. To this end, they agreed to hold a dedicated discussion on a bi-annual basis in the context of the Committee on Agriculture in Special Session to examine relevant trade-related developments across the three pillars of Market Access, Domestic Support and Export Competition in relation to cotton.
6. The dedicated discussions should be undertaken on the basis of factual information and data compiled by the WTO Secretariat from Members' notifications,

complemented, as appropriate, by relevant information provided by Members to the WTO Secretariat.

7. The dedicated discussions shall in particular consider all forms of export subsidies for cotton and all export measures with equivalent effect, domestic support for cotton and tariff measures and non-tariff measures applied to cotton exports from LDCs in markets of interest to them.
8. The Ministers reaffirmed the importance of the development assistance aspects of cotton and in particular highlight the work of the Director-General's Consultative Framework Mechanism on Cotton in reviewing and tracking of cotton-specific assistance as well as infrastructure support programmes or other assistance related to the cotton sector. They committed to continued engagement in the Director-General's Consultative Framework Mechanism on Cotton to strengthen the cotton sector in the LDCs.
9. The Ministers welcomed the positive trend in growth and improved performance in the cotton sector, particularly in Africa.
10. In this context, the Ministers underlined the importance of effective assistance provided to LDCs by the Members and multilateral agencies. They invited the LDCs to continue identifying their needs linked to cotton or related sectors, including on a regional basis, through their respective dialogues with development partners and national development strategies. They requested the development partners to accord special focus to such needs within the existing Aid-for-trade mechanisms/channels such as the EIF and the technical assistance and capacity-building work of relevant international institutions.
11. The Ministers invited the Director-General to continue to provide periodic reports on the development assistance aspects of cotton, and to report on the progress that had been made in implementing the trade-related components of the 2005 Hong Kong Ministerial Declaration, at each WTO Ministerial Conference.

18.3.12 Preferential Rules of Origin for the Least Developed Countries: The Ministers decided as follows:

1. With a view to facilitating market access for LDCs provided under non-reciprocal preferential trade arrangements for LDCs, Members should endeavour to develop or build on their individual rules of origin arrangements applicable to imports from LDCs in accordance with the following guidelines. These guidelines do not stipulate a single set of rules of origin criteria. Rather, they provide elements upon which Members may wish to draw for preferential rules of origin applicable to imports from LDCs under such arrangements.

A. Elements for Preferential Rules of Origin

2. Preferential rules of origin should be as transparent, simple and objective as possible. It is recognized that other than wholly obtained products, origin may be conferred by substantial or sufficient transformation, which can be defined in a number of ways, including through: (a) *ad valorem* percentage criterion; (b) change of tariff classification; and (c) specific manufacturing or processing operation. It is also

recognized that these methods in certain cases may be used in combination.

3. In the case of rules-based on the *ad valorem* percentage criterion, given the limited productive capacity in the LDCs, it is desirable to keep the level of value addition threshold as low as possible, while ensuring that it is the LDCs that receive the benefit of the preferential trade arrangements. It is noted that the LDCs seek consideration of allowing foreign inputs to a maximum of 75 percent of value in order for a good to qualify for benefits under LDC preferential trade arrangements.
4. The methods for the calculation of value should be as simple as possible. It is recognized that different methodologies are used to calculate the *ad valorem* percentage of value addition. This percentage may be determined on the basis of the principles of simplicity and transparency. For example, in case of methods used for calculation of foreign inputs, Members may exclude costs related to freight and insurance as well as international transportation costs. In case of methods used for calculation of local/domestic content, Members may include national or regional inland transportation costs.
5. In the case of rules based on the change of tariff classification criterion, a substantial or sufficient transformation should generally allow the use of non-originating inputs as long as an article of a different heading or sub-heading was created from those inputs in an LDC, notwithstanding that product-specific rule with different requirements may also be more appropriate.
6. In the case of rules that allow a specific manufacturing or processing operation for the purpose of conferring origin, such rules should, as far as possible, take into account the productive capacity in LDCs. For example, in a number of cases the use of process-based rules for chemical products has made such rules more transparent and easy to comply with. In addition, for articles of apparel and clothing it may be simpler to demonstrate a substantial transformation using such rules instead of the equivalent change of tariff classification.
7. Cumulation should be considered as a feature of non-reciprocal preferential trade arrangements. The core objective of cumulation is to allow LDCs to combine originating materials without losing the originating status of the materials and to jointly share materials or production. Certain non-reciprocal preferential trade arrangements provide illustrations of a range of cumulation possibilities, which Members may take into account in designing their preferential rules of origin. For example, such arrangements may allow bilateral cumulation (i.e. cumulation with the respective preference-granting country) as well as cumulation with other LDCs. Other possibilities include cumulation among GSP beneficiaries of a given preference-granting country and/or among developing country Members forming part of a regional group as defined by the preference-granting country.

B. Documentary Requirements:

8. The documentary requirements regarding compliance with the rules of origin should be simple and transparent. For instance, requirement to provide proof of non-manipulation or any other prescribed form for a certification of origin for products

shipped from LDCs across other Members may be avoided. With regard to certification of rules of origin, whenever possible, self-certification may be accepted. Mutual customs cooperation and monitoring could complement compliance and risk-management measures.

C. Transparency:

9. Preferential rules of origin for LDCs shall be notified as per the established procedures. The objectives of notification are to enhance transparency, make the rules better understood, and promote an exchange of experiences as well as mainstreaming of best practices.
10. The Committee on Rules of Origin shall annually review the developments in preferential rules of origin applicable to imports from LDCs, in accordance with these guidelines, and report to the General Council. The Secretariat shall annually provide the Sub-Committee on LDCs with a report on the outcome of such review.

18.3.13 Operationalisation of the Waiver Concerning Preferential Treatment to Services and Services Suppliers of LDCs: Recognizing the need to strengthen the domestic service capacity in LDCs with a view to making use of existing opportunities as well as any preferences afforded to them; and noting that no WTO Member had yet made use of the waiver since its adoption in 2011, the Ministers decided as follows:

1. The Council for Trade in Services was instructed to initiate a process aimed at promoting the expeditious and effective operationalization of the LDC services waiver. The Council for Trade in Services shall periodically review the operationalization of the waiver. The Council for Trade in Services may make recommendations on steps that could be taken towards enhancing the operationalization of the waiver.
2. With a view to accelerating the process of securing meaningful preferences for LDCs' services and service suppliers, the Council for Trade in Services shall convene a high-level meeting six months after the submission of an LDC collective request identifying the sectors and modes of supply of particular export interest to them. At that meeting, developed and developing Members, in a position to do so, shall indicate sectors and modes of supply where they intend to provide preferential treatment to LDC services and service suppliers.
3. Members, in their individual capacities, were encouraged at any time to extend preferences to LDCs' services and service suppliers, consistent with the waiver Decision, which have commercial value and promote economic benefits to LDCs. These preferences may accord, *inter alia,* improved market access, including through the elimination of economic needs tests and other quantitative limitations. In doing so, a Member may accord preferences similar to those arising from preferential trade agreements to which it is a party noting that preferential treatment, with respect to the application of measures other than those described in Article XVI of GATS, may be granted subject to approval by the Council for Trade in Services under paragraph 1 of the waiver Decision.
4. Members underlined the need for improved technical assistance and capacity-building to help LDCs benefit from the operationalization of the waiver. Special

focus should be directed towards the delivery of targeted and coordinated technical assistance aimed at strengthening the domestic and export services capacity of LDCs, making optimal use of existing Aid-for-trade channels such as the EIF and the technical assistance and capacity-building work of relevant international institutions. In this context, the LDCs were invited to include their services related needs in their respective national development strategies and in their dialogues with development partners. Members urged development partners to respond adequately to such needs.

18.3.14 Duty-Free and Quota-Free Market Access for LDCs: Recognizing that since the adoption of the Hong Kong Decision, Members had made significant progress towards the goal of providing DFQF market access on a lasting basis for all products originating from all LDCs, and that nearly all developed Members provided either full or nearly full DFQF market access to LDC products, and that a number of developing-country Members also granted a significant degree of DFQF market access to LDC products, the Ministers decided:

1. Developed country Members that had not yet provided duty-free and quota-free market access for at least 97 percent of products originating from LDCs, defined at the tariff line level, shall seek to improve their existing duty-free and quota-free coverage for such products, so as to provide increasingly greater market access to LDCs, prior to the next Ministerial Conference.
2. Developing country Members, declaring themselves in a position to do so, shall seek to provide duty-free and quota-free market access for products originating from LDCs, or shall seek to improve their existing duty-free and quota-free coverage for such products, so as to provide increasingly greater market access to LDCs, prior to the next Ministerial Conference.
3. Members shall notify duty-free and quota-free schemes for LDCs and any other relevant changes pursuant to the Transparency Mechanism for Preferential Trade Arrangements.
4. The Committee on Trade and Development shall continue to annually review the steps taken to provide duty-free and quota-free market access to the LDCs, and report to the General Council for appropriate action.
5. To aid in its review, the Secretariat shall, in close coordination with Members, prepare a report on Members' duty-free and quota-free market access for LDCs at the tariff line level based on their notifications.
6. The General Council was instructed to report, including any recommendations, on the implementation of this Decision to the next Ministerial Conference.

18.3.15 Monitoring Mechanism on Special and Differential Treatment: In view of the General Council decision of July 2002 to establish the Monitoring Mechanism, the Ministers decided as follows.

The scope, functions, terms of reference and operation of the Monitoring Mechanism shall be as follows:

1. The coverage of the Mechanism shall extend to all special and differential provisions contained in multilateral WTO Agreements, Ministerial and General Council Decisions.

2. The Mechanism shall act as a focal point within the WTO to analyse and review the implementation of S&D provisions. The Mechanism will complement, not replace, other relevant review mechanisms and/or processes in other bodies of the WTO.
3. The Mechanism shall review all aspects of implementation of S&D provisions with a view to facilitating integration of developing and least developed Members into the multilateral trading system. Where the review of implementation of an S&D provision under this Mechanism identifies a problem, the Mechanism may consider whether it results from implementation, or from the provision itself.
4. In carrying out its functions, the Mechanism will not alter, or in any manner affect, Members' rights and obligations under the WTO Agreements, Ministerial or General Council Decisions, or interpret their legal nature. However, the Mechanism is not precluded from making recommendations to the relevant WTO bodies for initiating negotiations on the S&D provisions that have been reviewed under the Mechanism.
5. The Mechanism can, as appropriate, make recommendations to the relevant WTO body that propose: (a) the consideration of actions to improve the implementation of a special and differential provision; (b) or the initiation of negotiations aiming at improving the special and differential provision(s) that have been reviewed under the Mechanism.
6. Such recommendations will inform the work of the relevant body, but not define or limit its final determination.
7. The relevant body should consider a recommendation from the Mechanism at the earliest opportunity. The status of recommendations emerging from the Mechanism shall be included in the annual report of the Committee on Trade and Development to the General Council.
8. The Mechanism shall operate in Dedicated Sessions of the Committee on Trade and Development. The Mechanism shall meet twice a year. Additional meetings may be convened, as appropriate. When in session, the Mechanism shall follow the same rules and procedures applied by the Committee on Trade and Development.
9. Monitoring of special and differential provisions in the Mechanism shall be undertaken on the basis of written inputs or submissions made by Members, as well as on the basis of reports received from other WTO Bodies to which submissions by Members could also be made.
10. Where the substantive matter falls within the purview of another WTO body, the Mechanism shall bring it to the attention of that WTO body so that the latter is in a position to provide the input.
11. The Mechanism shall be reviewed three years after its first formal meeting, and thereafter when necessary, taking into account its functioning and evolving circumstances.

18.4 Conclusions

Before the Ministerial Conference, the Director-General noted that even though significant negotiations had occurred and the negotiating package was stable, the Membership had failed to reach consensus.

In Bali, on the second day of the Ministerial Conference, the Indian Minister of Commerce and Industry made a strong statement arguing that food security was non-negotiable. The G-33 wanted food stocks acquired at administered prices not to be included in the aggregate measure of support (AMS) calculations.

The hard bargaining that ensued led finally to a compromise where Members agreed that they would refrain from using the WTO's Dispute Settlement Mechanism "in relation to support provided for traditional staple food crops in pursuance of public stockholding programmes for food security purposes". The decision was to be applied to those programs already existing by the date of the decision and that too with a peace clause until a permanent solution is found.

Finally, the Ministerial Conference provided momentum to the multilateral trading system after several years of deadlock. The Bali package was an important step in the right direction. Its main pillars: the Agreement on Trade Facilitation; the decisions on agriculture; and the decisions focusing on least developed countries were the first concrete results after twelve years of negotiations.

The main result in Bali, however, was the Trade Facilitation Agreement, designed to streamline customs procedures, increase transparency, foster customs cooperation and reduce red tape and redundancies in order to expedite trade flows. Trade facilitation was one of the original Singapore issues that developed countries had been promoting since 1996. In July 2004, trade facilitation was finally agreed upon as a topic of the DDA, while the other three: investment, completion and public procurement were dropped from the Doha Round talks.

The Bali package also included decisions on cotton, preferential rules-of-origin for LDCs, preferential treatment for services from LDCs, and duty-free and quota-free (DFQF) market access for LDCs along with mechanism on Special and Differential Treatment.

On the closing of the Conference the Chairman said, "What we have done here in Bali is truly extraordinary. We have negotiated a package that will bring food security to billions of the world's poorest. We have delivered an Agreement on Trade Facilitation that will inject up to a trillion dollars into the world economy".

He further said, "And we have agreed to a ground breaking suite of initiatives to help least developed countries benefit more from the multilateral trading system".

The Director-General opined, "We have put the 'world' back into the World Trade Organisation".

Though the Bali Conference laid foundation for further negotiations to conclude the Doha Development Agenda, the road ahead still remained full of hurdles.

19

Nairobi Ministerial Conference, 2015

19.1 Introduction

WTO's Tenth Ministerial Conference was held in Nairobi, Kenya, from December 15 to 19, 2015. Ms. Amina Mohamed, Kenya's Cabinet Secretary for Foreign Affairs and International Trade, chaired the conference. The provisional agenda of the Conference included the following items:

1. Overview of activities of the WTO.
2. Under this item of the agenda, Ministers were to be given the opportunity to review the operation and functioning of the multilateral trading system and to make general statements related thereto. Documentation available to delegations for the overview of WTO activities included reports from the Director-General, the General Council and other WTO bodies on activities under their respective mandates.
3. Action by Ministers.
4. Ministers were expected under this item of the agenda to take any action which they might have deemed necessary for the work of the WTO, including decisions on the accession of new Members to the WTO Agreement.
5. Date and venue of the Eleventh Session.
6. Election of officers.

The "Nairobi Package" adopted at the WTO's Tenth Ministerial Conference contained a series of six Ministerial Decisions on agriculture, cotton and issues related to least developed countries (LDCs). A Ministerial Declaration outlining the Package and the future work of the WTO was adopted at the end of the five-day Ministerial Conference.

Ms. Mohamed admitted that ministers "faced challenging moments", in concluding the Nairobi Package, which required an extra day of intensive negotiations to conclude. "Tough calls had to be made but we did bite the bullet".

"We have reaffirmed the central role of the WTO in international trade governance", she added. The decisions adopted have been given below:

Agriculture:

1. Special safeguard mechanism for developing country members.
2. Public stockholding for food security purposes.
3. Export competition.

LDC Issues:

1. Preferential rules of origin for LDCs.
2. Implementation of preferential treatment in favour of services and service suppliers of LDCs and increasing LDCs participation in services trade.

Ministers also welcomed the decisions taken by the General Council under regular work.

19.2 Ministerial Declaration

At the conclusion of the Conference, Ministers adopted a Ministerial Declaration containing three parts:

19.2.1 Part I: Preamble

1. The Ministers expressed their deep appreciation to the Government and people of Kenya for the exceptional organization and the warm hospitality they had received in Nairobi.
2. They noted that the Tenth Session took place at the twentieth anniversary of the WTO. On this occasion, they underlined the crucial importance of the multilateral rules-based trading system and reaffirmed the principles and objectives set out in the Marrakesh Agreement Establishing the World Trade Organization.
3. The Ministers reaffirmed the pre-eminence of the WTO as the global forum for trade rules setting and governance. They acknowledged the contribution that the rules-based multilateral trading system made to the strength and stability of the global economy. They also reaffirmed the value of the consistent practice of taking decisions through a transparent, inclusive, consensus-based, Member-driven process.
4. They noted with concern the slow and uneven recovery from the severe economic and financial crisis of 2008, resulting in lower global economic growth, depressed agricultural and other commodity prices, raising inequalities, unemployment and significantly slowing the expansion of international trade in recent years. They acknowledged that international trade can play a role towards achieving sustainable, robust and balanced growth for all.
5. The Ministers pledged to strengthen the multilateral trading system so that it can provide a strong impetus to inclusive prosperity and welfare for all Members and responds to the specific development needs of developing country Members, in particular the least developed country Members.
6. The Ministers acknowledged that international trade can play a major role in the promotion of economic development and the alleviation of poverty. They recognized the need for all the peoples to benefit from the increased opportunities and welfare gains that the multilateral trading system generates. The majority of WTO Members are developing country Members. They sought to place their needs and interests at the centre of the work in the WTO.
7. The Ministers reaffirmed the centrality of development in the WTO's work and committed to continuing to make positive efforts designed to ensure that developing country Members, and especially the least developed country Members, secure a share in the growth of world trade commensurate with the needs of their economic development.
8. The Ministers recognized the role the WTO can play in contributing towards achievement of the 2030 Sustainable Development Goals, in so far as they relate to the WTO mandate, and bearing in mind the authority of the WTO Ministerial Conference.

9. The Ministers recognized the importance of strengthened coherence in global economic policy-making. They also underscored the Marrakesh coherence mandate, and encouraged initiatives for cooperation with other international organizations in pursuit of the common objectives, while respecting the competence of each organization.
10. On the occasion of the WTO's twentieth anniversary, the Ministers acknowledged important achievements under the functions of the Organization described in Article III of the Marrakesh Agreement.
11. The Ministers reaffirmed the importance of work in regular bodies in furthering the objectives of the WTO Agreements and in facilitating meaningful exchange of information and sharing of experiences regarding the effective implementation and operation of their provisions. They took note of the WTO's trade monitoring work that, including trade policy reviews, had contributed consistently to the functioning of the multilateral trading system, by achieving greater transparency in, and understanding of, the trade policies and practices of Members.
12. The Ministers reiterated that the WTO shall remain the main forum to negotiate multilateral trade rules. Some progress has been made in the negotiations. At the Fourth Ministerial Session, a Development Round—the Doha Work Programme was launched for the first time in the history of the GATT and the WTO. They recalled the adoption of the Protocol Amending the TRIPS Agreement. They drew particular attention to the adoption of the Agreement on Trade Facilitation (TFA) as the first multilateral agreement since the establishment of the WTO. The Ministers welcomed the Decisions and the Declaration listed in Parts I and II of the Bali Ministerial Declaration and the subsequent General Council Decision of November 2014 on Public Stockholding for Food Security Purposes. They took note that much less progress has been made in agriculture and other central components of the WTO's negotiating agenda, namely NAMA, services, rules and development.
13. The Ministers acknowledged that the Dispute Settlement Understanding (DSU) continues to offer a means for the settlement of disputes among Members that is unique in international agreements. The system has dealt with a large and growing number of disputes, demonstrating Members' continuing confidence in it. They recognized that the increasing number and growing complexity of disputes present challenges to the system. They therefore committed to pursue and renew efforts to address current challenges and to further strengthen the system, including through effective implementation of the rulings and recommendations of the Dispute Settlement Body (DSB).
14. The Ministers recalled the commitments made by them at all of the previous sessions, as well as by the international community at the Fourth UN Conference on Least Developed Countries (LDCs) in Istanbul, to assist LDCs secure beneficial and meaningful integration into the multilateral trading system and the global economy. They recognized that LDCs remain vulnerable and continue to face structural difficulties in the global economy. The Ministers underscored the continued

importance of initiatives aimed at fully and meaningfully integrating LDCs into the multilateral trading system in a more effective manner.

15. The Ministers recognized the contribution of the Enhanced Integrated Framework (EIF) in mainstreaming trade in development policies of LDCs and building their trade capacity. This significant role in helping LDCs achieve their development objectives is duly recognized by the 2030 Agenda for Sustainable Development. Ministers are determined to further intensify their efforts to secure the necessary level of financial contributions to the program with the view to enabling the delivery of predictable trade-related support to LDCs, based on the programme needs as set out in the EIF Phase Two Programme Framework.
16. The Ministers recognized the importance of the Aid-for-Trade initiative in supporting developing country Members to build supply-side capacity and trade-related infrastructure and decided to accord priority to the LDCs' needs. The Ministers took note of the outcomes of the WTO global reviews on Aid-for-Trade, in particular the Fifth Global Review, and recognized the continuing need for this initiative.
17. The Ministers acknowledged the substantial progress in WTO's technical assistance and capacity-building, which focuses on the needs and priorities of beneficiary Members. They recognized that dedicated facilities such as the Standards and Trade Development Facility and the Trade Facilitation Agreement Facility are making an important contribution towards assisting developing country Members and LDCs to implement relevant WTO agreements. They also reiterated the importance of targeted and sustainable financial, technical, and capacity-building assistance programmes to support the developing country Members, in particular LDCs, to implement their agreements, to adjust to the reforms process, and to benefit from opportunities presented.
18. The Ministers celebrated the enlargement of the Organization by accessions in accordance with Article XII of the Marrakesh Agreement. They took note that the accessions of the Republic of Yemen, the Republic of Seychelles and the Republic of Kazakhstan to the WTO have been completed since the last Session. In particular, they noted with satisfaction that this Conference has completed the accession procedures for two least developed countries, the Republic of Liberia and the Islamic Republic of Afghanistan.
19. Recognizing the centrality and primacy of the multilateral trading system, the Ministers took note that WTO Members have also successfully worked and reached agreements in plurilateral formats.
20. The Ministers took note of the reports from the General Council and its subsidiary bodies. They welcomed the progress arising from these reports, and the Decisions stemming from them, in strengthening the effectiveness of the WTO as an organisation and the multilateral trading system as a whole.

19.2.2 Part II: Regular Work under the General Council:

21. The Ministers welcomed the following decisions adopted at this Session:

- Work Programme on Small Economies.

- TRIPS Non-violation and Situation Complaints.
- Work Programme on Electronic Commerce.

22. The Ministers further welcomed the adoption by the TRIPS Council of the Decision on the Extension of the Transition Period under Article 66.1 of the TRIPS Agreement for least developed country Members for certain obligations with respect to pharmaceutical products as well as the related Waiver Decision adopted by the General Council concerning least developed country Members' obligations under Article 70.8 and 70.9 of the TRIPS Agreement.
23. They welcomed the progress in the DDA, which is embodied in the following Decisions and Declarations adopted at the Tenth Session:

- Special Safeguard Mechanism for Developing Country Members.
- Public Stockholding for Food Security Purposes.
- Export Competition.
- Cotton.
- Preferential Rules of Origin for Least Developed Countries.
- Implementation of Preferential Treatment in Favour of Services and Service Suppliers of Least Developed Countries and Increasing LDC Participation in Services Trade.

19.2.3 Part III: Marginalization of LDCs

24. The Ministers strongly committed to addressing the marginalization of LDCs in international trade and to improving their effective participation in the multilateral trading system. Towards that end, they decided to ensure that all issues of specific interest to LDCs are pursued on a priority basis, with a view to strengthening them, making them commercially meaningful and, when appropriate, legally binding.
25. The Ministers reaffirmed their commitment to fully implement the Decision on Measures Concerning the Possible Negative Effects of the Reform Programme on Least Developed and Net Food-Importing Developing Countries, including differential treatment in line with the Marrakesh Decision in the context of the agriculture negotiations, in recognition of the challenges that these Members continue to face.
26. The Ministers reaffirmed their commitment to continue to address in every area of WTO work, in a substantive and meaningful manner, the needs of small, vulnerable economies (SVEs) and to favourably consider the adoption of such measures as would facilitate their fuller integration into the multilateral trading system. They decided to take into account the needs of SVEs in all areas of negotiations, without creating a sub-category of WTO Members.
27. The Ministers recognized the special situation of the Members acceded in accordance with Article XII of the Agreement Establishing the World Trade Organization who have undertaken extensive market access commitments at the time of accession. This situation shall be taken into account in the negotiations.
28. The Ministers reaffirmed the need to ensure that regional trade agreements (RTAs) remain complementary to, not a substitute for, the multilateral trading system. In this

regard, they instructed the Committee on Regional Trade Agreements (CRTA) to discuss the systemic implications of RTAs for the multilateral trading system and their relationship with WTO rules. With a view to enhancing transparency in, and understanding of RTAs and their effects, the Ministers agreed to work towards the transformation of the current provisional Transparency Mechanism into a permanent mechanism in accordance with the General Council Decision of December 14, 2006, without prejudice to questions related to notification requirements.

29. The Ministers agreed to reinvigorate the regular work of the Committees and directed the General Council to consider the need for adjustments in the structure of their subsidiary bodies in light of their relevance to the implementation and operation of the Covered Agreements.
30. The Ministers recognized that many Members reaffirm the Doha Development Agenda, and the Declarations and Decisions adopted at Doha and at the Ministerial Conferences held since then, and reaffirmed their full commitment to conclude the DDA on that basis. Other Members did not reaffirm the Doha mandates, as they believed new approaches are necessary to achieve meaningful outcomes in multilateral negotiations. Members had different views on how to address the negotiations. The Ministers acknowledged the strong legal structure of this Organization.
31. Nevertheless, there remained a strong commitment of all Members to advance negotiations on the remaining Doha issues. This includes advancing work in all three pillars of agriculture, namely domestic support, market access and export competition, as well as non-agriculture market access, services, development, TRIPS and rules. Work on all the Ministerial Decisions adopted in Part II of this Declaration will remain an important element of the future agenda.
32. This work shall maintain development at its centre and the Ministers reaffirmed that provisions for special and differential treatment shall remain integral. Members shall also continue to give priority to the concerns and interests of least developed countries. Many Members wanted to carry out the work on the basis of the Doha structure, while some wanted to explore new architectures.
33. The Ministers, therefore, agreed that officials should work to find ways to advance negotiations and requested the Director-General to report regularly to the General Council on these efforts.
34. While the Ministers concurred that officials should prioritize work where results have not yet been achieved, some wished to identify and discuss other issues for negotiation; others did not. Any decision to launch negotiations multilaterally on such issues would need to be agreed by all Members.

19.3 Outcome on Agriculture

A centrepiece of the Nairobi Package is a Ministerial Decision on Export Competition, including a commitment to eliminate subsidies for farm exports. DG Azevedo described it as the "most significant outcome on agriculture" in the organization's 20-year history.

"WTO members—especially developing countries—have consistently demanded action on this issue due to the enormous distorting potential of these subsidies for domestic production and trade", he declared. "Today's decision tackles the issue once and for all".

A number of countries are currently using export subsidies to support agriculture exports. The legally-binding decision would eliminate these subsidies and prevent governments from reverting to trade-distorting export support in the future.

Under the decision, developed members have committed to remove export subsidies immediately, except for a handful of agriculture products, and developing countries will do so by 2018. Developing members will keep the flexibility to cover marketing and transport costs for agriculture exports until the end of 2023, and the poorest and food-importing countries would enjoy additional time to cut export subsidies.

The decision contains disciplines to make sure that other export policies are not used as a disguised form of subsidies. These disciplines comprise terms to limit the benefits of financing support to agriculture exporters, rules on state enterprises engaging in agriculture trade, and disciplines to ensure that food aid does not negatively affect domestic production. Developing countries are given longer time to implement these rules.

Ministers also adopted a Ministerial Decision on Public Stockholding for Food Security Purposes. The decision commits members to engage constructively in finding a permanent solution to this issue. Under the Bali Ministerial Decision of 2013, developing countries are allowed to continue food stockpile programmes, which are otherwise in risk of breaching the WTO's domestic subsidy cap, until a permanent solution is found by the Eleventh Ministerial Conference in 2017.

A Ministerial Decision on a Special Safeguard Mechanism (SSM) for Developing Countries recognizes that developing members will have the right to temporarily increase tariffs in face of import surges by using an SSM. Members will continue to negotiate the mechanism in dedicated sessions of the Agriculture Committee.

19.3.1 Special Safeguard Mechanism for Developing Country Members: This mechanism is applicable in agricultural goods. It would enable them to raise their tariffs above the bound rates in the event of a fall in price of the imported product or an increase in volume of the imported product beyond certain levels temporarily. SSM would be an effective instrument to provide contingent protection to poor farmers in developing countries from negative shocks to import prices or from surges in imports.

The Ministers decided that:

1. The developing country Members will have the right to have recourse to a special safeguard mechanism (SSM) as envisaged under paragraph 7 of the Hong Kong Ministerial Declaration.
2. To pursue negotiations on an SSM for developing country Members in dedicated sessions of the Committee on Agriculture in Special Session.
3. The General Council shall regularly review progress in these negotiations.

19.3.2 Public Stockholding for Food Security Purposes: The Ministerial Conference decided as follows:

1. Members took note of the Ministerial Decision of December 7, 2013 and reaffirmed the General Council Decision of November 27, 2014.
2. Members shall engage constructively to negotiate and make all concerted efforts to agree and adopt a permanent solution on the issue of public stockholding for food security purposes. In order to achieve such permanent solution, the negotiations on this subject shall be held in the Committee on Agriculture in Special Session, in dedicated sessions and in an accelerated time frame, distinct from the agriculture negotiations under the Doha Development Agenda (DDA).
3. The General Council shall regularly review the progress.

19.3.3 Export Competition: The Ministerial Conference decided:

A. General:

1. Members reaffirmed their commitment, pursuant to the 2013 Bali Ministerial Declaration on Export Competition, to exercise utmost restraint with regard to any recourse to all forms of export subsidies and all export measures with equivalent effect.
2. Nothing in this Decision can be construed to give any Member the right to provide, directly or indirectly, export subsidies in excess of the commitments specified in Members' Schedules, or to otherwise detract from the obligations of Article 8 of the Agreement on Agriculture. Furthermore, nothing can be construed to imply any change to the obligations and rights under Article 10.1 of the Agreement on Agriculture or to diminish in any way existing obligations under other provisions of the Agreement on Agriculture or other WTO Agreements.
3. Nor can anything in this Decision be construed to diminish in any way the existing commitments contained in the Marrakesh Ministerial Decision of April 1994 on Measures Concerning the Possible Negative Effects of the Reform Programme on Least-developed and Net Food-importing Developing Countries and the Ministerial Decision of November 14, 2001 on implementation-related issues and concerns on, *inter alia*, commitment levels of food aid, provision of food aid by donors, technical and financial assistance in the context of aid programmes to improve agricultural productivity and infrastructure, and financing normal levels of commercial imports of basic foodstuffs. Nor could it be understood to alter the regular review of these decisions by the Ministerial Conference and monitoring by the Committee on Agriculture.
4. The Committee on Agriculture shall monitor the implementation of this Decision by Members in accordance with existing notification requirements under the Agreement on Agriculture.
5. The regular sessions of the Committee on Agriculture shall review every three years the disciplines contained in this Decision, with the aim of enhancing disciplines to ensure that no circumvention threatens export subsidy elimination commitments and to prevent non-commercial transactions from being used to circumvent such commitments.

B. Export Subsidies:

6. Developed Members shall immediately eliminate their remaining scheduled export subsidy entitlements as of the date of adoption of this Decision.
7. Developing country Members shall eliminate their export subsidy entitlements by the end of 2018.
8. Developing country Members shall continue to benefit from the provisions of Article 9.4 of the Agreement on Agriculture until the end of 2023, i.e. five years after the end-date for elimination of all forms of export subsidies. Least developed countries and net food-importing developing countries shall continue to benefit from the provisions of Article 9.4 of the Agreement on Agriculture until the end of 2030.
9. Members shall not apply export subsidies in a manner that circumvents the requirement to reduce and eliminate all export subsidies.
10. Members shall seek not to raise their export subsidies beyond the average level of the past five years on a product basis.
11. Members shall ensure that any export subsidies have at most minimal trade distorting effects and do not displace or impede the exports of another Member. To that effect, Members using export subsidies shall give due consideration to the effects of any such export subsidies on other Members, and shall consult, upon request, with any other Member having a substantial interest as an exporter with respect to any matter related to the export subsidies in question. The Member applying such export subsidies shall provide, upon request, such a Member with necessary information.

C. Cotton:

12. With regard to cotton, the disciplines and commitments contained in this Decision shall be immediately implemented as of the date of adoption of this Decision by developed country Members, and not later than January 1, 2017 by developing country Members.

D. Export Credits, Export Credit Guarantees or Insurance Programmes:

(a) Definition:

13. In addition to complying with all other export subsidy obligations under the Agreement on Agriculture and any other covered Agreements, Members undertake not to provide export credits, export credit guarantees or insurance programmes for exports of products listed in Annex 1 of the Agreement on Agriculture other than in conformity with this Decision. These export credits, export credit guarantees and insurance programmes comprise: (a) direct financing support, comprising direct credits/financing, refinancing, and interest rate support; (b) risk cover, comprising export credit insurance or reinsurance and export credit guarantees; (c) government-to-government credit agreements covering the imports of agricultural products from the creditor country under which some or all of the risk is undertaken by the government of the exporting country; and (d) any other form of governmental export credit support, direct or indirect, including deferred invoicing and foreign exchange risk hedging.

14. The provisions of this Decision shall apply to export financing support as defined in paragraph 13 provided by a government or any public body as referred to in Article 1.1(a) of the Agreement on Subsidies and Countervailing Measures.

(b) Terms and Conditions:

15. Export financing support shall be provided in conformity with the terms and conditions set out below: (a) *Maximum repayment term:* the maximum repayment term for export financing support under this Decision, this being the period beginning at the starting point of credit and ending on the contractual date of the final payment, shall be no more than 18 months. For developed Members, this shall apply from the last day of 2017. Existing contracts which have been entered into prior to the adoption of this Decision and are still in place, and are operating on a longer time frame than that defined in the preceding sentence, shall run their course until the end of their contractual date, provided that they are notified to the Committee on Agriculture and are not modified; (b) *Self-financing:* Export credit guarantee, insurance and reinsurance programmes and other risk cover programmes included within sub-paragraphs 13(b), (c) and (d) shall be self-financing and cover the long-term operating costs and losses of a programme. For the operations covered in the previous sentence, premiums shall be charged and be risk-based.

E. Special and Differential Treatment:

16. Developing country Member providers of export financing support shall be eligible to benefit from the following:

Developing country Members concerned shall have a phase-in period of four years after the first day of the implementation period by the end of which to fully implement the maximum repayment term of 18 months. This shall be achieved as follows: (a) on the first day of implementation, the maximum repayment term for any new support entered into shall be 36 months; (b) two years after implementation, the maximum repayment term for any new support to be entered into shall be 27 months; (c) four years after implementation, the maximum repayment term of 18 months shall apply. It is understood that where there are, after any of the relevant dates, pre-existing support arrangements entered into under the limits established in the subparagraphs (a)-(c) above, they shall run their original term.

17. Notwithstanding the terms of paragraphs 15(a) and 16 above, least developed and net food-importing developing countries shall be accorded differential and more favourable treatment comprising allowance for a repayment term in respect of them of between 36 and 54 months, for the acquisition of basic foodstuffs. Should one of these Members face exceptional circumstances which still preclude financing normal levels of commercial imports of basic foodstuffs and/or in accessing loans granted by multilateral and/or regional financial institutions within these time frames, it shall have an extension of such a time frame. The standard monitoring and surveillance provisions, as resulting from this Decision, shall apply to these cases.

F. Agricultural Exporting State Trading Enterprises:

18. Members shall ensure that agricultural exporting state trading enterprises are

operated in conformity with the provisions specified in paragraphs 20 and 21, in accordance with Article XVII, the Understanding on the Interpretation of Article XVII and other relevant provisions of GATT, 1994, the Agreement on Agriculture and other WTO Agreements.

19. For the purpose of the disciplines set out hereunder in this Decision, an agricultural exporting state trading enterprise shall be any enterprise which meets the working definition provided for in the Understanding on the Interpretation of Article XVII of the GATT, 1994 and is engaged in exports of products listed in Annex 1 of the Agreement on Agriculture.
20. Members shall ensure that agricultural exporting state trading enterprises do not operate in a manner that circumvents any other disciplines contained in this Decision.
21. Members shall make their best efforts to ensure that the use of export monopoly powers by agricultural exporting state trading enterprises is exercised in a manner that minimizes trade distorting effects and does not result in displacing or impeding the exports of another Member.

G. International Food Aid:

22. Members reaffirmed their commitment to maintain an adequate level of international food aid, to take account of the interests of food aid recipients and to ensure that the disciplines contained hereafter do not unintentionally impede the delivery of food aid provided to deal with emergency situations. To meet the objective of preventing or minimizing commercial displacement, Members shall ensure that international food aid is provided in full conformity with the disciplines specified in paragraphs 23 to 32, thereby contributing to the objective of preventing commercial displacement.
23. Members shall ensure that all international food aid is: (i) needs-driven; (b) in fully grant form; (c) not tied directly or indirectly to commercial exports of agricultural products or other goods and services; (d) not linked to the market development objectives of donor Members; and that (e) agricultural products provided as international food aid shall not be re-exported in any form, except where the agricultural products were not permitted entry into the recipient country, the agricultural products were determined inappropriate or no longer needed for the purpose for which they were received in the recipient country, or re-exportation is necessary for logistical reasons to expedite the provision of food aid for another country in an emergency situation. Any re-exportation in accordance with this sub-paragraph shall be conducted in a manner that does not unduly impact established, functioning commercial markets of agricultural commodities in the countries to which the food aid is re-exported.
24. The provision of food aid shall take into account local market conditions of the same or substitute products. Members shall refrain from providing in-kind international food aid in situations where this would be reasonably foreseen to cause an adverse effect on local or regional production of the same or substitute products. In addition, Members shall ensure that international food aid does not unduly impact established,

functioning commercial markets of agricultural commodities.

25. Where Members provide exclusively cash-based food aid, they are encouraged to continue to do so. Other Members are encouraged to provide cash-based or in-kind international food aid in emergency situations, protracted crises, or non-emergency development/capacity-building food assistance environments where recipient countries or recognized international humanitarian/food entities, such as the United Nations, have requested food assistance.
26. Members are also encouraged to seek to increasingly procure international food aid from local or regional sources to the extent possible, provided that the availability and prices of basic foodstuffs in these markets are not unduly compromised.
27. Members shall monetize international food aid only where there is a demonstrable need for monetization for the purpose of transport and delivery of the food assistance, or the monetization of international food aid is used to redress short- and/or long-term food deficit requirements or insufficient agricultural production situations which give rise to chronic hunger and malnutrition in least developed and net food-importing developing countries.
28. Local or regional market analysis shall be completed before monetization occurs for all monetized international food aid, including consideration of the recipient country's nutritional needs, local United Nations Agencies' market data and normal import and consumption levels of the commodity to be monetized, and consistent with Food Assistance Convention reporting. Independent third party commercial or non-profit entities will be employed to monetize in-kind international food aid to ensure open market competition for the sale of in-kind international food aid.
29. In employing these independent third party commercial or non-profit entities for the purposes of the preceding paragraph, Members shall ensure that such entities minimize or eliminate disruptions to the local or regional markets, which may include impacts on production, when international food aid is monetized. They shall ensure that the sale of commodities for food assistance purposes is conducted in a transparent, competitive and open process and through a public tender.
30. Members committed to allowing maximum flexibility to provide for all types of international food aid in order to maintain needed levels while making efforts to move toward more untied cash-based international food aid in accordance with the Food Assistance Convention.
31. Members recognized the role of government in decision-making on international food aid in their jurisdictions. Members recognized that the government of a recipient country of international food aid can opt out of the usage of monetized international food aid.
32. Members agreed to review the provisions on international food aid contained in the preceding paragraphs within the regular Committee on Agriculture monitoring of the implementation of the Marrakesh Ministerial Decision of April 1994 on Measures Concerning the Possible Negative Effects of the Reform Programme on least developed and net food-importing developing countries.

19.4 Decisions on Cotton

In addition, a Ministerial Decision on cotton stresses the vital importance of the cotton sector to LDCs. The decision includes three agriculture elements: market access, domestic support and export competition.

On market access, the decision calls for cotton from LDCs to be given duty-free and quota-free access to the markets of developed countries—and to those of developing countries declaring that they are able to do so—from January 1, 2016.

The domestic support part of the cotton decision acknowledges members' reforms in their domestic cotton policies and stresses that more efforts remain to be made.

On export competition for cotton, the decision mandates that developed countries prohibit cotton export subsidies immediately and developing countries do so at a later date.

Ministerial Conference decided as follows:

19.4.1 Trade Component:

A. Market Access:

1. The Ministers welcomed the progress made voluntarily by some Members towards providing duty-free and quota-free market access for cotton and cotton-related products originating from LDCs.
2. Developed country Members, and developing country Members declaring themselves in a position to do so, shall grant, to the extent provided for in their respective preferential trade arrangements in favour of LDCs, as from January 1, 2016, duty-free and quota-free market access for cotton produced and exported by LDCs.
3. Developing country Members declaring themselves not in a position to grant duty-free and quota-free market access for cotton produced and exported by LDCs shall undertake, as from January 1, 2016, to consider the possibilities for increased import opportunities for cotton from LDCs.
4. Developed country Members, and developing country Members declaring themselves in a position to do so, shall grant, to the extent provided for in their respective preferential trade arrangements in favour of LDCs, as from January 1, 2016, duty-free and quota-free market access for exports by LDCs of relevant cotton-related products included in the list annexed to this Decision and covered by Annex 1 of the Agreement on Agriculture.
5. The Ministers agreed to review the list annexed to this Decision in the Dedicated Discussions on cotton referred to in paragraph 14 of this Decision within two years, on the basis of updated trade statistics provided by Members on their imports from LDCs.
6. The Dedicated Discussions on cotton referred to in paragraph 14 of this Decision shall continue to address the following specific elements, based on factual information and data compiled by the WTO Secretariat from Members' notifications, complemented, as appropriate, by relevant information provided by Members to the WTO Secretariat: (a) identification and examination of market access barriers, including tariff and non-tariff barriers for the entry of cotton produced and exported

by cotton-producing LDCs; (b) reviews of market access improvements and of any market access measures undertaken by Members, including the identification of access barriers to cotton produced and exported by cotton producing LDCs in markets of interest to them; and (c) examination of possible additional measures for progressive and predictable improvements in market access, in particular the elimination of tariff and non-tariff barriers to cotton produced and exported by cotton producing LDCs.

B. Domestic Support:

7. The Ministers acknowledged the efforts made by some Members to reform their domestic cotton policies and which may contribute to the objective of reduction of the trade distorting domestic subsidies for cotton production.
8. The Ministers emphasized however that some more efforts remain to be made and that these positive steps are not a substitute for the attainment of the objective. In doing so, Members shall ensure that necessary transparency is provided through regular notifications and the subsequent review process in the Committee on Agriculture.

C. Export Competition:

9. The disciplines and commitments contained in the Ministerial Decision on Export Competition shall be immediately implemented with regard to cotton by developed country Members as of the date of adoption of that Decision, and by developing country Members not later than January 1, 2017.

19.4.2 Development Component:

10. The Ministers reaffirmed the importance of the development assistance aspects of cotton, and committed to continued engagement in the Director-General's Consultative Framework Mechanism on Cotton. They took note of the Director-General's seventh periodic report to the Membership on the development assistance aspects of cotton. They invited the Director-General to submit the next periodic report prior to the Eleventh Ministerial Conference.
11. The Ministers underlined the importance of effective assistance to support the cotton sector in developing country Members, especially the LDCs amongst them. They recognized that the Aid-for-Trade initiative, including through the Enhanced Integrated Framework (EIF), should play a key role in strengthening the cotton sector in LDCs. The linkage between this initiative and the development aspects of cotton should be reinforced to help formulate, on the basis of priorities identified by LDC cotton producers, multidimensional and integrated programmes and projects at the regional and sub-regional level, to be submitted to development partners.
12. The Ministers urged WTO Members and development partners to continue their efforts and contributions to enhance the production, productivity and competitiveness of the cotton sector in developing country Member producers, especially the LDCs. The beneficiaries of cotton development assistance were encouraged to continue carrying forward their domestic cotton sector reforms.
13. The Ministers recognized the importance of the role of Cotton Focal Points and

encouraged Members to enhance the experiences and information sharing amongst all interested parties in the cotton dossier.

19.4.3 Implementation and Follow-Up:

14. The Ministers undertook to continue holding Dedicated Discussions on cotton on a bi-annual basis, as indicated in paragraphs 5, 6 and 7 of the Bali Ministerial Decision on Cotton, including in particular, examining relevant trade-related developments across the three pillars of Market Access, Domestic Support, and Export Competition in relation to cotton.
15. The Ministers undertook to regularly monitor the implementation by Members of paragraphs 2 to 4 during these Dedicated Discussions on cotton, based on relevant Members' notifications to the WTO, complemented as necessary by Members' replies to specific requests for information from the WTO Secretariat.
16. The Ministers agreed to review the situation regarding cotton at the Eleventh Ministerial Conference, which they agreed to hold in 2017, and they invited the Director-General to report at that Conference on the progress made in implementing the trade-related components of this Decision.

19.5 Issues Pertaining to LDCs

The Nairobi Package also contains decisions of specific benefit to LDCs, including enhanced preferential rules of origin for LDCs and preferential treatment for LDC services providers.

The Ministerial Conference adopted a decision that will facilitate opportunities for least developed countries' export of goods to both developed and developing countries under unilateral preferential trade arrangements in favour of LDCs.

The decision in Nairobi builds on the 2013 Bali Ministerial Decision on preferential rules of origin for LDCs. The Bali Decision set out, for the first time, a set of multilaterally agreed guidelines to help make it easier for LDC exports to qualify for preferential market access.

The Nairobi Decision expands upon this by providing more detailed directions on specific issues such as methods for determining when a product qualifies as "made in an LDC", and when inputs from other sources can be "cumulated"—or combined together —into the consideration of origin. It calls on preference-granting members to consider allowing the use of non-originating materials up to 75 percent of the final value of the product. The decision also calls on preference-granting members to consider simplifying documentary and procedural requirements related to origin.

Key beneficiaries will be sub-Saharan African countries, which make up the majority of the LDC Group, the proponent for the Nairobi Decision on Preferential Rules of Origin for LDCs.

The Ministerial Decision on Implementation of Preferential Treatment in Favour of Services and Service Suppliers of Least Developed Countries and Increasing LDC Participation in Services Trade extends the current waiver period under which non-LDC WTO members may grant preferential treatment to LDC services and service suppliers.

The period has been extended 15 years until December 31, 2030.

The waiver allows WTO members to deviate from their most-favoured nation compulsion under the General Agreement on Trade in Services (GATS). 21 members have submitted notifications so far granting preferences to LDC services and service suppliers. The decision also instructs the WTO's Trade in Services Council to encourage discussions among members on technical assistance aimed at increasing the capacity of LDCs to participate in services trade. It also sets up a review to monitor the operation of the notified preferences.

19.5.1 Preferential Rules of Origin for LDCs: The Ministerial Conference decided as follows:

A. Requirements for Assessment of Sufficient or Substantial Transformation

1. When applying an *ad valorem* percentage criterion to determine substantial transformation, preference-granting Members shall: (a) Adopt a method of calculation based on the value of non-originating materials. However, Preference-granting Members applying another method may continue to use it. It is recognized that the LDCs seek consideration of use of value of non-originating materials by such preference-granting Members when reviewing their preference programmes; (b) Consider, as the preference-granting Members develop or build on their individual rules of origin arrangements applicable to imports from LDCs, allowing the use of non-originating materials up to 75 percent of the final value of the product, or an equivalent threshold in case another calculation method is used, to the extent it is appropriate and the benefits of preferential treatment are limited to LDCs; (c) Consider the deduction of any costs associated with the transportation and insurance of inputs from other countries to LDCs. This provision shall not apply to preference-granting Members who do not use the *ad valorem* percentage criterion as their main method for the determination of substantial transformation.
2. When applying a change of tariff classification criterion to determine substantial transformation, preference-granting Members shall: (a) As a general principle, allow for a simple change of tariff heading or change of tariff sub-heading; (b) Eliminate all exclusions or restrictions to change of tariff classification rules, except where the preference-granting Member deems that such exclusions or restrictions are needed, including to ensure that a substantial transformation occurs; (c) Introduce, where appropriate, a tolerance allowance so that inputs from the same heading or sub-heading may be used.
3. When applying a manufacturing or processing operation criterion to determine substantial transformation, preference-granting Members shall, to the extent provided for in their respective non-reciprocal preferential trade arrangements, allow as follows: (a) if applied to clothing of chapters 61 and 62 of the Harmonised System nomenclature, the rule shall allow assembling of fabrics into finished products; (b) if applied to chemical products, the rule shall allow chemical reactions that form a new chemical identity; (c) if applied to processed agricultural products, the rule shall allow transforming of raw agricultural products into processed agricultural products;

(d) if applied to machinery and electronics, the rule shall allow assembling of parts into finished products, provided that the assembly of parts goes beyond simple assembly.

4. Preference-granting Members shall, to the extent possible, avoid requirements which impose a combination of two or more criteria for the same product. If a preference-granting Member still requires maintaining a combination of two or more criteria for the same product, that preference-granting Member remains open to consider relaxing such requirements for that specific product upon due request by an LDC.
5. Preference-granting Members are encouraged to offer alternative rules for the same product. In such cases, the above mentioned provisions will be applicable to only one of the alternative rules.

B. Cumulation:

1. Recognizing that the development of cumulation possibilities should be considered in relation to the rules applied to determine sufficient or substantial transformation, preference-granting Members are encouraged to expand cumulation to facilitate compliance with origin requirements by LDC producers using the following possibilities: (a) cumulation with the respective preference-granting Member; (b) cumulation with other LDCs; (c) cumulation with GSP beneficiaries of the respective preference-granting Member; and (d) cumulation with developing countries forming part of a regional group to which the LDC is a party, as defined by the preference-granting Member.
2. Preference-granting Members remain open to consider requests from LDCs for particular cumulation possibilities in the case of specific products or sectors.

C. Documentary Requirements:

1. With a view to reducing the administrative burden related to documentary and procedural requirements related to origin, preference-granting Members shall: (a) As a general principle, refrain from requiring a certificate of non-manipulation for products originating in a LDC but shipped across other countries unless there are concerns regarding transhipment, manipulation, or fraudulent documentation; (b) Consider other measures to further streamline customs procedures, such as minimizing documentation requirements for small consignments or allowing for self-certification.

D. Implementation, Flexibilities and Transparency:

1. Developing country Members declaring themselves in a position to do so should, with appropriate flexibility, undertake the commitments set out in the above provisions.
2. No later than December 31, 2016 each developed Preference-granting Member, and each developing Preference-granting Member undertaking the commitments in accordance with paragraph 1 above up to that date or thereafter, shall inform the Committee on Rules of Origin (CRO) of the measures being taken to implement the above provisions.
3. Preferential rules of origin shall be notified as per the established procedures. In this

regard, Members reaffirm their commitment to annually provide import data to the Secretariat, on the basis of which the Secretariat can calculate utilization rates, in accordance with modalities to be agreed upon by the CRO. Furthermore, the CRO shall develop a template for the notification of preferential rules of origin, to enhance transparency and promote a better understanding of the rules of origin applicable to imports from LDCs.

4. The CRO shall annually review the implementation of this Decision in accordance with the Transparency provisions contained in the Ministerial Decision on Preferential Rules of Origin for Least Developed Countries adopted at the Bali Ministerial Conference.

19.5.2 Implementation of Preferential Treatment in Favour of Services and Service Suppliers of LDCs: The Ministerial Conference decided as follows:

1. Due to the extended period between the adoption of the Waiver in December 2011 and the notification of preferences in 2015, the Waiver is extended as of the date of this Decision until December 31, 2030. Preferences notified so far may, as appropriate, be extended accordingly.
2. Developed and developing Members, in a position to do so, that have not notified preferences under the Waiver are urged to redouble efforts to promptly notify preferences which have commercial value and promote economic benefits to LDCs.
3. Members shall give special priority to addressing regulatory barriers of interest to LDCs.
4. With a view to further increasing LDC participation in services trade and to complement notification of preferential treatment under the Waiver, Members are encouraged to undertake specific technical assistance and capacity-building measures to orient LDC service suppliers to preference benefits available so that such suppliers can utilize the preferences granted.
5. The Council for Trade in Services shall: (a) maintain a standing agenda item to review and promote the operationalization of the Waiver; (b) expeditiously consider approval of notified preferences relating to measures other than those described in GATS Article XVI, in accordance with the Waiver; (c) with a view to furthering the objectives of GATS Article IV, facilitate an exchange of information by Members on technical assistance measures undertaken to promote the increasing participation of LDCs in world services trade; (d) initiate a process to review the operation of notified preferences, on the basis of information provided by Members. In support of that process, Members may request WTO Secretariat inputs, as appropriate; and (e) further discuss any issues that may facilitate benefits provided under the notified preferences.
6. The Council for Trade in Services may make recommendations on steps that could be taken towards enhancing the operationalization of the Waiver.

19.6 Regular Work under General Council

Ministers also welcomed the adoption of Decisions covering a Work Programme on

Small Economies; TRIPS Non-violation and Situation Complaints: and a continued Work Programme on Electronic Commerce.

In another significant outcome from the Nairobi Ministerial Conference, WTO members representing major exporters of IT products agreed on December 16 on the time table for implementing a landmark deal to eliminate tariffs on 201 information technology products valued at over US$ 1.3 trillion per year.

Negotiations on the expanded Information Technology Agreement (ITA) were conducted by 53 WTO members, including both developed and developing countries, which account for approximately 90 percent of world trade in these products. However, all WTO members will benefit from the agreement, as they will all enjoy duty-free market access to the markets of the members eliminating tariffs on these products. The list of 201 products was originally agreed by the ITA participants in July 2015.

This breakthrough followed months of intensive negotiations among the ITA participants. Their review of "draft schedules" involved a process whereby each of them indicated over what time frame and how they intended to implement the elimination of duties on these products.

For every product on the list, ITA participants have negotiated the level of reductions and over how many years it will fully eliminate the tariffs. As a result of these negotiations, approximately 65 percent of tariff lines will be fully eliminated by July 1, 2016. Most of the remaining tariff lines will be completely phased out in four stages over three years. This means that by 2019 almost all imports of the relevant products will be duty free.

19.6.1 Work Programme on Small Economies: The Ministerial Conference decided as follows:

1. The Ministers reaffirmed their commitment to the Work Programme on Small Economies and took note of all the work conducted to date. They took note of the work carried out since 2013, including that on the challenges and opportunities faced by small economies when linking into global value chains in trade in goods and services, and instructed the CTD to continue its work in Dedicated Session under the overall responsibility of the General Council.
2. Furthermore, the Ministers instructed the Dedicated Session to consider in further detail the various submissions that have been received to date, examine any additional proposals that Members might wish to submit and, where possible, and within its mandate, make recommendations to the General Council on any of these proposals. The General Council shall direct relevant subsidiary bodies to frame responses to the trade-related issues identified by the CTD with a view to making recommendations for action.
3. The Ministerial Conference instructed the WTO Secretariat to provide relevant information and factual analysis for discussion among Members in the CTD's Dedicated Session, *inter alia*, in the areas identified in the Work Programme on Small Economies and, in particular, to continue its work on the challenges and opportunities experienced by small economies when linking into global value chains

in trade in goods and services.

4. The Ministerial Conference requested the Secretariat to also conduct work on the challenges small economies experience in their efforts to reduce trade costs, particularly in the area of trade facilitation.
5. The CTD in Dedicated Session shall continue monitoring the progress of the small economy proposals in WTO bodies and in negotiating groups with the aim of providing responses, as soon as possible, to the trade-related issues identified for the fuller integration of SVEs in the multilateral trading system.

19.6.2 TRIPS Non-violation and Situation Complaints: The Ministerial Conference took note of the work done by the Council for Trade-Related Aspects of Intellectual Property Rights pursuant to their Decision of December 7, 2013 on "TRIPS Non-Violation and Situation Complaints", and directed it to continue its examination of the scope and modalities for complaints of the types provided for under sub-paragraphs 1(b) and 1(c) of Article XXIII of GATT, 1994 and make recommendations to the next Session of the Ministerial Conference in 2017.

It was agreed that, in the meantime, Members will not initiate such complaints under the TRIPS Agreement.

19.6.3 Work Programme on Electronic Commerce: The Ministerial Conference decided regarding the 'Work Programme on Electronic Commerce' adopted on September 25, 1998 as follows:

1. To continue the work under the Work Programme on Electronic Commerce since the last session, based on the existing mandate and guidelines and on the basis of proposals submitted by Members in the relevant WTO bodies as set out in paragraphs 2 to 5 of the Work Programme,
2. To instruct the General Council to hold periodic reviews in its sessions of July and December 2016 and July 2017 based on the reports that may be submitted by the WTO bodies entrusted with the implementation of the Work Programme and report to the next session of the Ministerial Conference,
3. That Members will maintain the current practice of not imposing customs duties on electronic transmissions until our next session which we have decided to hold in 2017.

19.7 Doha Development Agenda

The Ministers acknowledged that members "have different views" on how to address the future of the Doha Round negotiations but noted the "strong commitment of all Members to advance negotiations on the remaining Doha issues".

"This work shall maintain development at its centre and we reaffirm that provisions for special and differential treatment shall remain integral", Ministers declared.

Ministers also stated that, while negotiators should prioritize work where results have not yet been achieved, "some wish to identify and discuss other issues for negotiation; others do not. Any decision to launch negotiations multilaterally on such issues would need to be agreed by all Members".

Director General Azevêdo acknowledged "persistent and fundamental divisions on the negotiating agenda" and said WTO members "have to face up to this problem".

"Members must decide—the world must decide—about the future of the Doha Round", he declared. "This impasse is already harming the prospects of all those who rely on trade today—and it will disadvantage all those who would benefit from a reformed, modernized global trading system in future".

The Nairobi Ministerial could break new grounds in the context of trade facilitation. Additional six countries—Myanmar, Norway, Vietnam, Brunei, Zambia and Ukraine—supported ratifications for the Trade Facilitation Agreement (TFA), bringing the number to 63 members that have formally accepted TFA, which will enter into force once two-thirds of the WTO membership has formally accepted it. For the first time in WTO history, the requirement to implement TFA was directly linked to the capacity of the country to do so. In addition, TFA states that assistance and support should be provided to help them achieve that capacity. The implementation of TFA has the potential to increase global merchandise exports by up to US$ 1 trillion per annum, according to the WTO's flagship World Trade Report released on October 26, 2015.

19.8 Conclusions

The outcome of the Nairobi Ministerial Conference is as expected and not surprising at all. Though the outcome is being claimed a historic one by WTO officials, but it is a setback to world trade and development, in particular for developing countries. The following conclusions have been drawn from the analysis of the business conducted at the Conference:

1. A few developed countries are taking stand that the 'world has changed' since the beginning of Doha Development Round. They want to move forward on two tracks—first, to take 21st century issues like competition, investment, government procurement, energy security, labour, environment, global value chains, e-commerce and regulatory coherence; and second, the rapid rise of emerging countries should make these countries to pay significantly more than agreed upon earlier. Taken together, these propositions clearly leads to the rejection of Doha mandate and implicitly call for a fresh mandate to start another round, comprising only the 21st century issues.
2. Re-affirmation of Doha Agenda has been divided. This is a diplomatic move to put Doha at back burner for the time being and eventually abandon it.
3. A new category of small and vulnerable economies is being created. This would imply emerging economies to open up more.
4. Abandonment of Doha will damage developing countries; particularly in agriculture sector because of high level of subsidies prevalent in developed countries which will deter market access to agricultural exports from developing countries. Gain to professionals in service sector in developing countries will also be curtailed as services negotiations have been put on the back burner.
5. Decision of export competition for farm products will disturb the balance of global trade in agriculture as the two more important remaining core issues—domestic

support and market access remained unresolved.

6. The pledge made by the EU and the US to phase out the total export subsidy on farm products by 2013 is still in practice and was hardly reiterated at the meet. What is sensible from developing countries' point of view to argue is that agricultural trade is highly discriminatory in nature essentially because of these primary issues that disturb the trade even now, i.e. domestic support and market access.
7. Export competition has the least intensity among the three—domestic support, market access and export competition—and distortion taking place due to export completion would be minimal compared to the other two bigger culprits—domestic support and market access.
8. The entire export subsidy given to the magnitude of US$ 5 billion on farm products is minuscule compared to domestic support amounting to US$ 360 billion a year.
9. According to World Bank estimate, abolition of export subsidy will yield 2 percent of theoretical gains to world agriculture. Instead what would have been significant is getting the commitment of phasing out of domestic support—the real dampener in global agricultural trade distortion.
10. India has to remove export subsidy on sugar—phasing out marketing and transport assistance via state owned enterprises. The US gets away with sweet deal on export credits and food aid.
11. Since 1995, the US has paid US$ 256 billion in subsidies to its farmers. The European Union handed out Euro 59 billion with subsidies to its farmers in 2014. Yet, they condemn India for giving out about US$ 40 billion as food subsidies. The average median income of a US farmer is US$ 84,649 per year almost 70 percent higher than that of a typical American household. Average income of farmers in India was pegged at ₹ 6,426 per month in 2012-13, according to the NSSO report.
12. According to International Centre for Trade and Sustainable Development (ICTSD), the US cotton subsidy under its new 2014 farm bill would lower global cotton prices by nearly 7 percent, causing losses to farmers in African countries and India to the tune of US$ 3.3 billion per year.
13. Duty-free and quota-free market access for exports of least developed countries was the decision of Hong Kong Ministerial Conference. It is not being fully implemented.
14. All decisions adopted at the Conference are either for extension or re-affirmation of decisions taken earlier and, in reality, no new trade negotiation took place at the meet. Developed countries are not willing to negotiate trade issues core to the development of developing countries.
15. Moreover, the conclusion of the highly ambitious TPP agreement and the prospects of quick conclusion of TTIP and TISA, all of which are being negotiated at the initiative of the US, outside WTO, pose a threat to the very relevance of WTO apart from being just a forum of dispute settlement.

The analysis of above facts manifests that Doha Round was only a development round in name sake for developing countries. The developed countries have led the foundation for burial of Doha Development Agenda by making diplomatic statements and giving divisive re-affirmation about it.

Developed countries are making commitments for phasing out export subsidies for the last few years. Similarly, duty-free and quota-free market access for exports of least developed countries is being committed since the Hong Kong Ministerial Conference. So far, nothing materialistic has happened for the developing countries. Global trade in agricultural products is highly distorted due to rich countries' subsidies. Negotiations in services have been put at the back burner.

The motive of these countries is to initiate new round for new issues. If they do not succeed in this, plan B in parallel moves in the form of TTP, TTIP and TISA is in progress. This will leave WTO as a mere dispute settlement body. Thus, the outcome of Nairobi meet is a setback, in particular for the developing countries.

Part III:
WTO: The Road Ahead

20

WTO: Issues, Strategies and Suggestions

20.1 The Background

The World Trade Organization (WTO) was established through Marrakesh Agreement signed by 123 founding Members on April 15, 1994. The WTO membership has risen to 162. Now, WTO Members account for 98 percent of world trade as compared to 91 percent in 1995.

At the very First Ministerial Conference in 1996, a plurilateral agreement on information technology was adopted along with establishment of work groups on three new issues, trade policy and competition, public procurement, trade and investment; and a work programme on trade facilitation. The Multilateral Trading System (GATT/WTO) completed 50 years in 1998. Developed Members emphasised for further negotiations on trade issues, while developing Members were of view that the implementation issue should be taken before the expansion. The need of integrating the developing countries into multilateral trading system was felt. Finally, a new round of negotiations was initiated at the Doha Ministerial Conference in 2001. "Doha Development Agenda" was adopted by Members at the Doha Ministerial Conference. The Doha Declaration listed 21 subjects, most of which were connected with negotiations, and other works including implementation, analysis, and monitoring of decisions and agreements. The Doha Work Programme was originally to be concluded not later than January 1, 2005.

The differences between the Members simmered on two lines. First, whenever developing countries raised the issue of non-implementation of agreements and non-realisation of due benefits for developing countries, the developed countries called for the extension of agenda, in particular 'Singapore Issues', and for starting a new round of trade negotiations. Second, on the question of agricultural subsidies provided for by developed countries, hampering the market access to developing countries' agricultural exports, the developed countries countered it by opening the platform for trade related environmental issues.

A package in July 2004 was agreed and it was decided to drop three Singapore Issues, namely, government procurement, trade and investment, and trade and competition policy, permanently from the Doha Development Agenda. On the fourth issue, namely, trade facilitation, a negotiation group was established. At the Hong Kong Ministerial Conference in 2005, a Declaration was made to establish modalities on agriculture and NAMA by April 30, 2006 and prepare draft schedules by July 31, 2006. It was resolved to complete the Doha Work Programme fully, and to conclude negotiations in 2006.

There were divergences on certain issues such as agricultural modalities, cotton subsidies and modalities on non-agricultural market access. Developed and developing countries both adhered to the traditional stands. Negotiations under Doha Round were suspended from June 24, 2006.

In order to restart the negotiations, two drafts of modalities for agriculture and NAMA, based on July 2008 negotiations, were circulated among the Members on December 6, 2008. Elements of political guidance were issued at the Geneva Ministerial Conference in 2011. But, the negotiations could only gain some momentum at the Bali Ministerial Conference in 2013. The Ministerial produced the first multilateral trade agreement since the WTO was established in 1995—the landmark Trade Facilitation Agreement (TFA), plus nine other accords regarding agricultural issues of particular concern to developing countries and special preferences for least developed countries. The success achieved in Bali was limited and conditional. Much depended on the outcomes of the Nairobi Ministerial conference. The outcome of the Nairobi was not satisfactory and resulted in a divisive reaffirmation of Doha Development Agenda. It was a setback for the developing countries, since distortions in global agricultural trade remained unresolved and services negotiations were put at back burner, resulting in curtailment of gains to professionals in services sector.

Table 20.1 chronologically presents important events in the evolution of WTO.

20.2 Issues for Consideration

This section discusses the issues that must be tackled to consolidate the success achieved so far under the WTO and to restore the WTO as a central negotiating forum in multilateral trade.

20.2.1 Agriculture: At the Ninth Ministerial Conference, held in Bali in December 2013, five priority items in agricultural agenda were taken up. These were:

1. Abolition of export subsidies.
2. Administrative reform of "tariff rate quotas" that are continually under filled.
3. Consent for developing countries to public stock holding for food security purposes.
4. Expanding the list of "green box" general services of interest to developing countries.
5. Restraining subsidies to cotton production by the developed countries.
6. Domestic support provided by the member governments. This issue is still unresolved and it is creating hurdles in the conclusion of the Doha Round.

A. Export Subsidies: At the Hong Kong Ministerial Conference, the Members agreed to eliminate, by 2013, all subsidies for agricultural exports, including financial contributions and other advantages gained from government supported export credit and insurance, food aid and state trading enterprises.

The commitment was diluted at the Bali Ministerial Conference in 2013. Members promised to apply extreme control in using any form of export subsidy and also promised to ensure, to the maximum extent possible, progress in eliminating all forms of export subsidies. But, these promises are conditional on a single undertaking that covers all elements of the DDA package.

Most of the countries expressed dissatisfaction to the Bali commitment. Developing countries insisted that the developed Members should accept hard limits, even elimination of the agricultural export subsidies.

At the Nairobi Ministerial Conference, Members again have set the time frame for the abolition of total export subsidies. Time will tell whether the real issue would be resolved or not:

Table 20.1: Milestones in the Evolution of WTO

General Agreement on Trade and Tariffs, 1947	October 30, 1947
Marrakesh Agreement	April 15, 1994
Establishment of the WTO	January 1, 1995
Information Technology Agreement	December 13, 1996
Comprehensive and Integrated Plan of Action for LDCs	December 13, 1996
Establishment of Work Group on Investment	December 13, 1996
Establishment of Work Group on Competition	December 13, 1996
Establishment of Work Group on Public Procurement	December 13, 1996
Approval to Goods Council for Work on Trade Facilitation	December 13, 1996
High Level Meeting for LDCs	October 10, 1997
Integrated Framework for Trade Related Technical Assistance for LDCs	October 10, 1997
70 WTO Members Reach a Multilateral Agreement on Financial Services	December 12, 1997
Adoption of a Comprehensive Work Programme on E-commerce	September 25, 1998
Establishment of Working Group on Trade and Transfer of Technology	November 14, 2001
Establishment of Working Group on Trade, Debt and Finance	November 14, 2001
Work Programme for New Round of Negotiations Adopted (Doha Round)	November 14, 2001
Withdrawal of Investment, Competition and Government Procurement Issues	August 1, 2004
Establishment of Negotiation Group on Trade Facilitation	October 12, 2004
Duty-free and Quota-free Market Access for LDCs' Exports	December 18, 2005
Suspension of Negotiations under the Doha Round	June 24, 2006
Resumption of Negotiations under the Doha Round	February 7, 2007
Draft Modalities on Agriculture Based on July 2008 Negotiations	December 6, 2008
Draft Modalities on NAMA Based on July 2008 Negotiations	December 6, 2008
Chairs Programme Launched to Support Developing Country Universities	January 26, 2010
Circulation of Elements of Political Guidance	December 1, 2011
Waiver on Services for Least Developed Countries	December 17, 2011
Decision on Work Programme on Public Stockholding for Food Security	December 7, 2013
Adoption of Bali Package	December 7, 2013
Trade Facilitation Agreement Adopted	December 7, 2013
Revised Government Procurement Agreement	April 6, 2014
Special Safeguard Mechanism for Developing Countries	December 19, 2015

B. Tariff Rate Quotas: The Bali Ministerial proposal would require countries with under-filled tariff rate quotas to accept quantities on a first-come, first-served basis, or to issue "automatic licenses on demand" up to the quota limit. However, the developing countries Members were exempted and the new provision would lapse after six years for all members unless renewed. The US chose to opt out of the new provisions.

C. Public Stock Holding for Food Security: The public stock holding for food security is the most contentious issue in the agricultural agenda. Funds spent on food stock piles are counted as an "amber box" subsidy. India proposed to count public stock holding funds as "green box" subsidies, exempt from any limit. The US and other agricultural exporters objected, fearing that an exemption would totally undermine any discipline on agricultural subsidies. At the Bali Ministerial Conference, it was agreed that WTO Members would use "due restraint" in making complaints against public stock holding for food security programmes (a peace clause), at least until the Eleventh Ministerial Conference in 2017.

As the time came to ratify the Bali Ministerial package as an integral part of the WTO accords in July 2014, India insisted that unless the 'peace clause' was immediately made permanent, and food security programmes were insulated from any WTO challenge, India would refuse to accept the Trade Facilitation Agreement. In November 2014, WTO Members agreed to a revised peace clause that committed them not to challenge India and other developing countries for exceeding the subsidy limits related to public stock holding programmes until a permanent solution is agreed upon.

D. Green Box General Services: The Bali Ministerial Conference accepted the proposal that the list of green box general services should be expanded to include land rehabilitation, soil conservation and resource management, drought management and flood control, rural employment programmes, issuing land ownership titles and settlement programmes. The expansion is subject to the provisions of Annex 2 of the Agreement on Agriculture that these and other green box measures shall meet fundamental requirements that they have no, or at most minimal, trade distorting effects on production (Table 20.2).

Table 20.2: Top Exporters of Agriculture and Cotton in 2013

(US$ billion)

Agriculture		Cotton	
European Union	156.3	China	17.5
United States	147.1	**India**	**11.3**
Netherlands	101.9	United States	7.5
Germany	87.6	Pakistan	5.3
Brazil	86.4	Australia	2.5
France	77.8	Turkey	1.9
Belgium	48.6	Italy	1.8
China	47.5	Germany	1.3
Spain	45.7	Brazil	1.2
Canada	45.3	Indonesia	0.8
Italy	42.6		
India	**42.3**		

Source: wits.worldbank.org.

E. Cotton Subsidies: The Hong Kong Ministerial Conference in 2005 issued a declaration calling on the developed countries to eliminate all forms of export subsidies by 2006 and to open their markets to cotton exported by LDCs on a duty-free, quota-free basis. The Bali Declaration was, however, much less crystal clear since it simply called for serious negotiations during 2014 to achieve a substantial reduction in subsidies, and for greater assistance to cotton producers in developing countries.

The main impediment to an agreement on cotton subsidies is the fact that developing countries are major exporters of cotton. The Hong Kong Ministerial Conference limited the target to cotton exports from developed countries.

F. Domestic Agricultural Support: In 2013, the European Union renewed its Common Agricultural Policy (CAP) until 2020. In 2014, the US Congress passed a new farm bill that restructures some key programmes and will guide US farm policy until 2018. In view of the fact that the US and the EU are the two countries most criticised for their agricultural subsidies, it is important to note that the hands of the respective trade ministers are almost fixed with respect to the legislative changes.

In July 2008 negotiations, the WTO Members wanted the US and the EU to sharply cut their AMS caps. Agreements on domestic support commitments are now much harder to achieve than in 2008 because of changes in market conditions and US farm legislations (Table 20.3).

Table 20.3: Actual Agriculture Producer Support Estimates, 2012

Country/Grouping	US$ billion	Percent of Production
Japan	52.0	61
European Union	112.2	23
Indonesia	24.9	21
China	167.1	18
Canada	7.6	16
Mexico	7.1	13
United states	33.5	9
Brazil	8.1	5
India	**13.8**	4
Australia	0.9	0

Source: OECD: Producer and Consumer Support Estimates Database.

20.2.2 Non-agricultural Market Access: Non-Agricultural Market Access issues are not as controversial as agriculture issues. Based on the July 2008 negotiations, which were in fact adjourned in the same year, a draft on modalities for non-agricultural market access was issued on December 6, 2008. The major issue is the reluctance of major developing countries to reduce their bound tariff rates closer to their applied tariff rates for manufactured imports. Developed countries also complained that the formulas, mentioned in the draft issued on December 6, 2008, applied to calculate tariff reduction only served to reduce bound rates, not lower the applied rates of most developing countries.

Table 20.4 shows pre-Doha and provisionally agreed post-Doha tariff averages for six major economies, both bound and applied rates with respect to NAMA. Applied tariff rates for manufactured goods are generally low, but average applied rates imposed by key emerging countries are quite high as compared to those imposed by major developed countries.

Table 20.4: Pre-Doha and Post-Doha Weighted Average Tariffs for NAMA

(percent)

Country/Grouping	Pre-Doha		Post-Doha	
	Bound Rate	Applied Rate	Bound Rate	Applied Rate
European Union	2.4	1.5	1.2	0.8
Japan	5.7	0.9	1.9	0.5
United States	4.2	1.4	1.6	0.7
Brazil	30.3	7.0	12.4	5.9
China	4.1	3.5	2.9	2.6
India	**30.4**	**7.8**	**11.6**	**7.7**

Source: Hufbauer, Jung, Miner, Moran and Schott (2015).

20.2.3 Services: The negotiations, which began in 2000 as mandated under Article XIX of the General Agreement on Trade in Services, were integrated into the single undertaking of the Doha Round. The services negotiations have been held up closer to the starting line than the target. Thus, progress on services is critical to the near term success and long-term viability of the WTO.

Under the Doha Round, the negotiations in services were focused on both liberalisation and new rule making in four major areas: domestic regulatory policies; safeguards; government procurement and subsidies; and special treatment for least developed countries. The negotiators argued that work on modalities for agriculture and NAMA had to advance before progress on services. The services talks were almost held up. The result of talks on new services rules was no better. The only area of progress was the Agreement to adopt a Waiver, at the Eighth Ministerial Conference in Geneva in December 2011, to allow Members to give preferential treatment to services from least developed countries. At the Nairobi Ministerial Conference, Ministers again took the decision to give preferential treatment to services and services suppliers from least developed countries. This was again reiterated at the Nairobi Ministerial Conference in December 2015.

20.2.4 Intellectual Property: Though the progress in the area of intellectual property is linked and to follow the achievements in preferential areas such as agriculture, non-agricultural goods and services, there are contentious issues pertaining to different aspects and areas of intellectual property.

20.2.5 Duty-Free Quota-Free (DFQF) Market Access: The Bali Ministerial renewed the call following the decision at the Hong Kong Ministerial Conference, for developed countries and for developing countries, to provide DFQF market access for exports of LDCs on 97 percent of their tariff lines.

The success on DFQF market access since 2005 has been limited. There are three main problems related to DFQF market access:

1. The 97 percent threshold, while seemingly generous, allows developed countries to exclude a handful of tariff lines that account for a large share of LDC exports;
2. The rigid rules of origin serve to exclude LDC exports that contain significant inputs from intermediate suppliers;
3. Some countries have not stepped up their own DFQF market access programmes. For example, Brazil and Russia have announced their programmes, but they have so far implemented nothing.

At the Nairobi Ministerial Conference, the Ministers adopted a decision on preferential rules of origin for the least developed countries.

20.2.6 Trade and Development: The WTO Committee on Trade and Development implemented a number of decisions taken at the Ninth Ministerial Conference in Bali, including holding a first session of the monitoring mechanism on special and differential treatment for developing countries. It also discussed the WTO's technical assistance and training activities and received members' notifications concerning market access for developing countries and least developed countries. It also began discussion on how to proceed with a review of the transparency mechanism for preferential trade arrangements.

There is dire need of bridging the gap between announcements made and the implementation of the promises. Though the current round of negotiations has been termed as a development round, very limited has been done for the development of poor countries.

20.2.7 Transfer of Technology: The Working group on Trade and Transfer of technology held a one day workshop in 2014, to discuss the relationship between trade and transfer of technology. It also explored possible recommendations to increase flow of technology to developing countries. But, the issue is that, in reality, very little has been done by developed countries on this front. To integrate developing countries into the multilateral trading system and for their development, developed countries have to transfer technology to developing countries as per the provisions prescribed in the WTO Agreements.

20.2.8 Building Trade Capacity: The developing countries, especially least developed countries, regularly complained of the difficulties faced by them in the implementation of their obligations under the WTO agreements. A number of programmes have been initiated to enhance and build the trade capacity of the developing countries.

A. Aid-for-Trade: Aid-for-Trade helps developing countries, and particularly least developed countries, in international trade. Many developing countries face a range of supply side and trade related infrastructure obstacles which constrain their ability to engage in international trade.

Fifth Global Review of Aid-for-Trade on 'reducing trade costs for inclusive and sustainable growth' took place in Geneva from June 30, 2015 to July 2, 2015. The Global Review analysed actions already taken by developing countries, regional commitments and their development partners to reduce trade costs and surveyed the extent of challenge remaining, and how it can be addressed in the context of proposed Sustainable Development Goals.

Aid-for-Trade flows to developing countries rebounded in 2012, with commitments rising by 21 percent after sliding by 14 percent in the previous year. OECD figures also suggested that support for trade for trade facilitation is growing and more funding is becoming available.

B. Enhanced Integrated Framework: The EIF for trade-related assistance to LDCs is a multi donor programme that helps LDCs to become more active players in the multilateral trading system. The EIF continued to grow in 2014, with a rise in the number of active projects in EIF countries. At present, 46 countries are receiving assistance to build stronger trade institutions and to address challenges, with Somalia becoming the latest LDC to join the EIF. After an independent evaluation, the EIF Steering Committee extended the programme into second phase when the current one ends in 2015. The EIF is supported by donor pledges of US$ 251 million and contributions of US$ 201 million as of December 31, 2014, up from US$ 190 million in 2013.

C. Standards and Trade Development Facility: The Standards and Trade Development Facility undertook research in 2014 in a number of developing countries, which led to recommendations for improving coordination between Sanitary and Phytosanitary (SPS) Committee and other multilateral agencies and facilitating safe trade. It also assisted in the development and implementation of numerous projects that promote compliance with international food safety; animal and plant health standards and facilitate market access. Throughout the year, several recommendations to further strengthen the operation of the Facility were implemented.

D. Technical Assistance and Training: The Institute for Training and Technical Cooperation (ITTC) reinforced the design and delivery of WTO technical assistance programmes and strengthened key aspects of these programmes. The WTO increased its training programmes for government officials, undertaking 324 technical assistance activities in 2014, compared with 279 in 2013. Although the overall total of activities was down two years ago, the number of participants benefiting from technical assistance continues to rise due to the growing use of e-learning, with an increasing focus on LDCs and Africa.

20.2.9 Special and Differential Treatment: Recalling the General Council decision of July 2002 to establish the Monitoring Mechanism; the Ministers at the Bali Ministerial Conference decided the scope, functions, terms of reference and operation of the Monitoring Mechanism for Special and Differential Treatment. The Special and Differential Treatment provisions are a part across all the WTO agreements.

The issue is the realisation of due benefits to developing countries, particularly least developed countries, from developed countries which are in a position to do so, under the Special and Differential Treatment provisions of the WTO agreements.

20.2.10 Dispute Settlement: In 2014, the DSB received 14 requests for consultations—the first stage in the dispute settlement process—and established 13 panels. The Dispute Settlement System should be reviewed taking into consideration the changing global trading environment.

20.2.11 Trade Policy Review Mechanism: The Trade monitoring reports revealed that trade restrictive measures introduced by the WTO Members continued to rise. Given the continuing uncertainties in the global economy, the reports stressed the need for countries to show restraint in imposing new measures and to eliminate more of the existing measures. WTO conducted 13 trade policy reviews in 2014 to examine the trade policies and practices of 21 WTO Members.

20.2.12 Trade Facilitation Agreement: Trade Facilitation Agreement is a multipart document, with tiers of obligations—more severe for developed countries and considerably less severe for the developing countries. It has a single principle; to curb red tape and corruption at sea ports and cargo airports and thereby drastically reduce the time and expenditure for merchandise to enter and leave a country.

Trade Facilitation Agreement does not require developing country Members to fully implement the agreement upon entry into force. The developing countries were encouraged to notify, by July 31, 2014, those commitments that they would implement at the start; those would be implemented after the transition period; and those that would be undertaken only after the attainment of the implementation capacity. These commitments were supposed to be annexed to the TFA and the Protocol adopted by the General Council in July 2014. 63 Members have ratified the Agreement till the conclusion of Nairobi Ministerial Conference. However, 107 Members must ratify TFA before it can be joined as a Protocol to the legal text of the WTO.

20.3 New Strategies

Since the deadlock is persisting in trade negotiations due to differences between the developed countries and the developing countries on certain issues, the developed countries are gradually adopting a new strategy. The developed countries are adamant on certain issues that are core to the interest of the developing countries. Developed countries are developing plurilateral agreements outside the WTO, which may render the WTO only as a dispute settlement body. The diplomatic statements and division in opinions indicates an end of the development round for developing countries. Developed countries are reluctant to resolve the problem of distortions in global agricultural trade. Negotiations on services have been put aside, also harming the interest of developing countries in professional services.

In response, the developing countries should prepare their strategy. First, the developing countries should stick to the traditional multilateral approach to expand and conclude trade negotiations as envisaged in the WTO based decisions and discussions among the WTO Members, including the Doha Development Agenda. Second, developing countries may allow plurilateral to multilateral approach or the new possibility developed by some developed countries consequent upon the deadlock in WTO talks since 2008, first initiating the plurilateral agreements and then making efforts to bring them within the WTO framework and, simultaneously, forming free trade agreements and bilateral trade agreements. The failure of the Ministerial Conferences might eventually lead to a spurt in free trade agreements and bilateral agreements among the countries, especially developed countries, that have emerged since the last four or five years.

20.3.1 Developing Countries: Possibilities of any successful outcomes on the trade negotiations, including the conclusion of the Doha Round are remote. Divergences on the positions adopted by the developed and the developing countries are very wide and, eventually, may make the multilateral trading system unsuccessful. The developing countries should devise their strategy to tackle contentious issues and to prevent the attempt of developed countries to dilute the development agenda, which is core to the interest of developing countries in coming years. The following issues are contentious and a proper strategy should be devised to address them.

A. Agriculture: The agriculture is most contentious issue to be resolved by the WTO Members.

- India wants a permanent solution to the food security issue. India's stand has been that the WTO should update the reference price of 1986-88 that is used in the formulae for calculating the food security cap or exempt schemes from the purview of subsidy caps. There is a little possibility of getting a permanent solution regards the issue of public stock holding for food security in the near future.
- The Doha Round of negotiations launched in 2001 has remained stalled since July 2008 due to non-convergence of the developed and the developing countries, basically over agricultural subsidies. Rich countries are not willing to abolish agricultural subsidies. The developing countries should bring all pending issues of the Doha Round on the table at the next Ministerial Conference scheduled in 2017.
- The US and the EU have renewed their agricultural policies, in 2014 and 2013 respectively, leaving no space for any reduction in farm subsidies. Hence, there is no question of solving the problem of domestic support provided by rich countries to the agriculture sector and eventually leading to the continuation of deadlock in the negotiations in other areas as well.

B. Non-agricultural Market Access: The issue, though less controversial, is linked to the solution of the issue of domestic support provided by rich countries in the agriculture sector. The developed countries want reduction in the bound tariff rates of developing countries so as to bring these closer to the applied tariff rates. The major issue is the reluctance of major developing countries to reduce their bound tariff rates closer to their applied tariff rates for manufactured imports, until the issue of domestic support to agriculture by the developed countries is resolved. Since there is no possibility of domestic agricultural support issue being resolved, the NAMA issue would remain unsettled as such.

C. Services: The negotiators argued that work on modalities for agriculture and NAMA has to advance before progress on services. Since there is still a deadlock in both agriculture and NAMA, no progress can be envisaged in the services sector. The services talks have almost languished.

D. TRIPS: Switzerland and the US had begun a campaign at the WTO to not renew a moratorium on "non-violation complaints and situations" for intellectual property rights that was to expire at the end of 2015. However, the Nairobi Ministerial Conference has extended the moratorium till 2017.

Apart from this, no progress has been made on the issues related to TRIPS as envisaged in the Doha Development Agenda, such as multilateral notifications and registration in the case of geographical indications and others.

E. Duty-Free and Quota-Free Market Access: There is need to do a lot in DFQF area. This is a part of the "Bali Package" agreed at the Bali Ministerial Conference in 2013. The developed countries indirectly indicated that if the developing countries falter in ratifying the Trade Facilitation Agreement (TFA), they will block the entire Bali Package. This approach manifests bickering on the Bali Package too.

F. Special and Differential Treatment: The envisaged benefits of the Special and Differential Treatment are that developed countries will provide a supportive environment to least developed countries, by providing preferential access to their markets and by providing technical and other assistance which is required to meet their WTO obligations. However, the unevenness that exists as regards developed countries and least developed countries in the terms of levels of development reveals some inefficiencies of the application of Special and Differential Treatment regime. The current Special and Differential Treatment system needs to be revised. However, the chances are no better.

G. Transfer of Technology: There has been only a provision on papers under the WTO agreements on transfer of technology, but in practice, nothing concrete has been done. The developed countries must sincerely provide incentives to their multinationals for transferring technology to the developing countries. The integration of developing countries into multilateral trading system is not possible, at least in the long-term, without the requisite technology transfer to them.

H. Building Trade Capacity: Though the Doha Round was named as the 'development round', little concrete has been done by developed countries for the development of the developing countries. The developing countries should raise the issues related to their capacity-building such as Enhanced Integrated Framework, Aid-for-Trade, Technical Training and Assistance, and others in the forthcoming Ministerial Conferences.

The developing countries should stick to their traditional multilateral approach for concluding trade negotiations as envisaged in the WTO based decisions and discussions among the Members, including the Doha Development Agenda. The problem of distortion in global agricultural trade caused by domestic support and limited market access should be resolved first. The developing countries should remain firm on the above mentioned issues as these are core to their interest.

In bargain, developing countries may allow plurilateral agreements among Member countries. The suggested strategy is first initiating the plurilateral agreements and then making efforts to bring them within the WTO framework. Each plurilateral agreement under the WTO auspices should be open to any WTO Member that later decides to join both to accept the obligations and enjoy the rights. There is a need to safeguard the interests of developing countries.

20.3.2 Developed Countries: Developed countries are forming regional and sectoral trade agreements for the last four to five years consequent upon stalemate in trade negotiations in the WTO. This trend and stalemate in trade negotiations may render WTO as a mere dispute settlement body.

In an effort to rebalance the NAMA deal, the developed countries adopted a new approach for sectoral liberalisation. Plurilateral talks in few sectors are now underway and future talks might be launched in other sectors. Because of inaction in the Doha Round, a group of WTO Members launched talks on Trade in Services Agreement. These negotiations are arranged on a plurilateral basis outside of the WTO.

Three plurilaterals: the Information Technology Agreement-2, the Environmental Goods Agreements, and the Trade in Services Agreement (TISA) might be concluded in the near future. There is a possibility that Investment Framework Agreement, Local Contents Requirements, Exchange Rate Practices and Public Enterprises are taken up in the next round of plurilaterals.

According to Article IX (3) of the Marrakesh Agreement, the incorporation of plurilateral agreements into the body of the WTO would require a three-fourth affirmative vote of all Members. In this way, plurilaterals, once brought in the WTO framework, would restore the WTO as the principal global forum for addressing new issues. However, this is a tough task.

Plurilateral agreements, that are either underway or would come in future, have been described below.

A. Information Technology Agreement-2: The prospects of bringing Mexico, Brazil, and other non-Member countries into the ITA-2 would benefit all countries. However, extending the commitments of current Members could lead to far greater gains. Current commitments do not include all IT products, nor do they eradicate non-tariff barriers that hamper trade in products already subject to tariff commitments. Talks have been held for more than a decade to expand the ITA in this direction, but not much progress was made until the breakthrough accord was reached between the US and China in November 2014.

B. Environmental Goods Agreement: After years of unproductive Doha Round talks, 14 WTO Members including the US, the EU, and China, in July 2014, decided to negotiate a plurilateral agreement on environmental goods to liberalize trade in environmental goods through tariff eliminations. Some other countries also joined the talks in 2015.

Though the level of aspiration of the current EGA talks is uncertain, they however seem modest with the inclusion of 54 product groups including air pollution equipments and waste water equipments. In March 2015, negotiators agreed on finalising an introductory list of around 600 products in categories.

C. Trade in Services Agreement: A plurilateral Trade in Services Agreement is the most important plurilateral agreement among the new issues. Launched by Really Good Friends (RGFs), a group of WTO Members that opened negotiations in 2014, the group included the world's largest advanced nations, accounting for more than two-thirds of global trade in services.

The TISA negotiation is not a part of the Doha round. TISA is a plurilateral effort designed, in the first occurrence, to meet the conditions laid out in GATS Article V. According to Article V, an agreement is essential to achieve "sizeable sectoral coverage" with respect to the volume of services trade, number of sectors, and modes of supply, and to abolish "substantial all discrimination" among its members. These services talks are taking place outside the WTO. In April 2014, TISA members circulated their first round of offers of market access concessions. The next round was held in February 2015. The stalemate has developed between developed countries and developing countries in the WTO talks, leading to the proliferation of bilateral trade agreements. The Doha Development Agenda (DDA) negotiations ran stranded almost seven years ago, in July 2008. In the intervening period, three mega regional negotiations occupied centre stage in world trade policy: the Trans-Pacific Partnership (TPP), the Regional Comprehensive Economic Partnership (RCEP) and the Trans-Atlantic Trade and Investment Partnership (TTIP).

African countries are also building their own regional cooperation. At the same time, many bilateral trade agreements are also taking place across the globe.

It is also being suggested that developing countries should allow the new plurilateral agreements, agreed by subsets of the WTO Members, to be added to the WTO framework without the unanimous consent of all WTO Members. This constitutional change would develop a new strategy, focusing on liberalising entirely new realms of global commerce, even if not all WTO Members are prepared to liberalise at the same pace.

Since some issues are too contentious for reaching agreement on rules that might tuck the policies of many WTO Members, the possible solution is to initiate plurilateral agreements that would establish rules of the road just for signatory members. Each agreement under the WTO patronage should be open to any WTO Member that later decides to join—both to accept the obligations and enjoy the rights. Thus, the first negotiating modality is a broad based approval of open plurilateral agreements. Such strategy would restore the WTO as the principal global forum for addressing new issues.

20.4 Conclusions

On July 28, 2015, the chief WTO spokesman opined, "that deadline will almost certainly not be met". He further said, "The gaps are very wide. The world's top economic powers have appeared unwilling to make concessions in key areas".

After the analysis of the facts and discussions in the preceding sections, some conclusions might be drawn regarding the WTO. The conclusions have been summarised below:

1. There is a definite failure on agricultural domestic support negotiations, since rich countries are not willing to abandon agricultural subsidies. The EU and the US have already re-enacted their long-term agricultural policies in such a way leaving no space for reduction or elimination of the farm subsidies.
2. On Non-Agricultural Market Access, the developing and developed countries are maintaining their positions and there is no possibility of convergence. The developed countries intend that the bound tariff rates of developing countries be brought closer to applied tariff rates. Further, the developing countries want the settlement of the issue of rich countries' farm subsidies before the NAMA issue.
3. In services sector, which was to follow the progress in agriculture and NAMA, no further progress is expected.
4. There has been no progress in the intellectual property area. There may be a face-off between developed countries and the developing countries in the forthcoming Ministerial Conference on certain issues relating to intellectual property rights in the pharmaceutical sector.
5. The Doha Development Round was started in 2001. The geopolitical circumstances in global trade environment have changed since then. The share of developing countries in world trade has increased substantially and, now, it accounts for more than one-third of the world trade. The trade interests of the Member countries have also shifted in the intervening period. Therefore, it is very difficult to make consensus on different trade issues. Doha Development Agenda might, most probably, remain an unaccomplished one.
6. So far nothing definitive is in sight for a permanent solution to public stockholdings. For a permanent solution, India had proposed either amending the formula to calculate the food subsidy cap of 10 percent which is based on 1986-88 prices or allowing such schemes outside the purview of subsidy caps. India has already given indication that it will not ratify the trade facilitation pact for the want of any visible progress in negotiations on finding a permanent solution on food security for public stockholding purposes.

In a nutshell, the trade negotiation stalemate might continue, as indicated by the developments that have happened so far. This might put the credibility of the WTO as a multilateral trade forum in question. Such an outcome, as explained in the suggestions given below, would be detrimental to the interest of developing countries, particularly the least developed ones. Consequently, it would give spurt to regional/free trade agreements between the countries, in addition to the possible efforts to initiate and bring the plurilateral agreements within the WTO framework.

Arthur A. Daemmrich quoted in Harvard Business Review on December 17, 2010, "that a stalemate has developed between developed countries and developing countries in WTO talks, leading to the proliferation of bilateral agreements". The following conclusions have been inferred regarding the prospects of plurilateral trade agreements:

1. Efforts are being made under a new approach, first to develop plurilateral agreements and then to bring them within the WTO framework. The work on plurilateral agreements on services, information technology-2, and environmental goods is already under way.
2. Countries are looking at shifting from a multilateral platform to a plurilateral one. According to a report prepared by the European Commission in 2013, the various forms of protection have risen in the last five years, ranging from stimulus measures to boost exports, pushing domestic goods over imported goods, completion of distorting policies packages and increase in import tariffs. The total number of measures introduced since 2008 has, according to the report of the European Commission, been 700. There have been two main reasons for this change. First, global unrest over the past few years has forced many countries to look inwards to protect labour markets and push domestic manufacturing and agriculture. Second, the WTO rules have been a deterrent for many countries wanting to boost local industry to sustain the domestic economy. Mega free trade agreements are taking place across the globe, making the shift from a multilateral platform to a plurilateral one for trade negotiations. However, this may not be in favour of the developing countries.
3. The Doha Development Agenda (DDA) negotiations were almost stranded seven years ago, in July 2008. In the intervening period, three mega regional negotiations occupied centre stage in world trade policy: the Trans-Pacific Partnership (TPP), the Regional Comprehensive Economic Partnership (RCEP) and the Trans-Atlantic Trade and Investment Partnership (TTIP). TPP is the US led 11 countries' partnership. RCEP includes the 10 countries from the Association of Southeast Asian Nations (ASEAN), plus six other nations including India, Brazil and China. TTIP is a big preferential trade agreement between the US and the European Union. These pacts might affect multilateral trade negotiations under the WTO platform. The EU and South Korea FTA that entered into force in 2011 increased the exports of the EU by 35 percent.
4. African countries are also building their own regional cooperation. At the same time, many bilateral trade agreements are also taking place across the globe.
5. The dismal progress in the Doha Trade Round and changing interest of the countries are encouraging them to form free trade agreements (FTAs). The US does not see any significant gains through a successful Doha Round. Consequently, it is focussing on regional agreements. Europe is crisis ridden to offer any major concessions. The Chinese economy is under severe strain with signs of slowdown.
6. For what is not achievable at the WTO for further liberalisation of trade and investment, the developed countries are trying to achieve them outside the agency.
7. TTP is important to the US because of its strategy to return to Asia.
8. Plurilateral agreements among developed countries and failure of talks in the WTO would be detrimental to the interests of developing countries.

9. The effect of the FTAs and bilateral agreements could well render the WTO irrelevant and the Doha Development Agenda (DDA) would be almost dead, unless the developing countries inject new life into the WTO.
10. This might put the credibility of the WTO in question. The failure of the multilateral trading system would manifest that the developed countries were not sincere on Doha Development Agenda and they merely coined it, to serve their own purpose, as the development round. The failure would eventually harm the development of the poor countries.
11. Developing countries, particularly the least developed countries, might be isolated further in world trade and most developed countries would trade amongst themselves in case the WTO loses its relevance as a multilateral trading forum.
12. The WTO is the only venue where trade rules can be reformed. This cannot be expected from the new generations of FTAs, particularly the mega regional trade deals under negotiation outside the WTO.

The cacophony of divergence between developed and developing country Members is certain at the next Ministerial Conference scheduled in 2017. This could be a part of the strategy adopted by the developed country Members. But, it would eventually damage the WTO as a multilateral trading forum. The formation of free trade agreements among developed countries including some emerging economies would have two implications. First, it would isolate poor countries from the global trade and harm their development. Second, it would work parallel to the World Trade Organization thereby undermining its relevance.

20.5 Suggestions

Both the developed countries and the developing countries should work together to retain the relevance of the WTO as a multilateral trade forum. The political leaderships might be involved to accomplish this objective. In this regard, the following suggestions have been made:

1. The entire WTO Member community should make sincere efforts to resolve the contentious issues such as agricultural domestic support, modalities on NAMA and public stock holding for food security purposes.
2. The developed countries should abandon farming subsidies being provided by them to their farmers. Simultaneously, the developing countries should bring bound tariff rates for NAMA closer to applied tariff rates.
3. Overcoming hurdles in Doha Negotiations requires high level of political attention. Leaders should strongly communicate that trade liberalisation is not a concession in general, but in a country's own interest to stimulate growth.
4. If the required success is not achieved on points mentioned above and damage to the WTO is eminent, it would be better to allow plurilateral agreements within the WTO framework as compared to free, regional or bilateral trade agreements between the countries outside the WTO. The plurilateral agreements could constitute a way of multilaterally shaping a trading system which is naturally gravitating towards differing levels of liberalisation between various countries. Each plurilateral

agreement under the WTO auspices should be open to any WTO Member that later decides to join, both to accept the obligations and enjoy the rights. There is a need to safeguard the interests of developing countries.

5. If plurilateral agreements take place among the developed countries only, which is generally happening, it will isolate the poor countries and would hinder their growth. Further, the WTO would lose its status as a multilateral trade negotiating forum, which also would not be in the interest of developing countries.
6. There are certain areas where bilateral or regional trade pacts may not be able to perform well such as the SPS and the TBT. The WTO's role as an arbitrator of trade disputes has been established and that needs to remain firmly entrenched as a key objective of the multilateral body to ensure that global trade remains fair.
7. Developed countries should implement the WTO provisions of transfer of technology to the developing countries for the development of developing countries and their integration into multilateral trading system.
8. Developed countries should make due efforts in helping the developing countries in building their trade capacity.
9. Developed countries have to give preferential and differential treatment to developing countries, if they are sincere in the development of developing countries and their integration into multilateral trading system.
10. Due concessions should be given by the developed countries in providing the market access for exports from the developing countries, particularly the least developed countries.

Appendix

List of 162 Members of WTO as on January 1, 2016

(Month, date and year of joining the WTO are given in parentheses)

Albania (September 8, 2000)	Croatia (November 30, 2000)
Angola (December 1, 1996)	Cuba (April 20, 1995)
Antigua and Barbuda (January 1, 1995)	Cyprus (July 30, 1995)
Argentina (January 1, 1995)	Czech Republic (January 1, 1995)
Armenia (February 5, 2003)	Congo (January 1, 1997)
Australia (January 1, 1995)	Denmark (January 1, 1995)
Austria (January 1, 1995)	Djibouti (May 31, 1995)
Bahrain (January 1, 1995)	Dominica (January 1, 1995)
Bangladesh (January 1, 1995)	Dominican Republic (March 9, 1995)
Barbados (January 1, 1995)	Ecuador (January 21, 1996)
Belgium (January 1, 1995)	Egypt (June 30, 1995)
Belize (January 1, 1995)	El Salvador (May 7, 1995)
Benin (February 22, 1996)	Estonia (November 13, 1999)
Bolivia (September 13, 1995)	European Union (January 1, 1995)
Botswana (May 31, 1995)	Fiji (January 14, 1996)
Brazil (January 1, 1995)	Finland (January 1, 1995)
Brunei Darussalam (January 1, 1995)	France (January 1, 1995)
Bulgaria (December 1, 1996)	Gabon (January 1, 1995)
Burkina Faso (June 3, 1995)	Gambia (October 23, 1996)
Burundi (July 23, 1995)	Georgia (June 14, 2000)
Cabo Verde (July 23, 2008)	Germany (January 1, 1995)
Cambodia (October 13, 2004)	Ghana (January 1, 1995)
Cameroon (December 13, 1995)	Greece (January 1, 1995)
Canada (January 1, 1995)	Grenada (February 22, 1996)
Cape Verde (July 23, 2008)	Guatemala (July 21, 1995)
Central African Republic (May 31, 1995)	Guinea Bissau (May 31, 1995)
Chad (October 19, 1996)	Guinea (October 25, 1995)
Chile (January 1, 1995)	Guyana (January 1, 1995)
China (December 11, 2001)	Haiti (January 30, 1996)
Chinese Taipei (January 1, 2002)	Honduras (January 1, 1995)
Colombia (April 30, 1995)	Honk Kong, China (January 1, 1995)
Congo (March 27, 1997)	Hungary (January 1, 1995)
Costa Rica (January 1, 1995)	Iceland (January 1, 1995)
Cote d'Ivoire (January 1, 1995)	India (January 1, 1995)

Indonesia (January 1, 1995)	Niger (December 13, 1996)
Ireland (January 1, 1995)	Nigeria (January 1, 1995)
Israel (April 21, 1995)	Norway (January 1, 1995)
Italy (January 1, 1995)	Oman (November 9, 2000)
Jamaica (March 9, 1995)	Pakistan (January 1, 1995)
Japan (January 1, 1995)	Panama (September 6, 1997)
Jordan (April 11, 2000)	Papua New Guinea (June 9, 1996)
Kenya (January 1, 1995)	Paraguay (January 1, 1995)
Kazakhstan (November 30, 2015)	Peru (January 1, 1995)
Korea (January 1, 1995)	Philippines (January 1, 1995)
Kuwait (January 1, 1995)	Poland (July 1, 1995)
Kyrgyz Republic (December 20, 1998)	Portugal (January 1, 1995)
Lao (February 2, 2013)	Qatar (January 13, 1996)
Latvia (February 10, 1999)	Romania (January 1, 1996)
Lesotho (May 31, 1995)	Rwanda (May 22, 1996)
Liechtenstein (September 1, 1995)	Saint Kitts and Nevis (February 21, 1996)
Lithuania (May 31, 2001)	Saint Lucia (January 1, 1995)
Luxembourg (January 1, 1995)	Saint Vincent & Grenadines (January 1, 1995)
Macao, China (January 1, 1995)	Samoa (May 10, 2012)
Macedonia (April 4, 2003)	Saudi Arabia (December 11, 2005)
Madagascar (November 17, 1995)	Senegal (January 1, 1995)
Malawi (May 31, 1995)	Sierra Leone (July 23, 1995)
Malaysia (January 1, 1995)	Singapore (January 1, 1995)
Maldives (May 31, 1995)	Slovak Republic (January 1, 1995)
Mali (May 31, 1995)	Slovenia (July 30, 1995)
Malta (January 1, 1995)	Solomon Islands (July 26, 1996)
Mauritania (May 31, 1995)	South Africa (January 1, 1995)
Mauritius (January 1, 1995)	Spain (January 1, 1995)
Mexico (January 1, 1995)	Sri Lanka (January 1, 1995)
Moldova (July 26, 2001)	Suriname (January 1, 1995)
Montenegro (April 29, 2012)	Swaziland (January 1, 1995)
Mongolia (January 29, 1997)	Sweden (January 1, 1995)
Morocco (January 1, 1995)	Switzerland (January 1, 1995)
Mozambique (August 26, 1995)	Seychelles (April 15, 2015)
Myanmar (January 1, 1995)	Tajikistan (March 2, 2013)
Namibia (January 1, 1995)	Tanzania (January 1, 1995)
Netherlands (January 1, 1995)	Thailand (January 1, 1995)
Nepal (April 23, 2004)	Togo (May 31, 1995)
New Zealand (January 1, 1995)	Trinidad and Tobago (March 1, 1996)
Nicaragua (September 3, 1995)	Tonga (July 27, 2007)

Tunisia (March 29, 1995)	Uruguay (January 1, 1995)
Turkey (March 26, 1995)	Vanuatu (August 24, 2012)
Uganda (January 1, 1995)	Venezuela (January 1, 1995)
Ukraine (May 16, 2008)	Vietnam (January 11, 2007)
United Arab Emirates (April 10, 1996)	Yemen (June 26, 2014)
United Kingdom (January 1, 1995)	Zambia (January 1, 1995)
United States (January 1, 1995)	Zimbabwe (March 3, 1995)

Bibliography

Books

Bhaumik, T.K. (2006), "WTO: A Discordant Orchestra", Sage Publications India Pvt. Ltd., New Delhi.

Chadha, G.K. (2001), "WTO and Indian Economy", Deep and Deep Publications, New Delhi.

Chakraborty, Debashis and Khan, Amir Ullah (2008), "WTO Deadlocked: Understanding the Dynamics of International Trade", Sage Publications Pvt. Ltd., New Delhi.

Das, Bhagirath Lal (2009), "World Trade Organisation: A Guide to the Framework for International Trade", Mittal Publications, New Delhi.

Das, M.R. and Chakraborty, T.K. (2004), "WTO: Opportunities and Challenges for Indian Banking", Himalaya Publishing House, Delhi.

GATT, July 1986, "Text of the General Agreement on Tariffs and Trade", Geneva.

Gulati, Ashok et al. (1994), "Export Competitiveness of Selected Agricultural Commodities", National Council of Applied Economic Research (NCAER), New Delhi.

Gupta, R.K. (1996), "Anti-Dumping: Countervailing Measures", Sage Publications, New Delhi.

Hufbauer, Gary, Jung Euijin, Miner Sean, Moran Taylor and Schott Jeffrey (2015), "From Drift to Deals: Advancing the WTO Agenda", Peterson Institute Report, Washington.

Indian Institute of Foreign Trade (1998), "Global Economic Challenges in the New Millennium", New Delhi.

Mattoo, Aaditya and Stern, Robert M. (eds.) (2003), "India and the WTO", International Bank for Reconstruction and Development, Washington.

Michalopoulos, Constantine (2001), "Developing Countries in the WTO", Palgrave, New York.

Parmita, Dasgupta (ed.) (2009), "WTO at the Cross Roads", Concept Publishing Company, New Delhi.

Rameshan, P. (ed.) (2008), "WTO, India and Emerging Areas of Trade", Excel Books, New Delhi.

Rao, M.B. and Guru, Manjula (2003), "WTO and International Trade", Vikas Publishing House Pvt. Ltd., New Delhi.

Sen, R.K. and Raj, J.F. (ed.) (2009), "WTO and Asian Union", Deep and Deep Publications, New Delhi.

United Nations Conference on Trade and Development (UNCTAD), "World Investment Report" (various issues).

—"Trade and Development Report" (various issues).

United Nations (1999), "The Millennium Development Goals and the United Nations Role".
—"World Economic and Social Survey, 1999".
Vasudeva, P.K. (ed.) (2005), "World Trade Organisation: Implications for Indian Economy", Pearson Education (Pte) Limited, Delhi.
World Bank, "World Development Report" (various issues).
—"Doing Business, 2012".
WTO, "Annual Report (Geneva)", (various issues).
—"Business Guide to the Uruguay Round", International Trade Centre UNCTAD/WTO and Commonwealth Secretariat, 1996, Geneva.
—"WTO Agreement Series: Agriculture", 2014, Geneva.
—"WTO Agreement Series: Sanitary and Phytosanitary Measures", 2014, Geneva.
—"WTO Agreement Series: Technical Barriers to Trade", 2014, Geneva.
—"Understanding the WTO", 2011, Geneva.
Yamazawa, Ippei (2000), "Developing Economies in the Twenty-First Century: The Challenge of Globalisation", Institute of Developing Economies, Japan.

Articles

AFP, "Progress Needed on Doha to Avoid Dangerous Situation: WTO", July 28, 2015, *The Economic Times*, Delhi.
Bhutani, Shalini, "WTO Needs Oxygen for Survival", July 30, 2015, *Deccan Herald*, Bengaluru.
Christian, Henn and Jean-Baptiste Le Hen, "The WTO Doha Trade Round: Unlocking the Negotiations and Beyond", November 16, 2011, International Monetary Fund, Washington.
Das, Abhijit, "Showing Spine at the WTO Negotiations", *The Hindu Daily*, July 16, 2015, New Delhi.
Dasgupta, Amit, "Can WTO Legitimately Make Global Trading Rules", August 4, 2015, *The Economic Times*, Delhi.
Dubey, Muchkund, "Implications of Doha for India", *The Hindu Daily*, December 24, 2001.
Dubey, Muchkund, "Implications of Doha for India", *The Hindu Daily*, December 25, 2001.
Editorial, "Rejection of an Imbalance", *Economic and Political Weekly*, Vol. XLIX, No. 32, August 9, 2014.
Ghosh, Soumya Kanti, "India's 93.2% Quandary at WTO, *Business Standard*, September 23, 2014.
Gulati, Ashok and Sharma Anil, "Agriculture under GATT: What it Holds for India?", *Economic and Political Weekly*, Vol. 29, No. 29, 1994.
Kanungo, Anil K., "Nothing Historic about Nairobi Ministerial", *The Financial Express,* December 23, 2015.
Lakshman, Sriram, "India, Brazil Cross Swords with US at WTO", *The Hindu Daily*,

June 24, 2015.

Mehra, Puja, "Centre Seeking Solution to WTO Subsidies Cap Issue", *The Hindu Daily*, June 30, 2015, New Delhi.

Narayanan, S. and Dasgupta, Jayant, "WTO at the Crossroads: India Must Ensure the Doha Mandate is Not Abandoned at Nairobi", *Times of India*, New Delhi, December 12, 2015.

PTI, "India Concerned over Pace of Deciding Agenda for Next WTO Meet in Nairobi", May 12, 2015, *The Economic Times*, Delhi.

PTI, "India Working with WTO for Permanent Solution on Food Security", July 22, 2015, *The Economic Times*, Delhi.

Ravi Kanth, D., "Doha Round: The Gloves are Off", *Economic and Political Weekly*, Vol. XLIX, No. 25, June 21, 2014.

Ravi Kanth, D., "WTO Upside Down: Trade Facilitation versus Agriculture", *Economic and Political Weekly*, Vol. XLIX, No. 36, September 6, 2014.

Sen, Agneshwar, "World Trade Organisation and Preferential Treatment", *Economic and Political Weekly*, Vol. XLV, No. 28, July 1, 2010.

Sharma, Pardeep and Gulati, Ashok, "WTO and Indian Agriculture", *Economic and Political Weekly*, March 10, 1995.

Sibananda, Sr. and Omphemeste, S., "Towards a Revised GATT/WTO Special and Differential Treatment Regime for Least Developed and Developing Countries", *Foreign Trade Review*, Vol. 50, No. 1, February 2015.

Varma Subodh, "Rich Bloc Wants Poor Nations to Cut Doles", *Times of India*, New Delhi, December 21, 2015.

Vishwanath, T.S., "Making a U-Turn on WTO", *Business Standard*, August 27, 2014.

Vishwanath, T.S., "The Mega Trade Agreement Session", *Business Standard*, September 10, 2014.

Journals, Periodicals, and Magazines

WTO, *World Trade Report* (various issues).

Washington Trade Daily

Foreign Trade Review

Business Standard

Indian Economic Review

Indian Economic Journal

Journal of Foreign Exchange and International Finance

Websites

www.wto.org

www.iisd.ca

www.ictsd.org

www.europa.eu

www.rbi.gov.in

www.dfat.au
www.imf.org
www.bis.org
www.worldbank.com
www.cecd.org

Index